This Book belong

Mrs. Amelia Ruzicka

3006. 58 ave.

Oakland, Calif.

Sr. 444

SUNSET'S COMPLETE GARDEN BOOK

PUBLISHED BY SUNSET MAGAZINE . SAN FRANCISCO, CALIFORNIA

FIRST PRINTING 20,000, SEPTEMBER 1939
SECOND PRINTING 10,000, OCTOBER 1939
THIRD PRINTING 10,000, DECEMBER 1939
FOURTH PRINTING 10,000, FEBRUARY 1940

Sunset's
COMPLETE
GARDEN BOOK

Edited by
RICHARD MERRIFIELD

•

Garden Consultant
NORVELL GILLESPIE

•

Illustrated by
NORMAN S. GORDON

1940 EDITION

LANE PUBLISHING CO.

SAN FRANCISCO

Contents

Note: For Garden "Movies," see Index.

The Book

WESTERN GARDENING is endlessly fascinating—and sometimes a little puzzling—because there are so many angles from which you constantly want to ask questions. You take any plant, for instance—and at once you wonder if it will grow well in the Pacific West, whether it is the right time to plant it, how to go about planting and caring for it month by month, and what it will look like when it comes up and blooms. You want to know when it will bloom, too, and perhaps you want to time its growth so that it will bloom in conjunction with other flowers.

So you have need for a Western garden book which tries to answer questions from all of these angles. Sometimes you want only to know what general care your garden needs this month; but at other times you must have the complete growing story of a given plant—in our particular soil and climate condition. Sometimes you need a picture to show how a certain elementary garden operation is done; or it may be a planting plan for a whole area of your garden. Oftentimes you will be planning along—sowing a border of fall or spring flowers, and you notice that a shrub or bulb is through blooming. Then you have prob-

lems at the beginning and end of the planting cycle. What do you do *after* the blossoms wither? There are vital things to be done. And so on all around your garden. The angle from which you want to fire your question is immensely important to you.

We have tried to arrange this book with that problem in mind. Each section is designed, as far as possible, to supplement the suggestions of each other section. The What-to-Do This Month and Bloom Calendars lead you naturally to the Growing Encyclopedia in the special how-to-do-it chapters—or the reverse, depending on your problem. For best results these different sections should all be consulted, just as you would look up references in an encyclopedia.

Space has made it impossible to cover, in the Encyclopedia section, *every* plant mentioned in the book. Often the garden matter under discussion has required mention of rare species or varieties—as in the Rock Garden lists. In most such cases the general growing directions under Annuals, Perennials, Bulbs, etc., may be followed for that type of plant.—R. M.

HOW TO
Plan Your Garden

PLANTINGS
INSURE PRIVACY

THE secret of successful garden - making is simply knowing how at every step. We will try to tell you, little by little, how to start and care for a garden in the Pacific West. We won't hurry over the garden terms used by the experienced— we'll stop and find out what they mean. For instance: "mulch." Will you agree not to smile if you know what a mulch is? Perhaps someone else doesn't, and later on perhaps you'll be pleased, too, at some explanation new to you.

Begin with a Plan

To begin your garden, take any sheet of paper and mark in the outline of your property, and the space taken up by your house, garage, barbecue pit, incinerator or garbage unit, clothes drier, drive, parking, etc.

For accuracy, rule your paper into squares or get square-ruled paper at a stationery store. Letterhead size is fine. Let each square represent a square foot; then take tape measurements of your lot, house, and of the main features, transfer them to the ruled paper, and you will be able to place your objects exactly. Draw the permanent features solidly. You might go over your penciling with ink.

Now, take several sheets of tracing paper. Lay one over your main plan. Thus you may sketch several garden plans without destroying the outline that is your groundwork.

Some landscape experts consider the lawn first, then frame a garden picture around it.

Others start at the boundaries of the lot and work inward.

We favor a different method for the newcomer to gardening. An expert, amateur or professional, is so familiar with planning, landscape design, and what role each object plays in the garden-to-be, that he has a clear picture and can begin anywhere. We are newcomers in this book. We'll begin by seeing a lot with its house or house-to-be, its unplanted soil, bare driveway and garage as a confused jumble. Our problem is: how to create order, beauty and comfort out of this confusion?

We'll do it by separating the parts of the property from one another and seeing how each one does play its role. As soon as you put a house on a lot, you divide the land into three parts. One is in front of the house, facing the street. The world passes there and judges you by the Front of your home.

The second part is the Service Area. It begins with your drive, includes your garage, garbage or incinerator unit, drying yard, and any other stationary equipment. If you have planned your home wisely you have grouped these to allow maximum space for your garden, and to make it easier to screen and beautify the more unattractive features.

Third and last, your garden has a part which goes by many names — private garden, rear garden, intimate garden, backyard garden, or out-

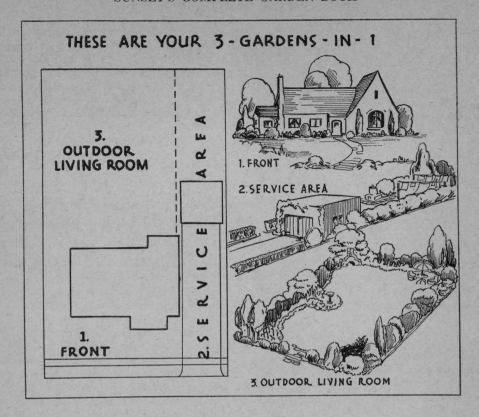

THESE ARE YOUR 3 - GARDENS - IN - 1

3. OUTDOOR LIVING ROOM

2. SERVICE AREA

1. FRONT

1. FRONT
2. SERVICE AREA
3. OUTDOOR LIVING ROOM

door living room. This is like another room of your home. We have a lovely Front because it meets the eyes of our neighbors; we beautify our Service Area to mask out ugly objects; but we have an Outdoor Living Room for ourselves alone.

The Front

The Outdoor Living Room is either private or only slightly visible to the public. The Service Area is partly open. The Front is open to the public eye.

A few homes have walls or thick screens of plantings in Front, but most follow the friendly American custom of allowing neighbors an unobstructed view of the house, unless the main garden is in front.

The Front may be broken down into the parking, entrance or garage drive, walk, lawn, plantings beside the steps, boundaries, plantings along the foundation of the house, and so on.

The Parking Strip

Some tie the lawn and parking in together by letting the same plants continue across to the parking. In some Front gardens you see a ground cover of flowers instead of a lawn, then the gray sidewalk, then more ground cover. Sometimes a hedge runs down the side of the lawn to the sidewalk, breaking off there and continuing in the parking. Such designs give the impression that the outside world is walking across your front lawn. It is wiser to let the parking be a unit by itself. There is one exception. If your lawn is planted with grass, grass will look well in the parking, too.

Plants for the Parking

For something a little different and in good taste for your parking, try Irish Moss. You have seen it between paving stones in patios. It spreads nicely, forming a fresh green mat, thick and mossy. Some prefer Lippia Grass because it asks for so little care — no lawn mowing, very little water — and grows in sun or shade, producing charming blossoms. A Front lawn planted to Lippia could be attractively continued into the parking. Small annuals or perennials, or low-growing shrubs may also be used.

The Lawn

Simplicity is beauty. We no longer clutter our lawns with iron deer, crowded flower beds and intricate paths. Modern homes have smooth lawns unbroken by plantings except for a tree or two or some specimen shrub. A specimen shrub is one with some unusual appearance. Sometimes it has silvery or reddish foliage, or bright berries, or a striking shape.

The best lawn, then, is a more or less unbroken, open center, accented by a special shrub or tree, and losing itself in the line of shrubs or other plants massed against the foundation of the house. For full information on Western lawns, see the lawn chapter in this book.

The Foundation

Foundation plantings soften the right-angle break between your house and the ground. Without them the building stands high and bare. But what a difference when you frame the picture. The house seems to settle into the ground, as if it had grown there. The right-angle is gone, the sharp edges are blurred.

Here again, divide your problem into its natural parts. On one or both sides of the door are windows. At the corners of the house you have sharp edges to be softened with foliage. Should your doorway have tall shrubs, or round ones of medium height? With an informal door, modify its austerity with shrubs of soft texture. On the other hand, you may want formality. Yours then will be clipped shrubs, along the base of your house with an eye to balance, and dark, upright shrubs. The choice depends upon your own personality, which your garden should express.

How to Group Foundation Shrubs

There are many foundation shrubs with distinctive shapes and textures from which to choose. Low ones should grow at the base of larger shrubs. The usual rule is to plant the low, sprawling kinds in front, and to increase their height gradually toward the tallest in the rear. How can you determine their shape? Some may be clipped, but it is better to buy those which grow naturally in formal contours. Unless you go in for formality, however, avoid regularity in these arrangements. Place a narrow one beside a squat, round one; a shrub of dark foliage behind a lighter-colored one, and the like. Always group them. A shrub standing alone against a foundation is a depressing sight.

Shrubs with small leaves are best for the average residence, although if your house is exotic — say, Spanish or Italian — use broad-leaved plantings, both trees and shrubs.

A few names of formal and informal shrubs suitable for Western foundation plantings, together with actual planting plans, are given here, but before you decide on this part of the Front of your home, consult the shrub chapter, the Dictionary-Encyclopedia part of this book, where an attractive grouping is suggested with each shrub mentioned; and your local nurseryman, too, so that you may see what these foundation plantings look like.

Shrubs for Western Foundations

Any of these shrubs will grow well in the Pacific West:

Strawberry Tree (*Arbutus unedo*) is an evergreen which likes either sunlight or partial shade, grows 8 to 15 feet, is hardy, has white flowers from September to December, and strawberry-like fruits. It belongs to the round-headed class.

Another evergreen is Azara, or *Azara microphylla*, a spreading, flat-sided shrub for either complete shade or full sunlight. Its greenish flowers are spicy to smell, and it blooms in February and March.

If you want a round, neat shrub, try Mexican Orange, *Choisya ternata*. Put it in sun or part shade, as an accent or specimen—that is, as a striking feature of your foundation plantings.

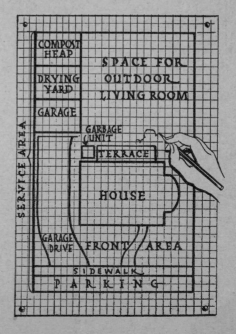

PLANTINGS MAKE EFFECTIVE SCREENS

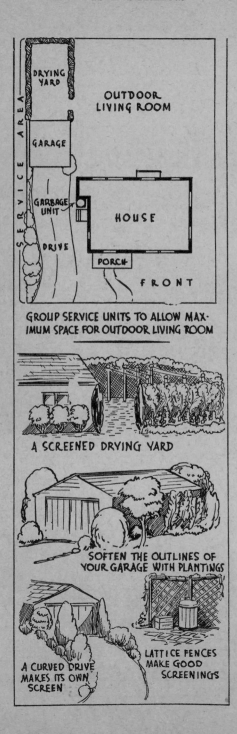

GROUP SERVICE UNITS TO ALLOW MAX- IMUM SPACE FOR OUTDOOR LIVING ROOM

A SCREENED DRYING YARD

SOFTEN THE OUTLINES OF YOUR GARAGE WITH PLANTINGS

A CURVED DRIVE MAKES ITS OWN SCREEN

LATTICE FENCES MAKE GOOD SCREENINGS

A graceful Cotoneaster of medium size which you might like is called the Franchet Cotoneaster —*Cotoneaster franchetti*. It is soft in texture, with red berries and arching branches. The berries come out in September and October.

If you have a Spanish-type home a Dracena Palm would be splendid at one of the corners. It finally grows 10 feet high, often 20 feet, either in part shade or sun. You could plant one in your patio, too. Its leaves are like swords. The botanical name is *Dracena australis*.

Natal Plum — *Carissa grandiflora* — makes a good foundation planting if you live in the Southwest, either inland or near the coast. It is an evergreen, growing 5 to 6 feet, and preferring sunlight. You can eat the red fruit. The white flowers bloom in June and July, and are large and fragrant.

Pittosporum tobira is interesting to know about. You may have heard of it as Japanese Pittosporum. It grows 6 to 10 feet, is symmetrical and bushy, and has dark green, shiny leaves, pale green underneath. The flowers are intensely fragrant, either white or yellow, and bloom from December to February. Pittosporums are wonderfully varied in shape and usefulness.

The Service Area

Some effort should be made to hide the less attractive features of the Service Area. Even the smallest garage can be made lovely with a climbing plant. A garbage or incinerator unit can be located in a corner and screened with a hedge, a lattice covered with climbing vines, shrubs or tall flowering plants. The driveway can be planted with grass, or any of the low-growing plants suggested for the parking.

If you can, have a laundry yard, with a high, narrow hedge or lattice fence, covered with vines, removing the waving garments and clothespins from your view as you sit down of an afternoon to enjoy your Outdoor Living Room.

Beauty in the Service Area

Here are some suggestions for Service Area plantings:

GARAGE: Escallonia, Italian Cypress, *Euonymus japonicus, Clematis montana rubens, Clematis jackmanii*, Genista, Oleander, Deutzia, *Eugenia myrtifolia, Cotoneaster pannosa*, Fuchsia.

PLANTINGS ALONG BASE OF HOUSE WHERE GARAGE DRIVE RUNS: Nasturtiums, English Ivy, Calla Lilies.

SCREENS FOR DRYING YARD, GARBAGE UNIT, VEGETABLE PLOT, ETC.: Hedge of Cypress, Hemlock, Pittosporum, Privet, Yew, Hawthorn, Arbor Vitae, Roses, English Laurel, Laurustinus.

The Outdoor Living Room

What you are aiming at in this garden area is privacy. You will want to relax and play informally away from the eyes of the public. To enjoy this privacy, your first thought must be, "How can I make my Outdoor Living Room a screened, enclosed area?"

If you have a large Outdoor Living Room, use trees or tall, thick-growing shrubs around the boundaries. If your place is small, use evergreen shrubs, such as: Thuya, Arbor Vitae, Juniper, Boxwood, Yew, Rhododendron or Azalea, or a high hedge of Privet or Cypress. For a very small place, try brick or stone walls overgrown with Virginia Creeper, or a lattice fence covered with Jasmine, Golden Gleam Nasturtiums or Passion-vine.

Try to design walls or fences so that they have niches where you can place a seat, statue, bird bath, or flower grouping.

Screens for a Skyline

Despite these plantings or fencings, you may still find the world intruding. Your neighbor's clothesline pole may peer over your most tasteful corner. A distant gas tank may rise horrendously on your skyline of shrubs. Therefore, plan background plantings with an eye to the skyline as well as to privacy.

Now, how will you use your Outdoor Living Room? A play area for your children? Or both that and a summer outdoor living space for the grown-ups? A little garden world kept only for the pleasure your care of it gives you? Or a formal garden where you may entertain your club, serving teas or buffet lunches?

Formal or Informal?

For an informal living area where the children may play and your family may bask, have plenty of lawn space — and the lawn should be sturdy.

Whether formal or informal, make your Outdoor Living Room easy to reach from the house. From the house you should be able to see the best vista of your garden. It should be a part of your home, another room, a real Outdoor Living Room.

Find Your Garden's "Axis Line"

A garden should lead the eye toward a vista. Landscape architects call this line, which leads to any natural terminal point, the "axis line". There may be more than one, depending on your garden's shape and size. At the end of the vista place some object to hold the interest, completing the picture as a period does a sentence: a pool, sundial, seat, group of shrubs, specimen shrub, piece of statuary, garden house, lattice fence, grouping of flowers in a niche, barbecue fireplace, bird bath, rock garden, etc.

The Informal Outdoor Living Room

For an informal garden you will want natural effects, graceful curves, and boundaries, borders or walks that are carefree in spirit. A little neglect, strange as it may seem, often aids in informal effect.

Sketch the Boundary

Now, having settled on the *personality* of your garden, you are ready to sketch a design. Indicate roughly the boundary space to be taken up by trees and shrubs. If you have space only for shrubs of medium height, allow a width of four feet for this border — more if you can. For a deep shrub background, allow seven feet or more. Make your shrub bed widest at the corners of your garden, and plan to have your tallest shrubs or trees there.

Shrubs are either low, medium or tall growers. The tallest go best in the back, medium next, the lowest in the front. It is good to forget or modify this rule now and then. It would be monotonous to plant in a row several shrubs all of the same

AVOID THIS · · · · · BY SCREENING OUT INTRUSIVE OBJECTS

height. It is better to put a medium shrub beside a tall one, then medium again, and low-growing shrubs in front of them.

Informality Means Curving Lines

Nor should the low foreground shrubs stand stiffly in straight lines. That would be formal. Let them curve in and out, not too much, but in a single "S" curve for each section of your space. Mark these "S" curves on your plan.

This brings you to your open space. What will you do with it? Part will be lawn, part flower borders. Flower beds in the middle of your lawn are hard to care for — the grass roundabout becomes trampled, and the lawn, in a wide ring around the bed, becomes cluttered. It is better to locate your flower borders like curving beaches between the mainland of your shrub background and the green lake of your lawn.

Make Flower Borders Wide

The wider a flower border the better. You will want many rows of flowers back in there. Along the lawn edge or the path, and in the foreground of the borders, plan for low-growing flowers, then higher and higher until they blend amongst your shrubs. The edges of these flower borders should follow the curving lines of the shrub bed.

For special plants suited to borders of every kind, see the chapters on annuals and perennials in this book.

How to Use Ovals in Planning

Your shrub background and flower borders determine the shape of the lawn and the space it will occupy. But before you decide anything finally, let's go back to the rule about the axis. One of the most beautiful shapes known is the oval. Try marking an oval diagonally across your garden, swinging it wide to touch the borders. Now revise your undulating border lines so that they curve in and out of the outline of this large oval. If you have room enough, you can have a few little bays where the oval does not touch — by marking in minor ovals. Thus you create a picture in which all the parts join together.

How to Vary This Planning

Anything that belongs in a garden will fit into such a plan. A Rose bed can be located in one of those bays. A rockery can rise in another. You can bring part of your background forward and locate a vegetable garden behind it, reached by a gap in the shrubbery, or gateway. Along one side of the garden you can have a perennial border, along the other side rows of bulbous plants. Instead of vegetables you might have a cutting gar-den apart from the main garden. This keeps your borders blooming to their fullest capacity, without being robbed of their blossoms.

The Formal Outdoor Living Room

This kind of garden is easy to design and hard to keep up. It needs care — clipped lawns and hedges, the shaping of shrubs, etc. It is more expensive and more work. Once you have achieved a trim look about your plantings, you won't want to let them grow shaggy — that takes constant attention.

Garden formality is simply balance. The simplest is a rectangular paved space with a hedge around it. Put a dark column-like tree or two at the corners, and its beauty increases. Add straight rows of bulbs along the hedge, set a fountain in the center, move a chair or two and a low table out there and your formal garden is complete.

You can build this rectangular shape into endless variations. Some formal gardens have several hedge rows arranged in a maze-like design. Cutting through this design you can have a walk bordered with flowers and leading to a vista — a pyramid-shaped tree to left and right; shrubs matching similarly, and so on. The central feature, the pool, statue or whatever you decided on, should be in the center of this balanced vista.

If you like circles, put a pool in the center, and curve the rest around it. Make everything carry out the idea started by the pool.

As with informal gardens, the best formal garden has an open center. You will also see, in the best formal gardens, simplicity. It is the secret of formal beauty. One statue is better than two.

A formal garden may be built around any geometrical figure, the rectangle, square, triangle, oval, circle, etc.

For a formal garden, you might have a paved terrace, with Irish Moss between the stones; geometrical lines leading toward a central feature, such as a pool; and neat flower borders, shrubs and hedges.

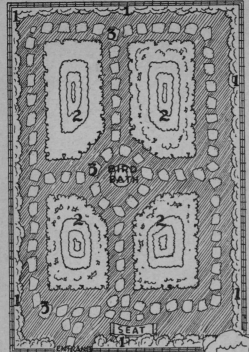

INEXPENSIVE FORMAL OUTDOOR LIVING ROOM

1. Either Climbing or Bush Roses, with background of green fence if possible.
2. Formal beds could consist of solid beds of flowers with edgings— i. e., pink Asters, bordered with blue Lobelia for summer display. For spring display, plant out Pansies in October. In between Pansies, plant Tulip, Daffodil, or Hyacinth bulbs. The Pansies are a gorgeous ground cover.
3. Walk consists of stepping-stones set in turf.

FORMAL OUTDOOR LIVING ROOM

1. Sugar Maple.
2. Hydrangeas or Pyracanthas.
3. Sugar Maple.
4. Hedge of Pittosporum, Privet, Yew, Laurustinus or Cotoneaster.
5. Flowers such as Japanese Anemone, Columbines, Asters, Campanulas, Chrysanthemums, Coreopsis, Delphiniums, Gaillardias, Marigolds, Irises, Lilies, Peonies, Pansies, Penstemons, Stocks, Snapdragons, Pinks, Violas, etc.
6. Red Escallonia.
7. *Cotoneaster pannosa.*
8. *Thuya beverlyensis.*
9. Red Escallonia.
10. Mock Orange.

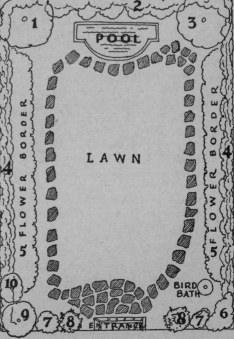

A MORE EXPENSIVE OUTDOOR ROOM

1. Japanese Purple-leaved Plum
2. Pfitzers Juniper
3. Fragrant Osmanthus
4. Daphne
5. California Toyon
6. Wild Tree Lilac
7. Golden Bells
8. Anemone Shrub
9. Rhododendrons
10. Azaleas
11. Portuguese Laurel
12. Mock Orange
13. Red Haw
14. Hydrangea Trophee
15. *Escallonia montevidensis*
16. *Prunus mume*
17. Scotch Broom
18. Common Snowball
19. *Hydrangea paniculata*
20. Abelia
21. Pink Weigela
22. Lilac
23. *Forsythia viridissima*
24. Azaleas
25. Common Magnolia
26. Andromeda
27. Irish Yew
28. Snowball
29. Selected Roses
30. *Pyracantha rogersiana*

AN INFORMAL OUTDOOR LIVING ROOM

1. *Juniperus meyeri*
2. Darwins Barberry
3. Common Snowball
4. Strawberry Tree
5. *Abelia schumanni*
6. Azaleas
7. Pink Weigela
8. Flowering Dogwood
9. *Forsythia fortunei*
10. *Spiraea van houttei*
11. Lilac
12. Ceanothus Gloire de Versailles
13. *Escallonia rosea*
14. *Genista newyrensis*
15. Japanese Pittosporum
16. Heathers
17. Pink Breath-of-Heaven
18. *Philadelphus Virginal*
19. Fuchsias
20. *Cotoneaster franchetti*
21. Mexican Orange
22. Monterey Pine

(*Continued on next page*)

A PLANNING GUIDE

On any sheet of paper, outline your garden area. Start your axis line from the natural point of entrance into the garden, or that place from which you will view the garden mostly—a door, gate, terrace, window, etc. Draw the line across diagonally (for best effect) to a corner, or near one. At that corner, plan a feature (pool, sundial, bench, or barbecue, etc.). A minor axis crossing the first will create charming nooks. Draw ovals around these axes. Inside the ovals is your lawn; outside, and curving in and out of the oval lines, are your borders and shrub backgrounds. This principle may be applied to gardens of any size or shape, with as many axes as your taste deems necessary.

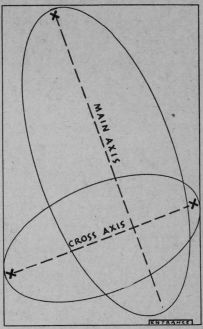

CLOTHE EACH AXIS WITH AN OVAL

(Continued from page 14)

23. Rhododendrons
24. English Laurel
25. *Cotoneaster thymifolia*
26. *Pinus mughus*, a variety of Swiss Mountain Pine.
27. *Pyracantha rogersiana*
28. Catalina Cherry
29. Daphne
30. Heathers
31. Flowering Dogwood
32. California Toyon
33. Barberry
34. Butterfly Bush, variety Isle de France
35. Mexican Orange
36. *Deutzia gracilis*
37. Arnold Flowering Crabapple
38. Lilac
39. Large-flowered Dogwood
40. *Viburnum laurustinus*
41. *Hydrangea paniculata grandiflora*
42. Kwanzan Flowering Cherry
43. Japanese Flowering Quince
44. California Cherry
45. Anemone Shrub
46. *Ceanothus thyrsiflorus*
47. Western Red Bud Tree
48. Simons Cotoneaster
49. Japanese Magnolia
50. European Spindle Tree
51. English Holly
52. Mountain Laurel

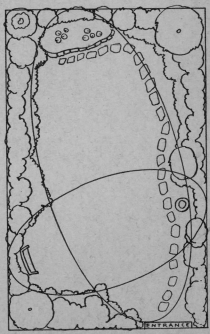

DRAPE OUTLINES OF BORDERS ETC,
ALONG THE OVAL FRAMEWORK

TWO FOUNDATION PLANTING PLANS FOR WESTERN HOMES

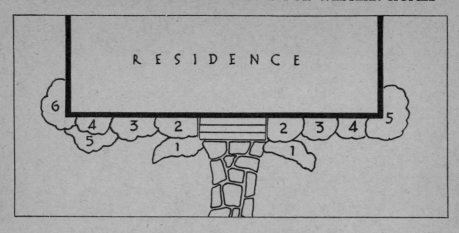

No. 1. FORMAL FRONT

1. *Juniperus sabina* (Savin Juniper)
2. *Veronica laevis*
3. Hydrangea in variety
4. Lilac hybrid
5. *Deutzia gracilis*
6. *Diervilla florida* (Weigela)

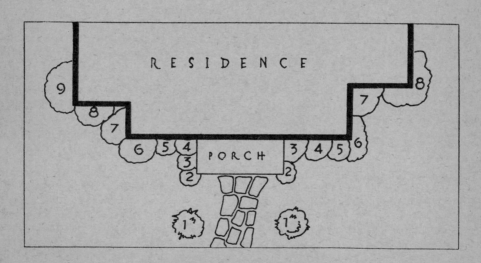

No. 2. FORMAL FRONT

1. *Taxus baccuta* variety *fastigiata* (Irish Yew)
2. Cotoneaster (one of the spreading types, as, *horizontalis*)
3. *Viburnum opulus sterile* (Snowball)
4. *Prunus laurocerasus* (English Laurel)
5. *Chaenomeles japonica* (Japanese Quince)
6. *Philadelphus virginalis* (Mock Orange)
7. *Juniperus pfitzeriana* (Pfitzers Juniper)
8. *Erica melanthera* (Black-eyed Heather)
9. *Pyracantha yunnanensis* (Yunnan Firethorn)

HOW TO
Have Good Soil

IN THE BEGINNING THERE WERE ROCKS

PLANTS LIVED AND DIED AMONGST THEM

You have a certain kind of soil in your garden-to-be. Let us see if we can find out what kind it is, what it is made of, and what you can expect of it. For your garden soil is the dinner table where your plants find their daily bread. Even though their life is the dimmest glimmer of awareness and feeling besides yours, they are alive in their world of plant life, and must eat to live. Their mouths are root hairs, drawing food from small particles of moist, rich soil.

What are these particles? What *is* soil, to begin with?

In the beginning, after the world cooled, there were rocks. Heat made them expand. Cold made them contract. Water froze in them, expanding them more. Cracks appeared. This happened to the biggest and smallest rocks. Winds hit and rubbed the littlest together.

Ages and ages passed. The mother rocks broke down. Plants lived and died amongst them, growing in the cracks, causing more breaking down because of the acids they excreted. When the plants died, they decayed, and the decayed plant matter mingled with the fragmentary, pulverized rock chips.

Rock is mineral. It does not grow cells or tissues, has no life, is not built to function as a living organism—so we say it is inorganic. Plants are organized to grow and reproduce, and be-cause they are living organisms we say they are organic.

The soil thus has two parts — inorganic and organic — mineral and plant. Imagine what happened during the prehistoric ages on this globe — millions of roots, leaves, mosses, rotted trees, stems, etc., falling, losing their identity as they decayed and were mixed with other mold which once grew in the sun, and with mineral grains which were once mountain crags.

How Soil Supplies Food

Plants cannot get their food from soil composed of hard-packed minerals alone. Air and water must circulate between the mineral particles; and this is exactly what the presence of organic matter makes possible. It holds apart the particles, makes the soil porous, collects and holds moisture, and finally furnishes food in the form of nitrogen, potash and phosphorous.

Not all the earth's covering is porous and rich in food for plants. The best part is on the surface. Below that you come to a layer of hard-packed particles, in appearance like the soil on the surface, but not as nourishing.

Below that you find clay, sand, rock, and mixtures of the three. You can tell them by their different colors and textures. They do not look as if plants could grow in them, and indeed they cannot. The surface soil seems warm, alive; the sub-soils are cold and dead-looking.

How to Judge Soil

Perhaps it may be hard for you to judge your soil. Try this test, then:

Take a clear bottle, or test tube, if you have one. Put a sample of the surface soil in it. Add five times as much water. Shake. Put aside to settle for an hour. Then look at it. The large parts drop first, the rest according to their size. You can easily see the proportion of sand, clay, vegetable matter, and gravel.

And here is how you judge what you see in the bottle or tube:

You have sandy soil if there is 5% clay or less.

You have sandy loam if there is 5%-10% clay.

You have medium loam if there is 10%-20% clay.

You have clay if there is 25%-30% clay.

You have heavy clay (adobe) if there is 35%-50% clay.

The Three Kinds of Soil

1. *Sand*: Your surface soil may not be rich enough. It may be sand, or mostly sand.

2. *Loam*: If it looks and feels like a perfect mixture of both sand and clay, and if in addition it looks as if a great deal of decayed vegetable matter, leaves, etc., were mixed with it, then you have the ideal garden soil — loam.

3. *Clay*: If your surface soil is sticky, thick, heavy, it is clay, or clayey.

Sandy Soil and Sandy Loam

Sand is not a cause for despair. It means good drainage, often too much. It is easy to work. The only trouble is that it does not have enough de-cayed vegetable matter in it to supply food. This organic matter, after the chemical changes it goes through in the ground, is called humus.

Don't pass over this tremendously important word — humus. If there is a big, magic Golden Key to successful gardening, its name is humus. This blackish-brown vegetable mold is the secret of soil fertility. The ancient Latins, who were skilled agriculturists, included all soil under this one word — for the Latin *humus* means ground. In a moment we will tell you how to manufacture it in your garden.

For the present, remember that the cure for a sandy soil or sandy loam is humus. When you mix them you get the ideal soil — garden loam.

Clay and Heavy Clay (Adobe)

Clay or adobe can be changed into good garden loam. They need changing for several reasons.

Adobe is hard to cultivate. It cracks when dry. Any soil that cracks in this way shows that it has heavy clay in it. Even a rather sandy loam may crack — that is what gardeners mean when they refer to "sandy adobe loam."

Clay and adobe soils keep out air and moisture because they are tightly packed. The tiny soil particles in them stick together, and even though these clays are wonderfully rich in food for plants, it is up to you to make the food available by adding whatever will keep the soil from pack-ing. It must be made porous. Plaster, coarse sand, wood shavings, horse manure, wood and coal ashes, peat, roots, bacterial cultures, or, best of all, decayed vegetable matter (humus), if spaded in, will lighten your soil.

So you see, we come back again to the Golden Key. You will meet it under many names, all meaning the same thing in the end: "decayed vegetable matter," "organic matter," "compost material," "humus," "leafmold," etc.

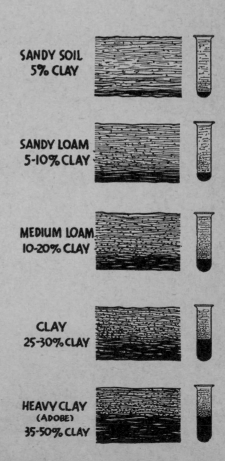

SANDY SOIL
5% CLAY

SANDY LOAM
5-10% CLAY

MEDIUM LOAM
10-20% CLAY

CLAY
25-30% CLAY

HEAVY CLAY
(ADOBE)
35-50% CLAY

PUT WINGS IN YOUR SOIL!

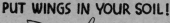

PEAT MOSS LIGHTENS HEAVY CLAY

humus
sand & = Loam.
clay

What Makes Garden Soil Good or Bad?

You already know one of the causes — the lack of a proper mixture of sand, clay and humus. There are two others, and for clearness we list all three: *texture*.

1. Poor physical condition — not enough humus.

2. Too much acidity or too much alkalinity.

3. The lack of some chemical element in the soil which plants must have in order to live.

1. How You Can Manufacture Humus Easily

There is only one way — Nature's way, which is to mix decayed vegetable matter with ordinary dirt, thus enriching it. Nature keeps adding to it with the dead tops of plants and falling leaves. Living creatures help Nature: earthworms help to bury this fallen vegetable matter; bacteria take the raw material and change it into plant foods.

Nature uses everything, even the merest blades of grass. You cannot do better than to follow her example. When you dig a weed, put it aside in a corner of the garden; rake leaves over there; heap your pruning there. You'll be surprised to see how much accumulates.

It is the gardener's gold; it is madness to throw it away or burn it — and if you will look under "Compost Heap" in this chapter you will see how to hasten its decay, destroy odors, and hide the entire pile under soil and behind a hedge or other screen.

This is one supply of humus. You either mix it into the soil when it is well rotted, or spread it on top after planting and then dig it in later.

Another source is leaf mold (decayed leaves).

Peat Moss and Its Uses

Thus we come by elimination to peat moss — a word which should be as fixed in your mind

as humus, for they are your two best garden workers.

Your local nurseryman, seedman or horticulturist will sell you a bale of peat moss for about $3.00. There are different kinds of peat moss. Sphagnum moss peat is one of the best. Peat moss is plant life that has decayed, but the decay has been artificially controlled to prevent complete decomposition. A United States Government bulletin states that it holds 15 to 30 times its own weight in moisture. It retains its identity for years, instead of breaking down rapidly as leaf mold does. During all that slow breaking down, peat moss continues to build soil for you.

Yet peat moss is not a fertilizer; nor is it a plant food. Nothing comes out of it. Its job is to lighten the heavy clays and make them more porous, and to enable sandy soils to hold moisture. This job it does more quickly than anything else. But — do not fail to keep adding other humus, preferably the decayed compost material, which, besides doing what peat does, also furnishes the plant with something to eat.

Peat moss should be well wetted when you mix it with soil, particularly sandy soil, because the moss has a drying effect, which is bad.

2. What to do About Acidity and Alkalinity

Some soils are acid. Others are the opposite of acid: they are alkaline. Some are neutral. It is important to know what you have because plants that thrive in one do not in the other, and vice versa.

How can you tell? Simple testing outfits are sold by horticulturists, costing from $2 to $10. Or any chemist could test the soil and let you know, for a small charge.

Alkalinity (too much salt) is treated with commercial aluminum sulfate or sulfur. Aluminum sulfate (sometimes spelled sulphate) is also sold by horticulturists. It is a material used in creating acid soils, in which you can grow Azaleas, Rhododendrons, etc. About a pound to 10 square feet is enough. Five pounds costs about 50 cents. More costs less, proportionately.

Acidity can be neutralized with lime. You can get lime very cheaply — about 50 pounds for 65 cents.

Most garden plants, however, like neutral soil — neither acid nor alkaline. You need not worry if you have an average garden loam — it is probably neutral.

WHAT A PLANT EATS

POTASSIUM

FOR STRENGTH

PHOSPHOROUS

FOR ROOTS-BLOSSOMS-SEEDS

NITROGEN

FOR NEW GROWTH

CALCIUM

FOR LEAF COLOR   *ROOT GROWTH*   *BACTERIA GROWTH IN SOIL*

IRON AND MAGNESIUM

FOR LEAVES   *STEMS*

CHLORINE, ZINC AND IODINE

FOR HEALTH

3. WHAT A PLANT EATS AND HOW TO FEED IT

Remember the third cause of goodness or badness in a soil — the lack of some chemical element which plants must have in order to live? Well, it's very simple. A plant must grow and keep on living. It gets oxygen and carbon from the air in the form of carbon dioxide, taken in through breathing pores in the leaves and green stems.

Then the plant needs moisture. This it gets from the soil — none of it enters through the leaves. It needs moisture because that is the only form in which it can absorb the food elements in the soil. They must always be in solution — like a convalescent on a liquid diet.

The plant's meal consists of nitrogen, potassium, phosphorus, magnesium, calcium, sulfur, iron, and other elements in small amounts. There is nitrogen in the air, but it is not in the proper form for plant use. Only its nitrate form can be taken directly. So tiny bacterial organisms in the soil change the air and soil nitrogen into a form the plant can use, potassium nitrate in solution. That is what happens to decaying organic matter in the soil — the bacteria are transforming it into an assimilable form for growing plants.

When you eat a dinner, your body uses one food element for your blood, another for the bones, another for the tissues, etc., like a general assigning different strategic parts of a military position to different parts of his army.

How a Plant Uses This Food

A plant does the same thing in various ways. It uses nitrogen to develop new growth, because nitrogen is the most important part of protoplasm — the vital substance of every living cell. It cannot do without it.

Potassium is used for added strength and for healthy growth.

Phosphorous helps the growth of roots, blossoms, and the maturing of the seeds.

Calcium, which is found in lime, favors a good growth of bacteria in the soil, aids root growth, and is partly responsible for a normal green in the color of leaves.

Iron and magnesium go to the leaves and stems, and help along that green leaf color, too.

Chlorine, zinc and iodine are needed in small quantities for general health.

You can easily see what may happen if any of these are missing — poor growth, no growth, sickly color, etc. The plant must have them all in the correct amounts.

If you have an average fertile soil, you probably have them all on hand. The main thing to look out for is a lack of nitrogen, and, perhaps, potassium and phosphorus.

How to Make Your Compost Heap

Whenever you cut your lawn, rake the grass clippings into an out-of-the-way corner. When you rake up fallen leaves, add them to your lawn clippings; when you pull a weed, toss it on the same pile. For this growing heap (and it will grow rapidly) of vegetable matter is worth

SOME SOURCES OF HUMUS
(Any Decayed Vegetable Matter)

TOPS OF PLANTS CUT OFF or FALLEN   PULLED WEEDS   FADED FLOWERS   FALLEN LEAVES   GRASS CLIPPINGS   VEGETABLE TOPS FROM YOUR KITCHEN

its weight in gold. In a few months it will be ready to use in every part of your garden, enriching the soil and helping to produce the masses of flowers you want.

When you design your garden, leave a space in back of the garage, beside it, in a far corner of the garden area, behind the vegetable plot or cutting garden, or any other spot that is not likely to be needed for anything else.

The size should be as large as you feel you can make it — 6 by 8 feet is a good size for a garden of moderate size. Smaller will do if you have a small lot.

Building the Pile

A compost heap should be deliberately built and maintained. The bottom layer should be soil, if you build a permanent concrete pit in the ground for your compost. If you do not wish to go to that trouble, just pile on your leaves and clippings until four inches or so have accumulated, then shovel a few inches of manure or old sod on top, and soil on top of that. Add the next leaves, etc., on top of that soil, and continue the process. Chemical compounds are on the market that hasten decomposition.

Soak the heap now and then — plentifully. Turn the entire pile over once a month. You will have some splendid humus in about six months. You will have no trouble with messiness if you follow these three directions:

1. *For Ugliness*: Screen the pile with a hedge or a trellis on which vines have been trained, or with any other medium-sized planting — a shrub or two, for example. Or run a little lath fence around it, paint the laths green and train vines, Climbing Roses, Sweet Peas, Honeysuckle, etc., along them.

2. *For Odor*: If the compost heap is built as directed, with layers of soil between the layers of compost material, you will have no difficulty with odors. Keep a layer of soil on top.

3. *For Flies*: When you are building your compost, add acid phosphate to each layer. Sprinkle on more when you fork over the heap. It will kill the maggots which otherwise would become flies.

How to Use Compost Material

1. In a few months remove humus from the bottom of the heap.

2. Lighten heavy clay soils with it by mixing with this rich, brownish-black decayed vegetable matter.

3. Make sandy soils more retentive of moisture by mixing with the same.

4. Use a light top dressing for your lawn — not to take the place of commercial plant foods but to supplement and work hand in hand with them.

5. Mix with garden loam when potting.

6. Mix with garden loam when preparing seed flats, and the soil beds for your cold frames and hotbeds.

7. Mix with soil of your flower borders.

8. Spread it on top of the soil around your Roses, shrubs and evergreens.

BUILDING A COMPOST HEAP

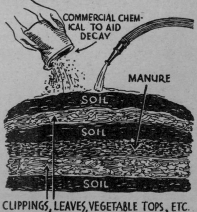

COMMERCIAL CHEMICAL TO AID DECAY

MANURE

SOIL

SOIL

SOIL

CLIPPINGS, LEAVES, VEGETABLE TOPS, ETC.

HOW TO
Start Your Plants

This is what you wait for with suppressed excitement when you start out to make a garden. This is what you work toward—the moment when you put the seeds into the soil with your own hands, seeds that will become blossoms, your own creations. Not all starting of plants is done with seeds—and this is one of the most fascinating things in gardening. You can cut a piece off a growing plant, set it in the earth, and it will become another plant. Sometimes you can place a leaf on the earth and it, too, sends down roots. You can cut a living bud out of a plant and slide it into the sliced bark of another, and it will grow. You can tie a twig from a shrub onto another shrub, and together they will grow more vigorously than before. You can lift a whole plant bodily from the soil, roots and all—anything from a grass blade to a tree—move it to another part of your garden, or from another garden to yours, replant it, and it will thrive in its new home!

Let us find out how to do some of these magical things.

How to Buy Seeds

First you need the seeds.

Buy quality seeds. Most seed packages cost 10 cents, some 5 cents, some 25 cents, some as high as $2.50. The cost often depends upon the newness of the variety.

Remember, each plant has its own requirements. Follow the cultural directions on the packages. Many have much in common, however, and general methods of propagation may in many cases be safely allowed.

Where to Start Seeds

Some seeds may be sown at once outdoors in your own garden; others must be protected in their earliest stages. Since the majority must be protected, and since with almost any seeds you will have the best results if you protect them, you will want to know how to provide this care.

Seeds need a rich, fine soil, careful watering, shielding from too much sun, from rains, wind, and from disturbance by birds, animals or others. The obvious answer is to start them in pots, pans, or boxes, either indoors or an otherwise sheltered place.

The best box (or seed flat as it is called) is 11 inches square and 3½ inches deep, outside measurement. The top is open. If the bottom has large cracks in it, fine; if not, drill a couple of ¾-inch holes, for water drainage later on.

Instead of a box you can use a shallow pot. They vary in size. It is best to use shallow fern pans for many seeds. A pan 10 inches in diameter and 3 inches deep will do for most seedlings. A seedling is the young plant just after it pokes its head above the soil, and until it grows 3 or 4 leaves and is transplanted from the seed flat or pan.

The Cold Frame

Gardeners often use a cold frame outdoors for protection from outside cold and heat, for early starting, and for forwarding partially hardened plants which have been started early indoors. A cold frame is like a small house with a glass roof. It is any wooden box with top and bottom knocked out, and a removable glass top (a window sash will do nicely). Three by 5 feet is a good size. The front might be 8 by 10 inches high, the back a few inches higher to let the water run off the glass.

This covering of glass absorbs the sunlight, warms the soil and makes your plants grow sooner. It wards off rain, cold, wind, and marauders. Place it in a sunny part of the garden, spade the soil beneath and on top of this fill in 2 inches or so of seed bed soil mixture (we'll tell you about that in a moment). This makes a fine drained seed bed that is free of weeds if the soil is mixed with sand and peat moss.

What a Hotbed Is

The cold frame may be any enclosure protected with glass, canvas, water-proofed muslin, or cheesecloth. Sometimes you will hear a cold frame called a hotbed; this means the soil beneath has been dug out to a certain depth and manure placed there instead, to supply heat; or that an electric heating unit has been put in under the soil. Sometimes electric heating cables are set 1 foot apart and 4 to 5 inches down.

There are many kinds of cold frames — all sizes, and ranging from the simple box and glass top above-described, to a permanent glass-covered shed, with walls of concrete. Some frames are built with a peaked roof, like that of a miniature barn, so that the top opens both ways.

The Lathhouse*

Another shelter, popular in California, is the lathhouse, which you can build for a few dollars in a corner of your garden, or beside the garage. Painted green, it makes an attractive structure with the sunlight making changing patterns through the crossed laths — and these changing shadows, by the way, form the principle on which a lathhouse is based: that of breaking the direct rays of the sun and not allowing them to concentrate too long on one spot.

The seed flats or pans are set on benches or boxes inside, and the laths admit light, but not enough light to allow injury from the sun during this tender germination period of the seeds. Laths are usually spaced one lath apart, although this is a little wide for a hot sun, and a little close if there is a scarcity of sunlight where you live.

How to Choose the Right Soil

Next you should think about the soil that you put into the seed flat, pan, pot or cold frame.

One good soil mixture contains 2 parts of garden topsoil, 1 part river sand (ask for No. 2 sand when you buy it from your nurseryman), and 1 part leafmold. Your nursery also sells leafmold. Mix these ingredients in the box, then sift mixture through an ⅛-inch sieve.

Before putting it into your seed flat, or pot, break up some old flower pots and strew the fragments on the bottom of the flat to allow water to drain, and also to hold the soil in. Take the coarser material that is left in your sieve and

* Full construction details for building a lathhouse will be found on pages 107-108.—ED.

TWO GOOD SOIL MIXTURES FOR YOUR SEED FLAT

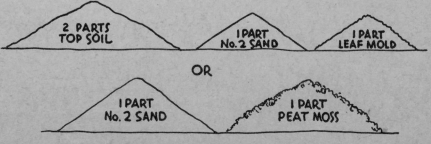

2 PARTS TOP SOIL   1 PART No. 2 SAND   1 PART LEAF MOLD

OR

1 PART No. 2 SAND   1 PART PEAT MOSS

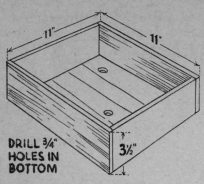

DRILL ¾"
HOLES IN
BOTTOM

AN IDEAL SEED FLAT

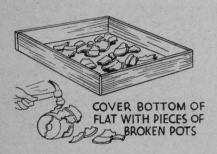

**COVER BOTTOM OF
FLAT WITH PIECES OF
BROKEN POTS**

SIFT SOIL MIXTURE INTO FLAT

MAKE FURROW 2" APART
⅛" DEEP

USE A
RULER

put that into the flat, or pot, covering the broken pieces. The sifted soil goes on top of that, to within 1 inch from the top.

No manure is needed in this mixture: it is a mistake to add manure at the time of your planting. If the topsoil used in the mixture seems to need enriching, add manure to it well in advance of the time you mix it up for seed planting; otherwise you will have decaying material around the seeds, and your seedlings may die. A greater percentage of the seedlings can be saved if powdered charcoal is spread on the surface of your seed boxes as soon as the young seedlings appear.

How to Have Weed-Free Soil

Many gardeners use equal parts of sand and peat moss instead of the soil-sand-leaf-mold mixture. It is free of weeds, immune to diseases, loose, porous and makes an ideal seed bed, especially for beginners. If you want to experiment with weed-free soil, bake any soil mixture in the oven for an hour or two, at 212 degrees Fahrenheit. The soil will burn if the oven is hotter.

The baking kills both weeds and diseases, such as damping-off fungi; but it requires some trouble to take such extreme precautions, and isn't wholly necessary unless you want to be sure of success with some very special plant. Formaldehyde dust or copper oxide dust are recommended to control damping-off.

If you have a heavy clay soil, mix it with equal parts of leafmold and sand. Leafmold is decayed leaves. Or you can mix with granulated peat moss. A clay soil cakes and hardens, and your small seedlings have a hard time breaking through.

Sowing the Seeds

Make shallow furrows 2 inches apart and about ⅛ of an inch deep, across the seed flat or bed, after firming the soil so that it won't settle after watering. A ruler will do for your furrow maker.

Snip off a corner of your seed envelope, hold over the furrow, and shake the seeds out. By holding the envelope firmly and tapping, you can gauge the number of seeds dropped.

Space the seeds so that they barely touch. You can't regulate this with fine seeds, but a little practice will show you how to strew them along thinly. Later on you will replant the seedlings farther apart, so don't be afraid of their coming up too closely together. It is wise to sow twice as many seeds as you expect to have plants.

Large seeds should be set down ¼ inch to ½ inch. The directions on the packages will tell you the proper depths. There is more danger in planting your seeds too deeply in heavy soil than in light or sandy soil.

Cover the smaller seeds only very lightly with sand. Medium sizes are covered ⅛ inch, the larger sizes ¼ inch. In general, cover to a depth which equals twice the seed's breadth.

How to Cover Seeds

Seed sowing is a simple operation, based on common sense rather than on any technical mysteries. The seeds of weeds will thrive under the most adverse conditions, but few flower seeds will. That is why you try to give them all the help you can.

The covering can be done with a small strainer or wire screen, sifting the sandy soil, or the peat and sand mixture, over the seeds. No. 2 sand can be used, and it is a good idea to put it in a Mason jar if you haven't a strainer or screen, and punch some holes in the top. Ordinary sifted garden loam may be used for covering, but sand will bring you less trouble with damping-off fungus. Sand insures a good drainage around the seeds, too.

After covering, firm the soil down around all seeds. Firm it with a block, pressed gently on the surface.

Authorities differ on the watering after planting. One holds that the pan or flat should be set in a few inches of water so that the entire soil mass is thoroughly wetted.

The majority, however, are for springling. Try both and test the results you get. In sprinkling, use a very fine spray, and sprinkle gently in order not to dislodge the seeds. Wet the soil well, but not enough to form puddles on the top, or to float some of the seeds away.

This moisture is important. Without enough water in the soil the seeds cannot germinate; therefore, keep the surface from drying out until the seedlings are up and the roots are growing down into the moist soil.

After your first watering, don't water again until the surface looks a little dry; then water again. Be sure not to let it really go dry, though.

How to Protect Seeds

Put several thicknesses of newspaper pages or wrapping paper over the seeds, but not touching them. Over this, put a sheet of glass if you can, tilting the glass slightly for ventilation. Do not shut out the air. Keep this covering on until the seeds sprout. This is done to keep the moisture in, and is especially needed in the summer heat when the soil bakes and hinders germination.

A HOMEMADE SOIL SPRINKLER

SHIELDING A FLAT WITH A LATH SCREEN

A SIMPLE COLDFRAME

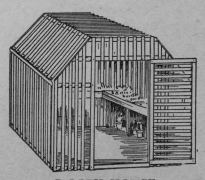

A LATH HOUSE

During the germinating period the seed box should be put in some place where it will be sheltered from direct sunshine, rain or wind. This is where you use your lathhouse, if you have one; or set it in cold frame, preferably one heated with manure or electricity, if you are starting your seeds early when the weather is cold. Lacking either, place it under a tree; and lacking that, set it in the open, but shield it with a lath screen, burlap or muslin, or on a shelf in the basement that is well lighted.

This is a critical time for many plants. During the first two weeks you must watch out for excessive drying of the soil, burning of the sun, usually low or high temperatures, or any sudden change of temperature. Any of these may prevent the growth of your seedlings. A 10-degree difference in day and night temperatures need not be regarded as such a sudden change.

If your first shoots show signs of wilting, give them more air and less water. Petunia, Poppy and Delphinium seedlings may survive the danger of damping-off if you give them more ventilation, and plant them farther apart in the seed bed.

When the first seedlings break through the surface, allow them more light, though not strong sunlight. Keep on sprinkling — daily for some seeds, twice or three times a week for others, according to the package directions, or other special instructions for individual plants in this book. Water deeply; remember that the roots must go down, and must find water 2 or 3 inches under the surface. On the other hand, do not water too often; it is less dangerous to water too little than too much.

How to Transplant Seedlings

Most of the seeds you sow in seed flats or pans will come up too close together to grow well like that for very long. That is one of the reasons for transplanting the young seedlings to other flats.

There are other reasons. Transplanting helps to develop a better root system, allows better aeration, and aids in the gradual hardening of the young plant so that it can stand the final shock of being set out in the open ground of your garden, where you want it to bloom.

Every nurseryman transplants his seedlings, and the wise home gardener will follow suit.

You may wonder why, if the soil in the open garden is good, the weather good, etc., seedlings cannot be transplanted directly there. In some cases they can. Calendulas and Sweet Peas will do just as well in the open, and so will others; but the majority will thrive better if you transplant them once or twice before planting in the open.

If the weather should change, or some other unfavorable condition come about, you might not be able to protect your seedlings. Besides, if they are in flats you can get at them easier to give them what care they need.

Wait for Second or Third Leaves

For your first transplanting, from one flat to another, wait until your seedlings show their second or third leaves. Then loosen the soil mixture around them. Do this with the greatest care. The soil should fall away from the roots. Pick each plant up gingerly and individually. A fork is good to lift them out with. Keep the roots shaded so that they will not dry out before you get them replanted. Wet paper or a cloth will do for this shading.

The bed into which the seedlings are to go should be prepared with care. The soil must be without lumps or clods, well spaced, pulverized and a little richer than the first flat.

Set the plants to 4 inches apart, depending on the size of the plant. If the transplanting is being done direct to the outdoor garden, set them as you want each plant to be when it blooms — that is, about 6 inches apart for the smaller plants, and from 12 to 18 inches for the larger.

After you have marked out where the seedlings go, make holes for them with a dibble. Make each hole small, ½ inch wide and 1 inch deep. A dibble is a short, pointed stick. You can buy one or whittle one from an old broom handle. Some prefer a pointed, some a rounded dibble.

Set the seedling in place and close the hole around it by thrusting the dibble into the ground ½ inch away. This compacts the soil around the roots. If you just pat around the plant with your fingers, or insert the dibble closer than ½ inch, the stem gets in contact with the soil but the roots do not, and there is an airpocket below the roots.

TRANSPLANT WHEN SEEDLING SHOWS A FEW LEAVES

STOCK SEEDLING

Another Good Method

One gardener in the San Francisco Bay Region, who has had much success with his plantings, uses a slightly different method, and recommends it highly. He waters his flat or cold frame the night before transplanting to it, makes his holes with a round dibble, than scatters a soil mixture into the hole around the roots and stem. He claims that the roots are not crushed together by this method, but spread out naturally, yet without any danger of air pockets or lack of contact with the soil particles. His mixture is half sand, half leafmold, screened.

After planting, water thoroughly. Continue to provide shading from the sun. If planted in the open ground, shade with inverted flower pots, berry boxes, tin cans, or anything else and keep shading for several days until they become established.

Harden them off, in the flat as well as the open, by gradual exposure to the sun and air. Transplanting is a shock, especially transplanting to the open ground. You had better transplant to another flat; then, if you have patience, to a cold frame, and finally to the open.

Before setting them out in the garden, give them a week in the open sun, with not too much water; this will slow down their growth a little so that there will be the least possible shock in transplanting.*

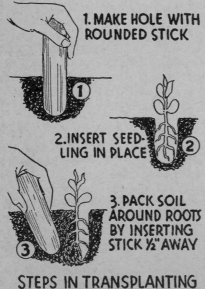

1. MAKE HOLE WITH ROUNDED STICK

2. INSERT SEEDLING IN PLACE

3. PACK SOIL AROUND ROOTS BY INSERTING STICK ½" AWAY

STEPS IN TRANSPLANTING A SEEDLING

* For information on how to transplant shrubs, consult the shrub chapter in this book.—ED.

How to Make Cuttings

To "make a cutting" means literally to cut off a part of a growing plant and set it in the ground to root.

Most cuttings are not too particular about the soil they will root in. A famous gardening expert simply puts them in sand. Some mix the sand with light soil, with more sand than soil. Others mix sand and peat moss, or topsoil and peat moss. In the nurseries ordinary No. 2 sand is used.

For Faster Rooting

Your cutting will root more quickly, and with more success, if you can give them warmth below the box you are rooting them in. Heat can be supplied electrically, or any other way. They will get more warmth if kept inside your greenhouse or the cold frame.

A deep box is best. Fill it with about 3 inches of sand or whatever mixture you wish to try. The rooting medium should be moist; therefore, to keep the moisture in, cover the box with a sheet of glass after planting.

Some cuttings root in a month, others take a very long time — even a year or more. You can see if they are rooting by digging them up — they do not mind it. When a few rootlets have grown, transplant to another flat containing good light soil. This transplanting — as in the case of all transplanting — gives them a better root system and hardens them so that they can stand the shock of being transplanted into the cool open ground of the garden.

Soft-Wooded Cuttings

Not all cuttings are alike, because, of course, not all plants are alike. First among the different kinds of cuttings are the soft-wooded ones, which root easier than the hard-wooded. You can test a soft-wooded cutting by bending a shoot of a plant. It is ready if it snaps off, but if it is too old or too young it just crushes.

The cut is made at a slant, below a joint, kept moist, then set about 1½ inches down in a pot or box and kept in the shade until the roots appear.

With this method you can multiply your shrubs, Roses, and many other plants during the summer. Cut the slips short — about 3 inches, leaving a few leaves at the top and removing all others. If the top leaves are large, trim them smaller — cut off squarely across the leaf a third, a half or even two-thirds of the way down. This reduces evaporation and gives the food that is stored in the stem a chance to produce new roots.

When planting, firm the cuttings solidly in the soil, do not forget the shading, and water carefully. It is rarely wise to plant them at once where they are finally to grow.

You can take soft cuttings from the following in the Pacific West; Abutilon, Arabis, Aubretia, Boronia, Cactus, Calceolaria, Forsythia, Fuchsia, Helianthemum, Hibiscus, Hypericum, Kerria, Lantana, Linum, Mahonia, Malvaviscus, Mesembryanthemum, Pentstemon, Petunia, Poinsettia, Rehmannia, Rochea, Salvia, Scabiosa, Sedum, Sophora, Streptosolen, Tecoma, Veronica and Viburnum.*

Hard-Wooded Cuttings

You can make an entire hedge of a shrub instead of a single plant standing alone. For example, a number of 6-inch lengths are cut from the branches of a Hydrangea or Privet. Tie them in a bundle and bury in sand, well covered, and keep the sand always moist. The well-lighted cellar is a good place to have your box of sand for this purpose.

The wood heals at the base by spring, and you can then set the cuttings in soil, leaving two buds above the ground. It is best to take these cuttings in midwinter or in the summer when the shoots are ripening. Cut off or cut down the leaves as you do with soft-wooded cuttings, and either push the bottom ends into the sandy soil or make a hole with a small stick. Do not crowd them. Water with light sprinklings two or three times a week.

_____
* See also list on page 30.—ED.

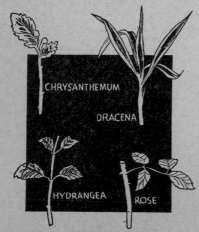

CHRYSANTHEMUM

DRACENA

HYDRANGEA   ROSE

SOME TYPES OF CUTTINGS

Some ripened wood cuttings may be rooted in the open, such as Azalea, Barberis, Fuchsia, Hydrangea, Kerria, Kolkwitzia, Leptospermum, Lonicera, Philadelphus, Rhododendron, Roses, Spiraea, Weigela, and others. It is best to root under glass Akebia, Bignonia, Cotoneaster, Cornus, Gardenia and Pyracantha.

Cuttings from Roots

These are very interesting to make. You will need a box, as with other cuttings. Fill it almost full, with light soil. Three inches is a good depth. Then select plants having somewhat thick roots. Cut the roots up. The pieces should be 1½ inches long. Scatter these pieces over the top of the soil and cover them with more soil, about ½ inch deep. After watering, put the box somewhere in the shade, covered with glass and paper.

Different methods are used successfully with root cuttings. Dracena, and most fruit trees, can be propagated this way, when the roots are cut into pieces 1 to 3 inches in length, planted horizontally in soil or peat moss, and given bottom heat if possible. Manure, by the way, is one way of furnishing this heat. You put a layer of it about 6 inches below the rooting soil.

Phlox, Bouvardia, Aralia, Oriental Poppies, and _Anemone japonica_ may be propagated with root cuttings. They do best under glass. Some others may be put out into the open ground — Wisteria, Iris, Hibiscus, Campanula, Camellia, Alstromeria and Robinia.

With some perennials you should let a small part of the end of the root stick out above the soil. They are planted in an upright position. This is done with Peony, Poppy, Bleeding Heart, Statice, Gypsophila, Gaillardia, Perennial Phlox, Stokes Aster, Anchusa, and others.

Leaf Cuttings

Not everyone knows that you can cut a leaf from certain plants, lay it on top of the ground, and make it send down roots. This can be done with Rex Begonia, _Begonia rex-cultorum_, Cotyledon, Echeveria, Gasteria, Hawarthia, Nymphaea, (the leaf-propagating kind), Tellima, the young leaves of Paulownia, and Gloxinia. These are fleshy-leaved plants, with much food stored within them.

Sometimes the leaf is used whole, sometimes shortened, or even cut up in pieces. When you cut them in pieces, leave a section of the heavy midrib of the leaf in each piece. Such pieces should be put in sand, several inches deep. They

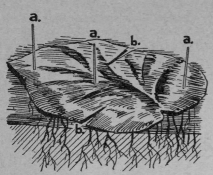

BEGONIA LEAF CUTTING
a. TOOTHPICKS TO HOLD LEAF
b. SLITS IN LEAF TO MAKE IT LIE FLAT

need warmth, too, so you'd better keep them in the greenhouse or cold frame, if you have one.

Rex Begonia leaves may be placed on top of moist sand in a box or cold frame. Hold them down with toothpicks or splinters, and keep them moist, shaded, and in an even temperature.

Heel Cuttings

This is one of the most successful ways of making a cutting, especially with Roses. You will have almost 100% good results. It can be done with any shrub, Cotoneaster, Pyracantha, Veronica, Ficus, Rubber Tree, Euonymus, Escallonia, Heathers, Daphne, Cryptomeria, Clethra, Ceanothus, etc. Here is how it is done:

In any plant you have a main stem, out of which grow sideshoots. There is always a slight swelling at the base of the sideshoot, where it joins the main stem. Take a sharp knife (a budding knife will do) and cut off the sideshoot, getting as much as you can of the swelling along with it. Will this injure the mother plant? Yes, it may; and that is why heel cuttings are best made from a branch you have already removed from the mother plant when pruning. In other words, the next time you prune a shrub, take one of the branches you have cut off, then select one of its sideshoots and carve out the heel or swelling as described above.

After you have carved out the entire swelling, pare it down until there is left at the hardened base of the sideshoot only a slight curve. Some plants will root much faster with heels.

When to Make Cuttings

In general, cuttings from shrubs should be made when they are dormant. In the West this is usually during the winter — any time in Novem-

ber, December or January. Some nurseries prefer to make cuttings of half-hardened wood in the summer. July and August are good months. Fuchsia, *Kerria japonica*, Beauty Bush, Crape Myrtle, Privet, Passion Flower, Mock Orange, Silver Lace Vine, Pomegranate, Scabiosa, all dormant Roses, Columbaria, and *Tamarix parviflora* come under this heading.

Root cuttings of Wisteria should be made at this time.

Make Green Cuttings in the Spring and Fall

Very soft, green cuttings are better made in the spring, from February 15th to May 15th. The trailing Ice Plants may be started at this time, as well as shrubby Calceolaria, Dianthus, Sun Rose, Blue Marguerite, Geranium and Pelargonium, all Pentstemons, and Fuchsia.

If you start green cuttings which are more ripened, the period between middle spring and early fall is best — May 15th to September 15th. Take Lilac cuttings early in June. Start Fuchsias in water or sand, and Aubretias after blooming. Others which may be started at this time are: Weigela, Streptosolen, *Poinsettia (Euphorbia) pulcherrima*, Oleander, Gazania, Golden Bells, Blue Marguerite, Deutzia, Daphne odora, hybrids of Bouvardia, and *Abelia grandiflora. Camellia japonica* cuttings are best taken in July or in August.

In the fall, between September 15th and the end of November, start your ripe wood cuttings — any kind of Cotoneaster, any kind of Spirea, Crape Myrtle, Geranium and Pelargonium, Bougainvillea, Flame Pea, Pansy, Viola, *Daphne odora, Begonia semperflorens*, Japanese Quince, *Kerria japonica*, and Weigela.

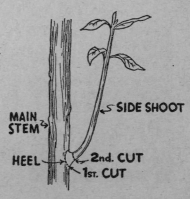

HEEL CUTTING

MAIN STEM
HEEL
SIDE SHOOT
2nd. CUT
1st. CUT

Some Plants You May Grow With Cuttings

Soft Green Cuttings (February to May)

Abutilon	Lantana
Aubretia	Malvaviscus
Begonia	Mesembryanthemum
Cactus	Pelargonium
Chrysanthemum	Pentstemon
Dahlia	Poinsettia
Dianthus	Rehmannia
Felicia	Salvia
Forsythia	Sedum
Fuchsia	Streptosolen
Geranium	Tecoma
Heliotrope	Verbena

Half Ripened Wood (July to September)

Abelia	Hydrangea
Azalea	Myrtle
Buddleia	Osmanthus
Choisya	Pleroma
Cotoneaster	Plumbago
Escallonia	Polygala
Eugenia	Pyracantha
European Bay	Thuya
Fuchsia	Veronica
Heather	Yew
Hibiscus	

Hard Wood Cuttings (December to February)

Boxwood	Jacaranda
Bougainvillea	Jasmine
Camellia	Lavender
Chorizema	Lions Tail
Daphne	Oleander
Euonymus	Oregon Grape
Deutzia	Solarum
Hoya	Spiraea
Hydrangea	Syringa (Lilac)
Holly	Weigela
Ipomea	

Cuttings That Will Root in the Open (November to December)

Azalea	Pelargonium
Barberry	Pomegranate
Dogwood	Poplar
Euonymus	Privet
Fuchsia	Rose
Grapes	Spiraea
Hydrangea	Syringa
Kolkwitzia	Tamarix
Lagerstroemia	Weigela
Lonicera (honeysuckle)	Willow
Mock Orange	

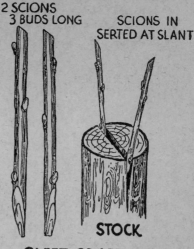

2 SCIONS 3 BUDS LONG   SCIONS INSERTED AT SLANT

STOCK

CLEFT GRAFTING

Grafting and Budding

In the West grafting is usually done in the autumn or spring. In autumn the tree has not yet become fully dormant (which means, literally, asleep); and in the spring the sap is beginning to flow.

Grafting is done to make a tree or shrub grow more vigorously and rapidly, or to add to the growing strength of a variety by grafting it onto another shrub or tree, which is already growing strongly. With some evergreens it is necessary to resort to grafting to get new plant stock, because they either refuse to grow from cuttings, or take too long to grow from seeds.

How to Begin

You work with two chief materials — a plant that is rooted in the ground (although there are exceptions), called the stock; and a piece cut from a twig, root or other part of another plant, which is grafted onto the stock, and is called the scion or cion. Scion means "child or descendant".

The stock and scion do not blend; each keeps its own individuality, except that their bark and wood grow together.

If you will cut a twig cleanly with a sharp knife, and study it, you will see first the outer bark, then green bark inside that. The first bark is firm, the second is soft. This soft tissue is called the cambium layer. It lies between the outer bark and the wood, and is a zone of cells which produces new growth. Cambium is from the Latin "cambio," meaning "exchange".

You can easily see how necessary it is for the growing tissue of cambium layer of the scion to come in contact with the growing tissue or cambium layer of the stock. This is the part that does the knitting together.

Cleft Grafting Is Simple

WHIP GRAFTING

Now, how do you go about this? There are several simple ways. One of the best known is Cleft Grafting. It is mostly used with nut and fruit trees. First you go to your stock and cut off short the branch or trunk on which the grafting is to be done. Split it down the center.

Next you cut off your scion from whatever plant, tree or shrub it happens to be on. It should be three buds long. The top bud is the scion's top; it is cut off close to that bud. You leave more room below the bottom bud, and whittle off that end in the shape of a wedge. Do this with two scions, because you must always insert two into the crack in your stock.

Now here's the main point. Remembering that the growing tissues must be in contact, put your scions into the crack at a slant, so that each is half clasped by the inner and outer bark of the stock. Cover over the entire surface with grafting wax; and later on cut out the weaker of the two scions, should both happen to grow — usually both do not. See picture on page 30.

Grafting Young Plants

Then there is Whip or Tongue Grafting. This is as common as the method just described, and as simple. The chances are you'll use it more because it is intended for young plants and small branches. Your stock and scion should be the same diameter. Cut both diagonally; that is, bevel the ends, and cut down into each beveled end. Fit the two parts together.

You need not use wax; merely tie securely with raffia or string saturated in grafting wax. The string should be strong enough to hold, yet weak enough so that it will break easily and not strangle the plant as it grows larger.

You can experiment with other forms of grafting, but most of them are variations of the above.

Budding

Inserting a bud in between the bark and wood of a plant is called budding. The reason for doing it is to obtain new growth fast, and in some cases to provide strong roots for subjects which ordinarily have weaker ones.

Pick out a branch which has more than the usual number of buds on it — indicating that it is healthy. Use a budding knife. Cut off the leaf, leaving a part of the leaf stalk. Cut downward, under the bark. When you lift out the bud it is like a tiny shield — that is why this is called Shield Budding. Then you make a T-shaped cut into the bark of your stock, down near the base of the plant, and on the north side. Cut just through the bark, not into the wood. Peel back the bark carefully and insert the shield-shaped bud. Put the bark back in place. Some turn the bud upside down to shed water. You can try both ways. Be very careful during this inserting, and make sure your bud fits flatly. Tie up with raffia, leaving the bud itself uncovered.

Sometimes the bud won't "take". If it dries up and turns brown, it hasn't taken; but if it is still fresh-looking in ten days it is a success, and you may cut the twine. Pacific Westerners should do their budding from June to September.

With budding, too, you may experiment with different methods. Patch Budding is harder than Shield Budding. You cut squares from the scion and stock and fit them. This may be easily done by the beginner. "H" budding, like its name, means that an "H" is cut in the stock and the scion is fitted to it.

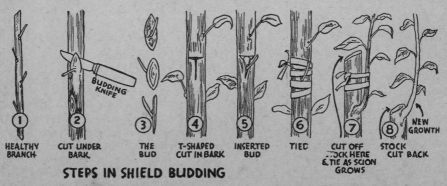

1 HEALTHY BRANCH   2 CUT UNDER BARK   3 THE BUD   4 T-SHAPED CUT IN BARK   5 INSERTED BUD   6 TIED   7 CUT OFF STOCK HERE & TIE AS SCION GROWS   8 STOCK CUT BACK   NEW GROWTH

STEPS IN SHIELD BUDDING

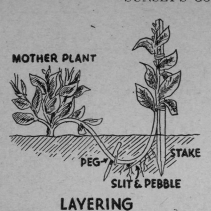

MOTHER PLANT

PEG
STAKE
SLIT & PEBBLE

LAYERING

April: *Saxifraga strachyii*, Stylosa Iris, Cacti, Delphinium, cuttings of Geraniums, Thalictrum.

October: Primrose, Bleeding Heart, Arabis, Aubretia, Coral Bells, Campanula, Veronica, Verbena, Petunia, Sedums, Cacti, Echeveria, Saxifraga, Phlox, Michaelmas Daisy, Astilbe, fibrous Begonia, *Francoa ramosa*, Thalictrum.

November: Primrose, German Iris, Armeria, Anchusa, Canna, Gaillardia, Geum, Sedums, Saxifraga, Thrift, Michaelmas Daisy.

December: Rudbeckia, Sedums, Cacti, Saxifraga, Phlox, Michaelmas Daisy, Lilies.

After these plants have finished blooming cut back the dead and unsightly tops. Then after about a week or two, lift the plants out of the ground carefully with a spade or trowel, and shake off the dirt. With a sharp knife cleanly cut the fibrous mass apart into individual plants, and replant.

Dividing

Sometimes you come across a garden direction which reads, "Divide Bearded Iris now," or "Divide clumps." Dividing — or simple division as it is often called — is done: (1) to break up an old plant, the root system of which has become so unwieldy that the plant can no longer function as it should; or (2) to gain several new, smaller, more vigorous blooming plants from one already growing.

Divide according to the following chart, delaying the dates in cold sections until the ground has warmed up in the spring.

January: Coral Bells, Michaelmas Daisy.

February: Thalictrum

March: Stylosa Iris, *Saxifraga strachyii*, Chrysanthemums, *Anemone japonica*, fibrous Begonias, Gerbera, Chrysanthemums, and Dahlias. ias, Gerbera, and Dahlias.

Layering

This is one of the most convenient ways of getting a new plant out of one that is already growing. You bend down a long branch, peg it to the ground, cover with soil, and stake the shoot to hold it firmly.

Before covering, make a slit halfway through the stem and insert a pebble there to hold it open. This helps new roots to form. Later on, when the branch has rooted well, you can separate it from the mother plant. Some of the plants which you can increase with layering are:

Laburnum, Berberis, Nerium, Cotoneaster, Pyracantha, Aubretia, Cantua, Lonicera, Philadelphus, Mandevilla, Alebia, Daphne, Magnolia, Cistus, Hoya, Euonymus, Cornus, Ampelopsis, Echium, Rhododendron, Azalea, Kalmia.

STEPS IN DIVIDING

(Experienced gardeners tear clumps apart with hands or handforks, doing less damage to roots than cutting)

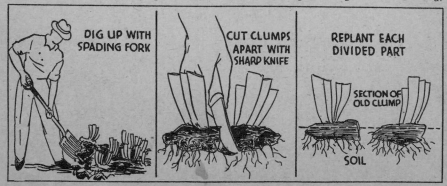

DIG UP WITH SPADING FORK

CUT CLUMPS APART WITH SHARP KNIFE

REPLANT EACH DIVIDED PART

SECTION OF OLD CLUMP

SOIL

The New Growth Hormone

At the present time we're on the threshold of a new way to make cuttings root faster. The Boyce Thompson Institute for Plant Research, Yonkers, New York, pioneered this work. Their investigations led to the development of a growth hormone chemical. This chemical makes certain hard-to-root cuttings root easily, and many others root faster. The manufacturers of the chemicals in a few instances are claiming advantages that as yet can't be guaranteed every time.

Briefly, it's necessary to dilute the growth hormone with pure grain alcohol or water, depending on which product is used. A small amount of the solution is poured into a drinking glass. Then the cuttings are placed in the glass for 18 to 24 hours, depending which product is used, so that just their basal ends absorb the solution. The cuttings are then ready to be rooted in flats of sand. Procedure from then on is the same as for all other cuttings, except that hormone-treated cuttings respond quicker.

Sketch 1. One-tenth gram Indole Acetic acid crystals (obtainable from Merck & Co., Rahway, N. J., for 65 cents) has been put in 10 cc. of pure grain alcohol. The solution is being drawn out, to which water will be added: one cc. of solution to each 100 cc. of water.

Sketch 2. The final solution prepared, cuttings (in this case Cascade Fuchsia) are stood in one inch of solution in a drinking glass. Best results are obtained if only the basal portions of the cuttings are in the growth hormone solution. Note the way the cuttings are tied in a bunch to keep them vertical. The cuttings should be allowed to stand in the solution 22 to 24 hours.

Sketch 3. The solution-treated cuttings should be inserted in coarse sand or top gravel. Top gravel insures perfect drainage. Sand sometimes packs too firmly.

Sketch 4. Three to 4 weeks later, Cascade Fuchsias are rooted nicely. They're at least 2 weeks ahead of cuttings started the old-fashioned way.

There's a great future for the growth hormone method, and great fun for amateurs who try it. Those unable to obtain the equipment pictured in Sketch 1 might try the new product, Hormodin A, which has a similar formula and gives similar results. Obtainable through garden stores. A 5 cc. bottle is $1.

HOW TO START SEEDS

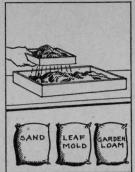

It is economical to buy quality seed. Carefully read and follow the cultural directions printed on the packet to get the best results, for each plant has its own requirements.

For soil drainage, break up old flower pots and cover the bottom of the seed box, in addition to boring holes in the bottom boards provided they are set with no space between.

Sift well-prepared soil composed of sand, leaf mold and good garden loam on top of drainage material through a fine-meshed sieve, filling box to about 1 inch of the top.

Firm the soil so it will not settle after water is applied by pressing down heavily on entire surface with a block of wood, making the surface perfectly level at the same time.

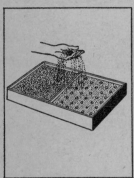

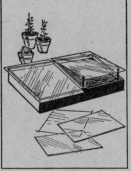

Scatter fine seed thinly over soil surface. Set large seeds down into the soil ¼ to ½ inch deep. Sift enough soil over the top of the seed box to lightly cover the seed.

Gently sprinkle seed flat by means of a fine spray so as not to dislodge the seed. Water thoroughly, then do not water again until soil surface shows indications of drying out.

Cover seed flat with glass slightly tilted to provide plenty of ventilation. To aid germination a couple of thicknesses of newspaper can be put under glass till seed sprouts.

Set seed box where protected from direct sunlight, winds or downpour—in lath house, cold frame or under a tree. If set in the open, shade with burlap, muslin or lath screen.

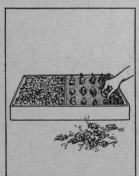

After the seeds sprout, keep the flat free from weeds. Also, thin out the little plants just as soon as they begin to touch so they do not grow up tall and spindly.

When fourth leaf appears lift out the plants with a fork and transplant into pots or box, using a little richer soil. Harden off plants by gradual exposure to sun and air.

In about two weeks set plants out into a garden spot prepared in advance by removal of stones and replacement of some of the subsoil with good garden loam and fertilizer.

After planting, carefully water the plants, so soil packs about the roots, then shade them for a few days by means of plant caps, improvised cardboard shields or inverted berry boxes.

HOW TO MAKE CUTTINGS

1. Every home gardener may have the fun of increasing favorite plants and shrubs by taking stem cuttings. Soft wooded plants, as geraniums and carnations; also shrubby, hard wood plants as roses and hydrangeas, can be grown by this method.

2. For rooting cuttings out of doors, use a flat with removable glass top. For 3 or 4 choice cuttings, use a flower pot in saucer of water as shown in Fig. 3. Provide drainage. Cuttings require moisture, protection from sun, and even temperature.

3. No general rules can be given for the soil in which cuttings should be started. Some gardeners prefer sand. In general, a mixture of peat moss and sand, or peat moss and loam is best. Experiment for yourself. The rooting medium must be moist.

4. Soft wooded cuttings root more easily than do hard wood cuttings. To test a soft wood cutting, bend a shoot of the plant. If it snaps off squarely as in *A*, it is ready. If it crushes as in *B*, the shoot is too old or too young for good results.

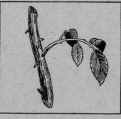

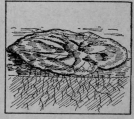

5. Above are pictured cuttings from a pelargonium taken in June. Note that cuts are made straight across, just below a joint. Such cuttings should be kept dry for 24 hours and then placed 1½ inches deep in pot. Keep shaded under glass until rooted.

6. Shrub cuttings can be taken either when the shrub is dormant in midwinter or in summer when shoots are beginning to ripen. Use a sharp knife and cut shoots 3 to 12 inches long, cutting below a joint. Above is shown a rose cutting taken in late summer

7. Above is a seed flat full of hardwood cuttings. Part of the leaves have been removed to reduce evaporation. The cuttings are set perpendicularly an inch or two deep. Some hard wood cuttings require months to root so they should not be crowded.

8. Certain fleshy leaved plants can be rooted by taking leaf cuttings. In the Rex begonia above, the leaf was simply placed on moist sand in a frame and held down with splinters. If kept moist, shaded, and at an even temperature, it will take root.

9. Some plants such as the dracena (as well as most fruit trees) can be multiplied with root cuttings. Cut a portion of the root into pieces 1 to 3 inches long and plant horizontally in moist peat moss, or soil. Such cuttings usually require bottom heat.

10. Another way to multiply woody or half woody plants is by layering. The method is to lay down a branch in midsummer, pegging it down as shown, then covering with loam. Keep watered and roots will form; then transplant. Provide a stake.

11. Some cuttings root quickly, others require a long time. Until cuttings are rooted they must be kept moist and warm. When rooted, transplant carefully to pots (firming the soil), and later to garden. Above is shown a properly transplanted holly tree.

12. The above suggestions will help you to grow plants from cuttings. For complete information, get "The Nursery Manual" by L. H. Bailey (The Macmillan Company, price $2.50). You may order it from SUNSET. Drawings used here are from this book.

HOW TO GRAFT

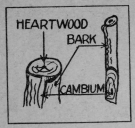

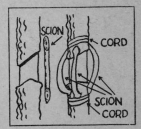

GRAPE END GRAFT

All plants have an outer and an inner surface. A mucilaginous growing tissue called the cambium layer unites these parts. In grafting, success depends upon forming a living contact between the cambium of a scion (a bud or shoot to be grafted) and the cambium of a sturdy root-stock.

Grafting deciduous trees is best done in late winter. Unless as an experiment, graft only related species — cherry on cherry, etc. Exceptions exist. Peach, plum, apricot, nectarine, and almond seem congenial, while quince has an affinity for apple, pear, loquat, and toyon. Freaks are fun!

Tools for grafting need not be expensive. Those essential include a knife for cutting scions; pruning shears; a saw; mallet and hand ax for splitting limb stubs; a heavy screw driver or other prying tool for opening clefts, and wax or tar to seal all of the cut surfaces afterwards.

Drawing above shows *end graft* (used principally for grapes). A root-stock and scion are matched for size, the square-cut ends butted tightly together and held in place by a peg forced into the pithy centers, and the perfect-fitting union bound very tightly with friction tape.

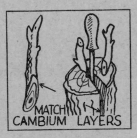

In *cleft-grafting,* saw limbs off squarely. Stubs left should have a diameter not greater than four inches. Wood and bark below the cut should be free of knots and blemishes. Leave a large limb, preferably on the south side to shade side grafts from sun and to utilize surplus sap.

Now with handax and mallet split limb stubs through their centers at right angles to the vertical, or tree trunk, line. A horizontal split holds grafts more securely. After splitting, force a screw driver (or other prying tool) into the cut until a half-inch cleft is formed. (See sketch.)

Scions should be taken from vigorous last season's growth. Cut them five inches long with four good buds. Sharpen lower end with two long cuts as indicated. Now fit scions one on either side, into the cleft. Match as nearly as possible the cambium layers of stock and scion as indicated.

Remove pry tool. Tension of wood should hold scions firmly. Wax carefully to exclude the air. A good grafting wax can be obtained at any seed store, or one can be made at home by melting together equal parts beeswax, resin and paraffine; it is applied hot, like asphaltum, with brush.

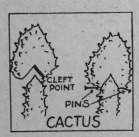

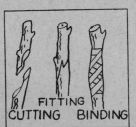

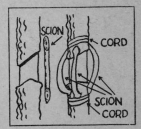

The *saddle* or *inverted cleft graft* is used principally on fleshy and succulent subjects. Scions are split or notched, and root-stocks are wedge pointed. Other than matching cut surfaces, no particular care is needed. Ordinary pins are used to hold scions in place until the union is made.

Whip or *tongue grafts* are used for small plants. Stock and scion of a size are cut on a long angle. Midway of this cut a transverse notch is made. Stock and scion are then fitted together, so that tongues interlock. The union is tightly wrapped with wax and friction tape to speed healing.

Evergreen and other difficult subjects are best *veneer grafted.* Stock and parent plant are placed side by side. A portion of bark of each is pared away and cut surfaces bound together with adhesive tape. When union is made the plant is severed from its parent and the root-stock beheaded.

Trees which have suffered trunk injuries can be saved by clearing out injured bark to live tissue and inserting vigorous shoots of last season's wood as shown. Shoots can be cut somewhat longer than wound and worked into place. Tie firmly, wax, and wrap with mud-filled burlap sacking.

HOW TO
Care for Your Garden

Your plants need, most of all nitrogen, potassium and phosphorous, so you must know where to get these and how to supply them.

Nitrogen

Source: Nature supplies nitrogen in nitrate form in barnyard and green manures. These manures are called organic plant foods, and include poultry manure, guano, blood and bone meals, etc.

Also included among them are the legumes, Vetch, Alfalfa, White Clover, etc. Inorganic plant foods also supply nitrogen, as: ammonium nitrate, sulphate of ammonia, etc. There is more nitrogen in these than in manures.

Use: While your plants are growing, add fertilizer containing nitrogen.

Phosphorus

Source: Manures also contain phosphorus, but in small amounts. Some is present in wood ash, but you will find most of it concentrated in super-phosphate, ammonium phosphate, raw phosphate rock, bone black, bone meal, and fish scrap.

Use: This type of fertilizer should be given to the plant after it has made its growth because its purpose is to help make the flowers and seeds, and aid the growth of the roots.

Potassium

Source: Like phosphorus, potassium is found in animal manure and wood ash, but in small quantities. You will find plenty of it, however, in carbonate of potash, nitrate of potash, kelp ash (seaweed), kainite, stems, tobacco, muriate and sulphate of potash.

Use: As in the case of phosphorus, apply it after the plant has made its growth, since its job is to build strong stems, and aid in the making of flowers and fruits.

How to Select a Fertilizer

You will find all the foregoing chemical elements present in complete commercial fertilizers. The best fertilizer should, besides containing the above, have in it other elements such as magnesium, chlorine, zinc, iodine and so forth in small amounts.

HOW TO FERTILIZE

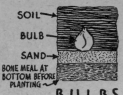

BULBS

ANNUALS or PERENNIALS

ROSES & SHRUBS

TREES

How to Apply Fertilizers

Bulbs: When shoots are 6-8 inches high, put fertilizer in a ring around the bulb, about 2 ounces to each bulb, if a fertilizer has not been put in at the time of planting. Bulbs like bone meal at planting time. You can use it freely. A fertilizer should be mixed with the soil in the bottom of the hole where the bulb is planted.

Annuals and Perennials: Scatter around each plant, and uniformly over the flower bed, watering well afterwards.

Roses: Roses like cultivated soil with plenty of humus. If the soil needs humus, add peat moss. When the buds start to form, put a half cup of commercial fertilizer around the bush, making sure that you keep it off the leaves and away from the stalk. Six to 8 inches from the stalk is a safe distance. Always apply water.

Ornamental Trees and Shrubs: For shrubs, follow the rule for Roses. If you are in doubt as to what chemical element is needed most, play safe with a complete commercial fertilizer containing the chief plant foods. Water thoroughly.

Trees: It is harder to tell when a tree needs fertilizing. This is because a tree's roots spread out so far, thus reaching more places where food can be absorbed. Each year spread fertilizer around the tree about 2 or 3 feet from the trunk, depending on the size of the tree. Distribute a pound for every year of the tree's age. After ten years, you can keep the amount down to about 15 pounds.

How to Fertilize

Much depends on this, if you are to get the best results. Here are some good rules for the Pacific West:

1. In the fall, right after the first rains, spread fresh and half-rotted manures on the soil. They should contain straw. After spreading, spade them into the ground.

2. During the growing season of shrubs and plants, apply well-rotted manure.

3. As your plants begin to blossom, help their flowers, growth and general health along with commercial fertilizers containing phosphorus and potassium besides nitrogen. Concentrated preparations of manure may be used at this time, too.

Commercial fertilizers usually contain a great deal of mineral fertilizers, though some kinds combine mineral and animal fertilizers.

You can tell pretty well what your garden soil needs as you get on with your gardening and the plants come up. If something seems to be wrong — if you have small flowers, weak stems, poor root growth, leaves lacking a rich green color, etc. — check back over the description of the needed chemical elements and what they do in the soil chapter of this book. You can then decide what is needed.

If you would like to know a lot about fertilizers, you can get information from your State Agricultural Experiment Station, or from fertilizer companies, the names of which the Garden Editor of *Sunset* Magazine will be glad to send you.

FERTILIZER CHART

Plants	Fertilizers and Amounts	When to Apply
Annuals	Balanced commercial fertilizer, elements preferably in the ratio 4-12-4 or 5-10-5. Three to 4 pounds per 100 square feet.	In spring, when preparing beds for planting. Work it into top 5 inches.
	Balanced commercial fertilizer, ¼ the above amount per 100 square feet.	When plants are in bud stage, apply once. For long-blooming kinds, 2 applications, 8 weeks apart.
Biennials and Perennials	Same as for annuals.	When new growth starts in spring. Work it into top 5 inches.
	One-fourth, same as for annuals.	After the above, apply at 6-week intervals till end of August.
Bulbs	Bonemeal. One-half inch bonemeal under 1 inch sand under each bulb.	At planting time.
House Plants, Porch and Window Boxes	Balanced commercial fertilizer, or house plant tablets. Apply in liquid form, usually 1 level teaspoonful or 1 tablet to 1 quart water.	When new growth starts in spring, and thereafter at 6-week intervals till end of October. Also, when planting (plants, not seed) or repotting, mix dry commercial fertilizer with soil.
Lawns: Old	Balanced commercial fertilizer, 3 to 4 pounds per 100 square feet. A rich thick lawn keeps weeds out.	As soon as last frost is out of ground, and thereafter at 6-week intervals till end of October.
New	Well-rotted manure, 2 inches for ordinary soils, 4 to 6 for heavy or sandy; plus balanced commercial fertilizer, 3 to 4 pounds per 100 square feet.	When preparing ground for seeding (preferably April or September). Spread commercial fertilizer over manure, and work them in 6 inches.
Hedges: Old	One pint balanced commercial fertilizer to each 15 feet of row, putting half on each side.	When new growth starts in spring, and thereafter at 6-week intervals till end of August. Work lightly into soil.
New	One pint balanced commercial fertilizer to each 20 feet of trench.	When planting. Spade thoroughly into bottom of trench.
Trees: Old	Allow 1 pound balanced commercial fertilizer for each inch of circumference of trunk, measured at height of 4 feet.	Once a year. Preferably spring, just as new leaves begin to develop, but can be done any time. Put it in crowbar holes circling tree at distance of greatest branch-spread, and 2 inches wide, 18 inches deep. Put 2 inches or soil in top of each hole.
New	Allow 1 pint balanced commercial fertilizer for each foot of diameter of the hole.	When planting. Spade thoroughly into bottom of hole.

THINGS TO REMEMBER

Always follow the directions that come with your fertilizer just as carefully as you'd follow your doctor's prescription.

Never, except when working it in, put commercial fertilizer on dry ground. First water the soil.

Never let any kind of fertilizer touch a plant— stalk, stem, foliage or flower. It burns them.

Always use only *well-rotted* manure. New manure sometimes brings harmful bacteria; always brings weed seeds and the wrong perfume.

Always test your soil once a year. Soiltex, a tester available at most garden stores, costs $1, and tells you whether anything's wrong, and what to do about it.

Never add lime to soil unless a test shows that soil needs it.

A Few Hints about Watering

There is more to watering than just operating the hose for 15 minutes after supper, before dark. Do not water much in the winter, unless it happens that you are doing a little planting, say, in February. The soil should then be both moist and firm around the roots. When you do your seed sowing around in April, water constantly. Bulbs planted in a sunny exposure should be watered profusely throughout the dry season.

Watering Northwest Lawns

Remember to water right after fertilizing your lawn (June is a good time to fertilize). In general, June is the time to start sprinkling or irrigating seriously. The lawn will need regular watering during the summer.

As fall comes on, do not give up watering because of foggy days or light rains. Your garden still needs good soaking through September, depending, of course, on the kind of weather you have any particular year.

Southwesterners

In the South instead of watering by sprinkling, make a basin around your shrubs, trees and plants, and let the water from the hose run slowly for an hour or two or until the soil will take no more moisture. In other words, flood your plants. It's a good idea to fill the water basin with manure after watering around shrubs. Then, when the soil dries, cultivate it a little.

Water generously in midsummer. August especially is a hard month for your garden. If you find that your water basins fill too soon, make mounds of soil around the shrubs, then flood them with a slow stream from the hose.

For annuals and perennials, dig a furrow between their rows, and let the water run down just as they do on large agricultural areas. The soil in all cases must become saturated, and then you must always cultivate (that is, loosen the topsoil) within a day or so. If you want to have the soil hold the moisture in, spread a mulch on it. Leaf mold, bean straw, peat and shredded cow manure are all good.

Keep a Notebook

Certain plants need especial watering attention at certain times of the year. Chrysanthemums from July to September, for example. It is wise to keep a notebook about such habits. In gardening, it is wise to concern yourself with one problem at a time — learn the habits of the plants you have set out, and learn about unfamiliar plants bit by bit, preferably when you start to grow them. This helps to keep you from becoming confused.

One more watering thought or two for the Southwest: Water early enough so that the foliage will be dry before sundown, in late fall. The temperature sometimes drops 30 degrees at night. Morning is your best time.

Pacific Central Gardeners

Watering during dry weather applies to you, too. This means regular watering during the summer. Avoid a superficial irrigating of the surface. Let the water go down deep. This is called slow irrigation.

If you do any transplanting, remember to water those plants well, whether trees, vines, shrubs or others.

Watering in General

Water your compost heap — the moisture helps to speed decay. Water plants before applying fertilizer, as well as afterwards; this avoids possible burning. If your garden slopes, it will need more watering than a level one. A sandy terrace dries up quickly; it should have twice as much water as a flat lawn.

Sprinklers are good, but you must let them stand in one place for some time before moving, because they spread water thinly.

You can tell when a plant needs water by the drooping or wilting of its leaves; but don't wait for that — some plants do not thus ask for help as soon as others.

Water according to the season. Evaporation is rapid in the summer, slow in winter. A plant just about to bloom needs more water than one which has finished. Different plants should be watered differently. Cacti need very little. Geraniums need a little more. Camellias need a lot. No plant except a bog plant should stand in nothing but water. Most others need good drainage.

Sprinkling lightly (except right after sowing seeds, and during germination period) is not enough. The roots turn up toward the surface — one of the causes of shallow-rooted lawns. Water deeply so that the roots reach far down — this stands them in good stead when the weather is extreme, and is especially important in regions of hot, dry summers.

WATERING CHART

Plant These in the Shade and Give Them Plenty of Water

Peruvian Lily	Dog-tooth Violet	Saxifrage
Sweet Alyssum	Bleeding Heart	Cineraria
Japanese Anemone	Foxglove	Indian Pink
Rocky Mountain Columbine	Geum	Meadow Rue
Wild Ginger	Columbine	Viola
Astilbe	Garland Flower	Violet
Begonia	Christmas Rose	Fairy Primrose
Calceolaria	Coral Bells	Polyanthus Primrose
Canterbury Bells	Musk Flower	Oxslip
Lily-of-the-Valley	Forget-Me-Not	Cowslip
Cyclamen		Flowering Sage

Give Plenty of Water to These Sun-Loving Plants:

Japanese Iris	Moss Pink	Violet
Poker Plant	Blue Bonnet	Tufted Pansy
Evening Primrose		Pansy

These Like Sun and Warmth, But Only Moderate Watering

Achillea	Australian Pea	Day Lily
Rock Cress	Globe Thistle	German Iris
False Wall Cress	Echeverias	Leucocoryne ixioides
Wild Hyacinth	Wild Wallflower	Perennial Blue Flax
Firecracker Flower	California Poppy	Monkey Flower
Harvest Brodiaea	Blue Marguerite	Penstemon
Mariposa Lily	Blanket Flower	Common Garden Petunia
Corn Flower	Gypsophila repens	Cinquefoil
Shasta Daisy	Sneezeweed	Cornflower
Coreopsis	Sun Rose	Mourning Bride
Dwarf Morning Glory	Sunflower	Verbena
Wild Larkspur	Coral Bells	Indian Pink

For Very Little Water

Sand Verbena	Rock Rose	Jerusalem Thorn
Ovens Acacia	Red-flowered Gum	Sweet Pittosporum
Kangaroo Thorn	Pink-flowered White	Matilija Poppy
Baileys Acacia	Ironbark	Spanish Broom
Summer Lilac	Anemone Shrub	Stokes Aster
Bottle Brush	Red Ironbark	California Fuchsia
Cassia	Honey Myrtle	Scotch Broom
Wild Lilac	Oleander	Lions Tail

Western Garden Enemies

Plants become ill just as human beings do. When you walk or work amongst them in your garden, watch out for trouble. You are your garden's physician. Anything that looks wrong probably is wrong: a spot on a leaf, a leaf eaten away, tiny objects clinging to a branch, etc.

Gardens are attacked by, (1) insects, (2) diseases, and (3) miscellaneous pests.

1. INSECT PESTS

Insects must eat — that is why they come after the growing things in your garden. There are two main kinds: biting insects and sucking insects. The biters are controlled with stomach poisons placed on the leaves they eat. The suckers do not get their food from the surface of the plant, but from its juices, and must be fought with "contact insecticides".

2. PLANT DISEASES

Fungi or bacteria may be the cause of the trouble if you are unable to discover actual insects about a troubled plant. These are controlled with spraying or dusting of the plant. In some cases, the soil must be disinfected. In still other cases, when you find that the disease is transmitted by an insect from one plant to another, the insect has to be controlled.

3. MISCELLANEOUS PLANT PESTS

These include gophers, slugs, snails, squirrels, etc. They are killed with special preparations of poisoned grain, metaldehyde baits, and stomach poisons.

Biting Insects

When you come across leaves which seem to have been eaten away in part or entirely, or roots, tubers, or another part of a plant with an eaten look, your garden is being visited by biting insects. Some biters burrow into fruit and lay eggs there. Some tunnel into other parts of the plant. Most of the biting insects can be killed with lead arsenate. All the control measures given in this chapter are sold under various trade names. Just ask in your garden store or nursery. In the table, you will notice, most of the biting insects are beetles, caterpillars, grasshoppers and worms, and the chief remedy is lead arsenate spray or dust.

Sucking Insects

Sometimes you will shake a flower and tiny specks like pepper will fall out. Or you may see a leaf unnaturally curled, and sticky to the touch. At other times a tiny insect will jump from a leaf if you disturb it.

You may see a cluster of things like minute barnacles or little eggs clinging to a stem or twig. Or you may not see any insects, but only a strange yellowing of the leaves, tender young leaves stunted and curling, distorted buds, discoloring of the plant, blackening, fungus growing in a sticky mass of honeydew, stunted flowers, or little galls on stems or the upper parts of leaves.

When you notice any of these signs, the trouble is some sucking insect or other. None of them do all of these things; each has its specialty.

Note in the table on the next page that a combination oil-nicotine spray is the remedy in most cases here, and that the pests are spiders, and the tiniest mites, bugs or flies.

Fungous Diseases

If there are gray, powdery growths on your plants; tiny red, brown or black pustules (elevations looking like pimples or blisters); holes in the leaves; red spots on the fruit; dying buds; soft brown spots; curled, distorted leaves; black spots on your Roses; or premature falling of leaves — the trouble is probably fungi (microscopic plant organisms, living as parasites on your plants).

Note, in the table, the importance of Bordeaux mixture in controlling fungous diseases.

Bacterial Diseases

When your leaves, twigs or branches die in an unaccountable manner, they may be attacked by some bacterial disease or blight. Potatoes, tomatoes and celery so attacked may sometimes be controlled with Bordeaux mixture. Peaches and walnuts are probably doomed, however, although you can try the same control measure with them. It is sometimes effective with peaches.

Miscellaneous Plant Pests

Most of the time you will see these "in person," and so will know that they are around. Snails can either be hand picked and stepped on (wear gloves if you are squeamish about handling them); or can be killed with poisoned bait. The latter is the better.

Other pests which succumb to poisoned bait — and usually one preparation will do for them all — are sowbugs, slugs, and earwigs. Special ant poisons are on the market.

Moles are caught with regular mole traps. Squirrels, gophers and rabbits are discouraged with poisoned barley, which you can also buy. Success has been had in gopher control with fumigating, non-explosive bombs which are ignited, dropped in the holes, and the holes covered. Gophers, however, are best trapped.

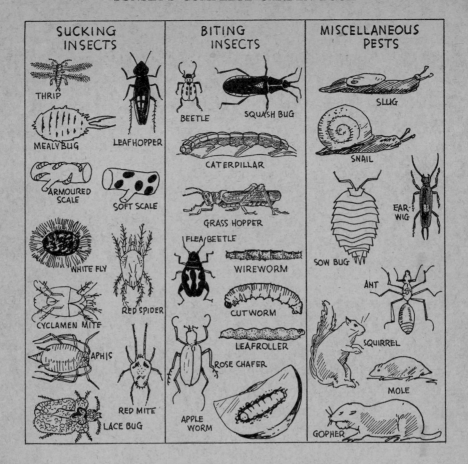

HOW TO CONTROL BITING INSECTS

BITING INSECT	CONTROL MEASURE	REMARKS
Twelve Spotted Beetles (Diabrotica)	Dust containing fluorine compound	Larvae eat roots and tubers. Adults eat plants, trees
Flea Beetles	Bordeaux mixture	⅛ in. long. Blue or green. Shiny. Eat leaves
Weevils or Snout Beetles	Dust containing fluorine compound	
Rose Chafers	Lead arsenate spray mixed with molasses	Tiny Beetles. Long legs. Brown. Eat foliage
Wireworms	Paradichlorobenzene mixed with topsoil but not touching stems	Larvae of Chick Beetles. Live in soil. Eat potatoes, beets, beans. Asters, Chrysanthemums. Long and slender.
Squash Bugs	Nicotine spray	Gray-brown, marked with orange. Attack melon and squash vines
Bulb Flies	Burn bulbs	Larvae eat bulb centers
Leafrollers and Leaftiers	Lead arsenate spray or dust	Caterpillars seen on apples, cherries, etc. Eat foliage. They roll and tie up leaves. Spray in summer
Caterpillars	Lead arsenate spray or dust	Attack foliage. Are cocoons of moths and butterflies. Spray when larvae first appear
Apple Worms or Codling Moths	Lead arsenate spray or dust	Worms in apples. Two broods a year. Spray when emerging from eggs

HOW TO CONTROL BITING INSECTS—(Continued)

BITING INSECT	CONTROL MEASURE	REMARKS
Artichoke Worms	Lead arsenate mixed with nicotine dust	They tunnel into artichokes. Burn the wormy heads, or dust every other week when heads are forming.
Cutworms, Army Worms	Poisoned bait (on sale at seed store—comes in container)	Larvae of insects which fly at night
Grasshoppers	Poisoned bait (see above)	Attack flowers and vegetables

HOW TO CONTROL SUCKING INSECTS

SUCKING INSECTS	CONTROL MEASURE	REMARKS
Aphis	Rotenone, pyrethrum, or oil-nicotine spray	Also called plant lice. Fat bodies, thin legs. They curl and stunt leaves and flowers. Make stickiness in which fungus grows
White Flies	Combination oil-nicotine spray	White bodies, white wings. Excrete stickiness as do aphis. Kill when young. They suck plant sap
Mealybugs	Combination oil-nicotine spray	Waxy. White. Size of grain of wheat. Suck sap. Secrete honeydew stickiness as above. Look for them on trees, shrubs, perennials. Ants protect them
Greenhouse Orthezia	Combination oil-nicotine spray	Mostly found in greenhouse. Spray every 6 weeks
Thrips	Nicotine spray or dust	Look like pepper. Lurk in flowers. Suck juices of fruit, foliage, flower
Leafhoppers	Nicotine spray or sulphur	$1/8$ in. long. Winged. Green, yellow, or spotted. They jump. Suck juices; kill tissues. Look for them on roses, apples, beets, grapes and other plants
Red Spiders	Combination oil-nicotine spray	Red or yellow and in between. Suck juices. Make leaves turn yellow. May kill tree or plant, or cause it to lose leaves
Cyclamen Mites	Combination oil-nicotine spray	Pale green. Found on Cyclamen. Attack leaves, buds. Look for curling, distortion, discoloration.
Lace Bugs (California Christmas Berry Tingid)	Combination oil-nicotine spray	Look for them on underside of Christmas Berry leaves. They make plants black, sticky; distort leaves
Chrysanthemum Midges	Combination oil-nicotine	Also called gall flies. Make galls on leaves, stems. Look for larvae with magnifying glass. Galls distort buds, leaves

What Your Pest Kit Should Contain

1. A hand sprayer of the fly-spray type, if you have a small garden. A pressure sprayer is better if your garden is larger.

2. A small bellows or piston-duster for dusting.

3. A container of lead arsenate, which can be dusted or sprayed on leaves and fruit to control biting insects.

4. A container with a contact insecticide (pyrethrum, rotenone, oil-nicotine, etc.) for the control of sucking insects, etc.

5. A container of nicotine, rotenone, or sulphur dust for low-growing plants, where you can reach the undersides of leaves better than you can with a spray.

6. A container of Bordeaux mixture for controlling fungous and bacterial diseases.

7. A container of poisoned bait for earwigs, snails, grasshoppers, sow bugs, army worms, slugs, cutworms, etc.

With the foregoing inexpensive equipment you will be ready at any time to do battle with almost any pest or disease which attacks your garden.

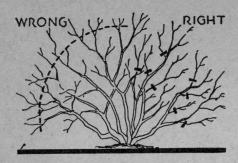

WRONG   RIGHT

How to Prune in the Pacific West

The most important thing to remember about pruning is that it sends the energy of a plant where you want it to go. Here are some of the familiar problems you can solve by correct pruning:

Dead or Injured Limbs: Dead, broken or diseased branches should be cut out as soon as possible with a sharp saw. Paint over the cuts with a commercial cauterizer.

Shaping: Shrubs, trees, Roses, etc., may be shaped by pruning to conform to the original idea you had when you planted them. Most specimen shrubs are so treated.

More Bloom: A plant can be made to bloom more abundantly by pruning. Deciduous shrubs, for example, should be pruned after flowering to encourage vigorous bloom for next season.

Light and Air: If a plant is too thick in the center, so that little light and air reach the interior, thin it out by pruning amongst center branches.

Larger Flowers: Remove the small buds which have come out beside the larger ones. The strength goes into the remaining larger bud. When you do this you are disbudding.

New Growth: You can bring about new stem growth by heading back, which means pruning so that the outward growth is cut back toward the main stem.

Pruning on top will increase the foliage and branches toward the sides. If you prune the roots, the plant will stop growing somewhat, but will develop more fruit and blossoms for you.

More Energy: Energy can be kept in the plant by removing flower stalks. This method is called topping.

When to Prune in the West

It is a good plan to go over all your trees and shrubs once a year at least, to cut out the superfluous, dead, diseased or broken branches, thin out the interior, force new growth, and trim up generally for shape.

Shrubs and trees which come to you from the nursery should be looked over before planting to see whether they need pruning.

There are no hard and fast rules for pruning growing shrubs and trees. Each one has its peculiarity, and the best plan is to write down the names of those growing in your garden, then familiarize yourself with its habits just before you prune it.

There are a number of general rules, however, which you can apply safely. For example, the time to prune any shrub or tree depends on when the plant blooms. Spring-blooming deciduous species are pruned after the blooming period, as are some evergreen kinds and you recall that "deciduous" means those trees which lose their leaves each year; it comes from the Latin, "deciduous," meaning "falling off". When you prune one of these you are inducing the formation of flower buds for the next season.

Summer and fall-blooming shrubs are usually pruned in the late fall and winter. New growth comes out by spring, bearing new flowers.

Many evergreen shrubs have indeterminate blooming periods; these may be pruned at any time of the year.

Three Important Rules for All Pruning

1. Use sharp, well-adjusted tools. You will need a strong pair of hand shears, a pruning saw that is preferably curved, pole shears so that you can reach the high limbs, and a pair of two-foot shears.

2. With all woody plants prune to a lateral or bud, leaving no outjutting stubs to die back, because sometimes they die back farther than you want them to and no new growth starts there.

3. When you prune, you leave a wound. The small cuts will usually heal themselves. Large wounds, over five inches in diameter, should be

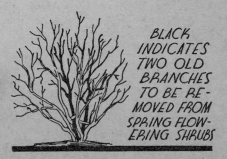

BLACK INDICATES TWO OLD BRANCHES TO BE REMOVED FROM SPRING FLOWERING SHRUBS

painted with a commercial cauterizer, which prevents decay and diseases and allows the wound to heal naturally.

Vines

Very little pruning is needed except to watch for and remove dead wood and scraggly growth. When a vine refuses to come into bloom dig down with your spade and cut off a few of the roots. This encourages blossoms on the old wood. You can help along your Wisteria by this method.

Pruning Western Roses

With Roses as with other plants, it is well to have in mind what your aim is in pruning. You want fewer and larger flowers from your Roses. In general, the way to get them is to prune severely. This must be done even when you plant them—remembering to make outside cuts for open bushes, and to leave no stubs whatever above the buds.

Hybrid Teas

In the Pacific West we plant Hybrid Teas more than any other kind of Rose, for it is here that they grow to special perfection. The ideal is to have a spreading bush, with its branches springing from the base. To achieve these, take care to remove all dead, weak, unripe, useless or interfering shoots, leaving no stub ends.

Next, the remaining shoots are shortened, leaving only 3 or 4 leaf-buds; this conserves the strength of the bush.

Mention has been made several times of cutting back to leave no stub. Here is a good rule to follow when you cut Hybrid Teas back to out-pointing buds: cut ¼ inch above the bud. If you are farther out, a stub is left; if you are in closer, you may cause injury to the bud itself.

Avoid under-pruning — remove at least two-thirds of last season's growth. The directions apply to practically all Hybrid Tea Roses. But you must remember the special needs of individual varieties, too. Betty Uprichard and Isobel need more pruning,while the Pernet Roses such as Golden Emblem, Queen Alexandria and Souv. de Claudius Pernet are pruned less.

Hybrid Perpetuals

These are grown mostly in colder climates, and resist frosts better than do the Hybrid Teas. Frau Karl Druschki, Paul Neyron, etc., should be pruned more severely than the Hybrid Teas because they are rank growers. Weak shoots especially should be pruned very much; the strong shoots need the least pruning.

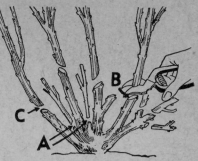

PRUNING ROSES

(A) Remove all weak and scraggly growth from around base.
(B) Shorten remaining canes by removing about ¾ of the previous year's growth.
(C) Make cuts slanting, cutting about ¼ inch above leaf buds. Use good tools.

Climbing Roses

Little pruning is necessary for Climbing Roses. Generally speaking, cut out the dead branches, remove old wood each year, and tie up the new canes which tend to sprawl.

Pruning Hedges

Privet should be sheared several times each year. Other hedges are shaped after they bloom —the Japanese Barberry and Quince, for instance, as well as Lilacs, Spiraeas and some of the Viburnums. With all these, clip only lightly.

An evergreen hedge should be cut back when the new growth becomes dark and stiff. These hedges take different shapes, which must be borne in mind during pruning.

The rectangular evergreen hedges are Hemlock, California Privet, Hornbeam and Yew; these should be made wide at the bottom, and narrower at the top, to admit light to the lower branches.

Conical hedges are other Privets, White Pine, Spruce, Retinospora, Barberry, and Arbor-vitae; the tops of these should be rounded, somewhat blunt, and narrower than the base.

How to Prune Shrubs

With most shrubs, a light thinning is often wiser than too heavy pruning. Unless you are striving for a formal effect, why not let your shrubs grow as freely as possible, especially those in the background of your borders?

You'll probably want to keep those in front of the house well shaped, as well as any specimen shrubs in your rear garden; but unless a background shrub is crowding itself or others, in trouble, or too rampant, let it take its natural shape.

Dead wood should be cut out. Cut it close to the main branch or trunk.

A new branch starts off in the direction of the bud, and the next blooming of the shrub will be on this new wood which is produced after pruning. If you want the new branches to spread outward, cut back to *outside* buds. For inward growth, cut to *inside* buds. It is better, however, rarely to cut for inward growth, since this will tend to crowd the interior of the plant and choke off its sunlight and air circulation.

Trees

When you transplant a tree, prune it severely. Do not try to keep too much of the top for immediate effect.

In pruning any tree, make your cuts with a sharp instrument, close to the main branch or trunk. As with shrubs, cut to outside buds so that new growth will spread outward.

There is a special way to cut. Cut upward on the under side about a foot from the main trunk or branch. This cut keeps the bark from stripping down. Then make a cut on the top side, a little farther out. The branch then falls, leaving a stub a foot or more in length. Finally, you cut off this stub close and parallel to the trunk or branch that is left, making sure you cut closely, so that nothing is left which might catch water and possibly lead to decay. Paint the wound, if it is over 5 inches in diameter, as directed under "Pruning Shrubs."

Tree Surgery

There are certain tree operations which come under the head of "Tree Surgery," although they are allied to pruning. Sometimes a tree branches upward into two secondary trunks, and the crotch is not strong enough to support the two heavy developments. If you suspect a tree of having a weak crotch, prune it first on the weaker side, or on both. If it still is weak and seems to be in danger of splitting, the tree needs surgery and you had better call in an expert to support the crotch with cables or bolts.

A tree needs surgery when its health seems endangered by the loss of heavy limbs during storms; when it is split in two; when its crotch is weak; when it is suffering from large cavities in its wood; and when wounds from pruning show decay.

SOME SHORT CUTS IN WESTERN PRUNING

Deciduous Shrubs

(Those which lose their leaves in the fall)

Unless otherwise noted prune after flowering or while dormant.

Azalea mollis—Remove suckers and dead flower heads.

Berberis (deciduous varieties)—Thin only.

Calycanthus—Prune for shape only.

Caryopteris—Cut back heavily the year's growth.

Cercis (Red Bud)—Prune only to shape.

Cornus (Dogwood)—Thin out if necessary and prune to keep in bounds. Red barked varieties grown for winter effect, cut down to within 1 and 2 inches of base about May.

Cydonia japonica—Remove suckers and prune laterals to short spurs.

Deutzia—Remove all old flowering wood.

Diervilla (Weigela)—Vigorous pruning of old wood.

Euonymus (deciduous varieties)—Thin out wood if too thick and shorten straggly growth. Prune berried varieties after fruiting only.

Exochorda grandiflora—Remove old flowering wood.

Forsythia—Prune laterals to 2 to 4 buds, after flowering only.

Fuchsia—If branches were killed by frost in winter, cut back to living wood or to ground after danger of frost is over. In mild localities and when used against walls, cut back laterals to 2 to 3 buds in early spring.

Hibiscus—Thin out old wood.

Hydrangea—Cut back season's growth to 2 to 3 buds and thin. After flowering considered best time.

Jasminum fruiticans—Very little pruning.

Kerria—Remove old wood to ground.

Kolkwitzia amabilis (Beauty Bush)—Suggest vigorous pruning of old wood.

Lippia citriodora—Prune to shape; gets very straggly.

Lonicera (bush varieties)—Remove old wood.

Magnolia (deciduous varieties)—Some of smaller varieties really in shrub class. No pruning.

Peconia moutan (Tree Peony)—No pruning except removal of old flower heads. Remove suckers from grafted varieties.

Philadelphus (Mock Orange)—Vigorous pruning old old wood to ground.

Ribes (Currants)—Remove old wood.

Spiraea—Cut out all old wood. Variety Anthony Waterer can be cut to ground when dormant if pink foliage is desired in spring.

Symphoricarpus (Snowberry)—Most attractive if cut to ground after fruiting.

Syringa (Lilac)—Remove flower heads and suckers. Thin young shoots if twiggy. English authorities recommend that old plants which have become too tall and leggy be cut to within 3 feet of ground in spring before flowering. This will sacrifice a season's bloom.

Viburnum (deciduous varieties)—To shape only.

Evergreens

Unless otherwise noted prune in spring.

Abelia—Very little pruning; thin if necessary.

Arbutus unedo (Strawberry Tree)—Thin out dead wood. Leggy stems can be cut back hard to force bushier growth.

Aucuba japonica—Little pruning unless straggly when will stand cutting of stems to 2 to 3 feet of ground to force new growth.

Azalea indica—Remove old flower heads and suckers, especially on grafted bushes.

Azara microphylla—Little pruning. Leggy bushes can be cut back after flowering.

Berberis (evergreen varieties)—Thin if necessary by cutting old exhausted stems to ground. Best time to prune is winter.

Buddleia—Varieties *Globosa* and *Alternifolia* pruned only if straggly by shortening stems after flowering. Other varieties cut back hard.

Buxus (Boxwood)—Natural shaped bushes best left unpruned. Keep dead wood thinned out for air to penetrate.

Camellia—Two methods. Prune only to shape or size or thin out and clear heavily.

Cassia—Prune only when too straggly by cutting back. Usually very early bloomer so delay pruning until after bloom.

Cestrum—Will stand hard pruning.

Choisya ternata—Thin out twiggy stems to help control mealy bug, and prune for size when necessary.

Cistus (Rock Rose)—Cut off old flowers and ends of shoots when plants are young, to form bushy shrubs. Older plants require very little pruning and resent being cut into hard old wood.

Coprosma—Prune for shape only.

Coronilla—Variety *Emerus* may be cut back hard. Variety *Glauca* requires very little pruning.

Cotoneaster—Usually little pruning required, especially if berries are cut.

Daphne—Prune very little. Ends of main shoots may be cut back if bush is too large. Don't cut laterals as these are the flower stems.

Diosma—Variety *Ericoides* may be pruned hard. Variety *Purpurea* (also known as *Agathosma villosa*) requires pruning only if too straggly.

Duranta plumieri (Golden Dewdrop)—After severe weather is over, cut back any wood injured by frost.

Elaeagnus—Little pruning. If bushes are straggly, shorten longest shoots.

Erica—Larger varieties may be cut back fairly hard at or after flowering time. Dwarf varieties are improved by removing old bloom after flowering.

Escallonia—May be cut back hard.

Euonymus (evergreen varieties)—Prune very little unless for hedge.

Fabiana imbricata—Cut back hard after flowering as apt to become straggly.

Genista (Broom)—When young cut back growing points several times during summer to encourage bushy habit. On older bushes shorten longer growths after flowering if necessary.

Iochroma—Prune quite hard after danger of frost is over. Quite tender.

Kalmia—Remove flower heads only.

Lantana—Will respond to hard pruning.

Lavandula (Lavender)—Prune hard.

Leonotis leonurus (Lions Tail)—Prune heavily to prevent getting straggly. Heavy pruning will cause later bloom.

Leptospermum—Will not break from old wood.

Ligustrum (Privet)—Prune hard in winter or spring.

Lonicera (Honeysuckle)—Usually cut hard, and old wood thinned if confused in line.

Mahonia (Hollygrape)—Pruning not usually necessary but may be cut hard.

Myrtus—Little pruning required.

Nandina domestica—Little pruning required.

Nerium (Oleander)—Often cut back hard every third year and old flowering wood removed every year after flowering.

Osmanthus fragrans (Sweet Olive)—Thin shoots when necessary.

Parkinsonia aculiata (Jerusalem Thorn)—Thin shoots when necessary.

Pernettya mucronata—Pruning rarely required and then only thinning.

Philadelphus mexicanus—Prune hard if you want form.

Phillyrea—Will stand hard pruning.

Photinia—Shorten long shoots if straggly.

Pimelea ferruginea—Prune only to shape.

Pittosporum—Prune for shape and size.

Polygala—Little pruning required.

Prunus (evergreen varieties)—Thin out when growth is heavy, and prune to shape.

Psidium cattleianum (Strawberry Guava)—Usually requires little pruning.

Pyracantha—May be pruned heavily in cutting berries.

Raphiolepis (Hawthorn)—Prune very little.

Rhamnus (Buckthorn)—Will stand hard pruning.

Rhododendron—On young plants points of shoots may be removed to encourage sturdy growth. If old bushes should become too large, cut back overgrown branches to old wood before flowering in spring. A season's bloom will be lost but better growth will be secured. General pruning: remove all faded flower heads to prevent development of seed pods and on grafted varieties remove suckers.

Rosmarianus officinalis—Prune to prevent becoming too straggly.

Ruta graveolens (Rue)—Will stand hard pruning when necessary.

Ruscus aculeatus (Butchers Broom)—Prune very little.

Salvia (shrub varieties)—Prune to prevent becoming too straggly.

Senecio grayii—Prune to shape only.

Solanum—Don't prune until after severe weather is over. Will stand heavy cutting back.

Spartium junceum (Spanish broom)—When young thin shoots can be cut back quite often to form bushy growth. Mature shrubs can be cut back quite heavily.

Teucrium (Germander)—Will stand heavy pruning.

Veronica—Prune as needed to shape.

Viburnum (evergreen varieties)—Prune only when necessary; little required.

Vitex—Pinch back ends of branches in spring.

HOW TO PRUNE IN THE WEST

Make sure all pruning tools are sharp and well-adjusted. Dull tools leave harmful wounds.

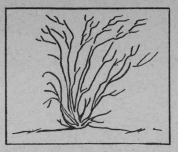

Most deciduous shrubs for garden purposes flower in the spring. Prune right after flowers drop, not in the fall.

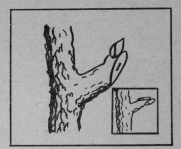

Prune to inside buds for inward growth, outside buds for outward growth. Usually the latter.

Shear your Privet hedges three to five times each year, depending on how rapid the growth is.

When new growth is dark and stiff, cut back evergreen hedges.

California Privet, English Laurel, Yew and Hemlock hedges are pruned wide at bottom, narrow at top, to admit sunlight.

Prune evergreen shrubs in the spring, unless otherwise noted.

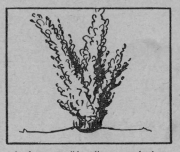

As far as possible, allow your shrubs to retain their natural shapes.

A poorly balanced tree. Tree-pruning should seek to restore well-balanced development. This needs a tree-expert.

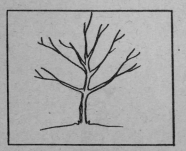

A well-balanced tree, with wide branches and wide crotches. Needs annual pruning.

Small wounds under two inches heal of themselves. Paint larger ones with commercial cauterizer.

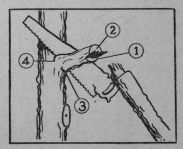

When pruning trees, cut and undercut branch at (1) and (2), undercut at (3), then saw down close at (4).

HOW TO
Grow Annuals

ANNUALS LIVE FOR ONE YEAR

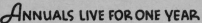

ANNUALS bring results for only a few cents' investment. They grow and blossom quickly, so that you feel you are getting somewhere in your first garden. Best of all, they are brilliantly colorful, so profuse in their blossoming that in a few short weeks you can make every corner of your garden blaze with flowers.

"Annual," of course, means "yearly" — and these plants are called annuals because a year is usually the span of their lives. With most of them, you must sow their seeds each year, although some will be your guests longer. Few, though, are at their best after the first year.

So you see that annuals are not permanent. During the short period of their stay, however, they pay marvelously for their board and keep.

Offhand you would say, "Plant them anywhere," because there are so many things annuals will do for you. Some are tall, some low growing. Some you will plant and prize for their looks, others for their fragrance. Some annuals will even bloom at night for you.

Different annuals will:

Give quick foliage effects in the place of shrubs.

Grow in partial shade.

Serve as low edging plants at the sides of the lawn or in front of the flower border.

Grow in the rock garden.

Provide masses of color.

Decorate window boxes.

Make good house plants.

Decorate the foundation of your home until you can get in your shrubs.

Beautify your garage driveway, the strip between the property line and drive, or parking out front.

Act as a ground cover.

Fill in bare spots between bulbs, perennials, shrubs.

Save gardening expense for you if yours is a rented house.

Keep you supplied with unequalled cut flowers for vases, etc.

Act as screens, grow on arbors, trellises, etc. (annual vines).

Fill in odd spots beside steps, walks, entrances, on slopes, placed where the lawn mower won't go, etc.

Conceal ugly objects, the garage, a tree stump, a brick wall, etc.

Fill your garden with fragrance.

Is it any wonder people love annuals so—and especially here in the Pacific West, where much of our climate encourages the germination of their seeds, where our rains speed their growth and the springs are ideal for their blooming, and finally, where our dry, warm summers do their share in ripening the plants and scattering the seeds?

Then, too, many annuals are natives of the West—California Poppy, Gilia, Clarkia, Godetia, Lupine, and California Bluebell, for example.

The Planting and Care of Annuals

There are general hints, applying to most annuals. Buy new seeds, not old. Buy from reliable dealers. And here is an actual opportunity to make use of the directions in the chapter on "Planting" in this book, when you sow these seeds.

All annuals need sunlight, though some will get along with only partial sunlight. Even these, while they try to oblige you by growing without much sun, do better if you give them more.

Most annuals need good soil. A few will do their best for you in poor soil, but they are exceptions.

The soil should be well prepared, with decayed manure added. See the chapter on "Soil" in this book.

In California it is best to sow most annuals in the autumn. They will flower during the coming spring. In the milder parts of California, however, annual seeds may be sown out of doors at the beginning of each season, although in colder months it is necessary to sow them in flats.

If You Live in the Northwest

In the Pacific Northwest, if you are sowing in the fall, do not put the seeds in too deep; don't put them in until the first frost arrives; and be sure the soil is in good condition. Annuals which may be sown outdoors in the fall in the Northwest are:

Snapdragon, Clarkia, Phlox, Pinks, Rose-of-Heaven, Cosmos, Pansy, Poppy, Centaurea, Mignonette, Godetia, Larkspur, Petunia hybrids, Candytuft, Pot Marigold.

When these germinate in the spring, thin them out soon. Better sow these seeds where you want the plant to grow, because transplanting of early seedlings may mean the loss of many of them.

When your annuals come up in the spring and have a dozen leaves, pinch off the top bud or buds. This will make the growth stockier; the plants will branch out and develop more and larger flowers at the sides for you.

As they grow older, pinch off any smaller buds growing out beside larger ones. The strength that was to have gone into the growth of the two buds will be concentrated in the one that is left. This is one of the ways in which the large blooms are created by specialists.

After annuals attain their full growth they may start declining. You can make any of them continue to bloom for a while if you are careful to remove all seed pods as they appear.

Annuals for Special Places

For Foliage: Amaranth — has vivid foliage, showy flowers. Summer Cypress — use along walks, and against shrubs. Leaves turn purple-red. Plant is bushy.

Partial Shade: Larkspur, Tasselflower, Sweet Alyssum, Cornflower, Pansy, Candytuft, Lupine, Godetia, Clarkia, Petunia hybrids, and China Aster.

NATIVE WESTERN ANNUALS

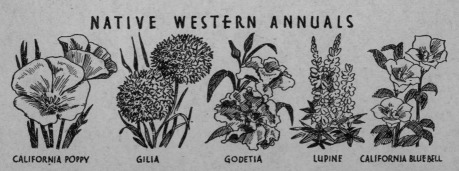

CALIFORNIA POPPY   GILIA   GODETIA   LUPINE   CALIFORNIA BLUEBELL

**USE ANNUALS
FOR LOW EDGES**

Flower Border: Phlox or Godetia will give you masses of color. When you lay out an annual border, put the tallest growing annuals at the rear, the next in front of them, and the smallest edging annuals in front.

If your border is placed against a wall, its width should be 4 or 5 feet, depending on the length of the wall—narrower for a short wall, wider for a long one. Arrange plants so that you will have passageways which allow you room to cultivate, pick flowers, and weed. In an annual border you will find that it is hard to sow plants so that they will come up at just the distances apart you desire. This is corrected by thinning them out after they are up. But try to space them, even so—6 to 18 inches apart, depending on the size the plant will be.

Godetia, a native of the West Coast, is especially good for annual borders in the Pacific Northwest, as are Phlox and Petunia. These are all highly colorful, Phlox being used for masses of color, Petunia for its long blooming period, and Godetia for its conspicuous bright-green leaves and large satiny blossoms ranging from crimson to purple, pink, mauve and white.

Among the low-growing annuals for the edge of your lawn or front of the border, you will find these excellent in most parts of the Pacific West:

Pansy, Kingfisher, Daisy, Verbena, *Clintonia pulchella,* Chinese Pink, Mignonette, dwarf Celosia, English Daisy, Forget-Me-Not, Sweet Alyssum, Virginia Stock, dwarf Floss Flower, *Lobelia erinus,* Portulaca, dwarf Candytuft.

For the background of the border, plant the taller annuals such as:

California Bluebell, Calliopsis, Cosmos, Canterbury Bells, Larkspur, African Blue Daisy, Amaranth, Salpiglossis, Giant Spider Plant, Hollyhock.

Rock Garden: Some gardeners advise against putting vigorous annuals in a rock garden, and this is good advice when you are growing special rock garden plants which are very particular about their surroundings.

Where you are not attempting to grow such rarer plants, you may with safety work in a few low-growing annuals, such as Sweet Alyssum, Chinese Pinks, Pansy, Gazania, Phlox, Tassel-flower, California Poppy, Rose Moss, Candytuft, and dwarf varieties of Ageratum, Snapdragon, Marigolds, Scabiosa and Petunia.

Window Boxes: Sweet Alyssum, Nasturtium, Primrose, Mignonette, Ageratum, Browallia, Calendula, Candytuft, Nemesia, Baby Blue Eyes, Pansy, Petunia, Portulaca, Verbena, Virginia Stock.

Low Edging Plants: Dwarf Floss Flower, Sweet Alyssum, English Daisy, dwarf Celosia, *Charieis heterophylla,* Chinese Pink, Kingfisher Daisy, dwarf Candytuft, *Lobelia erinus,* Virginia

**USE ANNUALS FOR TEMPORARY
PLANTINGS BETWEEN SHRUBS**

Stock, Forget-Me-Not, Portulaca, Mignonette, *Schizopetalon walkeri,* garden Verbena, Pansy.

Masses of Color: The following are white — Babysbreath, China Aster, Primrose, Sweet Alyssum, Summer Chrysanthemum, Moonflower, Sweet Peas, Petunia, Four o'Clock, Clarkia, Candytuft, Cornflower, Godetia, Scabiosa, Zinnia, Snapdragon, Cosmos, Larkspur, Stocks.

Yellow may be had among these: Tasselflower, California Poppy, Chrysanthemum, Four o'Clock, Zinnia, Sweet Sultan, Calendula, Gaillardia, Salpiglossis, Dimorphotheca, Hunnemannia, Marigold, Snapdragon, Nasturtium, Everlasting, Sunflower, Cockscomb.

Purple, blue and shades in between: China Aster, Forget-Me-Not, Phlox, Zinnia, Browallia, Chinese Forget-Me-Not, Gilia, Poppy, Verbena,

Phacelia, Morning Glory (dwarf variety) Petunia, Candytuft, Love-in-a-Mist, Stock, Larkspur, Cornflower, Lobelia, Scabiosa, Salpiglossis.

There is a large selection among the reds, oranges and intermediate shades: Cosmos, Amaranth, Stocks, Candytuft, Primrose, Hollyhock, Nasturtium, Salpiglossis, Sunflower, China Aster, Everlasting, Larkspur, Nemesia, Sweet Sultan, Cornflower, Zinnia, Statice, Gilia, Cockscomb, Gaillardia, Poppy, Verbena, Tasselflower, Snapdragon, Phlox, Four o'Clock, Clarkia, Flax, Petunia, Scabiosa.

House Plants: Sweet Alyssum, Lobelia, Browallia, Pansy, Snapdragon, Petunia.

Foundation Plants: If yours is a new home, just built, there may be some reason why shrubs cannot be put in at once; and even if they can, they may look sparse until they attain their growth-to-be.

If you are moving into a rented house, there may be bare-looking spaces at the base of or between the foundation shrubs. Until these spaces are filled in by the bottom spreading of the shrubs (as the result of top pruning), or by the perennials which you will plant later, sow annuals for a temporary effect of a full planting. Petunias, Marigold, Zinnia and Summer Cypress are fine for this purpose and all have good foliage, which is what you especially want.

Parking, Driveway, Strips: The parking may be planted with a ground cover of Rose Moss, Sweet Alyssum, or balcony-type Petunia, or with low-growing plants, annuals, biennials, or perennials. Since most parkings are fairly sunny, you may take your pick of almost any of the low annuals. The soil of a parking is perhaps more often neglected than that of any other part of a piece of property—remember that it must be as carefully prepared as any other.

Since you will want plenty of clearance room in the strip in the middle of the drive, the same would hold true there.

The strip between the property line and the driveway can be planted with any annual if it is sunny. If limited sunlight reached it, plant any of the annuals mentioned under "Partial Shade" in this chapter. Four-o'Clocks and Cinerarias are good, too. Summer Cypress, Petunia, Marigold and Zinnia wil provide you with foliage to take the place of shrubs.

Ground Cover: Many of the low-growing annuals will do, depending on the location of the place you want to cover—although you will be wiser to put in something more permanent, evergreens and perennials. Ground covers are used mostly on steep banks where you cannot work very well with a mower, and since banks are such a problem you will not want to go to the trouble of reseeding them each year.

However, annuals will do for a temporary effect, and the following have the virtue of reseeding themselves: Petunia, Poppy, Sweet Alyssum, California Poppy, Candytuft, Pansy (although it is better to resow Pansies each year), Floss Flower, etc.

Bare Spots: There are times of the year when few perennials are blooming and your borders will look dull. These are the best times to use annuals, selecting, preferably, those which sow themselves: Calendula, Cornflower, Petunia, Shirley Poppy, Larkspur, Snapdragon, Zinnia, Sunflower, Babysbreath, Balsam, Cosmos, Four-o'Clock, Marigolds, Clarkia, Love-in-a-Mist, Tobacco, and Godetia, as well as those mentioned in the paragraph above.

Your selections should be for color chiefly, but it is well to have in mind the heights of the annuals you sow. You won't want tall ones thronging the front of your perennial border and blotting out perennials which will be coming into bloom from time to time. Put the tall ones in back, therefore, and the lower ones grading down to the front.

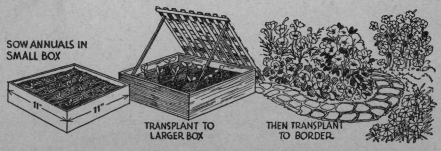

SOW ANNUALS IN SMALL BOX

11"   11"

TRANSPLANT TO LARGER BOX

THEN TRANSPLANT TO BORDER

Annuals can either be sown directly in the border or cultivated in pots, and the pots set here and there for the time being among the perennials.

Another method is to sow seeds in flats, transplant them to the cold frame, and finally transplant them to the perennial border. In this way you obtain your effects faster, instead of having to wait for seeds to germinate in the border itself.

Many perennials are unattractive after blossoming; others, after being cut back, are out of the garden picture entirely until they grow up again. Some of the perennials which should by all means be helped out with annuals are: Canterbury Bells, Foxglove, Bleeding Heart, Virginia Bluebell, and Oriental Poppies.

The main rule to follow is this: Fill in with annuals wherever a gap occurs, among shrubs, perennials, bulbs or anywhere else. Bulbs especially need this interplanting because they become ugly after the blooming period.

Quick Bloom: Candytuft, Love-in-a-Mist, Mignonette, Cornflower, Forget-Me-Not, Babysbreath, Calliopsis, Poppy and Larkspur.

Cut Flowers: Snapdragon, Cosmos, Summer Chrysanthemum, Ageratum, Browallia, Gaillardia, Phlox, Pinks, Larkspur, Calendula, Babysbreath, Calliopsis, Lupine, Poppy, Marigolds, China Aster, Mignonette, Salvia, Nasturtium, Scabiosa, Salpiglossis, Stocks, Verbena, Tree Mallow, Sweet Sultan, Zinnia, Sunflower.

Fragrance: Lupine, Candytuft, Sweet Pea, Nasturtium, Phlox, Verbena, Snapdragon, Mignonette, Larkspur, Pansy, Sweet Sultan, Pinks and Stocks.

Screens: The climbing annual vines can be used for a wide variety of things—trained to decorate the bare front or sides of the garage; trellises on the porch or for screening unsightly parts of the garden such as the compost heap, garbage unit or drying apparatus; covering stumps of trees, walls, etc.; or acting as a temporary vine on a pergola, arbor, or elsewhere until you get a slow-growing woody vine established. Annual vines are also used for high and low walls and are lovely when allowed to hang down. Some vines worth growing are:

Balloon Vine, Canary Bird Vine, Cardinal Climber, Chilean Glory Flower, Climbing Foxglove, *Cobaea scandens*, Cypress Vine, Gourds, Hyacinth Bean, Japanese Hopvine, Moonflower, Morning Glory, Nasturtiums, Scarlet Runner Bean, Sweet Pea, *Thunbergia alata, Thunbergia gibsoni.*

USE ANNUALS FOR ODD PLACES

Other annuals, such as Sunflower, Hollyhock, and Cosmos, do wonderfully when you want to screen any tall bare space in a hurry until you get your more permanent plants in.

Odd Spots: There are dozens of these in every garden—beside the back steps, on either side of the garage door, at a corner of the house, along a walk, around a garden bench, at the basement door, etc. You can turn them into delightful little garden spots with annuals.

No corner need be too humble, to seemingly unimportant to lack the magic touch that will give it beauty—and annuals will always be your standbys to produce that beauty quickly.

After the annuals come biennials, which live for two years. After the biennials come perennials, which grow and bloom slower but live several years. Some plants have annual and perennial varieties. You will find this distinction always noted in the Growing Encyclopedia in this book. Some of the longer-living flowers do not do so well after the first year, and so you pretend they are not biennials or perennials, but treat them as annuals. The Pansy is an example. It is a perennial, but you have better results with it if you sow new seeds each year.

HOW TO GROW ASTERS

1. One of my favorite summer flowers (among the annuals) is the China aster which I grow successfully in my Seattle garden. I particularly like the Sunshine variety but grow also the shaggy giants that have been popular for so many years. In my opinion, success with asters lies in keeping the plants growing vigorously.

2. The first step is to buy good seed—from Sunset advertisers of course! A wilt-resistant strain is now available and should be used by all who have had trouble in growing this flower. By planting both early and late varieties, the flowering season will be prolonged. Order your seed now for April planting.

3. The last of February I decide where in the garden I shall set my aster plants and then prepare the place by covering it with a layer of well-rotted manure. Spring rains will then carry the fertilizer into the ground. Asters do best in a rich, porous soil. Do not plant in the same place twice in succession.

4. Before the seed arrives I prepare the seed flats. First a layer of gravel is placed in the bottom for drainage and the flat is then filled with rich loam, leaf mold and sand, sifted together. Some gardeners advise baking the soil but I have not found this method necessary. Provide a pane of glass for covering top of seed flat.

5. I sow seed under glass in March or April. After thoroughly watering the soil, let it drain for several hours. Then plant seed in rows, covering with about half an inch of soil. Press firmly. Keep the pane of glass over the top until plants are up, then remove during the day. Work to develop sturdy plants.

6. While waiting for plants in seed box to develop I finish preparing their place in the garden by spading in the manure and working in plenty of wood ashes; commercial plant food also is often needed. The ashes furnish potash and lime which asters seem to require. After spading, work soil until well pulverized.

7. In May when danger of frost is over, I transfer the plants to the open ground which has been watered and raked smooth in advance. Set plants a foot apart, firming carefully. Locate aster bed in full sun—at least in Coastal regions. I plant in beds so that the plants support one another and give a good splash of color.

8. Asters have many enemies. Dust the plants thoroughly with nicotine dust and use an all-round garden spray regularly. Keep plants growing vigorously and if one of them develops yellows, pull it up immediately. Aphis are particularly bad and must not get a start. Wilt can be avoided by planting a wilt-resistant strain.

9. Do not overlook the all-important feature of cultivation. I use the hoe religiously and keep the ground loose at all times. Always cultivate after watering. During extremely hot weather, it will be well to mulch the plants with peat moss to keep the roots cool. A manure mulch is too likely to harbor injurious insects.

10. As plants come into bud, give them a good feeding of commercial plant food, applying it according to directions on the container. After applying plant food, water plant thoroughly so that fertilizer will be in solution. Avoid getting it on leaves or stems. Sensible use of plant food produces an abundance of bloom.

11. Over-watering of asters is likely to cause root rot. I thoroughly irrigate my plants whenever necessary and then depend upon cultivation rather than on daily sprinklings. A heavy stream of water will break down the blooms. Keep faded blossoms cut off and remove all dead or diseased leaves from the plants.

12. Asters are lovely as cut flowers. Cut blooms with long stems and plunge deep into cold water, removing all lower leaves that would be immersed. Then if you would get the greatest joy out of your bouquets, share them with others. By so doing your asters will have fulfilled all that can be expected of them. Try it!

HOW TO GROW PANSIES

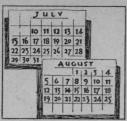

1. The size and quality of pansies depend largely on the seed. Instead of buying ordinary seed, spend a few cents more and get the Giant strains, sturdy of stem and with large, exquisite blooms. Sunset Garden Editor will be glad to tell you where to buy such seeds.

2. The best time to plant pansies is as soon as seed is ripe—usually from July 10 to August 25, but along the Coast fall plantings can be made all through September to bloom in winter or early spring. Around San Diego and Los Angeles pansies can be planted any time of year.

3. Remember that pansies like cool weather so plan your plantings accordingly. In mountain states and where winters are severe winter protection is necessary. Under proper conditions seed planted in spring will bloom in summer and fall in most parts of Sunset Land.

4. Prepare seed bed very carefully using a fine soil mixture of rich loam, peat moss and well-rotted manure. When the mixture is pulverized, tamp the surface until smooth and then soak the soil thoroughly to a depth of several inches. A good seed bed is most important.

5. Sow seeds broadcast or in drills, covering lightly with finely sifted soil. Thumb tack burlap or muslin over frame and water seeds with a fine spray through this cover. Leave covering on until plants sprout; then remove to allow more air. Never let seeds dry out.

6. While seeds are sprouting and tiny seedlings developing, the soil must never become dry, but on the other hand it must not be kept too damp—either is fatal. Water daily but with a very fine spray. Protect from sun during middle of day. Plants must be kept cool.

7. In four to six weeks seedlings will be ready to plant out into the garden. If possible transplant but once; too many transplantings will weaken the plants. The garden soil for pansies must be rich, and well drained so that winter rains will not stand around roots.

8. Fall planted pansies will appreciate the winter sun but be sure that they will be somewhat shaded as warmer weather comes on. In Southern California pansies that are to bloom in late spring are usually located on north or east. Reaching for the light develops long stems.

9. Instead of planting pansies in geometrical, formal beds, use them as a ground cover for the spring bulbs, as a carpet for the rose garden, in clumps in the rockery or as borders for paths and beds. Plants set eight inches apart form a compact growth that is desirable.

10. Pansies are best treated as annuals but the blooming season can be prolonged by clipping off seed pods and long, scraggly runners. Cultivate lightly without disturbing the roots. A mulch of peat moss is excellent during warm weather in order to keep the roots cool. Water often.

11. Rather than to plant seeds, you may prefer to buy pansy plants, but remember always to buy from reliable Western plant men and pansy specialists. Select your colors carefully and plant in harmony. Get good plants and pinch back most of the blooms before planting.

12. In general, violas thrive under the same conditions as pansies. In fall it is a good plan to take up your violas, shake off the old soil, divide clumps and reset, applying plant food to stimulate a good growth of late bloom. There are many named varieties of violas.

HOW TO GROW SWEET PEAS

1. I plant sweet peas in late fall for spring and early summer bloom. This is my method. Choose a spot in your garden where the sweet peas will receive plenty of sunlight in the forenoon, but not in the afternoon.

2. Prepare your soil in early fall for the longer the ground lies turned over and in a rough state, the more mellow it will be, and the happier your sweet peas. Sweet peas require deeply dug and quite rich garden soil.

3. Mark off a space 2 feet wide and the desired length. Apply a liberal coat of well-rotted manure. Bonemeal and (in some soils) lime are also beneficial. Use cow manure if soil is light, barnyard manure if soil is heavy.

4. Beginning at one end, spade a ditch across one end of your space, removing the dirt therefrom and placing it at the opposite end of the plot. Remember sweet peas love deep spading —2 feet deep is about right.

5. Now throw the dirt from your second row of spading into the first ditch and so on until the last row, which is filled with the dirt from the first ditch. This is "trenching." Mix manure thoroughly with the soil.

6. For late fall planting, select the Late or Summer Flowering Spencers, a strain which produces quantities of good bloom. Buy the best seed possible, getting variety of colors. Seeds advertised in Sunset are dependable.

7. Wait for a pleasant day in November or December when the clods break up easily and loosely. Then rake your soil thoroughly and plant seeds an inch apart and an inch deep. Cover and firm soil with foot.

8. Watch for pests. If slugs take your first sprouts, apply one of the poison baits for slugs and snails. If birds are your enemy, cover the tiny seedlings with a screen or wire netting until the plants are well established.

 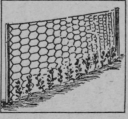  

9. When plants are three inches high, thin to a foot apart, pinching out the top for sturdy growth, leaving about four leaves on the plant. Now give each little vine a twig support as the wind may twist and ruin it.

10. When plants have reached a height of six or eight inches, put up the permanent support. Chicken wire of coarse mesh is good in all but the hottest climates where bamboo or string support is better. Tie lightly.

11. After the last rains, hoe well and mulch with peat moss or manure; otherwise constant hoeing will be necessary to keep soil friable. After rains cease, irrigate plants thoroughly once a week. Avoid sprinkling the foliage.

12. Now enjoy the delicate beauty of your flowers. Pick them regularly, keep seed pods picked off. When plants start flowering, apply commercial plant food occasionally. Spray regularly to eliminate aphis.

HOW TO
Grow Perennials

PERENNIALS LIVE
SEVERAL YEARS

JANUARY
DECEMBER

JANUARY
DECEMBER

JANUARY
DECEMBER

A PERENNIAL lives several years. All the wonderful things you can do with perennials spread out from this simple fact. With perennials you can have flowers blooming in regulated succession of color, throughout the year, in many localities of the Pacific West. You can have wide, deep, permanent borders like whole seas of color-harmony between the island of your lawn and the mainland of your shrub-and-tree background.

Perennials are to many the most interesting plants in the garden. Something new happens amongst them every day — new leaves appear, new buds come out, new flowers take the places of the faded ones. No other plants keep blossoming so continuously. Best of all, many perennials do not lose their vigor after the first couple of years, but keep improving.

But it is the color possibilities of perennials which endear them to all Pacific Western garden lovers. It is even possible to have one color dominate each month of the year, white for May, blue for June, yellow for July and so on.

Although each perennial has its likes and dislikes as to soil, care, moisture, sunlight, etc., most of them grow well in a neutral soil, that is, neither acid nor alkaline; most of them thrive in a combination of sunlight and shade, although some do better in one or the other; and most care neither for too much moisture nor too little, but a medium amount.

How to Plant Perennials

Annuals come into bloom quickly for you, but perennials take a long time—a year, two years, sometimes even three. Because of this you will naturally ask yourself the question: "Shall I grow perennials from seed or get plants from the nursery that are all ready to set out in my garden?"

The answer to this depends a lot on your patience, and how long you are willing to wait for flowers. If you grow them from seed you have the satisfaction of having grown your own plants literally from the ground. On the other hand, with many perennials you may have better success with nursery plants.

In California, if you sow seeds from May through August of this year you will have blossoms next year. Even nursery-grown perennials that are due to flower in the spring must wait until next year, no matter how early you put them in the border now. However, there are a number of fall-blooming perennials which may be obtained in gallon cans at nurseries, if you are eager for flowers the same year.

Sowing the Seeds

With most perennials seeds, both in the Pacific Northwest and California, screen the soil very finely into your seed bed, using a mixture of peat moss, sand and good topsoil from your garden. Smooth and firm the soil before any seeds are put in—this can be done with a flat board. Don't press heavily; a light firming will do. Then make straight rows with a knife and plant the seeds three times the depth of the seed. Cover the seed with soil, smooth, and firm again with your board—lightly as before.

After that you use a fine spray to water lightly. Keep the soil moist but not saturated. Watch that crusts do not form on the surface.

Note for Northwesterners

Extra care is needed when you sow late in the fall in the Northwest. Your seed bed should be cool, damp, and kept so with shading (a lath screen will do) during the germination period.

In the Northwest most perennials raised from seed will bear flowers the second year. It is generally thought better to sow in the spring than in the fall, because seeds then have a chance to grow into plants and gather strength before cold weather comes. In the fall spring-sown plants can be transplanted from flats, pots, cold frames, etc., into their permanent places in your open garden.

If, however, you do sow seeds outdoors in the fall, wait until the first white frost, which should come in late November. These seeds will not sprout until spring, but will come up all right then, and you may have blossoms that year.

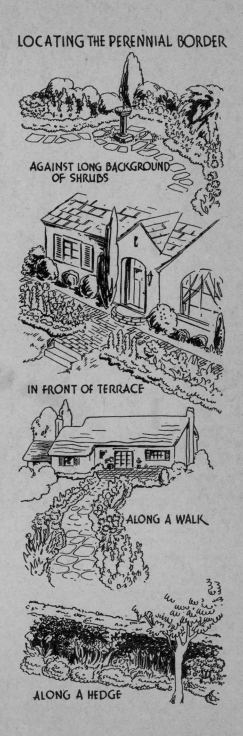

LOCATING THE PERENNIAL BORDER

AGAINST LONG BACKGROUND OF SHRUBS

IN FRONT OF TERRACE

ALONG A WALK

ALONG A HEDGE

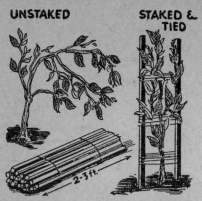

UNSTAKED   STAKED & TIED

2-3 ft.

STAKE TALL PERENNIALS

Planting Directions

Follow the general rules for planting in the chapter, "How to Start Your Plants," plus these special ones for perennials. Make your planting holes large enough so that the plant to be set in has enough room for its roots to spread with no crowding.

The holes should be spaced a little closer than half the height of the plant. This rule varies with some. If you are transplanting a field-grown nursery plant, or one from your own garden proper, mark off 18 inches between holes. They may crowd as they establish themselves and grow, but you can thin them out later next season. Don't worry about this; it is always necessary to go over your perennial groups each year, respacing them, etc. This is a regular part of their care.

If you are growing Phlox or Delphiniums, give them still more space to grow in.

With this wide spacing, your perennial beds and borders may look sparse during the first year. This is an excellent time to fill out not only with annuals but bulbous flowers, which we shall learn more about presently.

When the plant is set, scatter topsoil down around the roots, being careful not to cram them together, and when the hole is filled, firm the earth around the stem. This firming should be done well. Then you give the plant plenty of water, so that the soil will settle still closer around the roots, without leaving any air pockets down there.

After watering, take some compost (decayed vegetable matter from your compost heap), or peat moss, or even dry soil, and spread it around the base of the plant to keep the moisture in. This is a mulch.

The Care of Perennials in the West

In return for the years of beauty which they bring to your garden, perennials ask that you give them a few minutes of care each day, and certain attentions from time to time. There is no getting away from it—a perennial border, small or large, is a responsibility. But the rewards are worth it.

Pick off all faded blossoms, and burn them to kill thrips or other pests clinging to them. By doing this, you allow the plant to use its energy to develop new flowers. You also keep the seed from setting.

Next, watch for pests—both insects and diseases; and as soon as anything suspicious appears, go after it with your spray or duster.

Keep supplying moisture. As the blooming period begins, set aside a time each week for putting liquid manure around the roots of each plant. It would be well to work in some bonemeal, compost, wood ashes or lime with such plants as Irises, Phlox and Delphinium.

Cultivation is an art, too. A hoe may be all right for potatoes but not for perennials. Use a small, rakelike hand tool. Cultivate around each plant once a week during the summer months. Do not bear in too deeply—you may injure the roots. Cultivate right after watering. With this regular stirring of the soil you will not be troubled with weeds.

Throughout the growing season you might add mulches of peat moss, spreading around the stems to hold in the moisture.

With planned care you can make the attending of your perennial border a pleasant task, performed in small chunks, day by day. Keep a little record of each perennial you grow—noting the date you planted it, the date it blooms, its color, likes, dislikes, etc.

Set aside a time for cleaning up in the fall, putting all litter, weeds, etc., on the compost heap, pulling up stakes and daubing some green paint on them, and whatever else you can think of to trim up the garden. Speaking of stakes, either make a number of these of various sizes, two or three feet long and so on, or buy them and have them ready at all times for supporting your perennials. The stakes are pushed into the ground a few inches from the plant, and the plants are secured to them with raffia or a twine that will not cut the stem. Unstaked plants sprawl miserably, and a plant left unstaked during its early growing period and staked belatedly will never have the naturally strong upright position it should have.

Soil and Upkeep of Perennial Border

Generally speaking, you will have satisfactory results if you provide your perennial bed with a soil that is rich in humus—for perennials are heavy feeders. Give them a soil that is a good medium in every respect — neither light nor heavy, neither acid nor alkaline, and neither soaked nor dry.

When you prepare this soil, treat it as shown under "Soils" in this handbook. That is, if the top or undersoil looks dead, not rich and fertile, mix with it well-rotted manure, commercial humus, matter from the compost heap, or leafmold.

If your soil is heavy, use humus to lighten it. The humus will make it easily workable, and retentive of moisture. If the soil is light, humus will bind it and keep its fertility from leaching out. Mix half a quart of bonemeal with every bushel of compost or other humus.

Preparing the Bed

Spade up the perennial bed to a good depth. Go 2 feet down. There may be some plants already growing if you have moved into a house formerly occupied. Don't kill them. Lift them out with care, allowing a lot of soil to cling around the roots. Dig a small trench near by and heel them in (See Index for "Healing in"). You can do it with perennials in the same way.

Stir up or break up the subsoil as you do with a lawn, and scatter drainage material on the bottom—broken pots, gravel, etc. On top of that, pile about 5 inches of good rich soil, then a layer of well-rotted manure. Tamp down firmly.

Fill up with rich medium soil. Bring in some good topsoil if you have none; or you may experiment with the improvement of what you have. Keep packing all this down hard, and build it up until it stands above the surface of the rest of the garden. It will settle.

Now turn the hose on your soil bed—it hurries the settling. After three weeks it should be ready.

As your border or bed develops, spread a mixture of manure and a complete commercial fertilizer on it and work into the soil. Perennials are much helped by sheep manure, hardwood ashes or bonemeal, applied every year. After three years or so, you will find that these manure applications, though necessary, have soured the soil. You can prevent that by applying slaked lime every two years.

The top of your perennial bed should be loose, a thing to watch if your soil is naturally clayey.

PICK OFF FADED BLOSSOMS

This is so that you can stir the surface easily with your hand cultivator. Manure, sand, or fine wood ashes spread around now and then help to keep it loose.

When you are ready to sow or plant, rake over the settled bed and level it off. The outcome of this thoughtful preparation will mean that you'll have flowers sooner, and more of them.

In the Northwest, watch that looseness of the topsoil in the early spring particularly because that is when your weeding is done oftenest. Do less fertilization, too, or you will have plants that do not mature before cold weather sets in, which will mean the loss of bloom.

This talk about soils has been placed after those on planting and care because so much that has to do with soils for perennials is really after-care. Renovating old perennial beds is an example of this.

Renovating Old Beds

Perennials eat so much that every three years or so you should repeat the soil-preparation just described. Since you will want to replace them in good condition after the bed is renovated, take up each plant with soil adhering to its roots and heel it in.

Then remove the old surface soil, putting it aside for some other use. Make a mixture of new soil, loam, compost, etc., prepare it with tamping, leveling, watering, etc., as above directed, and replant the perennials you have temporarily removed, remembering as you do so to put them back with the greatest care.

WATCH FOR PESTS

Some of your perennials will have grown so thickly that they will need dividing. Break up these heavier, massed root clumps and reset them as separate plants. Irises will surely need this attention.

Designing a Perennial Border

Someone has said, "A perennial border takes time, patience, and a knowledge of the plant material in it." Let's start with the "time". Most of us are so eager to get our garden started that we rush ahead with a border for perennials as if we were working with annuals. But perennials demand careful soil preparation, forethought and planning. Let's go back to first principles to see why this is so.

What you want in your perennial border is a continuous blooming of glorious, varied flowers, more than anything else. You are aiming at a succession of blossoms, either one color dominating each month, or different color harmonies succeeding each other, one group of flowers coming into bloom after another finishes and a whole border constantly changing like the variations of a colored theater spotlight. To achieve this you must take time to plan, time to prepare, time to find out when perennials bloom and how to schedule them so that they will make the harmonies you want. "Make haste slowly" as you plan your border.

Patience

How about "Patience"? You may be impatient to have a huge, blazing border of perennial flowers. It is usually better to start with a modest one. A large border costs money and takes good slices of your time and strength for its maintenance. A small border is easier all around.

It takes patience, too, to make a plan on paper, deciding your colors from month to month, and then looking up plants that will have those colors at those times.

It takes patience to keep records in a notebook so that you will be able to plan for year after next by referring to the planting and blooming dates of your perennials.

Finally, it takes patience to care for this kind of a border. Yet, curiously, no one ever seems to mind all this. Perennials pay back these attentions a thousandfold. It seems as if magic were at work when you see these plants blooming, producing more and more flowers, and repeating the performance the next year, better than ever! Still more magical are the changing hues of a perennial border throughout the blooming seasons.

Where to Have the Border

The best place is in front of a long background of shrubs and trees. This is in most gardens against the back or sides of the lot. If you have a hedge or fence for the background, locate the border in front of it.

Another perennial border may be placed along the front of the house, among or in front of the foundation trees and shrubs. In any case, it will probably lie in front of shrubbery, a wall or other barrier and will come forward to the edge of the lawn or open area.

Locate a border so that it does not come too close to the larger roots of a tree, where you will not be able to dig down far enough to prepare the soil properly. Place it also so that it is sheltered if possible from too much wind, which might damage the more delicate of your flowers.

The Plan

Lined or graph paper is good for this purpose, or you can rule one yourself, allowing ⅛ of an inch to a foot. In the back, indicate where your shrubs are. They probably take up from 3 to 5 feet. Your border, should be, if you have space enough, 6 to 10 feet wide. Ten feet looks much smaller on the ground than it does in one's imagination, especially when you remember that a good perennial border is by no means a single row or two of plants, but several rows, going back like the first rows of seats in a theater.

On this sheet of paper trace the outline of your bed, showing whether it is long and narrow or short and wide, curving its lawn-edge as you intend it to be when you stake it out in the ground, and so on.

In the background, have shrubs, trees, and possibly vines, if there is a wall. Evergreen shrubs serve you best. They have attractive foliage, resist drought, and are not attacked by diseases or pests.

The outer curving edges of your border should harmonize with the shrubbery, swinging in where the shrubs do, and undulating outward where a group of shrubs protrudes.

Within the border itself the usual rule is to place tall perennials at the rear and low ones in front; but the best gardeners are open minded on this, the wisest knowing that there are many places for low-growing kinds in the rear, nestling around the bases of larger ones and filling up the undergrowth of the border. Here and there a tall spire gives exactly the accent you want among the low and medium plants toward the front; and medium sizes all along the low-edging foreground may be used to relieve the monotony.

Some Afterthoughts

Roses are not very satisfactory in a perennial border. A well-known gardener who has tried to add them for their color has come to the conclusion that they should have their own place elsewhere in the garden.

There are times during the year when bare spots appear in the best of borders. A group of plants may bloom a little late; others will finish blooming and leave a gap which is not even covered up by other perennials coming into bloom in front, at the sides or in back. To offset this, plant a few annuals before the gap is due to occur. With a little forethought — finding out how long it will take for a given annual to blossom — you can plant it far enough ahead so that it does its work for you right on time.

Bulbs are also used for this purpose, especially in shady borders.

Narcissus is one of the best for this. Any of its varieties will do. In the Southwest these additions of annuals and bulbs will carry on your color schemes so well that you will have flowers throughout the year.

One of the most attractive ways to group perennials is to have several plants of each kind or

variety in a cluster, creating a massed effect with their different colors. This is indescribable when placed against a background of flowering shrubs. A prominent Northwest gardener has successfully used such arrangements both against flowering shrubs and those valued chiefly for their foliage—Spiraea, Japanese Snowball, double Japanese Kerria, the Barberry family, dwarf Weigela and Deutzia.

Background of the Border

In California, your background of evergreen shrubs should occupy at least 3 feet. If it is to be tall, you might plant it with such shrubs as Common Myrtle, Strawberry Tree, Japanese Pittosporum, English Laurel, or *Viburnum lucidum.*

A border background of medium height could include Japanese Privet and another Privet variety, *Ligustrum lucidum; Cotoneaster harroviana;* and dwarf Myrtle.

If your background is a wall or fence, plant shrubs which can be trained flat against it. Narrow-leaved Pittosporum is good for this and is a beautiful weeping type of shrub. The Pyracanthas can be trained to grow flat, as can the true evergreen Pear, Pyrus kawakami.

In the Northwest, if you have a fairly wide and long border, use Common Lilac, which is dense and tall, with plenty of blossoms and good foliage. It can be used in masses of different sizes, placed here and there along the background. In the foreground, in front of the Lilacs, Bridal-wreath, Virginia Mock-Orange, White Kerria and the Lemoine Deutzia are fine for small groups. All bear flowers early in the season, which blend well with your Lilacs, and all of them give good foliage during the entire season.

At the farther ends of a long border like this, you will need something different to finish off your background. You can get an interesting effect of distance with the gray-foliage shrubs — such as Garland Spiraea (also called Snowgarland), and Cherry Eleagnus.

There should be some plantings for accent in the background — red Cedars, a Pine or Fir, Dogwood, Flowering Peach, etc., and, if you have room enough, great coarse shrubs in the farthest rear, a Witchhazel or Buckthorn. To complete your landscape, have a tree, if you can, rising against the sky.

Cypress, and Rhododendron Boule de Neige are valuable plantings for backgrounds in the Northwest. The latter is a dense bush, like a mound, with snow-white flowers. The Red Cedar above mentioned is very picturesque with its upright, spreading shape, and reddish-green leaves.

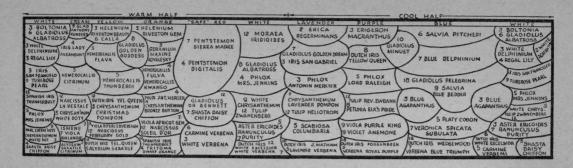

A Planting Plan for Perennials

The possibilities in color schemes for perenial borders are many. We are indebted to Charles Gibbs Adams, Southern California landscape architect, for the following tips:

The blue garden is always a joy if given backbone by a few accents of rich deep purple. Blue is the harmonizer in almost any scheme. The white border is charming, especially if it lies in a garden rich in color. It's thrilling at night in lighted gardens.

A scheme in the French blending of blue, lavender, pink, and a bit of purple, combines daintiness with richness.

For warmth, nothing equals a rich blending of cream, yellow and orange, with a little accenting of deep clear red, or of velvety brown. For spring you can secure certain irises, like the Spanish Thunderbolt, or such Tulips, as Blackboy or La Tuilpe Noire; for summer, try brown English wallflowers; for fall, bronze heleniums, like good old Riverton Gem, or any of several brown or bronze pompon chrysanthemums; for winter our native *Fritillaria lanceolata*.

For the Blue Garden: Choose from among the following for winter: *Iris stylosa*, Iris Purple King, perennial Forget-Me-Not, the blue strain of *Primula obconica*, Hyacinth Queen of Blues, blue Dutch Roman Hyacinth, Dutch Iris Wedgewood. If one uses annual fillers, ideal winter ones are Nemesia Blue Gem and dwarf Jubilee Gem Cornflower.

For Spring Blue: *Linum narbonense*, Iris Frederick, *Campanula portenschlagiana*, *Salvia farinacea* Blue Bedder.

For Summer Blue: Verbena Blue Triumph, Platycodon, Agapanthus, and *Veronica spicata*. Good annuals are *Browallia speciosa Major* and Cornflowers.

For Autumn Blue: *Campanula isophylla* and *Isophylla mayi* and *Salvia pitcheri*. Good annuals are Love-in-a-Mist and Ageratum, except in frosty regions.

Good Blue Annuals: Lobelia Crystal Palace, and *Nemophila insignis*.

For White: Choose for winter perennial Candytuft, Daisies, *Iris stylosa*, and Snowflakes. So scarce is good winter white that you must depend on annuals somewhat, especially Stocks, Violas, Snapdragons, and, in shade *Primula chinensis*.

For Spring: Iris San Francisco, or Easter Morn, Platycodon, Freesia, Giant Purity, Hyacinth, Daffodil and Ranunculus.

For Summer: White Delphiniums, *Lilium regale*, perennial Phlox, especially Mrs. Jenkins, white Agapanthus, and *Crinum powellii*.

For Autumn: *Aster ericoides*, Boltonia, Japanese Anemone, single and double, Mexican Tuberose, and pompom Chrysanthemums of low stature.

Yellow: For winter nothing equals Reinwardtia or Golden Flax. Most nurseries, however, sell it as *Linum flavum*, a plant with but half its beauty. Alstromeria is lovely in shady locations. For frosty spots, winter Aconite is a jolly standby.

Ideal for Spring: Calliopsis, Ranunculus, Daffodils (early blooming variety, February Gold), Iris Happy Days, Calla, *Hemerocallis thunbergii*, and *citrina*.

For Foregrounds, or Bulb Covers: *Alyssum saxatile*, and A. *citrinum*.

For Summer: The finer dwarf Goldenrods, Rudbekias, and Nasturtium Golden Gleam.

The rainbow scheme here diagrammed follows, in general, the lines of the spectrum, with white added for leavening and extra generosity shown as to the precious blues. Perhaps even more satisfying would be the use of either the warm half or the cool half alone. The pattern could be repeated, working the opposite way from the center.

HOW TO START A PERENNIAL BED

SPADE DOWN
TWO FEET

BREAK UP
SUB SOIL

SCATTER
DRAINAGE MATERIAL

ADD FIVE INCHES
OF RICH SOIL

ADD LAYER OF MA-
NURE. TAMP DOWN

FILL IN WITH RICH SOIL
ABOVE GARDEN LEVEL

WATER TO HASTEN
SETTLING

LEVEL OFF
AFTER SETTLING

NOW YOU ARE READY
TO PLANT

HOW TO GROW DELPHINIUMS

1. The adventurous gardener prefers to grow delphinium from seed. Buy the best seed obtainable (we can give you the names of reliable dealers if you wish), and you can develop fine plants. Delphinium seeds are sown in late summer when the seed is fresh to produce good, healthy clumps in the fall.

2. Delphinum prefer a rich, well-drained, light soil. A good mixture for the seed bed consists of equal parts of garden loam, coarse sand, and peat moss. Sift this mixture through a ¼ inch sieve into the seed box and place the frame some distance above the ground to protect seedlings from snails.

3. Firm the soil with a wooden block and then moisten. Sow the seeds in shallow drills (this facilitates transplanting), and cover with this same soil mixture just enough to hide the seed. Keep the loam moist with a rose spray, but never flooded. Shade each flat with burlap or dark heavy paper.

4. Fresh seeds require about 10 days to germinate, and stragglers may require 15 to 20 days. As soon as two or three true leaves appear, seedlings may be transplanted to a second box which is filled with the same soil mixture plus a small quantity of bone meal. Set about two inches apart.

5. In early spring the plants are ready for their permanent location in the garden. They are sun-lovers, but will endure partial shade, and require a rich, sandy loam. In preparing the bed dig at least two feet deep, depositing a small quantity of gravel in the lower twelve inches to insure drainage.

6. From time to time, enrich the soil with quantities of bone meal, wood ashes and limestone. Do not allow strong fertilizers to come in contact with the crowns of the plants. A small trench around each plant will keep them sufficiently moist. When they commence to bloom, feed them with plant food.

7. For the best effect, delphiniums should be planted in groups. Set plants two feet apart with the crowns about two inches below the surface. A group of a dozen plants of the same variety is much more beautiful than one in which every plant is different in size and color. Use as backgrounds.

8. When the plants have bloomed in the spring, cut just below the withered flowers, and when the new growth appears, remove the old stalk close to the ground. By so doing, it is very possible to have two or three crops of flowers each year. Delphinium are delightful with pink, rose, white or yellow.

 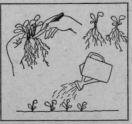  

9. Delphinium may also be propagated by division and cuttings. February and March are the best months to divide clumps. If the season is warm, however, they are often ready in January. The young shoots should be just breaking through the ground when divided. Never disturb when dormant.

10. To divide, dig the plant carefully, without breaking the roots. Wash off the dirt so that the shoots can be seen. Cut the clump into pieces, each containing two or more good shoots and ample roots. Dust the cut with a sulphur, have the soil in the new bed prepared and plant immediately.

11. When shoots are two inches high, cuttings may be taken. Dig the earth away exposing the crown of the plant. With a sharp knife remove the shoots, taking a thin heel of the crown. Place in water for two hours. Dust the plant crown with sulphur. Start cuttings in a pot or seed flat in sand.

12. Keep the soil moist while they are striking root, and in a partially shaded location. If they dry out, they will die. It takes five to seven weeks for cuttings to root. At the end of this time, they may be transplanted to three-inch pots filled with sifted leaf mold. Transplant later to the garden.

HOW TO GROW CINERARIAS

1. For shaded spots in the garden or as potted plants for porch or patio, no flower is lovelier than the cineraria. Cinerarias come in a wide range of colors, blues, purples and crimsons, as well as many variations of these shades. The flowers are borne in trusses, rising above large leaves.

2. Generally speaking, most cinerarias are considered as annuals but in Coastal California the plant becomes semi-perennial. Under favorable conditions, the plants tend to reseed themselves, occupying the same place in the garden year after year. It is one plant that thrives under pines.

3. Many amateur gardeners prefer to buy plants of cinerarias, but it is not difficult to grow them from seeds. Plants can be purchased at practically any time of year. Be sure to buy the choicest of seeds and the finest of plants. Your garden catalogues will indicate varieties, colors, etc.

4. For late winter bloom, seed should be planted the preceding summer; for summer bloom, the preceding fall. Seeds planted now should bloom next August. From Marin County south the plants grow beautifully in the open without protection but they will not stand extremes of cold or heat.

5. Cineraria seed is very fine and great care must be used in planting. Sift together equal parts of peat moss, sand and rich loam, and fill shallow flats or seed pans. Level soil, press down firmly, and water thoroughly. Then sprinkle seed on surface as evenly as possible and press the soil lightly.

6. Do not cover seed with soil, but place pane of glass or a piece of wrapping paper over flat or pan; raise glass slightly at one side to admit air. At all times keep the surface of the soil moist but do not over water or the seedlings may damp off. Water with fine spray. Keep flat in shade.

7. When seedlings show a second pair of leaves, prick them out carefully into a larger flat, filled with light porous soil with plenty of leaf mold or peat. The root system of cinerarias is very shallow so keep young plants well watered. Transplant the tiny seedlings about two inches apart.

8. Do not transplant to the garden too quickly. Six to eight weeks growth is usually required to produce sturdy plants with sufficient root systems to withstand life in the open. If necessary transplant a second time into a larger flat. Remember that taller varieties make a coarse growth.

9. Give cinerarias happy surroundings in your garden. They love lush green vegetation and revel in ferns and other woodsy things beneath trees. Be sure that soil is rich, porous and acid. The more leaf mold and peat moss you add, the better. Pine needles provide a good acid condition.

10. Give your cinerarias plenty of water but do not water from the top when plant is in bloom. Each truss bears many blossoms and the weight of these, heavy with moisture, will break the stems. Do not plant within range of sprinklers. Cultivate lightly because of shallow roots.

11. Cinerarias are subject to leaf miner, a difficult pest to control; also to aphis, sow bugs, etc. Keep the plants growing vigorously at all times, spray regularly with an all-round garden spray and trap snails and sow bugs. As flowers die, cut them off to encourage another crop of lovely blooms.

12. Cinerarias are attractive when massed in beds or borders in combination with fuchsias, ferns, columbine, foxglove, violets, violas and primroses—all of which enjoy a semi-shaded situation. The blossom of the cineraria is lovely as a cut flower. Place loosely in a low container

HOW TO GROW CARNATIONS

1. Carnations are exceptionally easy to grow in most Pacific Coast gardens. They may be propagated by seeds, layers and cuttings. Of several good types available I prefer the fragrant Chaubaud Giants (the new strain) 85% of which come double from seed. The flowers are very fine.

2. In our Washington climate this Chaubaud strain (do not confuse with the old Chaubauds) blossoms six months after sowing of seed. January is, therefore, our best time of planting for summer bloom. If plants are wanted for winter blooming indoors, seeds may be planted in June.

3. In colder sections of Sunset Land it is best to prepare the soil in the fall and store it in the basement until needed. I usually fill my seed flats in the fall so that they are all ready to use when January comes. A sifted garden soil with peat moss or leaf mold is quite satisfactory.

4. January has now arrived. Thoroughly soak the flat containing soil and let it stand until the next day to drain. Then plant the seeds in shallow drills one-eighth inch deep with sifted soil to cover. Pat down firmly. Finish with a thin layer of peat moss. Keep in sunny window.

5. When seeds come up (in about five days) watch for damping off. Semesan or sulphur, used according to directions on container, will help to solve this problem. Water seedlings with very fine spray. When plants are four weeks old they should be ready for their first transplanting.

6. The first transplanting is to pots or paper containers. I make pots of heavy butcher paper, paraffined and pinned together. These paper containers are set close together in a large box or flat. The soil used in the transplanting pot is of loam, peat moss and well-rotted cow manure.

7. After transplanting, the plants are likely to grow rapidly and soon appear to shrivel at the ground, this shriveling condition extending up the stalk. Do not be alarmed at this for it seems to be a natural condition with the dianthus family. Keep plants growing vigorously as possible.

8. The first of April the plants, pots and all, may be placed in a cold frame for hardening before planting directly in the garden. I sink the pots in the ground so that the top of the pot is level with the soil in the cold frame. Final transplanting is usually done about the middle of April.

9. If one does not wish to bother with sowing seed, sturdy plants of carnations can be bought about April first from the nurserymen. As with the buying of seed, it pays to buy the finest strains. (Sunset Garden Editor will tell you where the best seeds and finest plants may be purchased.)

10. Carnations like a good, rich soil with full exposure to the sun. As the plants grow and come into bloom apply a commercial plant food at least once a month, following directions given on container. Keep plants well watered, and faded blooms picked off. Staking plants is advisable.

11. In the fall those plants liked best may be lifted, cut back and brought inside for winter bloom. Otherwise leave them in the garden. In colder sections plants should be given some protection after ground is frozen. Carnations left in the ground over winter often produce inferior bloom.

12. Many carnation growers prefer to discard the less desirable plants each fall and to increase their finer ones by cuttings. Take cuttings shortly after blooming season is over, using the hard, green wood from one of the lateral shoots. Root cuttings in sharp, clean sand, transplant in spring.

HOW TO

Grow Bulbs

AND TUBEROUS-ROOTED PLANTS

A BULB is just a plant in miniature, having inside it the flowers, leaves, etc., waiting only for warmth and moisture to make it grow rapidly into a complete blossoming plant. This, in addition to the great beauty and lasting qualities of many bulbous plants, is why they are such favorites with home gardeners everywhere in the Pacific West.

Most of us, in everyday conversation, lump all the bulbs, tuberous roots and other variations under the word "bulb," but it is important to know the difference for identifying and for planting purposes.

All bulbs and tuberous roots grow at the bottom of the plant, either between the crown (base of stem where roots join on) and roots, or as protuberances from the roots or lower stem.

True Bulb: An onion is a true bulb. It contains the future flower within its fleshy scales. Hyacinths and Lilies are also true bulbs.

Tubers: Dahlias, Sweet Potatoes and Potatoes are examples. A distinction is sometimes made between tubers and tuberous roots — the former having eyes, as Potatoes do, the latter having none.

Corm: A corm is a hard, solid, flat bulb, not fleshy like the Onion. Gladiolus and Ixias are propagated with corms.

Rhizomes: A rhizome is a sort of stem which runs along the ground, either on the surface, or wholly or partially buried. It sends down roots, sends up shoots at its upper end, and acts as a food storehouse for the growing plant. It occurs in the Irises.

Where to Plant Bulbs

Bulbous flowers can be used everywhere in the garden — on the lawn, at its edges, in the various borders, the rockery, in window boxes, in formal beds, and even in the water garden. If you have a woodsy garden or garden corner, bulbs planted naturalistically will make it ten times as charming as it would be without them.

Bulbs are easy to grow, too, delighting in both sun and partial shade, and asking for only a little attention.

Before deciding on what bulbs to plant, first look over your garden for sheltered spots, where the wind will not whip your plants, and where the sun does not blaze enough to burn foliage.

Some people like to tuck bulbous plants in at the bases of any tall-growing shrubs which have few leaves near the ground. In the spring you have a surprising burst of color there, when you do this. Or you may have a few deciduous trees which will allow just enough sunlight to filter through their leaves to satisfy the bulbs preferring very little, but not too much sun.

If you have a large garden, you might set aside a plot for a cutting garden for bulbs alone, or

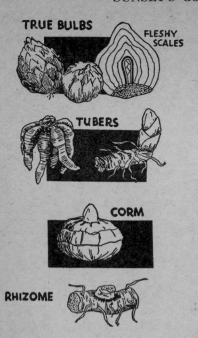

TRUE BULBS — FLESHY SCALES

TUBERS

CORM

RHIZOME

a rich soil with plenty of leafmold and humus. Others would rather grow in a light soil containing sand. Most of them, however, do well in a good sandy loam; and bulbs are so accommodating that some will even grow for you in heavy clay or its opposite, a nearly pure sand.

It is best to loosen heavy clays for them, though, with wood ashes or sand. Leafmold should be mixed in. If you mix manure with the soil, be careful not to let it come in contact directly with your roots or bulbs; they are sensitive to manure. Bonemeal is a fine application — spread it over the soil after your planting is done.

When you prepare to set bulbs in your perennial border, dig as deep a hole as possible and lay drainage material on the bottom. All bulbs require good drainage, for although they like a moist situation they will fail to thrive if the roots stand in water or come in contact with sour soil. For drainage material, use gravel, small stones, or broken pots, then cover with sand. Fill in with this sand until it is 6 inches below the surface, then add soil mixed with leafmold and sand. This will give the roots a porous medium for their growth.

How to Plant Bulbs

Bulbs are set in at various depths. The following table is the correct one to follow in the Pacific West:

	Inches Deep	Inches Apart
Gladiolus	4-6	6-10
Bulbous Iris	3-4	6
Hyacinths	4½	8
Tulips	7	6-10
Narcissi	5	5-10
Lilies	8-10	12
Ranunculus	2	8

Generally speaking, plant them at a depth equal to twice their diameter; but this is not always correct. Usually it is better to set them in deeper. Choice bulbs should be set on a layer of sand, 1 to 2 inches deep, since this provides good drainage and prevents decay. To avoid decay with ordinary bulbs, be sure the base is

include them among annuals, perennials, and biennials you are growing apart for cut flowers.

Not the least important of the uses and places for bulbs is in the perennial border, where they can be used to fill up ugly gaps left by perennials which have finished with their period of bloom.

Naturalizing is a favorite method of bulb planting. It is suited to park-like areas, wild spots beyond the lawn, edges of woodlands, etc. The bulbs which can be planted best in quantity, and which multiply even though you neglect them, are usually selected. Crocus is the best known, but you may also use Winter Aconite, Snowdrop, Daffodils, some of the late-flowering Tulips, and many others. In planting them, you can either make holes in the soil for each bulb, or turn back the sod, place the bulbs in position, and put the sod back again. The soil should be moist and soft.

Not only should suitable parts of your garden be chosen for bulbs, but your selections of individual bulbous plants should be made with care. Like all other plants bulbs have their likes and dislikes — it is necessary to know their needs; and especially, if you plan a succession of bloom, you will need to know when they will produce flowers.

Soil Preparation

Bulbs are not all alike in their soil preferences. Bulbs which grow best in wild, woody areas like

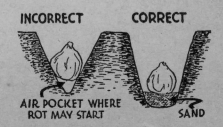

INCORRECT   CORRECT

AIR POCKET WHERE ROT MAY START   SAND

WHEN TOPS ARE BROWN, CUT DOWN TO SURFACE

firmly planted — if there is any space left between the base and the soil, water may collect there, causing rot.

There are general rules, too, for the distances between the plantings. Distances are based on the size of the bulb and the kind of total planting you plan to have. If you want a natural effect, plant them closer together, especially the low-growing varieties and our native bulbs of the West. You may also set them a little closer together if you intend to take them up every year. If they are to remain in the soil undisturbed, however, arrange the above distances between them, to allow for their growth and development.

Care of Bulbs

Like all Gaul, this is divided in three parts: watering, fertilizing, and care after blooming.

Care concerning water really begins before you plant. The soil should not be watered before setting bulbs. That starts growth too soon. When the top growth develops too early, you sometimes have short-stemmed flowers. Instead, you want the root system to get under way. This should be remembered especially if you live in a warm region, and do your bulb planting in the fall.

If you do happen to set them in a moist soil, and the top growth starts soon, as it will, then keep on watering. Otherwise the sprouts will dry up.

In northern climates this needn't bother you. Frosts and freezing hold back the top growth. The roots get their start first. But in the South, winter temperatures are high enough to start this growth at any time.

Next comes fertilizing. This, too, begins before you plant. Scatter a little bonemeal in the bottom of the hole prepared for the bulb. This is the safest fertilizing method. Most bulb growers avoid using manures. They do more harm than good.

A well-rotted manure may be mixed in the soil, though, as noted above. Native bulbs and Lilies are exceptions — do not mix manure with their soil. If you apply commercial fertilizers, remember that they are risky with bulbs unless you know exactly how to handle them.

After bulbous plants bloom, you have the choice of taking them up and storing them, leaving them in the ground, or dividing them. Tulips and Hyacinths should be taken up. Wait until the foliage is brown before digging. Dry them, and store in a box of sand or sawdust. Narcissi may be left in the ground. They will keep blooming for half a dozen years — although their flowers will be small after a while.

Don't dig, cut back or divide until the tops are brown — with any bulbous plants. The leaves must mature after the flowers finish blooming. If they do not mature, you may not have blossoms next year. If someone mistakenly does cut them down ahead of time, dig the bulbs up and replant them in an out of the way spot.

When the foliage is brown, cut back to the ground with a knife or pruning shears and toss the tops on the compost heap.

Some bulbous plants which have been left in the ground will thicken into clumps. Instead of digging and storing, or leaving in the soil, you divide them. To do this, wait until the foliage has died down. Dig up the whole plant, with plenty of soil clinging to this root-clump. Break up the clump into smaller parts, as you would a breakfast roll. This will give you several plants instead of one. Replant anywhere, in suitable soil — that is, in soil like that from which you took the clump.

In all cases, it is wise to familiarize yourself with the care - requirements of the particular bulbs you are growing.

Suggestions for Your Selection

Narcissus or Daffodil. These are grown by almost everyone who loves flowers. Narcissus blooms can be had from November until the latter part of April, simply by selecting different varieties of Narcissi. We have mentioned these first because, of all bulbous plants, they are the best for you to work with if you are a beginner. Narcissi grow in partial shade and under deciduous trees. Very little effort is needed on your

71

part, once they are planted. They return each year. Set them 5 inches deep. They are not particular about soil, but it is well to give them a good, deep, porous garden loam. They make lovely cut flowers, and are especially attractive when set out in naturalized drifts and allowed to increase as they wish. In cold sections give them a mulch in the winter.

The large trumpet Narcissi are the so-called Daffodils. King Alfred variety is all yellow, with a frilled trumpet. The Emperor is not so big, but is less expensive. Golden Spur is the earliest; Spring Glory is a bi-color yellow trumpet Daffodil with white petals.

The smaller trumpet varieties include Sir Watkins, yellow: Conspicuous (Barri), with yellow petals and cup edged with orange red; Laurens Koster (Poetaz), which has clusters of white flowers having yellow cups (this can be grown in water); Orange Cup (Poetaz), yellow edged with orange cup; Paper Whites, same as Chinese Sacred Lily but pure white; and Soleil d'Or, which has a shallow chalice, and bears clusters of yellow flowers with an orange cup (this, too, can be grown in water).

The shallow-chaliced Narcissi include the *Poeticus ornatus* variety, bearing a white cup edged with scarlet; and Evangeline (Leedsii), with white petals and a yellow chalice.

The Jonquil, another type of Narcissus, is fragrant, with golden-yellow flowers.

The Double Narcissus variety includes Von Scion and Golden Phoenix. The Doubles are yellow.

Tulips. These are as familiar to most of us as Narcissi, but for some reason are not grown as much. For one thing, Tulips do not propagate so easily as do Narcissi. Nevertheless, they are magnificently colored flowers, and there is a vast variety to choose from — the Darwin, Cottage, Breeder, etc. Tulips are most satisfactory when placed in a hardy border. Use moderately rich, well-drained, light soil. Watch that they do not dry out after they sprout. In Southern California one must plant them a little deeper than in colder climates. Eight inches is a good depth; 7 inches elsewhere. They do well where it is partly shady,

so that you can plant them under your deciduous trees with good results. Gophers may come after them; if they do, surround the plants with a wire netting. Your Tulips will bloom in April when the Hyacinths do, and also at the close of the Narcissus season.

It is getting harder and harder to tell the different varieties apart; modern hybridization has merged the old forms of Darwin, Cottage and Breeder so much that most of them blend into one another.

Best known among the Darwin Tulips are the varieties Baron de la Tonnaye, rose pink; Clara Butt, soft rose; Rev. H. Ewbank, deep lilac, and City of Haarlem, cardinal red.

The Breeder Tulips come in shades of brown and purple, which are not found in the Darwins. Bronze Queen is buff and golden bronze, with brown tones. Dom Pedro is coffee brown and mahogany. Louis XIV is gold and purplish bronze, and Lucifer is rose and terra-cotta outside and orange inside.

Cottage Tulips bloom later than the others. If you are trying for yellow shades, use these: Mrs. Moon, bright yellow; Inglescomb Yellow, a rich yellow; Inglescomb Pink, rose-pink.

Hyacinths. A Hyacinth is a colorful, fragrant flower, charming in mixed bulb borders. The soil should be rich and sandy, with good drainage. They like more sun than Tulips do, but will grow in partial shade. Give them plenty of water, and protection from the wind. In the Northwest, winter mulches should be given them. When planting in the Southwest, put them in deeply to keep the top growth from starting too soon, and put some leaves and laths over the bed to keep the ground cool. This will prevent too rapid growth.

Lilies. Lilies suited to your garden should be selected. Some varieties stand more sun than others—Madonna and Regal, for example. Many others thrive in complete shade. A marvelous succession of bloom may be had with Lilies in the Northwest particularly. You can have Madonna Lilies blooming in June, followed by Regal Lily, and others coming into flower through July, August and early September. Lilies require a light garden loam and perfect drainage. Some

Lilies have roots at the base; others have roots at the base and on the stem. The latter are planted 10 inches deep; the others 2 or 3 inches.

The Gold-banded Lily of Japan is white, with crimson dots, and a golden band down the middle of each petal. The botanical name is *Lilium auratum*. Rose shades outside the petals, and yellow inside, make the Regal Lily (*L. regale*) one of the most handsome of the true, trumpet-shaped Lilies. *Lilium henryi* is soft orange and blooms in August in Southern California. *L. speciosum rubrum* is also an August bloomer, bearing rosy white flowers with red spots. A white variety of this is *L. speciosum album*.

Then there is the Madonna Lily, which we have mentioned. It blooms in June in California. A California native is the Leopard Lily (*L. pardalinum*), which is deep orange with maroon dots. Finally, among these best-known, easy-to-grow Lilies for the West, there is the familiar Tiger Lily (*L. tigrinum*), which as you know is heavily dotted over its orange-red flower.

Gladiolus. Like Narcissi, these are easy for the beginner to grow. A good thing to know at the outset is the general pronunciation. More and more gardeners have decided upon "Gladiolus" for both singular and plural, with the accent on the "o". Differences of opinion, however, are the spice of gardening, so if you prefer Gladiolus for the singular, and Gladiolus, Gladioli or even Gladioluses for the plural, stick by your guns. After all, the "i" ending is Latinly correct, although the world often ignores this in the process of anglicizing a word; and as for the last-named above, well, there is such a word as galluses!

Gladiolus or Gladioli, then, as you like, are odd-looking in their bulbous state, for they are corms, flat and hard, not fleshy. They grow in any good garden soil, preferably a sandy loam, and need no fertilizer during the first year. The plants will eat up the soil's nourishment, so that you will have to add nourishment from time to time to make up for what is lacking. Buy corms from a reliable dealer to be sure they are free from thrips.

Planting depths vary. Five to six inches is good for a light soil; 4 for a heavy loam. Locate them where they will have plenty of sunlight, such as in your borders or — and this is an excellent idea — in a separate cutting garden, for the Gladiolus is a cut-flower primarily. It blooms only briefly in the garden. When the growth is vigorous, supply them with water.

An enormous number of varieties have been developed in the past two decades or so. Here is a selected group suitable for the Pacific Western localities.

Orange Queen primulinus hybrid, apricot with orange shades; Maiden's Blush primulinus hybrid, salmon with yellow throat; Alice Tiplady primulinus hybrid, deep orange; Souvenir primulinus hybrid, deep yellow.

And here is a similar group: Mrs. F. C. Peters, lilac; Virginia, red; Mr. W. H. Phipps, deep pink; Mrs. Leon Douglas, begonia rose; Prince of Wales, light apricot-salmon; E. J. Shaylor, deep rose, ruffled; Halley, delicate salmon-pink; Dr. F. E. Bennett, deep peach-red; Mary Pickford, cream with yellow throat; Purple Glory, deep maroon; Marie Kunderd, white with a suggestion of pink in the center of petals, ruffled; Rose Glory, rose pink, darker in the throat, and ruffled; Byron L. Smith, lavender-pink on white ground.

Bulbous Iris. These are exotic flowers, with long, slender grasslike foliage. Irises are best thought of as cut-flowers, like the Gladiolus, although they make good backgrounds for borders. Their colors range through yellows and oranges, violet and lavender. There are various kinds, English, Dutch, Spanish, etc., although it is hard for a layman to tell them apart. But it is good to know what you are growing, for you must not give the Dutch or Spanish Irises any water in the summer. Since they originate in a southern climate, they are much easier to grow here on the Pacific Coast than on the Atlantic. As a matter of fact, America's supply of Dutch Irises comes from Oregon and Washington.

Irises like a soil that is warm, sandy, well-drained, and sunny. In the South you can plant them early; in Washington, plant them early in November. In California they start to grow right away, and their leaves are above the surface during the winter. Flowers appear in April.

Plant your Dutch Irises in groups, or behind other plants. This is because their stems are rather poor-looking. But these are long-lasting plants, even so.

Among the Spanish Irises are the varieties Cajanus, which is yellow; and King of Blues. The variety of Dutch Iris known as Imperator is a deep blue; Golden Glory is yellow.

Anemone. These give you brilliant colors in the spring—reds, purples, lavenders, whites and pinks. The tuberlike roots are set in 3 inches down. If you find it hard to tell which is the top and which the bottom of the tuber, look for fibrous threads—that is the top; and for the smooth side—that is the bottom. We in the West have a corner on the lovely St. Brigid and De Caen types which cannot be grown in other parts of the country except the South. They thrive in California. Set them out early in spring in Pacific Northwest but in fall in California.

One of the best is the Japanese Anemone, which is best increased by dividing the roots in the fall or early spring. Anemones like a peaty or sandy loam, with well-rooted manure added. Semi-shade is the best location.

Ranunculus. A Ranunculus looks like a buttercup. They look so well side by side with Anemones that they are often spoken of together, as if they were twins. Their roots are odd—a mass of small tubers resembling claws. When planting, set so that the claws point downward. Ranunculus bulbs are usually dry when you buy them. Better soak several hours before planting. Three inches is a good planting depth. In the South, give them half and half sun and shade; in the North, let them have full sun. The soil should be sandy, drained, and fertilized with manure. When you plant them in your borders or flower beds in September, October, and November, you have blooms from March to June.

Crocus. Plant Crocuses preferably where there are few other flowers—though they will be as gay under some trees, in half shade, informally along a garden path, in a border, rockery or on a terrace. They look best when allowed to grow naturally along a lawn or the edge of a grassy wood. You will be astonished at the way they multiply. Very little care is needed; mainly, keep out weeds. Blooms will come in January if you set the bulbs from September to December. The soil should be rich, acid, moist and well fertilized.

Freesia. Here is another multiplier. All kinds of colors are offered—salmon-pink, golden-yellow, carmine-red, white, and near blue. Freesias do well on the Coast of California, but must be grown in greenhouses in the North. The small bulbs are planted with their points upward, about 3 inches deep. Locate them in a sunny spot, where there will be warmth, drainage, and a light but rich soil. They make good cut-flowers not only because of the waxy, fragrant flowers but because they last well in water. It is best to plant them before October. They mix well with Narcissi or other spring-blooming bulbs, or are beautiful when scattered through shrubbery.

Varieties of Freesias are: Splendens, deep lavender; Purity, white; and Yellow Prince, pure yellow.

Watsonia. Most people associate the color white with Watsonias, but there are also salmon, apricot, rose and pink hybrids. These hybrids are better than the white, and are worth your interest—though few gardeners who have grown the classic white Watsonias would ever omit them. Plant them early, during September and October, in sunny positions. They will not mind a little shade. Plant 6 inches deep, a foot apart. Let them stand in the ground after blooming; cut the leaves back when they turn brown. If you live where it is cold in winter, better dig the corms up and either replant or store them until early fall. They do not like winter cold. Otherwise, no other care is necessary—not even watering. They look well in mixed borders, placed in the background with bulbous Irises and Delphiniums.

Clementina, salmon-rose, J. J. Dean, rose, and Fanny Lyon, apricot-buff, are colored varieties of Watsonias.

Ixia. These brilliant, cup-shaped or star-shaped flowers blossom from March to June. It's a pity they are not used so much as formerly. They are grown in full sun. Their corms are planted either in early spring or throughout the autumn.

Sparaxis. A sun-lover. Red and white color combinations, with flowers something like the Ixia.

Calla Lily. This has a large white or yellow flower, something like the thrown-back cowl of a friar. A large yellow spoke stands alone in the center, like a torch. Calla Lilies are easy to grow, requiring a moist soil, plenty of water, either sunlight or partial shade, and applications of manure now and then. To propagate them, you divide their thick, chunky roots. There is a yellow variety, *C. elliotiana*, which has green leaves spotted with cream.

Amaryllis. If you have a love for old-fashioned things, why not revive the custom of growing Amaryllis? They are especially good for the interior regions, where there is a high summer temperature. You plant the large bulbs just below the surface with the neck exposed. Don't be alarmed when the lilylike foliage dies—it always does; and then the flower stalk protrudes.

Tigridia. A garden novelty. The green bud opens in the morning and closes at sunset—and never opens again. Yet in that brief lifetime so much intense beauty and brilliancy are crowded in that gardeners, who for a long time did not like to bother with them, now are seeking them eagerly.

Tuberous Begonia. If the soil is mixed with leafmold and sand, and good drainage is provided, these are not hard to grow. Their flowers are large, with orange, yellow, pink, rose and white shades. Set the tubers 2 inches deep, with the concave side up, in a shady corner or fern garden. Do not disturb them.

Oxalis. This rapid spreader is used as a ground cover. The pink, lavender, yellow, white or rose flowers blossom from January to March. Good varieties for the West are: Bowiei, rose; Bermuda Buttercup, yellow; Grand Duchess, white, pink or lavender.

Chionodoxa. These little blue or white flowers go best in the flower border. Offsets from the bulbs are planted in the fall, September to December. Varieties are: Luciliae, light blue; Sardensis, darker blue.

Scilla. Some call this the Wild Hyacinth, a name more suited to its slender grace. Its flowers are like nodding bells, blue, white, and lilac. You'd like them in your wild garden or rockery. Sibirica, blue, Campanulata, blue, pink and white; and Clusii (peruviana), deep blue, are good suggestions.

Brodiaea. Here's another California native. Its colors are tempting—you have a choice of violet, with *B. grandiflora*; crimson, with *B. coccinea*; or lavender, with the common *B. capitata*.

Calochortus. Another native. *C. amabilis* is yellow; *C. amoenus* is rose pink; *C. albus*, white; *C. benthamii*, yellow again; *C. venustus* (the "true Mariposa Tulip") has yellow flowers with a black spot on each petal; and *C. venustus oculatus* is white or cream, with tints of lilac.

Erythronium. You may recognize this better as Dogtooth Violet or Fawn Lily. They naturalize in shady borders or grassy slopes. They are dainty little plants, and you would like the varieties Californicum White Beauty, white with a maroon spot at the base of the petals; *Californicum bicolor*, white and yellow; Hendersonii, light purple; and revolutum Rose Beauty.

Fritillaria. Unless you like oddities, you might not care for Fritillarias. They are bell-shaped flowers nodding from slender stems, which sounds all right, but their odor would interest only a botanist. Recurva is orange scarlet; Parviflora is purple.

Camassia. This is a Western bulb, and is very easy to grow. Camassias were favorites of Pacific Northwest Indians, who grew them, not for the rich blue flowers, but in order to steam and eat the sweet, nutty bulbs. Camassia is a rapid multiplier, needs no winter protection, and asks only for a little moisture before it blooms.

HOW TO GROW BULBS

LILIES
8 - 10" DEEP

NARCISSI
5" DEEP
5"- 10" APART

TULIPS
7" DEEP
6"- 10"
APART

Select lilies suitable to your garden. Soil for most—a light garden loam, wood soil or peat, and no alkaline or lime. Provide perfect drainage. Keep roots cool in the shade of other plants.

Plant narcissi as early as possible. Charming when naturalized in drifts and left to increase. Excellent for cut flowers. Plant them in light sandy soil with plenty of leaf mold or peat. Give them winter mulch in cold sections.

Tulips are most satisfactory planted in groups in hardy border in moderately rich, well-drained light soil. Never allow them to dry out after they sprout. Great variety to choose from—Darwins, Breeders, Cottage. Try a few of each.

4½" DEEP
8" APART
HYACINTH

SOUTH AFRICANS

BULBOUS IRIS
3"- 4" DEEP
6" APART

Hyacinths—fragrant, colorful flowers, attractive in mixed bulb border. Like rich, sandy soil, abundance of water, perfect drainage, sunny situation, protection from wind. Mulch in winter if danger of alternate freezing and thawing.

South African bulbs are admirably suited to California gardens because of similar climatic conditions. This group includes *freesias, tritonias, ixias, baboon flower, watsonias.*

Try some *English, Spanish* and *Dutch* iris which are quite distinct from the usual bearded iris type. These grow from small bulbs and have grass-like foliage. Plant in warm sunny position. No summer water for Spanish and Dutch.

3 EARLY BULBS FOR ROCK GARDENS

3 BULBS FOR NATURALIZING

4 **WEST COAST NATIVES**

Grape Hyacinth, Glory-of-the-Snow and Spring Snowflake are ideal for the rock garden. These are hardy and dependable in most situations and can be left in the ground to grow and multiply undisturbed for years. Plant them 2-4" deep.

Plant these in colonies and leave to grow undisturbed for years. Winter Aconite—very easy culture. Snowdrop —particularly effective in thin woodland spots. Crocus—fine planted at edge of trees, some straying into lawn area.

Calochorti—fine for slopes in leaf mold, sand and grit. Avoid alternate freezing and thawing. *Brodiaea* — naturalizes in most soils under trees. *Erythronium* — best in moist well-drained spots. *Fritillaria*—lily-like flower. Many sorts.

2½" DEEP
6" APART
ANEMONES AND RANUNCULUS

GLADIOLUS
4"- 6" DEEP
6"- 10" APART

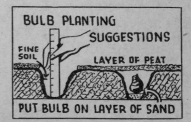

BULB PLANTING SUGGESTIONS
FINE SOIL
LAYER OF PEAT
PUT BULB ON LAYER OF SAND

Anemones range in color from white through blue and purple; Ranunculus through yellow, orange and red. Fine cut flowers. They like rich, sandy, porous soil and protected positions. Soak bulbs prior to planting Ranunculus.

Gladiolus are hardy everywhere in summer. Plant any month in the year in warmer sections. Like sandy loam, full sun, perfect drainage. Use in borders or in separate cutting gardens. Try some primulinus as well as exhibition types.

Plant most bulbs three times their depth, varying with soil and climate. Ideal bulb soil—loam, sand and leaf mold or peat moss. Set bulbs at bottom of hole on sand. Avoid contact of bulb with plant food. Winter mulch in cold sections.

HOW TO GROW DAHLIAS

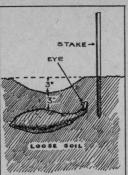

Above is my picture taken May 20th—just before I was planted. I might have been planted earlier but later plantings produce good fall bloom.

May 21. This morning my master is digging the garden. He's spading ground at least 18 inches deep and pulverizing the soil until it is very fine.

May 23. I'm being planted. Study the picture above to see just how they did it. Later that depression in the soil will be filled in with dirt.

Every few days my master stirs the ground around me so I can breathe better. I like to have the ground kept damp but not wet while I am young.

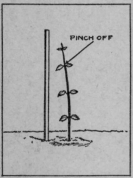

Today I had grown so high that I had several sets of leaves on my stem, so my master pinched off my top to make me grow bushy and strong.

Now that I am growing I need plenty of water, but I like to have the ground cultivated thoroughly after watering. I am tied with raffia to my stake.

Aug. 1. At last I am getting buds, but in order to have my flowers the very best, my master removes some of the buds. Picture shows how he does it.

Aug. 5. Now that my buds are starting to swell, my master puts plant food around me regularly, following the directions given on the package.

Whenever aphis bother me, I'm sprayed with nicotine sulphate solution. This keeps me healthy and strong. I'm growing fine, my buds are bursting.

This morning the whole family came out to see me. I just heard my mistress say that the San Leandro flower show is next week. Will they take me?

Early this morning they cut off my best bloom, removed the lower leaves, plunged my stem into hot water for a minute and then cold water.

Well, here I am at the Dahlia Show and look what I'm wearing! No wonder I got first prize; I came from good stock, and I had intelligent care!

HOW TO GROW GLADIOLI

1. The ease of culture and comparative freedom from disease and insect enemies make the gladiolus a most satisfactory flower. Be sure to order your bulbs from reliable dealers. As soon as bulbs arrive, the package should be unwrapped and the bulbs put in a cool, dry place.

2. When you buy from reliable dealers you are assured of good bulbs, or corms as they are generally called. A thick, high-centered bulb is better than a thin, flat one because it is younger and more vigorous. Generally speaking price depends upon whether or not the variety is a new one.

3. Any good garden soil will grow gladiolus. If of a clay or adobe, sand or peat moss should be added. Spade in well-rotted manure the fall before planting but do not use fertilizers at planting time. Gladiolus enjoy a sunny situation. Dig soil to a depth of at least a foot; pulverize.

4. Bulbs may be planted five or more inches deep and four to six inches apart, depending upon size of bulb. In Southern California plantings can be made almost any time but spring is conceded to be the general planting time all along the Coast. Plan for a succession of bloom.

5. Gladiolus require thorough waterings—not mere sprinkling. To conserve moisture and to keep the soil in good condition, cultivation is important all through the growing period. Before flowering a top dressing of commercial plant food should be given, watering soil thoroughly.

6. Slender stakes, or bamboo, painted green, make attractive supports for the spikes. Use strips of cloth or raffia instead of cord to tie the blossoming spikes. Deep planting also helps to keep the plants from falling over. Continue to apply plant food as the plants come into blossom.

7. The gladiolus surpasses most flowers for keeping qualities when cut. Cut the spikes as buds start to open with a sharp knife rather than with shears to avoid bruising. In cutting, leave about four strong leaves to develop bulbs for next year. Put spikes into cold or ice water immediately.

8. Gladiolus may be planted in rows or beds, but lend themselves also to borders among shrubbery or flowers. Of course they are most easily cultivated and cared for when grown in rows. Some of the smaller types are especially lovely in rock gardens. Study your catalogue pages for colors.

9. Cultivation should be continued after blooming season to develop strong bulbs for the next season. Less water is needed after flowering. As soon as foliage turns yellow, about four to six weeks after blooming, it is time to dig the bulbs. The man pictured should be using a hoe.

10. When digging, cut off the tops close to the bulbs and dry well in the air and sunshine for several days. Cure indoors for a few weeks and store in a cool, dry cellar in flats or boxes. 40 to 50 degrees is a good temperature. In the warmer sections it is not necessary to dig the bulbs in fall.

11. The bulbs should be cleaned about six weeks after digging and the roots and bulblets removed. Bulblets are cared for the same as bulbs and will flower the second year if one wishes to bother with them. Bulblets should be planted very early in spring, otherwise they may not mature.

12. A satisfactory crate for storage can be made of four-inch boards for the sides and lath laid fairly close together for the bottom. Two feet square is a good size for such crates. Peat moss is a satisfactory packing for bulbs. Gladiolus may be grown from seed but not satisfactorily.

HOW TO GROW IRIS

There are three common types of iris—the Tall Bearded with which we are most familiar; the Siberian and Japanese seen growing around pools; and bulbous for rock gardens. This movie applies only to Tall Bearded!

For the finest of Iris go to western growers. The garden editor of Sunset Magazine will be glad to give you the names of reliable growers in your community. Study your iris catalogs for descriptions of the many varieties.

Tall Bearded Iris are best planted in June, July and August in the northern part of Sunset Land and September and October in the south, but it is possible to plant them at almost any time.

 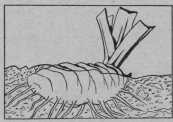 

Select a sunny, well-drained place for your bearded iris. They will not thrive in shade. A hillside or terrace is good. Plant in loam if possible. If soil is acid a little lime or wood ashes will help. Avoid heavy fertilizers.

To plant, spade soil deeply and work ground carefully. Set rhizome as shown with roots spread out, two-thirds of rhizome covered and the rest exposed. Cut back leaves before planting. Set plants a little more than a foot apart.

Water new plantings but do not soak. When plants are established, forget them. But if fall rains are late, start watering in fall to encourage new growth. Keep free from weeds. If your ground freezes, mulch in late fall.

Bearded iris are lovely as cut flowers. Rather than cut the foliage of prize varieties, substitute gladiolus leaves. Change water every day, trimming back stems. Lovely combined with fruit blossoms and roses.

When leaves die down in late summer and plants grow shabby, pull out the dried leaves. Rake out dead leaves and other garden debris to discourage borers. If borers get in trim away all injured parts.

When the clumps of Iris become crowded, usually every three years, either cut out the center, replacing with new soil or take up the clump, break it up and replant, trimming off the top third of the leaves as shown.

HOW TO
Grow Shrubs

USE CONIFERS
FOR DARK ACCENTS

There are two kinds of shrubs. One loses its leaves in the fall. Instead of using many words, it is simpler to describe it as deciduous. Dee-sid'-you-us. The other kind keeps its leaves, staying green. It is called evergreen.

A tree has one stem; a shrub may have many. Trees may stand attractively by themselves; most shrubs must stand in groups to look their best.

Shrubs fit naturally only into certain parts of your garden. You can use them for hedges, along your house foundation, at doorways, entrances, corners, and around the boundaries of your lot. Some shrubs are colored or shaped with such uniqueness or unusual beauty that they stand by themselves as individuals. Such shrubs are called specimens.

In general, shrubs go best wherever you want a permanent, low or medium-sized effect, a middle step between your flowers and trees.

What to Look for When You Select Shrubs

It is better to have a few kinds of shrubs than one of each of many kinds. With a few you won't have to study up so much on their care. As with all plants, there are general rules for planting and caring for shrubs, but each species has its own pet likes and dislikes. It is wiser to know a lot about a few than a smattering about a number. You get better results.

Your garden picture will have more strength, restfulness and unity if you follow the above suggestion.

Next, consider the work you want a shrub to do for you. You will want some to provide backgrounds of rich green. These shrubs you buy for their foliage. Mirror Plant is of this kind. Perhaps you know it as Coprosma. Its appeal lies in its glossy leaves. Other shrubs are valued for their blossoms. You like the familiar look of Rose leaves, but it is the Rose's flower that you love. So with Escallonias, Camellias and many others. Then there is the berrying group. When you think of Cotoneaster you think of fat red berries, clustered against the green foliage. The Firethorns belong to this group of brilliant berried plants.

In your garden's background, plant the shrub you value for foliage, unless it is so unusual that it merits a foreground location. Background shrubs should have coarse leaves, so that your outdoor living room will be enclosed as with a thick screen. They should be vigorous growers —you will want them tall. In front of them, put smaller-leaved shrubs, and those which you prize for their flowers, berries, special shape, or other good points.

The very showy shrubs, the specimen shrubs, should be planted with much taste; too many will steal the show from one another, like several prima donnas in an opera. Use these for accents. Do you know music? In waltz time you have three beats—one, two, three; one, two, three, etc. The "one" is accented—remember? —as if you said it aloud and whispered the rest. That beat stands out. An accent in gardening stands out, too, is noticeable. Hence it is good taste to use it sparingly.

Growing Habits, Soil and Exposure

What is a growing habit? You can see examples of it in human beings. Some naturally spread sideways, some shoot up tall and slim. Shrubs as just as original. It isn't wise to force a shrub out of its natural way of growing. You can't push a slim fellow down into a round, chunky shape—he'll just grow up slim again if he can. He never looks right, if forced. Buy a round shrub to begin with.

You can find a shrub to suit almost any shape or location. Think of the variety these growing habits suggest:

Dense	Tall	Open
Coarse	Round	Short
Tapering	Conical	Sprawling
Drooping	Columnar	Spreading

There's a shrub for each kind.

Before buying a shrub, be sure it will grow in the soil of your garden. It would be a waste of money to plant a Rhododendron in a heavy alkaline soil that had no drainage. It is easy to learn what soil you have. Ask any skilled gardener or nurseryman, or apply a test like that given in our soil chapter.

Think of the exposure, too. Often a plant fails to thrive only because a simple fact has been disregarded. Sun-loving shrubs languish in the shade, and vice versa. Strong winds can be harmful to shrubs, yet some shrubs resist wind admirably. See the lists of shrubs for special exposure at the end of this chapter.

The actual selecting of a shrub, then, goes something like this in a thoughtful gardener's mind: "I have a corner. I want a tall, narrow shrub for it. It must grow that way naturally, fit into my garden picture and thrive in this soil and exposure. I want such-and-such, but will it grow well here?" Then this wise gardener looks over his catalogue or garden book, checks his list of wills and won'ts against the descriptions, and emerges triumphant from his hunt with a shrub for his corner. And—it thrives for him. This is what garden experts mean when they say, "Consider sun, shade, soil, etc., and select accordingly."

Winter Care of Western Shrubs

If you live where there are snowfalls, prepare for the cold in this way:

When the leaves of your deciduous shrubs fall, first prune, then tie up the branches and wrap in several thicknesses of burlap. Tie the burlap so that the wind will not whip it away. When the following spring is well advanced, remove this covering. If you take it off too early, the plants may thaw out too rapidly and die.

The same precaution should be taken with the Roses which the catalogues describe as "half hardy," meaning that they are not robust enough to endure unfavorable conditions without help. This care should be taken with any Roses you have budded or grafted—they easily become frost victims.

You Can Grow Shrubs from Cuttings

A cutting is a piece of a plant which you cut off and plant by itself. It grows into a new plant. But you must know what piece to cut, and how to plant and care for it. For more detailed information, cuttings under "How to Start Your Plants," in this book. You can make cuttings from Cotoneasters, Spiraeas, Firethorns,

SHRUBS HAVE VARIOUS SHAPES

PYRAMIDAL   LOW BRANCHING ROUND HEADED PROSTRATE COLUMNAR

SHRUBS ARE USED FOR:

HEDGES...

FOUNDATION PLANTINGS...

DOORWAYS.

ENTRANCES...

CORNERS...

BOUNDARIES...

SPECIMENS.....

Fertilizing Your Shrubs

When you plant a shrub, you want it to grow immediately, Nitrogen causes immediate, healthy growth. Manure contains nitrogen. Therefore, before planting a shrub, see that its soil-to-be is well mixed with manure.

Then again, the plant's growing roots must be able to penetrate the soil easily. In other words, it must be porous. Manure with its bulkiness makes a soil porous.

With shrubs, as with other plants, keep in mind the wisdom of "balanced fertilizers." Too much nitrogen will make your shrubs grow a lot, but it will not make them strong. Nitrogen-carrying fertilizers such as ground blood or nitrate of soda are good, if not used to excess. For strength and hardiness, use bonemeal and acid phosphate.

Planting

Put it down on your calendar that November is the best planting month for shrubbery, evergreens particularly, if you live in a mild region along the Pacific Coast, and especially if you live near Puget Sound. The soil is still warm; you can work it easier. It contains plenty of moisture, yet not too much, as in the spring. The nurseries have more selections to show you than later on. Then, when you have put in your shrubs in the fall, along come the rains, making the roots grow, which in turn force the spring growth of the tops.

Protect a Shrub before It's Planted

If you can, plant your shrubs right away, where they are to go. If this is not possible, dig a trench for the shrubs which come to you with their roots bare. This protection is needed to prevent exposure of the roots to the sun, or drying out.

The trenching is called "heeling in" and is nothing more than a temporary planting. The idea is to cover the roots and keep them moist. Sometimes shrubs will dry in transit, in which case you had best bury them, tops and all, for several days in moist earth.

Dig the trench about 2 feet or more deep, and 2 feet wide. Put the shrubs in upright as if you were planting a hedge, but don't crowd them. Shovel the soil loosely around them without packing, and then hose them thoroughly until there are puddles. This watering will make new fiber form.

When you are ready to plant them in their final home, you'll find that they lift out easily;

Hydrangeas, English Laurels, Golden Bells, Weigelas, Butterfly Bushes, and many others. Any month during the summer will do for the starting of cuttings. Early February and late October are good months, too.

but even so, handle them with care, because a shrub or any plant undergoing the process of transplanting is like a person who is weak from hunger, or like a fish gasping for its native element. The proof of this is that if you uproot any plant and leave it without soil or water on its roots, or if you transplant it without giving it the care it must have, it wilts and dies.

Digging a Shrub's Home

Perhaps your shrubs will not arrive too early for planting, and nothing will happen to hinder your putting them in immediately. If that is the case, prepare the holes for them before they come.

Dig the ground deeply, throwing the topsoil into one pile, and the poorer undersoil into another. Dig a hole large enough, both in depth and diameter, 15 to 20 inches deep, to allow the shrub to spread its roots. With your fork, break up the bottom of the hole to allow good drainage. This is especially important if the bottom is hardpan.

When you fill in, after setting the shrub in place, use as much of the topsoil as you can, more around the roots than at the surface. It will be well to examine your topsoil to see whether it is heavy or poor. If it is, mix it with sand and peat moss.

Those shrubs which you are placing near the foundation of the house may need extra attention as to their soil, for builders sometimes leave rubbish or bad soil there. In that event you may have to dig it up and cart it off in your wheelbarrow, and bring better soil from another part of your property.

Planting Bare Root, Balled, Canned and Boxed Shrubs

Your nursery will prepare different shrubs in different ways according to the requirements of their root systems. Some will come to you with bare roots, others with roots in a ball of earth and burlap wrapped around the ball, others in boxes, and still others in tin cans.

Before planting a bare-root shrub, prune back its roots, fill up not quite to the top, and tamp. With practically all bare-rooted plants, prune back at least one third of the top growth in order to encourage a strong root system.

With a balled shrub, do not break the ball but set the shrub, ball and all, down into its hole. Fill in loose earth around it, and when partly so filled, cut the string at the top, pull back the

TIE IN BURLAP FOR WINTER IN THE NORTHWEST

top of the burlap covering, and go on covering with soil.

Shrubs which are hard to transplant are root-pruned by the nurseryman a year before transplanting, and are then prepared for transplanting by allowing them to take along with them the soil they are used to. A balled shrub costs more because it costs money to prepare it in this way.

When a balled shrub is received from the nursery, immerse the ball in water so that the roots will have had a thorough soaking before the shrub is planted.

If you receive a canned plant, use your tin-snips to cut the can away. Remove it very carefully. If the plant comes boxed, make sure the hole it is to go in is big enough for the box. When the plant is set, you can remove its box and fill in the hole as you do for balled shrubs.

Care after Planting

First, prune the branches. Even heavy pruning is wise. This balances the loss of roots which always happens when a plant is dug up for transplanting.

Also, after planting, water often; and if it is an evergreen shrub, spray the foliage twice a day until new growth appears. When the shrub is well established, give it some commercial plant food. The directions will be on the package. You can also add well-rotted manure, spading it into the soil. During the first year, continue these surface applications, either with decayed manure, marsh hay or straw.

In general, for all shrubbery, and trees, too, fill up the hole about three quarters full of soil, using as much topsoil as you can. Flood with water until the water comes up to the top; let it settle; then flood again.

Moving a Shrub within Your Garden

If you transplant a shrub from one part of your garden to another, there are important

SPECIMEN SHRUBS MAY STAND ALONE

things to remember for the Pacific West. The operation is in 5 parts: (1) preparing the plant for transplanting, (2) digging up the plant, (3) taking it to its new location, (4) planting, (5) caring for it after planting.

Make sure first that the shrub you want to move is vigorous and healthy. It should have vigorous roots, a well-balanced top, and no diseases or insect pests. Spray such plants with whatever spray is needed for its special trouble (consult Encyclopedia in this book, under name of each shrub).

When to Transplant

There are two kinds of shrubs—evergreen and deciduous. "Deciduous" means that the plant loses its leaves and grows them again. Evergreen stays green.

Deciduous shrubs should be moved in the fall, or before the leaves grow in the spring. Moving at other times requires extra care. Midwinter or fall are best along the Coast; the roots have more time to grow and get used to their new home before the summer heat comes.

Inland, in the cold parts of the valleys and mountain regions, transplant only in the spring. You may experiment with fall transplanting here if you put a good mulch around the plants to keep the ground from freezing down to roots.

One way of doing this is to wrap the tops with burlap for protection from the winds in the winter. At the base put straw or manure, and soil on top of that.

If you live in a warm region, your fall transplanting should be done only if there is plenty of water.

In general, do not transplant during the warm weather, unless you can buy your shrubs packed in tin cans—these may be planted at any time.

How to Move Western Evergreens

When you move an evergreen shrub, leave plenty of soil around the roots. Evergreens transpire heavily, and this transpiration should

be reduced. Spring is the best time, anywhere, a little before the first leaves come out on the deciduous plants.

Winter transplanting is all right where the winters are mild. Summer transplanting may be done in humid climates, but you must give the plant plenty of moisture. If there is an out and out wet and dry season in your locality, transplant only in the wet season.

Follow the above directions for moving shrubs, being careful not to injure the roots. It is best to begin your digging a little way off from the plant. This saves more roots from being cut off. Keep as much earth around the roots as possible.

Good pruning of all new, tender shoots or growths is recommended before attempting to move.

Plant at the same depth the shrub grew in before. A Rhododendron is a shallow-rooted plant, however; such plants should be placed almost on the soil surface.

After the Planting

A support may be needed for a transplanted shrub or tree. A tripod made of three poles, tied at the apex, is good. Guy wires are also used.

Evergreens need warm soil, and coolness and moisture in the atmosphere. You can give them these by mulching and watering. This care helps the root growth and holds back the top until the new roots are established.

For the moving of very large shrubs or trees, you will probably call in your nurseryman, since that requires equipment not usually found around the average home — horses, block and tackle, grabhooks, chains, a crew of three to five men, etc.

The Shrubs Which Lose Their Leaves in the Fall

Some of us shudder at the thought of bare, leafless branches in the wintertime. To others, there is a particular beauty about them. For these last, who enjoy the feeling of seasonal changes, deciduous shrubs are as much prized as evergreens.

Most deciduous shrubs do best in Northwest and Pacific Central localities, but there are many well suited to the Southwest, too, among them the following:

Deciduous Shrubs for Southwest Gardens

Japanese Quince	Hydrangeas
Common Snowball	*Deutzia gracilis*
Weigela	Japanese Rose
Golden Bells	Beauty Bush
Dwarf Flowering	Crape Myrtle
Almond	Smoke Tree
Flowering Pomegranate	Rose Acacia
Dwarf Flowering	Pussy Willow
Almond	Indian Currant
Sweet Shrub	Blue Chaste Tree
Double Rose Deutzia	*Viburnum carlesi*

Deciduous Shrubs for Northwest Gardens

Fireleaf Aralia	Hydrangea
Japanese Maple	Japanese Rose
Russian Almond	Beauty Bush
Azaleas	Japanese Privet
Common Sweet Shrub	Sweet Mock Orange
Siberian Pea Tree	Ninebark
Blue Spiraea	Common Smoke Tree
Ceanothus Gloire de	Smooth Sumac
Versailles	Bridal Wreath
European Cranberry	Dwarf Snowberry
Bush	Coral Berry
Dogwoods	Lilacs
Filbert	Tamarisk
Cotoneasters	Fragrant Snowball
Flowering Quince	Snowballs
Deutzias	Weigelas
Russian Olive	Roses
Cork Bark Bittersweet	Scotch Broom
European Burning Bush	February Daphne
Golden Bells	Flowering Currant
	Rose of Sharon

Deciduous Shrubs for Pacific Central Gardens

Flowering Peach	Snow Crab
Azalea mollis	Purple-Leaved
Sweet-scented Shrub	Flowering Plum
Dogwood	Flowering Almond
Deutzia	Pomegranate
Crape Myrtle	Bridal Wreath
Tree Peony	Indian Currant
Chinese Azalea	Snowball
Pea Tree	Winter Sweet
Japanese Quince	Crabapple
Pearl Bush	Japanese Flowering
Hydrangea	Cherry
Mock Orange	Sumac
Barberry	Ural False Spires
Blue Spirea	Lilac
Golden Bells	Double-flowering Kerria
Beauty Bush	Smoke Tree

Flowering Currant	Lemon Verbena
Snowberry	Fuchsia-flowered
Tamarisk	Gooseberry

The Shrubs Which Stay Green

Evergreens are used more in Pacific Coast gardens than anywhere else in the country. Nowhere else can you see such a variety of berries, flowers and foliage. An evergreen is a year-round plant, and there are two kinds — those which are broadly called broadleaved evergreens (although they do not all have broad leaves), and those which bear cones and are therefore called coniferous. The planting methods and care of both are the same.

Evergreens may be planted almost at any time during the year. They are delivered to you balled or in pots. Ask for large sizes if you want an immediate effect; but if you can wait, buy them in a younger state — they will be stronger. Make the planting holes at least two, and preferably three times as large as the pot or ball. Be sure the subsoil, the earth at the bottom of the hole, is broken up. Do not break the ball. An evergreen hates to have its roots disturbed. It may die. Fill in loose soil, pack it, and water right away.

Evergreen Shrubs for Southwest Gardens

Abelias	Breath of Heaven
Strawberry Tree	Golden Dewdrop Shrub
Flowering Maple	South African Daisy
Butterfly Plant	Tree
Aster fruticosa	Heathers
Kurume Azaleas	Silverberry
Blue Barleria	Apple Blossom
Adenocarpus	Escallonia
Azara	Brooms
Summer Lilac	Euonymus
Camellias	Cape Jasmine
Japanese Box	Fuchsias
English Boxwood	Grevillea
Bird of Paradise	Hibiscus
Magic Flower	Carpenteria
Darwins Barberry	Hydrangeas
Red-leaved Japanese	Sun Rose
Barberry	Hollies
Orange Jasmine	Bush Honeysuckles
Cassia	Privets
Night-blooming Jasmine	Mallow
Red Cestrum	Laurels
Flowering Oak	Lions Tail
Mexican Orange	Oregon Grape
Cotoneasters	Japanese Mahonia
Daphne	Bottle Brushes

Myrtles
Banana Shrub
Nandina
Oleander
Sweet Olive
Poinsettia
California Holly
Pittosporums

Dwarf Pomegranate
Rhododendrons
Yellow Heliotrope
Pyracanthas
Trumpet Bush
Purple Princess Flower
Viburnum
Brush Cherry

Evergreen Shrubs for Pacific Central Gardens

Abelias
Flowering Maple
Acacias
Andromeda
Strawberry Tree
Gold Dust Plant
Azaleas
Boxleaf Azara
Darwins Barberry
Summer Lilac
Box
Red Melaleuca
Bottle Brush
Camellia
Cantua
Natal Plum
California Wild Lilac
Mountain Lilac
Orange Cestrum
Ceanothus Gloire de
    Versailles
Mexican Orange
Flowering Oak
Rock Rose
Mirror Plant

Evergreen Dogwood
Scorpion Senna
Cotoneasters
Prostrate Cotoneasters
Cigar Plant
Broom
Daphne
Breath of Heaven
Eleagnus
Heathers
Escallonias
Eugenia
Evergreen Euonymus
Pineapple Guava
Fremontia
Fuchsias
Silk Tassel Bush
Bridal Veil Broom
Cape Jasmine
Grevillea
Hakea
Sun Rose
Golden St. Johnswort
Chinese Hibiscus
English Holly

Dutch Holly
Mountain Laurel
Lantana
Bay Tree
Laurels
Lavender
Australian Tea Tree
Privets
Honeysuckle
Banana Shrub
Oregon Grape
Myrtle
Nandina
Oleander
Hollies

Pittosporums
Princess Flower
Catalina Cherry
California Evergreen
    Cherry
Pyracanthas — better
    known as Firethorn
Burning Bush, etc.
Yeddo Hawthorn
Coffee Berry
Rhododendrons
Matilija Poppy
Rosemary
Veronicas
Viburnums

Evergreen Shrubs for the Pacific Northwest

Abelia grandiflora
Kinnikinnick
English Laurel
Azaleas
Bamboo
Barberries
Boxwood
Camellia
Cotoneasters
Brooms
Daphnes
Euonymus
Heathers
St. Johnswort
Hollies
Laurels
Lavender
Andromeda catesbaei

Privet
Honeysuckles
Magnolia grandiflora
Oregon Hollygrape
Nandina
Japanese Spurge
Photinia serrulata
Pernettyas
Pyracanthas, also
    known as Firebrush,
    Firethorn, etc.
Rhododendrons
Skimmia japonica
Common Gorse
Veronica
Viburnums
Vinca
Yuccas

A DECIDUOUS
SHRUB OR TREE · · ·

· · · LOSES ITS LEAVES
IN THE FALL

· · · AND GROWS
MORE NEXT YEAR

AN EVERGREEN
—IS EVER GREEN

How to Select Conifers for Your Garden

You have been acquainted with coniferous (cone-bearing) evergreens since childhood. That is what a Christmas Tree is.

It is so hard to make a distinction between coniferous shrubs and trees that we are treating them under one heading. The distinction isn't important. Some of the shrubs are taller than some which are, strictly speaking, trees, and vice versa. In either case, the planting and care do not differ from those for broad-leaved evergreens.

Most conifers are symmetrical in shape, broad at the base and tapering to a spire at the top, like a Christmas Tree, although some, the semi-creepers, for example, are low and sprawling.

Conifers have a thousand uses. They grow well behind a garden bench, sundial, or other feature. They make impressive accents at corners, and backgrounds for flower borders. Because of their density, they are perfect for screening out ugly objects beyond your lot. Austrian Pine, Scotch Pine, Red Pine, American Arbor Vitae, White Pine and Canada Hemlock are excellent screens.

You can classifly them conveniently in six groups. The pyramid-shaped conifers include Hemlocks, Pines, Spruces and Firs. They are used to decorate lawns, avenues, and corners. Other conifers which can be recommended as specimens for Western lawns are:

White Fir	Austrian Pine
Nikko Fir	Red Pine
Veitch Fir	Douglas Fir
Chinese Juniper	Umbrella Pine
Pfitzers Juniper	Upright Japanese Yew
European Larch	American Arbor Vitae
Japanese Larch	Oriental Arbor Vitae
Oriental Spruce	Giant Arbor Vitae
Colorado Spruce	Canada Hemlock
Swiss Mountain Pine	Carolina Hemlock

Thread-branched Japanese Cypress

Conifers of medium size, such as the Junipers, Yews, Retinosporas, and Arbor Vitaes, can be used in backgrounds and along the foundation of your house. Gates, doors, corners of buildings, drive entrances, ends of terraces, at the bottom of steps — all sorts of places can be splendidly accented with these.

For locations requiring a formal touch, use the straight-standing, slim, columnar conifers — the Junipers, Cedars and Arbor Vitaes.

Globe Arbor Vitae, however, is shaped like its name, and in company with Mugho Pine is used along the foundation wherever you want low, round plantings. For the best effect, combine such globe-shaped shrubs with taller ones in back of them.

The semi-creepers of which we spoke, such as Savin Juniper and Pfitzers Juniper, are placed in the foreground, flanking steps, or at the corners of a lawn, around pools, under trees, etc.

Lastly, there are the prostrate types, *Pachysandra terminalis*, Sun Rose, Spring Heath, *Cotoneaster microphylla*, English Heather, etc. These are planted under trees, on banks, in rockeries, and other spots where you want what is called a ground cover.

Shrubs for Dry Locations

Kangaroo Thorn	Strawberry Tree
Salt Bush	Tree Anemone
Andreans Broom	Dogonaea
Flannel Bush	Shingle Heath
Catalina Cherry	Punk Trees
Lemonade Berry	Mountain Cherry
Templetonia	Australian Bluebell
Japanese Barberry	Five-leaf Aralia
Russian Olive	Siberian Pea Tree
Cherry Eleagnus	Sun Rose
Indian Currant	Privet

Shrubs for Border Backgrounds

These will do well in most Western border backgrounds: Chinese Redbud, Flowering Dogwood, Hawthorn, Flowering Crab, Double Flowering Cherry, Sweetbay, Deutzia, Rose of Sharon, Beauty Bush, Everblooming Honeysuckle, Mock Orange, Spiraea, Viburnum, Cotoneaster and Red-berried Photinia.

Shrubs for Shade

Aucuba	Viburnum
Camellia	Rhododendron
Mahonia	Azaleas
Hydrangea	Japanese Barberry
Abelia grandiflora	Japanese Box
Five-leaf Aralia	Coral Dogwood
Sweet Shrub	Wintercreeper
Common Boxwood	St. Johnswort
Flowering Dogwood	Mountain Laurel
Golden Bells	Privets
Japanese Holly	Oregon Hollygrape
Daphne	Coralberry
Drooping Leucothoe	Snowberry

Shrubs That Withstand Wind

Laurustinus	Common Myrtle
Kangaroo Thorn	Catalina Cherry
Salt Bush	Pittosporum
New Zealand Holly	Broad-leaf Acacia
False Olive	Bottle Brush

Silverleaf Cotoneaster   Oleander
Hakea   Monterey Cypress
Myoporum   Germander

Shrubs for Gravelly Soil

Acacias   Winter Cassia
Wild Lilac   Rose Box
Mexican Orange   Rock Rose
Scotch Broom   Fragrant Broom
Salt Bush   Spotted Rock Rose
Canary Island Broom

Shrubs for a Steep Slope

Roses   Five-leaf Aralia
Japanese Barberry   Honeysuckle
Coralberry   Dwarf Broom
Trailing Roses

Low-Growing Shrubs—under Three Feet

Wilsons Barberry   Rose Daphne
Buxus sempervirens   Drooping Leucothoe
   suffruticosa   Oregon Hollygrape
Rock Cotoneaster

Drooping Shrubs

Golden Bells   February Daphne
Japanese Rose   Slender Deutzia

Medium-Sized Shrubs—Three to Six Feet

Abelia grandiflora   Adams Needle
Box   Flame Azalea
Thorny Eleagnus   Holly Barberry
Evergreen Burningbush   Japanese Barberry
Japanese Holly   Sweet Shrub
Mountain Laurel   Lemoine Deutzia
Japanese Privet   Japanese Quince
Oregon Hollygrape   Kerria
Firethorn   Coralberry
Leatherleaf   Fragrant Viburnum
Viburnum   Crimson Weigela

Shrubs for Hedges

Japanese Barberry   Common Lilac
Darwins Barberry   Bush Honeysuckle
California Privet   Laurustinus
English Privet

Tall Shrubs

Dogwood   Privet
Cotoneaster acuminata   Honeysuckle
   (nepalensis)   Mock Orange
Cotoneaster harroviana   Prunus
Euonymus japonicus   Lilac
Golden Bells   Common Snowball
English Holly   Weigela

Specimen Shrubs for the West

A specimen shrub is like a person who takes one of the leading parts in a play. There must be something about it that makes it more attractive, or more distinctive in some way, than other shrubs. Its habit of growth, that is, its shape, should be unusual, first of all — the familiar Japanese Maple, a shrubby tree, is a good example. When you look over some specimen shrubs, you will find your own favorites, and it is impossible to tell ahead of time which kind of distinctive feature you will like — a special type of bark, colorful twigs, an irregular or graceful shape, odd foliage, the flowers, etc. Here are some names to give you an idea:

Chinese Abelia is copper colored, striking, and easy to grow. *Aralia sieboldi* has large, glistening, dark-green leaves like the palm of your hand. It does well in indoor pots. Strawberry Tree is liked for its red, strawberry-like fruit and dark-green leaves. Japanese Aucuba has scarlet berries and large, glossy leaves. *Cassia artemisioides* is gray, with golden-yellow flowers.

Thorny Eleagnus is arresting in a close-up view, but not at a distance. Its leaves point, and are olive-green above, silvery underneath. Australian Brush Cherry is ruddy colored, graceful and impressive. *Euonymus japonicus* is smooth, straight standing, with silver, white or yellow foliage markings. English Holly is very hardy on the Pacific Coast, an old-fashioned favorite. Plant it in the shade in the Southwest.

Oregon Hollygrape is claimed as a native of Northern California. Its lustrous foliage is like holly, and it bears yellow flowers in dense clusters in the spring, with purple berries later. Nandina is sacred to the Japanese. It is a favorite with Californians, looks like bamboo, is bronze-red when young, then dark green, has striking red color in winter, and bears pink flowers and red berries. Japanese Pittosporum, the landscape architect's favorite, is dense, round, with a fine symmetrical shape. Makes a rich foliage-mass, and has creamy-white fragrant flowers.

HOW TO GROW WESTERN SHRUBS

Study SUNSET, the advertising as well as the editorial columns. In this all-western magazine you will find many ideas for making your home more beautiful with shrubbery, trees and plants.

This month after reading SUNSET, go into your garden. Look around. See where you can improve your home by adding a few well-chosen shrubs—at house corners or as backgrounds and hedges.

Now that you know where shrubbery is needed, get out your garden catalogs and make out your order. Or, better still go to a good nursery and make selections. SUNSET advertisers are reliable.

Before your shrubbery is delivered, get your soil ready. Dig ground deep, throwing top soil into one heap and poorer undersoil in another. If top soil is heavy or poor, add sand and peat moss.

When shrubs arrive, dig hole large enough and deep enough to allow roots to spread out. Fork up bottom of hole so that the shrub will have better drainage. Very important if soil is hard pan.

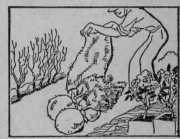

Examine stock when received and, if possible, plant immediately. Otherwise dig trench and temporarily set bare-root plants therein. Meanwhile protect balled and canned specimens from sun and wind.

Plants that arrive looking like the specimen above should be carefully set into hole after roots and top have been pruned back. Spread roots in all directions; shovel loose soil around roots; tamp.

Set balled plants as shown in sketch. Fill in loose earth about root ball but do not break ball. When hole is partially filled, cut cord at top of ball, turn back top of burlap, cover with soil.

For "canned" plants, cut can with tinsnips and remove carefully. If plants come boxed, be sure hole is large enough for box; remove box when plant is set. Fill holes with soil as for balled plants.

For all shrubbery and trees, fill hole ¾ full of soil—using as little subsoil as possible—flood to top with water, repeating as soil settles in hole. Mulch top with loose soil and wet peat moss.

After planting, water whenever necessary; spray foliage of evergreens twice daily until new growth appears. As plant becomes established, give commercial plant food, following directions on package.

When your shrubbery, trees and plants are growing, look around and see if it isn't worth while to have an attractive home. Fall and winter is planting time on the Coast. "It's not a home until it's planted!"

HOW TO GROW FUCHSIAS

1. Grow fuchsias in your SUNSET garden. You will love their graceful, bell-like flowers in clear tones and shades of red, purple and soft pink. They bloom freely and are especially desirable for the coast gardens of California. Here's how!

2. Probably the simplest way to get a start of the fuchsia is to buy the plants in tin can containers from some reliable Pacific Coast nurseryman. They may be planted at practically any time of the year but fall is preferred.

3. Fuchsias can be grown also from cuttings. For summer cuttings, take short, chunky pieces about 3 inches long from young growth, cutting below a joint. Bury ⅔ their length in a sunny box of damp sand until rooted.

4. When making cuttings in midwinter, take them from well-ripened wood. Cut pieces 12 to 18 inches long, severing below a joint. Plant them ⅔ their length in a sandy hole in the garden or in trenches for later transplanting.

5. Then, too, fuchsias can be grown from seed. (The English seed houses carry it.) Sow the seeds in flats in early spring, using a soil mixture of 2 parts garden loam, 1 part sand and 1 part leaf mold, all three sifted together.

6. Before transplanting seedlings or rooted plants to the garden, remember that the fuchsia is happiest where the temperature ranges between 50 and 60 degrees. Set plants in shade or at least where there is little sun.

7. Set each plant in a large hole with plenty of good drainage. Put the plant on a shovelful of sand and fill hole with good rich soil; water thoroughly and firm soil around plant. Be sure the ground is well loosened before planting.

8. Once planted fuchsias require little care. Give them plenty of water, especially when young, and every spring mulch with well-rotted manure or, better yet, dig in commercial plant food. Do not let plant food contact plant.

9. Allow fuchsias to grow naturally or train them flat against a wall by removing lower branches and fastening main stems to wall. When a bushy or low-growing effect is desired, pinch out tops of plant to stimulate spreading.

10. Where winters are severe, dig small fuchsias in fall, pot them and carry over until spring in a dry cellar; then replant. In California along the Coast no winter care is necessary except doing the necessary pruning.

11. Fuchsias make lovely bouquets even though they soon perish. Cut long sprays from under sides of branches, plunge into cold water and then arrange flowers so that the "bells" hang gracefully over sides of bowl.

12. Those interested in learning more about the varieties of fuchsias should join the Fuchsia Society. Write the garden department of SUNSET Magazine for particulars about the Society and where to buy plants and seeds.

HOW TO
Grow a Lawn

THERE used to be a saying that a lawn had to be centuries old before it could be good. If anyone tells you that, just smile. You can have a perfect lawn in from six months to a year, thanks to Western lawn specialists who have studied grasses.

Almost every Pacific Coast home has a lawn, many of them lovely, yet the percentage of really good lawns is small. This is because most people do not remember that after all a lawn is just a collection of plants — grass plants — and that you have to give them a chance to grow healthfully just as you do other plants.

If you follow the simple directions given here, you should have the cherished dream of every home owner — a smooth, velvety, carpetlike lawn, the perfect setting for your house and your garden.

It will look spacious, no matter how modest in size your place is, because you will be too wise to overcrowd it with plants or walks. Yet for all its appearance of spaciousness, your good taste in design will not allow it to occupy too much of your lot, but will fit its size and shape properly into your landscape picture.

The Foundation of Your Lawn

Take spade or shovel and a wheelbarrow if you have or can get one. Thrust the spade from 2 to 5 inches into the surface of the area that is to be your lawn. Toss your first shovelful of this surface earth into your wheelbarrow, then keep on until you have removed the whole top from your lawn plot. Wheel each load of this surface layer over to a corner.

There is a reason for this. The surface earth is the richest. Moreover, grass has roots, like any other plant; these roots sometimes grow down 3 inches from the top, though usually 2. You'll want to let them feed on the best soil you have.

You move that soil out of the way temporarily so that you can get at the next layer. Now you dig again. Dig down 6 or 8 inches this time. Move that to another corner, but be sure to remember which layer is which and count the wheelbarrow loads. This layer, too, has a use — we'll come to it in a moment.

You don't dig any more, but you use the fork on the heavy clay subsoil which you have reached after removing the top layers. If you have a pickax, so much the better. Break the clay up well.

Now you're ready to work back up again, layer by layer. The clay subsoil is going to provide drainage for your lawn. Did you know that you could regulate the speed with which your lawn soaks up water?

Look carefully at your subsoil. It is very sandy? Then the water from the rains and from your hosing will escape too fast. It needs thickening. Your thickening materials are clay and peat moss. If there is no clayey soil in your

BUILDING THE LAYERS

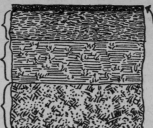

REPLACE TOP SOIL
SPREAD THRU SCREEN

MIX 2ND LAYER
WITH PEAT MOSS

BEGIN TO BUILD UP
HERE. IF CLAYEY,
LOOSEN SUBSOIL
WITH COARSE SAND,

SPREAD 1" MIXTURE OF
PEAT MOSS, WELL-ROTTED
MANURE; WORK IN TO
LAYER OF TOP SOIL

SMALL GRAVEL , WOOD ASHES MIXED WITH CLAY FOR DRAINAGE. IF SANDY
MIX WITH PEAT MOSS AND CLAY TO THICKEN.

land, your local seed merchant or nurseryman will tell you where you can get some.

The peat moss is a brown substance that looks a little like sawdust, except that it is dry. Your seed store has it for sale. It is used for mixtures and surface coverings, but its use is not for enriching the soil, as some people imagine. For further complete information on this important substance, look under "Peat Moss" in the Index.

If your soil is heavy and clayey already, loosen it with coarse sand, small gravel and wood ashes, well mixed with the clay. This will allow the water to drain.

You are now finished with the bottom layer. To which corner did you move the second layer? That is the layer which stores moisture under the roots of your grasses. You counted the wheelbarrow loads—remember? The purpose of that is so that you can dump into your lawn plot, on top of the subsoil, an equal number of wheelbarrow loads of well-soaked peat moss, or as many as the budget will allow. Then bring over that second layer, load by load, and mix up in equal quantity with the moss.

You're almost ready to sow the lawn seed, but first you have to remember that the lawn will want to eat. Plants are hungry things. What do they eat? Plant food. That is what it is called. They need humus — decomposed organic matter. You can add humus to your top soil by getting, first, some mushroom bed fertilizer. This is a mixture of soil and stable manure discarded by commercial mushroom growers after it is unfit for the culture of mushrooms. Most fertilizer dealers have it for sale. If you can't obtain it, substitute well-rotted manure.

Mix it with peat moss or some well-rotted manure, and spread over your lawn plot an inch thick. Fork this into the soil, working it in to the depth of 3 inches. This makes the earth able to retain moisture and plant food for your grass plants.

After you fork in the humus, rake the soil over to pulverize any clods or lumps which have formed, and level the whole with a rake.

Give it a good sprinkling. Keep sprinkling regularly for three to four weeks.

Four weeks? Yes; it seems a pity to have to wait that long before you do anything else, after all the excitement of getting the layers ready, but it pays. During that time most of the weeds you'll ever have trouble with will have a chance to sprout, and you can pounce on them as they appear.

It is a mistake to dig and plant a lawn in the same day. It takes several weeks thoroughly to rot all organic matter in some soils, and until this matter is completely rotted, you should not sow the seed. If you are a patient person and want the best results you can get, it might be well to wait even more than four weeks.

After four weeks or so, fork the soil over down to three inches. Get the weeds out by the roots.

Now you are ready to sow the seed.

More lawns suffer from too much seed than too little. A pound of good lawn grass seed is enough for 150 to 250 square feet, depending on the mixture. Few lawns, you know, are made up of one kind of grass; the best lawns are mixtures.

Most lawn seeds like a slightly alkaline earth condition, although Kentucky Bluegrass will do better in neutral soil, not too alkaline; and the Bents and Fescues, which you will meet later, prefer acid soil.

Slightly acid or neutral soil helps keep down the weeds, while encouraging the growth of your grasses. You can keep your soil from being too acid, however, with a moderate application of dehydrated lime — about 2 to 4 pounds to 100 square feet. But if you are treating an established lawn with lime, don't put it on the surface — it makes weeds grow.

But we are getting ahead of our story. Your most natural first question is: "What seed shall I use?" A lawn specialist will always answer your question with another question: "What will you use your lawn for? Is it to be a fine lawn, not to be walked on much, or at all? Or will the children play on it?"

Lawn Grasses for California

If you want a fine lawn, not for hard usage, you have your choice of several grasses for the interior valleys of California and the Pacific Coast. (For Washington and Oregon see "Additional Lawn Notes for the Pacific Northwest," farther on in this chapter.) If you want grasses for hard use, in California, get a mixture of Kentucky Blue Grass, Chewings Fescue, Pacific Rye and White Clover.

No one grass thrives everywhere. Soil and climate conditions are often different even within small areas — within a block, sometimes within a single garden. A mixture is therefore better than a single kind of grass. The grasses in the mixture which are best suited to your conditions will predominate. A mixture is flexible in this way; a single variety is not.

One of the West's outstanding lawn experts says that various mixtures of Astoria Bent, Kentucky Blue Grass, Chewings Fescue, Bermauda Grass, Rye Grass and Canada Blue Grass are best for Western lawns.

Astoria Bent (*Agrostis capillaris* variety)— Astoria Bent is not like other Bents. It doesn't grow surface runners. Its growth is upright and its color is truly grassy, not the dull blue-green of the other Bent grass. The "Astoria" refers to Astoria, Oregon, of which region the grass is a native.

This Bent has a creeping root system, resulting in a dense turf which throttles weeds. Best of all, it is hardy, and does well on many kinds of soil, although best on acid soil. It likes its soil heavy with plenty of humus.

You have to watch it when it first comes up, for what is called "damping off." This is a fungus which occurs when you have sown the seeds too thickly, or have watered the seedlings too much. Control it by dusting with Semesan.

Kentucky Blue Grass (*Poa pratensis*)—The Kentucky Blue Grass lawns may turn somewhat brown in the winter, but are very pretty during the spring, summer and autumn. It is a splendid grass to have in a mixture, although weeds are likely to get ahead of it because it takes some time to make a close turf.

Chewings Fescue (*Festuca rubra*) — New Zealand is the home of this form of Red Fescue. You will like its fine leaves and feel that it is a

A MIXTURE of GRASS IS BETTER THAN THIS

KENTUCKY BLUE GRASS   ASTORIA BENT   RYE GRASS   CHEWING FESCUE

SINGLE VARIETY of GRASS

Adaptable and Flexible

Inflexible - may not grow well for you

lovely grass, but do not use it singly on the Pacific Coast. It belongs in mixtures here.

RYE GRASS — This is a hard usage grass — good to have in mixtures where you do not wish a lawn for looks alone. Besides the Pacific Rye recommended for California a few paragraphs back, there are Australian Rye and Perennial Rye. The only trouble with Rye Grass is that it is hard to cut, and shows injury from the mower.

BERMUDA GRASS — This is a low, creeping plant, sending out surface runners and rooting at the joints, which makes it hard to dislodge

How are you going to sow this evenly? Divide your lawn plot into four equal parts; divide the seed likewise. To have even distribution, sow first across one way, then the opposite way, and last diagonally.

Cover the seed lightly with $\frac{1}{8}$-inch to $\frac{1}{4}$-inch of top soil. Do this by "tucking" with your rake — that is, instead of the usual back and forth movement, chop lightly toward you. This will not cover every seed, but will be sufficient.

After tucking, screen humus through a $\frac{1}{2}$-inch mesh, and broadcast it thinly, barely cover-

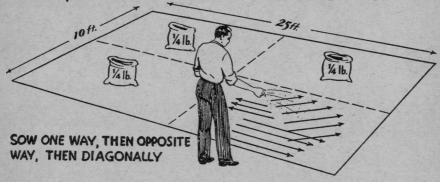

250 Sq.ft. DIVIDE IN 4 PARTS - DIVIDE SEED LIKEWISE

10 ft.

25 ft.

¼ lb.

¼ lb.

¼ lb.

SOW ONE WAY, THEN OPPOSITE WAY, THEN DIAGONALLY

once it is well established. But it makes a dense sod, and is good in hot climates despite its drawbacks. Do not water it too much.

CANADA BLUE GRASS (*Poa compressa*)—Here is another hot climate grass. Of late years it has been used in the hottest parts of the San Joaquin and Sacramento Valleys. Its color is a bluer green than Kentucky Blue Grass, and it is more tufty than Kentucky.

Getting the Seed Sown

Your choice of grass mixtures will depend on the amount of sunlight and shade in your garden, too. It is hard to grow grasses in the shade; few grasses are suitable, and even those need top dressings and fertilizing often.

The best sowing times are in the fall or early spring months. A leading expert favors the fall, although he admits that after 6 or 12 months no difference can be noticed in the finished lawn. In most parts of California a lawn may be planted any month except when there is frost.

Let us say that you have bought a pound of some good mixture, enough for 250 square feet.

ing the surface. If you plant during dry summer months, cover with a small layer of coarse sand instead.

The sand prevents baking or waterlogging of the soil. Do not cover this young seed with anything that will decay while the seeds are trying to sprout. Some manure sold is not well rotted, and during the summer months especially it is hard to make manure rot.

A good way to protect the seed while it germinates, and to hold moisture until the young roots are established, is to "mulch." A mulch is any covering material placed on the surface of the soil, intended to prevent evaporation. It conserves moisture, protects roots or low-growing plants from frost or heat, prevents puddles, keeps the soil open, supplies plant food and keeps down weeds. A mulch, you see, does a lot of work for you, despite its odd name.

Some mulches contain well-rotted manure, peat moss, mill shavings, rice hulls, or other light materials. Rice hulls, though, will be full of weed seeds; and strong winds blow the hulls away.

Peat moss holds the moisture, and is the best mulch for a newly planted lawn; but don't mulch too heavily — the seedling grass won't be able to break through.

After covering the seeds, roll with a light roller, one weighing not more than 75 pounds, and about 24 inches wide. Lacking a roller, use a foot board, or put a large box lid on the ground and step on it. Do not roll if the soil is wet. Finally, sprinkle with your hose nozzle adjusted to a fine spray. Use extra-special care. Let no water collect on the surface.

Caring for the New Lawn

During the days that follow, do not let your lawn area dry out. Bright sun, or a strong wind kills many newly planted lawns. Keep sprinkling with the fine nozzle, keeping the soil moist, not wet, until the first seedlings appear.

This first appearance is a delicate time for the Bents and finer grasses. You had better treat them with Semesan to be safe — a level teaspoonful to a gallon of water. Stir it well. This will prevent the damping off, as well as "brown patch."

By this time you'll be all agog for your first mowing. If you know these few mowing rules, you'll become the family expert.

Mow when the seedling grass is 3 to 4 inches high. Have the mower sharp. Do not mow in

ALWAYS MOW DIAGONALLY,
THEN NORTH & SOUTH

the same direction — mow diagonally, then north and south. This will give your lawn an even texture.

Do not have the mower's blades too low; if you cut off most of the grass' leaf it won't have anything to breathe with—for all plants breathe with their leaves. Also, the mower might pull up the smaller grasses by the roots.

Lastly, remove the weeds in a week or two; get them up by the roots and either sprinkle some fertilizer where the weeds were, so that the grass will spread and grow there, or plant new seeds there. During the summer, mow once a week.

Keep on watering, when your grass is established. Give it 3 or 4 thorough waterings a week; this is much better than light daily sprinklings. There should be plenty of moisture in the soil at all times.

Feeding the Lawn

In California, where more watering is done than elsewhere, you should top-dress your lawn twice a year, once in the spring, once again in late fall. The modern method is to use a top dressing of bonemeal mixed with peat moss. Rub in the dressing with the back of your rake.

FERTILIZE LAWN
1. EARLY SPRING
2. EACH SUMMER MONTH
3. FALL

How and when to fertilize? — that is the question. The answer is: frequently. Once a month during the growing season. If you do it often, don't do too much at a time. Frequent fertilizing will give your grass a uniform, rich green color, together with continuous growth and the elimination of weeds.

Top Dressing

The ideal program is to apply the top dressing of bonemeal in early spring. Then during each summer month use one of the commercial plant foods, following directions given on the container. Always water the lawn thoroughly before using concentrated plant foods, and then give it another hosing to dissolve every particle of the concentrate. In the fall give the other top dressing of bonemeal.

Here are a few general hints to note about fertilizing lawns. The University of California College of Agriculture strongly recommends that any manure used be well rotted, to assist the decay of plant foods and make the nitrogen in them avilable to the plant. Sheep manure especially is freer from weed seed than other manures.

Be careful with lime—it may burn your young grass. A top dressing of peat moss alone for a well established lawn is not sufficient — plant food is necessary.

Summer Care of Western Lawns

Summer is the time of year when your lawn needs more intelligent care than at any other time. You will use your lawn constantly in midsummer, and the summer weather will be hard on the grass, yet your pep may be at too low an ebb for much garden work.

Even so, if you live along the Coast, give the lawn 2 or 3 good soakings a week. In the warm valleys, give it a daily soaking, or at least every other day, depending on the heat. Just sprinkling will result in shallow rooting and weak growth of the grass. You won't like the color, either. The moisture ought to go down 4 inches or more.

A. B. Lambert, director of the Lambert Gardens in Portland, Oregon, advises: "There's one simple and always reliable means of determining the need for water. If you can shove the long blade of a pocket knife into the ground up to the hilt, it is moist. If you can't then just keep on soaking."

Watering without feeding, however, will exhaust the store of food there is in the soil for your grasses. Water makes a soil solution of the plant food, and the warmer the weather the more the plants absorb this solution. This is why you apply extra plant food in the summer. Otherwise the grass stops growing and succumbs to the sun.

Your mowing should be regular, not cutting too short, and remembering that a new lawn should be cut more often than an old one.

In the West it is not wise to roll the lawn heavily, at any time. Our soils incline to pack naturally; we have to keep them open to admit water.

Additional Lawn Notes for the Pacific Northwest

Although you can start your lawn any month in the year, in the Coastal sections of the Northwest some months are better than others. Here is a list given in the order of preference:

1. April
2. May
3. September.
4. March
5. August
6. June
7. July
8. February
9. January
10. December
11. November
12. October

The first 6 are the best. East of the mountains only the first 6 are suitable at all.

Grass Mixtures

Much that has been said about lawns in general applies in Washington and Oregon. It still holds true here that a mixture of seed is best, because grasses vary in their characteristics. Some make a good growth early in the spring, others do their best during hot weather, and still others during the fall or winter.

A mixture allows replacing as the seasons change, with the result that you have a good-looking lawn all year. That is much better than one which looks its best during only a few months.

You can have an extra-fine lawn in the Northwest with a mixture of Bent Grasses, Fescues, and Blue Grasses. The most beautiful of the Bents is Seaside Creeping Bent, but this is also the most expensive and particular as to its surroundings.

A more useful Bent—and not as particular about moisture and soil—is Astoria, native of

Oregon. Colonial Creeping Bent is all right, too.

Rhode Island Bent and Red Top are not the creeping variety, but are satisfactory.

Among the Fescues, the best for your purpose are Sheeps Fescue and Chewings.

With the Blue Grasses, you have two good choices—either Kentucky Blue Grass, for general use; or Shadyland Blue Grass, if your lawn is shady. Your seed store will have mixtures which blend all these grasses.

Summer Care in the Pacific Northwest

The summers are hot in Eastern Oregon and Eastern Washington, but even here, east of the Cascade Mountains, you can use the same mixtures. The reason is that the requirements for lawns are pretty much the same everywhere in the world, and good lawn grasses are only slightly affected by changes in climate conditions. As was remarked in the general discussion on lawn, the grasses in the mixture which are best suited to the existing conditions will thrive.

All lawns in the Northwest prefer a slightly acid soil. The Bent Grasses won't grow well if lime is applied, so you'd better never use lime here—it sickens the grasses and helps along the weeds.

Water once or twice a week, and thoroughly. Mow every 5 to 7 days.

If you have bare spots in the lawn, take your rake and stir the surface, give it a little fertilizer, and plant some more seeds there. There's usually a cause—hard wear, or perhaps unsuitable soil. If you can, it is well to discover the cause, then remove it.

Go after the weeds, of course. Pull the large ones out or kill them with a teaspoonful of ammonium sulphate in the weed's center over the crown. Your small weeds will disappear if your lawn is fertilized, cut and watered properly. It doesn't pay just to pull out the weeds, unless you make your lawn grass take possession of that empty space.

Fertilizing

If you overlook fertilizing during the fall, be sure to do it the first nice day. It will make a big difference in your lawn next summer. Grasses in the Northwest, you see, make much of their root growth during the months of winter, and this growth is helped by a good supply of the mineral elements in fertilizers. Your plant food should contain phosphates and potash.

Ground peat (some call it horticultural peat moss) is easily applied. You take off the wires and burlap covering, and scuff the material off the side of the bale with a steel garden rake. When peat is baled it is compressed to save space in the shipping; that is why it should be broken up well before you use it.

Then you scatter it evenly over your lawn area, and with a lawn broom make believe you are trying to rake it off. Actually you are brushing it into the grass, and only raking off the coarse particles. These coarse particles will make a good mulch for your perennial and bulb beds, or your shrubbery.

THE RESULT OF YOUR CARE —
A SUCCESSFUL BEAUTIFUL WESTERN LAWN!

HOW TO GROW A WESTERN LAWN

Now that his new house is erected and the outside workers are off the job, Johnny Jones is ready to start the preparatory work on his lawn in earnest.

During the excavation no under-soil was thrown out where the lawn was to be, but valuable top soil was saved and piled up at one side ready for later use.

The first step of construction he takes is to fork up the lawn area, rake it, break up earth clods and remove all rocks and debris not conducive to good grass growth.

He next considers his under-soil, and finding it too stiff and poor adds necessary lacking elements in the form of a liberal amount of sand and well-rotted strawy manure.

Taking the house steps as the fixed point for his grade he sets up grade stakes strung with stout cord and with Junior's help drags a flat board over the surface to level it.

He has a home-made lawn roller (made according to directions given in the Portland cement book) which he pulls lightly over the surface to compress the under-soil gently.

For his seed bed he spreads a top 2-inch layer of loam, using top soil saved from the excavation, screened together with humus supplied in the form of good dairy manure.

He rakes the seed bed finely, rolls it lightly a second time, allows it to weather so that weed seeds will germinate prior to seeding, and hoes out weeds as they spring up.

Quality grass seed is important. Jones buys his seed from the best store in town, knowing that they will give him the kind of mixture and the quantity he needs.

Being ready to sow, he divides up the area, apportions seed, and broadcasts in two directions, lengthwise and crosswise at right angles in order to cover completely.

After sowing, he carefully rakes in the seed with long light strokes so the tiny grass seed is well mixed with fine soil particles, and then lightly rolls it the third time.

To complete his planting, he waters thoroughly with light spray attached to his garden hose, being careful not to stand on newly seeded area, repeating this for several days.

When the grass is 3 inches high he mows it with a good five-blade mower, and thereafter weekly, being most careful that the mower does not drip oil on the lawn.

To keep maturing lawn conditioned he always waters as needed, and feeds the soil regularly with dependable commercial plant food applied as directed on the package.

He keeps a lookout for stray weeds—eradicating the few that appear with a patent weed gun. Having used good seed and reliable commercial plant food there are few weeds.

This picture of his family gathered to admire his fine lawn is a dream come true and is a fitting and adequate reward for any effort Johnny Jones has expended upon it.

HOW TO
Build a Rock Garden

TILT ROCKS TOWARD CENTER FOR DRAINAGE

PLAN for your rockery at the time you plant your entire garden, so that it will fit naturally into the whole design. To make it do this, think of it as a terminal point—that is, a main feature of the garden toward which the eye travels.

The best places for rockeries are by no means confined to the regular corners of your garden, or to odd out-of-the-way nooks, although these are excellent spots. Sometimes a rockery becomes the whole garden. There are many such in the state of Washington, which in itself is like a huge rock garden. Sometimes it will be the central feature, adorning a pool. It depends on the shape of your garden. If it is on sloping land, you might build a rock wall or two for terraces. If you have an irregular boundary, yours will probably be the nook-and-cranny kind. If you have rolling land, a low, rambling rockery would be charming. For a flat, rectangular garden, center the rockery as the chief feature of interest, subordinate it as the terminal point of a secondary axis line, or place it in one of the corners, preferably one of the far corners, so that you can see it from your house.

How to Get the Rocks

Avoid rocks with too-freakish colors. They rob the color interest from your plants. Rocks can be bought at nurseries, although many an automobile returns from its owner's vacation laden with choice stones from mountain streams, stony fields, etc. There may be enough rocks already on, or under, your own garden.

Preparing the Ground

Spade the soil well, about a foot down, depending on the size of the rocks. They will look more natural if they lie half submerged, than if you dump them on the surface (see illustration). This also gives them a firm setting — the soil which will hold your plants will not be disturbed by joggling of the rocks. All rocks must be placed to slant toward the center so that rain or other water will run downward, inside, reaching plant roots which have groped inward amongst the rocks, preventing outside soil and plants from being washed away, and preventing puddles of standing water from forming in crevices.

The Shape and Size

The size depends largely on the space you have, and your own preference. It's a good rule, though, not to make a rockery too large to begin with. You can enlarge it whenever you wish.

Sixteen feet is a good length. Mark it out on the ground. Make the outline irregular. A wavy oval shape is good. Through the center it might be seven feet, and less than half that at the two ends. Unless you have it placed so that you can walk around it, as one does around a piece of statuary at a museum, have the back higher than the front. Three to fourteen inches is a good front elevation; three feet is not too high for the back. This back slopes steeply toward the front. From the central and highest point to the two ends of your wavy oval the sloping will be more gradual,

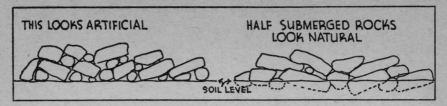

THIS LOOKS ARTIFICIAL

HALF SUBMERGED ROCKS LOOK NATURAL

SOIL LEVEL

since the distances are longer. Plan not only for an irregular edge as you look down at the outline drawn on the ground, but for irregularity in elevation — that is, an undulating skyline. This adds interest.

A Few General Rules

1. The principle behind the building of any kind of rock garden, low, high, rambling, wall, etc., is always the same. Allow for drainage and a cool root run. Stone chips or gravel mixed with the soil speed the water along the inward-slanting rocks, and these rocks carry the water down to the bottom of the pile.

2. Arrange for drainage at the bottom. The best way is to scatter old broken bricks, pieces of rock, gravel, mortar, etc., after your excavation is made. Cover with soil, then place on top of this soil the main rocks.

3. Set the higher rocks farther back. If they overhang those beneath they will keep the sun and air away. Follow this rule especially when building a rock wall. Let the wall or bank slope inward.

4. When arranging rocks, besides sloping them inward and down, so that they rest on their broadest bases, place them so that they also form bays or pockets which will hold the soil for your rockery plants. If you plant dwarf shrubs, the soil of these bays should be as deep as the root system of each shrub requires.

5. A rock wall higher than three or four feet is not as attractive or easy to build as two walls, placed like steps, one behind the other, with a space on the landings for soil and plantings. Use the heaviest rocks at the base. This terraced arrangment is very good along banks which slope down to a sidewalk or lawn. Plant the wall while constructing it.

Soil for a Rockery

The best all-around soil, suited to the largest number of rock garden plants, is this:
¼ stone chips
¼ clean sand
¼ humus (decayed vegetable matter)
¼ good light loam.

You will modify this from time to time to suit the special requirements of individual plants, but the above is a good starter.

Winter Care

Begin early in the fall, Northwesterners. Set out rock plants in August or September, but not later than early October. Plants must get a footing or they will be heaved out by the soil's heaving and thawing. If you find them heaved out during the winter, put them back in firmly. Cover with Oak leaves, or any non-smothering material. Remove weeds. If soil cakes, stir and loosen. Put stone chips under the collars of plants sensitive to dampness. Mix leafmold with sand or stone chips; spread on the soil to keep soil from forming a hard surface.

Make sure all roots are covered before winter. Peat moss is a good covering.

Rockery Plants You Can Grow

SHADE: Ferns, Haberlea, Ramondia, Bluebells, Trillium, Corydalis, Dragonhead, Ladyslipper.

PART SHADE: *Polemonium reptans, Polemonium humile,* mossy Saxifrages, Anemones, Primroses, Forget-Me-Nots.

SANDY SOIL AND SUNSHINE: Statice and Spurge, Rock Roses, Evening Primrose, Succulents, Toad Flax.

MOIST SOIL: *Myosotis palustris, Soldanella alpina, Penstemon gracilis, Mimulus alpina,* Dracocephalum, Primulas, Anemones, Ladyslipper.

FOR A SHADED ROCK WALL: *Erinus alpinus,* Australian Violet, Primulas, Arenarias, Campanulas, *Saponaria ocymoides, Iberis sempervirens,* Violas, Saxifrages, small Veronicas, Arabis alpina, *Corydalis lutea, Hypericum coris,* Primulas in variety.

FOR A SUNNY WALL: Androsace, Sweet Alyssum, Aubretias, *Armeria maritima, Arabis alpina* (*albida*), Campanulas, *Cerastium tomentosum, Convolvulus mauritanicus,* Dianthus, *Gypsophila repens, Globularia nana cordifolia, Iberia sempervirens, Iris pumila, Phlox subulata, Thymus serpyllum coccineum,* Helianthemum, Sedums.

DWARF SHRUBS FOR ROCKERIES: Excellent dwarfs will be found among the Veronicas, Sun Roses, Lavenders, Fuchsias, Hypericums, Mesembryanthemums, Lithospermums, Daphnes, Cotoneasters, Convolvulus, Brooms, and Barberries.

Sunset-tested Rock Garden Plants

ALPINES

Aethionema Warley Rose
Androsace sempervivoides, lanuginosa, primuloides
Anemone hupehensis, blanda, apennina
Aquilegia jonesii, pyrenaia, caerulea
Astilbe simplicifolia
Campanula piperi, lasiocarpa, raineri, laurii
Cyclamen neapolitanum
Daphne petraea
Erodium chamaedryoides roseum
Geum borisi
Leonotopodium alpinum
Lewisia howellii, tweedyi, fincheri
Mimulus cardinalis
Pentstemon rupicola
Peonia brownii
Phlox rigida, diffusa
Primula marginata, rosea grandiflora, auricula
Ramondia pyrenaica (Northwest only)
Saxifraga longifolia var. Tumbling Waters

ANNUALS

Alyssum in var.
Anagallis
Arctotis breviscapa
Asperula setosa
Brachycome iberidifolia
Convolvulus minor
Diascia barberae
Eschscholtzia
Gilia tricolor
Lobelia, dwarf
Mesembryanthemum tricolor
Nemophila insignis
Phacelia campanularia
Platistemon californicus
Portulaca
Saxifraga cymbalaria
Sedum caeruleum

BULBS

Allium in var.
Brodiaeas in var.
Calochortus in var.
Chionodoxa lucilae
Colchicums
Crocus, species, such as *imperati, Sieberi, susianus* and *Tomassinianus*
Dodecatheons in var.
Erythroniums (Dogtooth violets)
Fritillarias

Galanthus elwesii (Snowdrop)
Iris in var.
Lilium pomponium, chalcedonicum
Milla biflora
Muscari azureus (Grape Hyacinth)
Narcissus in var. (dwarf Daffodils)
Scilla campanulata and *nutans* (Bluebells)
Tritonia crocata
Tulips (species not hybrids)
Zephyranthes in var.

(Southern California and Southwest)

Agave in var.
Arctostaphylos uva-ursi (Kinnikinic)
Azalea obtusa
Ceanothus prostratus
Cereus viridiflorus
Chamaecyparis nana
Convolvulus cneorum and *mauritanicus*
Cotoneaster in var.
Crassula in var.
Daphne blagayana and *cneorum*
Echeveria in var.
Erica in var. (Heather)
Fuchsia pumila, ises (dwarf)
Genista dalmatica (Broom)
Helianthemum in var.
Hypericum repens
Japanese maples, dwarf
Juniperus procumbens
Lithops in var.
Lithospermum prostratum
Mammillaria in var.
Mesembryanthemum aurantiacum and *speciosum*
Opuntia vulgaris
Picea albertiana conica (dwarf Spruce)
Rhododendrons in var.
Rochea versicolor
Sedum in var.
Thymus serpyllum, album and *coccineum*
Veronica buxifolia, chathamica, cupressoides

PERENNIALS

Anemone pulsatilla
Arabis albida
Arenaria montana
Armeria caespitosa
Asters in var. (dwarf perennials)
Calceolaria polyrrhiza
Campanula isophylla alba, miranda, garganica
Ceratostigma plumbaginoides
Clintonia andrewsiana
Dianthus in var. (dwarf Pinks)
Geraniums, species
Iberis sempervirens (dwarf Candytuft)
Linaria alpina
Nepeta mussini
Potentilla cinerea
Primula in var. (Primrose)
Saponaria ocymoides var. *grandiflora*
Thymus in var.

Miniature Gardens—Window Boxes

There are two methods to follow. One is to grow plants right in the box. The other is to grow them in pots and set the pots in the box at blossoming time, with the pots concealed by the soil. If you like the first way, the box must be deep, and there should be a layer of gravel at the bottom. Keep the pots somewhere else when the plants aren't in flower. Meanwhile, you keep still other plants, which are in flower, in the box, and thus rotate them. You may arrange with your local nurseryman or florist to keep you supplied with flowering plants. When they are out of season he takes them back and cares for them. You save yourself a mess to clean up.

The less lazy method is more gratifying, if you have a gardener's soul. You make permanent plantings. You have better results with vines and bulbs. As for the mess, you spread newspapers around and go to it.

Wooden window boxes are best. Metal ones demand more watering, and store heat; concrete and terra cotta boxes dry out, and are heavy. Wood retains moisture. Redwood is best. Make holes in the bottom, two holes to every square foot. Cover holes with pieces of inverted crockery. Add an inch of gravel. Fill up with rich loam mixed with peat, sand and fertilizer. Not too much fertilizer. Tamp down. Moisten. Leave two inches between the top of the box and the surface of the soil.

Don't crowd the plants. Roots have to have room. Have small hand sprayers for insects. Divide perennials as you do in regular borders. Cut off faded flowers of annuals. It's better to water thoroughly rather than often.

Suggested Plants for Window Boxes

FOR A HOUSE OF BROWN SHINGLES: Golden Gleam Nasturtiums, Yellow Alyssum, Blue Violas and Calceolarias.

A KITCHEN WINDOW BOX: Chives, Tarragon, Thyme, Rose Geranium, Rosemary, Lavender, Marjoram and Sage.

POT PLANTS FOR A SUCCESSION OF BLOOM: Hyacinths, Schizanthus, Cinerarias.

DROUGHT RESISTANT FOR A WEEK END COTTAGE: Geraniums, *Nepeta mussini*, Carnations (Chabaud strain), and *Alyssum saxatile*.

SPRING BULBS FOLLOWED BY ANNUALS: Snowflakes, Muscari, Freesia, Daffodils, Narcissus. Plant mixed Nemesias between bulbs, lift bulbs when through blooming.

DWARF SHRUBS FOR AN EVERGREEN EFFECT: Pimelea, *Euonymus mycrophylla*, *Veronica buxifolia*, Cuphea; Cytisus.

ON A NORTH WALL: Felicia (blue or pink), *Saxifraga crassifolia*, Heuchera, Violas, Primulas, *Campanula sophylla*.

FRAGRANCE THROUGH AN OPEN WINDOW: *Daphne cneorum*, Dark Heliotrope, Jonquils, Mignonette, *Yerba buena*.

OLD STANDBYS: (Inexpensive and satisfactory). Ageratum (blue, grows 8 to 12 inches), Browallia (amethyst, 1 foot), Calendula (yellow-orange, 15 inches). Candytuft (12 inches), Lobelia (blue, trailing), Mignonette (tinged with red, not particularly colorful, but blends well), Nasturtiums, of course, Nemesia (comes in dainty colors, 1 foot), Nemophila (Baby Blue Eyes), Pansies, Petunias, Single Pinks (16 inches), Portulaca (low growing), Sweet Alyssum, Virginia Stocks, Verbena.

Cacti and Succulents

To grow these from seed, first take a clean flower pot. Put broken pieces of an old flower pot in the bottom. Add a tablespoonful of charcoal for drainage. Mix half and half coarse sand and peat moss, sift, and fill to within 1 inch of top of pot. Set the pot in pan of water, until soil is damp. Tamp the soil surface.

Mix a little sand with fine seeds and sow by tapping the package. April to mid-July is the best planting time. For larger seeds, mark off surface into 1-inch squares. Moisten a toothpick, pick up a seed, and set one seed at each corner of every square. Sift fine sand over seeds to depth of a seed's diameter, then cover with ¼-inch coarse sand to conserve moisture. Place grass over top of pot, and cheesecloth over glass. Keep soil moist by setting the pot in water from time to time. A sunny window is the best location. When you see growth, put a match between the pot and glass. Remove glass when germination is completed—(germination period depends on varieties). Shade from sun and draughts at this stage. When second leaves of succulents, or several groups of cactus spines appear, transplant to another pot. Don't water for 24 hours, then less than before. Wait until warm weather before re-transplanting to open ground (6 to 18 months, depending on variety). Seeds may be started in flats by the same method.

HOW TO GROW HOUSE PLANTS

POTTING

ROCK

DRAINAGE HOLE MUST BE KEPT OPEN

WATERING

FEEDING

ROOT SYSTEM TOO SMALL TO STAND FEEDING

INSECT PESTS

1. In potting or repotting plants, allow sufficient space to spread roots. Have pots scrubbed clean, cover drainage hole with rock as indicated. Soil mixtures vary but a favorite one is composed of 1 part garden loam, 1 part well-rotted manure, 1 part peat moss, and a little sand.

2. Water house plants only when soil is dry on surface. Let water run gently but soak soil thoroughly. Never pour water on foliage. An hour after watering, pour out any water that has been gathered in the saucer beneath the pot. During cold weather water in morning, using tepid water.

3. Never use plant food (solid or dry) when soil is dry. Soak soil first and allow a few hours to elapse before applying. Never let plant food touch stem, foliage or flowers. If roots are weak, avoid artificial feeding. Always follow directions given on package of plant food—they vary.

4. Look out for insect pests on house plants. Generally a forceful stream of water will clean plants of aphis or red spiders. Use an all-round garden spray every few weeks. Keep all dead leaves and wilted flowers picked off for these harbor disease. Wash occasionally with soapsuds.

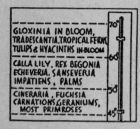

GLOXINIA IN BLOOM,
TRADESCANTIA, TROPICAL FERNS,
TULIPS & HYACINTHS IN BLOOM

CALLA LILY, REX BEGONIA
ECHEVERIA, SANSEVERIA
IMPATIENS, PALMS

CINERARIA, FUCHSIA
CARNATIONS, GERANIUMS,
MOST PRIMROSES

CHRISTMAS CHERRY
45° - 50°

CUT BACK AFTER FOLIAGE HAS DROPPED

POINSETTIAS
60°-65°

OLD STEMS PLACED IN WATER WILL ROOT

FREESIAS

Cover ½ inch Deep

Before Blooming 50°-55°

When in Bloom 60°-65°

5. Temperatures at which house plants are kept is important. Study chart above. Keep flat pans of water near plants to provide humidity. Fresh air is essential, but avoid drafts. Group your plants so they can be cared for with a minimum of work. Few plants can stand 70°.

6. Take up Christmas (Jerusalem) cherries in fall and repot, taking care not to disturb roots. When acclimated, place in sunny window. Give plenty of water. Later when berries and leaves begin to drop, prune back plant and put in cool place, watering sparingly. Transplant in spring.

7. Poinsettias do best at 60° to 65°, and kept fairly moist, during bud and bloom. When lowest leaves begin to drop off, withhold water gradually and then keep entirely dry. When only naked stems remain, store pot in warm, dry place until May; then cut stems and repot or transplant.

8. In early fall obtain freesia corms and dry them for a week or two in the sun. Plant several in one pot. Place in cool room out of sun (slightly watering) until corms sprout, then bring to sunny window. Never soak freesias but sprinkle lightly with tepid water. When in bloom keep at 60° to 65 .

PRIMROSES

CYCLAMEN
45° - 55°

PROPERLY PLANTED WITH UPPER HALF EXPOSED

THE GARDEN NOTE BOOK

by Alfred Putz

Fully Illustrated

9. Most primroses can be grown from seed. Sow in spring for winter bloom. Water primroses carefully—never pour water into heart of plant. Avoid using leaf mold or peat moss on this plant; it may cause yellows. Never let primroses become root bound. Keep in sunny window; no drafts.

10. Keep cyclamen cool, giving plenty of light, but avoiding direct rays of sun. When blossoms drop and leaves yellow, withhold water until soil is dry. Pull off wilted leaves and dust top of corm with charcoal. Set aside to rest, watering occasionally until growth starts, then water freely.

11. These sketches, together with the information contained in captions, are found in "The Garden Note Book," an excellent garden guide by Alfred Putz. Published by Doubleday Doran and Company, price $1.50. The book contains 218 pages. Sunset will order the book for you.

12. The book described in previous paragraph is not exclusively about house plants. It includes much on pruning, planting, propagating, and other garden practices. There are 52 chapters and each chapter starts off with a drawing, showing just how to garden. We recommend it heartily.

HOW TO
Make Garden Furnishings

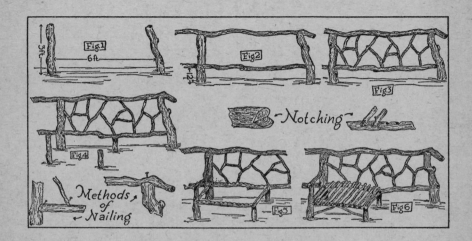

A Rustic Fence and Seat

CEDAR and Juniper are the best woods. Seasoning the wood is optional. To bend straight limbs, heat in boiling water, then bend and wire in position to dry. Use sharp tools. Tools needed: hammer, rip saw, rasp, chisel, sharp knife, and drills. Build the combination fence and seat diagrammed here as follows:

Have the upright posts 4 to 5 inches in diameter and 4½ feet long. The rails are 2 to 3 inches in diameter and 6 feet long. The top rail is 12 feet. Dead or green wood may be used for cross pieces. Set posts in the ground 1½ feet deep. Notch their tops (see Figure 1 and sketch labeled "Notching"). In these notches you lay your 12-foot top rail for nailing. Set the bottom nail 12 inches above the ground, notching this time as in Figure 2. Nail in place. Notch the ends of all cross pieces (you can see how long to make them by measuring or holding in place). Spring them into place—note in the sketch how each is a little bent, showing that it is sprung.

A rustic seat can easily be added to this fence (see Figures 5 and 6). In particular note the small sketches showing how to nail and notch.

With these few principles you can build benches standing alone, tables, chairs, and other simple kinds of rustic garden furniture.

Amateur wood workers should send to the Superintendent of Documents, Washington, D. C., for Farmers' Bulletin No. 1582 (5 cents), which tells how to treat wood for bark worm before using.

Wood well suited to almost any rustic gadget you might want to build can be bought in most wood yards. The designer of the fence shown here is B. E. Koehler of Hollywood.

How to Build a Barbecue Fireplace

Have a concrete foundation beneath your brick superstructure. The foundation can be 4 inches thick. Three inches are below ground, 1 inch above. Order 200 common brick. Secondhand bricks are cheaper and more weathered looking. Get a sack of cement and 3 sacks of sand for your mortar. Lay the bricks as the diagram shows. Insert the iron bars at "A-B" after second brick course is laid. For these grate bars, get ½-inch round iron rods; space them 3 inches apart from the front to the rear. Let them run the full length, side to side, so that the firepan can slide easily between the firebox and the grill sections.

Lay brick carefully and you will come out right where the first vertical course, the sixth course from the bottom, makes a shoulder. The shoulder is to support the 3/8-inch-thick iron plate for the oven floor which you see in the plan's first section. It also supports the grill mesh at "C" on the right.

Position "D" for the grill mesh is lower, nearer the fire, for greater heat. Make this position by raking out inside joints between the fourth and fifth brick courses while mortar is fresh, to make a groove on three sides which lets the mesh slide into place. The mesh should be 3/16-inch iron rods, 1 inch apart, in a metal frame.

Note the brick wall in the pit's center, separating the firebox section from the grill. The opening in this wall lets the firepan slide from one section to the other over the grate bars. It is two brick courses high. The span has an iron bar support, 1/2x2 inches x2 feet. Another iron bar of the same size, is put over the opening between firebox and chimney. Twenty inches long is enough. Your firebox is brick on two sides,

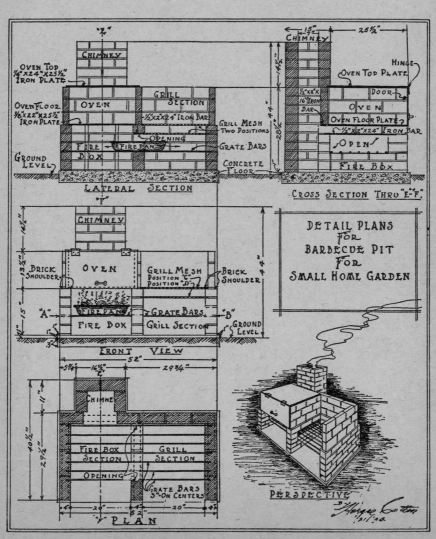

(Designed by Horace George Cotton, Landscape Architect)

open at the front, covered on top with an iron plate which makes the oven floor, and open in the rear into the chimney.

The oven section has brick on three sides, and a 3/8-inch iron floor. The oven's front and top are covered with two 1/4-inch-thick iron plates hinged together. These stay detached from the brick, and are removable. Make a seat where the metal plate rests on the brick. Smooth the brick with neat cement; seat plate in the soft cement before dry. Use the metal floor and top of the oven as hot plates if you wish, for keeping food warm.

While wood is fiercely burning, keep it in the firebox to heat the oven. When you have a bed of coals, slide the firepan into the grill section for grilling purposes. If you want to use the oven and grill at the same time, have two firepans. To make a firepan, get a heavy metal drip-pan, and drill 1/2-inch holes in the bottom 2 inches apart for draft. Best fuel is Oak. Other hardwoods also O.K. Total cost of fireplace and materials, about $10.00, if size is same as shown herewith. For different size, follow same plan but change proportions. It should not take more than three or four hours to make this pit.

A Thatched Roof Garden House

This rustic retreat, which measures 6½ feet by 13½ feet, is big enough for several persons at one time. Arthur O. Johnson, well-known Western architect, designed it. The specifications are flexible. For instance, instead of a thatched roof of palm leaves you may substitute any similar thatching material, shingles, or simply vines which you train over the understructure as a roof.

This garden house will accommodate one or more card tables and the chairs which go with them. If you wire your shelter for electricity its usefulness will be doubled. The best wood to use in building is Redwood, although Cedar, Oak, Spruce, stained, are good, too. Paint Pine if you use it. The dimensions given in the diagram are exact, but you may change the size of your garden house to larger or smaller by keeping the same proportions. That is, to make it one tenth larger, one third smaller, or any other size, have every measure one tenth larger or one third smaller, etc.

Vines make good plantings, since they provide you with shade. A few small shrubs — not too many — placed at the corners of this garden house (see small sketch), will tie it into your main garden. If you paint the little house, avoid white.

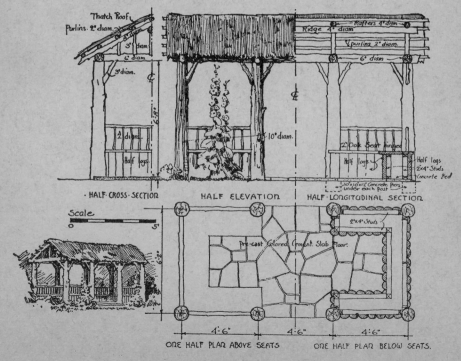

How to Build a Lathhouse

The lathhouse should, as nearly as possible, face so that the laths run north and south. The windy side should be solid or screened with glass.

Note that in this plan, we suggest instead of ordinary plastering laths, 1x2 inch battens, milled with a groove on top to provide a run-off for rainwater, thereby eliminating the drip that is so harmful to some plants. If ordinary laths are used, remember that they are only 1½ inches wide, and so the spacing between them should be 1½ inches.

Use treated lumber for all foundation members. Carefully level, plumb, and square up different members as you frame the structure.

When completed, paint the lath house. Recommended are: green (prepared house paint, 3 coats); white (cold water paint, one or 2 coats—preferably 2); or stain (prepared shingle stain, 2 coats).

BILL OF MATERIALS

Mark	Title	Pieces	Size	Length	Description
A	Mudsill	3	2"x 6"	16' 0"	No. 1 Heart Common Redwood (Paint with Creosote)
B	Mudsill	4	2"x 4"	16' 0"	No. 1 Heart Common Redwood (Paint with Creosote)
C	Studs	15	2"x 4"	8' 0"	No. 1 Heart Common Redwood (Cut to length shown)
D	Studs	6	2"x 4"	2' 0"	No. 1 Heart Common Redwood (Cut to length shown)
E	Purlins	5	2"x 4"	16' 0"	No. 1 Heart Common Redwood (Shaped 1 edge)
F	Rafters	20	2"x 8"	5' 0"	No. 1 Heart Common Redwood (Bandsaw 2 edges to radius)
G	Plates	1	2"x 4"	16' 0"	No. 1 Heart Common Redwood
H	Girders	2	2"x 4"	16' 0"	No. 1 Heart Common Redwood
I	Cripples	12	2"x 4"	4' 0"	No. 1 Heart Common Redwood (Cut between Studs)
J	Bench Frame	12	2"x 4"	4' 0"	No. 1 Heart Common Redwood (Cut to length shown)
K	Bench Frames	7	2"x 4"	16' 0"	No. 1 Heart Common Redwood (Cut to length shown)
L	Bench Frame	2	2"x 4"	4' 0"	No. 1 Heart Common Redwood (Cut to length shown)
M	Bench Frame	16	2"x 4"	4' 0"	No. 1 Heart Common Redwood (Cut to length shown)
N	Bench Frame	4	2"x 4"	2' 0"	No. 1 Heart Common Redwood (Cut to length shown)
O	Bench Frame	6	2"x 4"	4' 0"	No. 1 Heart Common Redwood (Cut to length shown)
P	Bench Frame	4	2"x 4"	1' 0"	No. 1 Heart Common Redwood (Cut to length shown)
Q	Bench Top	10	1"x10"	16' 0"	No. 1 Heart Common Redwood (Cut to length shown)
R	Bench Top	9	1"x10"	4' 0"	No. 1 Heart Common Redwood (Cut to length shown)
S	Siding	170' 0"	1"x 6"		V-joint redwood rustic
T	Battens	70	1"x 2"	18' 0"	Clear redwood to pattern
U	Battens	140	1"x 2"	4' 0"	Clear redwood to pattern
V	Battens	70	1"x 2"	3' 0"	Clear redwood to pattern (Cut to length shown)
W	Battens	70	1"x 2"	7' 0"	Clear redwood to pattern (Cut to length shown)
X	Trim	3	1"x 4"	16' 0"	Clear redwood surfaced 4 sides (Rabetted on back)
Y	Trim	2	1"x 4"	16' 0"	Clear redwood surfaced 4 sides (Shaped one edge)
Z	Trim	2	1"x 8"	18' 0"	Clear redwood surfaced 4 sides (Bandsaw 2 edges to radius)
X2	Trim	2	1"x 4"	8' 0"	Clear redwood surfaced 4 sides (Cut to length shown)

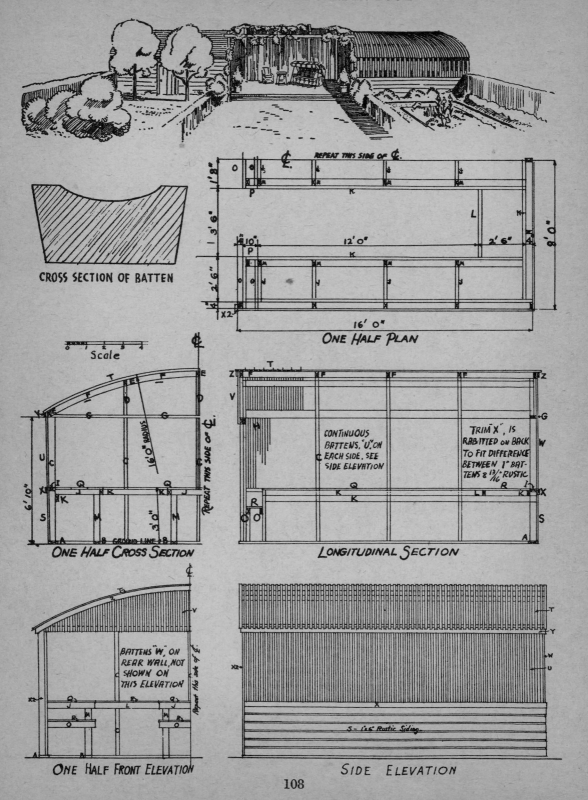

CROSS SECTION OF BATTEN

ONE HALF PLAN

Scale

ONE HALF CROSS SECTION

CONTINUOUS BATTENS, "U", ON EACH SIDE, SEE SIDE ELEVATION

TRIM "X", IS RABBITED ON BACK TO FIT DIFFERENCE BETWEEN 1" BATTENS & $\frac{13}{16}$" RUSTIC

LONGITUDINAL SECTION

BATTENS "W", ON REAR WALL, NOT SHOWN ON THIS ELEVATION

ONE HALF FRONT ELEVATION

S - 1x6" Rustic Siding.

SIDE ELEVATION

MEMO

Calendar

AN IMPORTANT secret of garden success lies in knowing what needs to be done each month. Months differ; each has its characteristic gardening significance. In January you get out your notebook of last year's garden record, and open a new one for the new year. This is the month of planning. In March you are starting seedlings in flats or pots indoors. In April you are planting outdoors. Then through the summer months little is done beyond maintenance. But you begin to think of perennials in August, and to start them. The new fall bulbs are on the market in September, to be started in October. November is the transplanting month, and the time for a general garden clean-up.

This Memo Calendar is divided into the twelve months of the year, then subdivided into Pacific Western gardening regions. Not everything that can or should be done in the garden is listed, naturally, since not even a good-sized library could exhaust the possibilities. But you will find much fact and much suggestion here, and perhaps the inspiration for a garden notebook of your own, worked out for the year 'round.

One of the most frequent uses of this Calendar will be the discovery of what *may* be planted in any given month. With this information you can quickly look up the plant in the Dictionary-Encyclopedia (page 150) and find how the plant is grown. Or if the Calendar suggests that such and such a time is best for fertilizing your lawn, look up "Lawns, fertilizing of," in the Index, for the correct way to carry out the suggestion. In this way you can make this book work for you, delivering up needed facts almost automatically.

WHAT TO DO IN JANUARY

PACIFIC CENTRAL

This is the busy garden month. Planting, transplanting, spraying and cleaning up all need your attention. Clean perennial borders. Divide large clumps. Plant Roses now. Prune Rose bushes and dig around plants.

Lawns: Work soil to depth of six inches to let rains do their work. Pruning, Spraying: Not safe to postpone any longer. Whitewashing trunks is excellent. Prune Grapes, Raspberries, Loganberry, Blackberry, Dewberry, Gooseberry, Currants.

All Lilies should be planted before end of January. Transplant Primroses. Ranunculus bulbs may be planted until the end of this month. Tulips, Daffodils also, but best planted October-November.

Sow seed under glass of Virginia Stocks, Mignonette, Cornflower, Snapdragon, all spring-blooming annuals. Bulbs of Tulips, Crocus, Snowflake, Dicentra, Freesia, Regal Lily and other hardy Lilies, Narcissus, Peony, Hyacinth, and of other spring-blooming bulbous plants may be planted now, if fall planting was delayed, and weather is good.

Good month to dig up conifers, Roses, evergreens, deciduous trees, shrubs, for transplanting.

Subdivide hardy Aster or Michaelmas Daisy, Delphinium, Shasta, Daisy, Valerian, Gaillardia, Geum, Heuchera, Penstemon and Phlox.

Hedges, Windbreaks: Plant new hedges; fertilize old ones. Privet, Wild Cherry, Pittosporum—all are good for Northern California. Good for windbreaks: Acacia, Causarina, Escallonia. Plant now, five feet apart, with more space, however, for English Laurel.

PACIFIC SOUTHWEST

Good time to start your garden notebook, jotting down bulbs, annuals, perennials, cuttings, shrubs, seeds, dates, locations, etc.

January and February are good months for planting and moving trees, shrubs, vines.

Cut Chrysanthemums and Dahlias to the ground now. If you need the space for other plants, heel in Chrysanthemums and Dahlias in some other part of the garden.

Good time to change paths, or transfer groups of plants to new locations. Pruning and fertilizing in general can be done now. Do not prune spring flowering material until after blooming period is past, however. Prune Pyracanthas and Cotoneasters as soon as berries have disappeared.

There are still such bulbs on the market as Anemones, Ranunculus, Tuberous Begonias, Lilium auratum, Lilium rubrum. Gladiolus corms may be planted this month, but do not expect blooms until latter part of May.

Seed sowing, except for seeds of hardy annuals, is inadvisable now because of the cold nights.

Prune Roses about the middle of this month —except the ramblers and one-time blooming climbers like Belle of Portugal which should be pruned in June after their flowers are gone. Prune heathers as soon as the blooming season's over. Prune Hydrangeas back to just above the second joints on last season's growth. Fuchsias should be pruned towards the latter part of the month.

Complete the task of dividing perennials. Discard the old woody roots in the center of the clumps and use the new ones around the outside.

PACIFIC NORTHWEST

This is the time to do your planning indoors for the year's gardening. A good time, too, to make your compost bed. Spread soil over compost materials to speed decay. Moisture helps also, as does spading the mass to increase bacterial activity.

To protect half hardy plants from frosts, mulch the ground around and over them this winter while ground is frozen. Don't mulch too heavily—plants cannot then push their way up. If you use leaves, straw, etc.,try light covering of brush, with mulch over it.

Start your rock garden now, if you haven't one. Gather suitable rocks every time you take a drive this winter.

Spray, with dormant type spray, every deciduous tree, shrub and bush during January or February.

Divide perennial plants; move those that are not in proper location and order the new ones you want. Don't overlook ground peat or compost. Here are some common dependable annual plants you may never have grown and may want to try. Feathered Cockscomb (Celosia plumosa): Good for background planting. Love Lies Bleeding, Amaranthus caudatus): Good for background planting. Unusual flower spikes. Handle plants in the same manner as Josephs Coat (Amaranthus tricolor). Sow in spring. Mexican Fire Bush or Summer Cypress (Kochia): Plant in open ground when frost danger is past. Strawflower (Helichrysum): Sow out of doors fairly early in the spring. Also: Calliopsis, Blanket Flower (Gaillardia), Painted Tongue (Salpiglossis), Globe Amaranth (Gomphrena), Pot Marigold (Calendula).

WHAT TO DO IN FEBRUARY

PACIFIC CENTRAL

Sow seed under glass of Calliopsis, Gilia, Shirley Poppies, Delphinium, Lobelia, Ageratum, Arctotis, Coreopsis, Stocks, and others for early blooming.

Continue to plant out hardy annuals for early blooming. Many spring blooming plants may still be planted, weather permitting. Continue to dig up conifers, deciduous trees, evergreens, shrubs, Roses, for transplanting.

If winter has been severe, cut back to new shoots: Delphiniums, Peonies, Physostegia, Thalictrum, Gerbera, Salvia, Phlox, Columbines, Doronicum, Anemone, Campanula grandiflora, Cannas.

Dig, fertilize perennial border. Apply calcium nitrate if your soil cakes. Plant out hardy varieties of flowers—Sweet Peas, Nasturtiums, Snapdragons, Poppies, wild flowers. Cuttings from Hydrangeas, Syringas, Viburnums, Fuchsias, Lilacs, Weigelas, Lantana, Deutzia, may be started now.

February is a good time to start a perennial border. Get young plants. Begin with background. Plant evergreens or tall shrubs by getting balled roots. Turn soil well; fertilize richly. Draw a plan on paper to work from.

These bulbs and roots may be planted now: Agapanthus, Alstromeria, Amaryllis belladonna, Anemone, Astilbe, tuberous-rooted Begonia, Boussingaultia, Crocus, Bleeding Heart, Cyclamen, Cinnamon Vine, Freesia, Snowdrop, Gladiolus, Gloxinia, Snowflake, Regal Lily and other hardy species, Daffodil, hardy Water Lily, Peony, Balloon Flower, Tuberose, Ranunculus, Sparaxis tricolor, Tiger Flower, Montbretia, Tulip, Watsonia, Calla, Zephyr Lily.

PACIFIC SOUTHWEST

Take up and divide these perennials: Shasta Daisy, Columbine, Helenium, Anchusa, Valerian, Michaelmas Daisy, Coreopsis, Dianthus plumarius, Erigeron, Gazania, Geum, Helianthus, Heuchera, Pentstemon, Phlox, Physostegia, Salvia, Veronica. Set new Roses; there is still time. Plant Gladiolus now for May-June bloom.

Sow seeds of hardy annuals in coldframe or open ground. California wild flowers will germinate by spring, planted now. Cut down Poinsettias.

Watch for aphis on your Lily shoots. Apply fertilizer to soil around Iris; keep it away from rhizomes, however. Leave Dahlias in ground another month. Look at your stored tubers now to see if they are drying out.

Look over your Chrysanthemum plants. Are new growths up? If you do not plan to take cuttings this spring, dig up old plants when new shoots appear; divide and reset.

For blooms in June, sow these seeds now: annual Phlox, Larkspur, annual Chrysanthemums, Godetia, Clarkia, Nasturtiums, Calliopsis, Candytuft, Poppies. Protect seeds from birds with coarse cheesecloth or chicken wire. Plan a cutting garden. Plant in rows, leaving space for cultivating, irrigating, spraying. Plant in the same row all flowers having same season of bloom; you can then remove them after they bloom without disturbing the others.

Remember to water your plants before applying fertilizer. This avoids possibility of burning.

PACIFIC NORTHWEST

Trim up any rock garden plants and shrubs that need it now. Notice any bare spaces; you can insert in them those plants you have desired so long. Plants with good balls of earth may be safely transplanted now. Watering is seldom necessary when planting is done this month, if soil, already moist, is firm around roots. See that all plants are firm in their positions. Ideal time to sow seeds indoors. Sow in small, clean pans.

Plants easily raised from seed are Adonis vernalis, yellow; Alyssum saxatile compactum, yellow blooms early in spring; Armeria Ruby, deep rose; Alpine Aster, mixed colors; Aubrietia, pink, lavender, purple; Bellis perennis, pretty colored Daisies; Campanula carpatica (Blue Bell); Cheiranthus allioni (Siberian Wallflower); Cheiranthus linifolius erysimum, mauve; Dianthus in variety, especially D. caesius, pale pink, and deltoides, bright pink; Erigeron aurantiacus hybrida, yellow-orange Daisies; Gypsophila repens, creeping growth, starry white flowers; Heuchera, pale pink to crimson; Iberis sempervirens, white Candytuft; Lupinus nootkatensis, purple, white; Myosotis alpestris, varieties Victoria, Royal Blue, Ruth Fischer, blue Forget-Me-Nots; Polyanthus in variety, all shades of blue to purple; Primroses; Papaver alpinum, wide color range; Coonara Poppies, pink, salmon, saffron, orange-scarlet, old gold; Primula japonica, mixed; Primula bulleyana, lovely shades; Primula pulverulenta, old rose; Saponaria ocymoides, creeping plant, rosepink; mossy Saxifrages; Sedums (Stone-

WHAT TO DO IN MARCH

PACIFIC CENTRAL

Water the garden during dry weather. Make cuttings of Chrysanthemums now from suckers about base of plant. Plant tubers of tuberous Begonias in flats or open ground. Spray apples and pears with Bordeaux mixture and lead arsenate from time leaves appear until fruit sets.

Lawns may be put in from the 15th of March on, provided soil has warmed up sufficiently. Rake vigorously old lawns, working out old grass. Open up sod with fork or with block of wood having long spikes driven into it. Reseed if necessary, covering with light mulch. Apply the more concentrated fertilizers to lawn or flower garden.

Continue planting Gladiolus bulbs.

Last month usually in which deciduous trees, shrubs, Roses can be safely dug up and transplanted. Seed of many late spring and summer blooming annuals, and some perennials, may be safely sown in open, usually about 15th of the month, weather permitting. Good time, too, to set out plants of annuals for early spring blooming.

Prune evergreens before new growth starts. Potted plants left over may need repotting for long growing season ahead. Prune Diervilla and other flowering shrubs soon after flowers are past. Eucalyptus and Acacia may be planted now. Prune Hydrangeas, Poinsettias, Fuchsias.

And don't forget the weeding! Look for snails and slugs under leaves, litter, etc.

PACIFIC SOUTHWEST

March means warmer days, but, because of possible rains, keep cultivator handy. Anything in your plant list, from trees to annuals and perennials, may be set out now. German Iris blooms this month. Daffodils and late flowering Narcissi open in March. Do not cut down the leaves of the latter until brown.

Pick blossoms on Sweet Pea vines. Prune shrubs that are through flowering — also ber-ried shrubs. Fertilize all shrubs, trees, established vines. Never fertilize seedlings, or put fertilizer in soil where you plan to sow seed at once. Add extra food when plants are growing vigorously.

Take up, divide and reset Dahlias that have been in the ground all winter. Keep planting Gladioli for bloom in mid-June. Tuberous Begonias may go in now. Wait until April to make cuttings of your old Chrysanthemum plants. March cuttings often damp off.

Rake the lawn, get out dead runners, cut close, and sow Bluegrass and Clover on top. Water well, add commercial fertilizer when new grass is growing good. Plant any hardy seeds in the flower garden — Marigolds, Petunias, Zinnias, Asters, and perennial seeds should wait until warmer weather in April or May.

Spray Roses with nicotine solution for aphis, also with arsenate of lead for leaf-eating insects. Tobacco dust around base of plants keeps off many pests. Dusting sulphur is good for mildew; apply in morning so that the sun will liberate the fumes.

PACIFIC NORTHWEST

Prune and spray fruit trees or bushes before sap flows and buds burst. Give trees coating of lime and sulphur, or oil emulsion — very effective for certain scale insects. Spray thoroughly; it pays.

Prune or plant shrubs, Roses, ornamental trees, hedges. Fertilize trees and bushes this month. Divide and replant old clumps of perennial plants. Plant Sweet Peas early. Plant Gladiolus early.

Many annual flowers can be planted now. Sow these broadcast over perennial and bulb beds and among shrubbery plantings: Alyssum, Little Gem, Clarkia, Godetia, Poppy, Calliopsis, French Marigold, Eschscholtzia, Blue Lace Flower, Pansy, Arcotis, Bachelor Button, Candytuft, Pinks, Snapdragon, Scarlet Flax, Sweet Sultan.

Suggestions: Try Ageratum this year. The variety Little Dorrit Blue is a good edging plant. Combines with Sweet Alyssum. The tall Mexicanum (lavender-blue) is good for cutting. Also good for bouquets is annual Babysbreath (Gypsophila elegans). New to Northwest gardeners, but good to grow, is Chinese Forget-Me-Not (Cynoglossum amabile) — Gentian-blue, fragrant, long blooming, and thrives almost anywhere. Annual Gaillardia makes a fine cut-flower. Try Salpiglossis in the open ground this year, for better luck. Let it take care of itself, but thin out if needed when six inches tall. Good for cutting are the improved Mourning Brides or Scabiosas.

Plant tender annuals indoors early this month, in flats, hotbed, coldframe. Transplant to garden in mid-April.

WHAT TO DO IN APRIL

PACIFIC CENTRAL

Watch for slugs, aphis, etc. Go over all your plants regularly with a spray. Keep garden free from debris and weeds. Look over Iris clumps this month for overcrowding; divide and replant after blooming season.

This month sow seeds of Asters, Zinnias, Cosmos, Marigolds, Coreopsis, Double Lark-spur, Mignonette, Centaurea, Phlox drummon-di, Stocks, Salpiglossis, Ageratum, Gypso-phila, Dianthus, Sunflower, Chrysanthemum, Arctotis, Myosotis, Schizanthus, Verbena.

Trim spring-flowering shrubs after bloom-ing, using a sharp knife. Set out slips in the fall when the plant is dormant.

A very good month in which to sow grass seed for lawns. Dahlia tubers may be planted now, but usually best in May or June. Seeds of summer blooming annuals may be sown now. Continue planting Gladiolus bulbs.

Apply commercial fertilizers about flower-ing plants coming into bloom. A good month usually in which to apply commercial fer-tilizers to lawns.

Watch Roses carefully for mildew, aphis, spraying periodically or dusting with agricul-tural sulphur for mildew, spraying with nico-tine preparations for aphis as they appear.

April is a month of great garden beauty in the Bay Region. Prepare perennial border. Take cuttings of Chrysanthemums and propa-gate in frames, also Carnations, Pentstemons.

Subdivide Delphiniums (2-year-old clumps) now. Examine for heart rot, remove diseased portions, treat with dry sulphur. Fertilize soil before replanting Delphinium divisions. Plant in groups two or three feet apart.

PACIFIC SOUTHWEST

All seeds may be planted now with no fear of frost or cold weather. Continue to plant Gladiolus bulbs, setting them in a group rath-er than singly. Dahlia tubers may be set out in sufficiently moist soil. Water until sprouts are eight inches high. Plant Dahlia seeds in seed box now. Chrysanthemum cuttings may be taken and planted in moist sand. Use tips only. Water sparingly, in a. m. Transplant when roots develop to two-inch length. Plan to place in the garden in May. Good month in which to renovate your Bermuda lawn. Rake the lawn well, loosening the Bermuda; then cut close. Sow two pounds of Bluegrass and one of clover to every 1,000 square feet. Cover lightly with peat and commercial plant food.

Do not cut down Narcissi leaves until they turn brown. Good summer flowers to plant in April are: Calliopsis, Candytuft, Bachelor Button, annual Chrysanthemum, Dianthus (Pinks), annual Phlox, annual Larkspur, Nigella, Linaria, Zinnias, Cosmos and Petunias.

Wild flowers are out now. Make a trip to the desert to get acquainted with the native flora. Attend the spring flower shows for new flowers you may want to grow next year. Have you tried Ixia, Sparaxis, Spanish Iris, Tritonia and Scillas?

Watch Roses for thrips, aphis; spray. Watch for mildew; use dusting sulphur. Use arsenate of lead for leaf-eaters. Keep slugs from Del-phiniums with coarse coal ashes or powdered lime scattered on ground.

PACIFIC NORTHWEST

Still too early in most years to plant flower seeds outdoors, but you can try in a small way. Buy seeds early; plant about one-fourth of each packet this month if weather is good. You may have annual flowers much earlier, if seed is sown now. Make early plantings in small beds, in sunny, sheltered places. Trans-plant later about mid-May.

Lawns: If you plan a new lawn planting this spring, prepare ground now. Give it a good surface cultivation every week with rake or hoe. Mix in fertilizer, compost or peat. Post-pone planting of lawn seed until end of April or early May in the Northwest. It will grow faster in warmer weather.

Suggestions: Don't expect great results from the cheapest seed and equipment or poor land. Don't expect your garden to put up a good fight against insects and bad weather, if you starve it for plant food and moisture. Do not let insect pests and diseases get a start.

Plant Tigridias (or Mexican Lilies) in April. These bulbs will bloom through late summer well into the fall. In the vicinity of Portland, Oregon, Tigridias should for safety be taken up in the fall and stored. An Os-wego, Oregon, gardener leaves Tigridia bulbs in the ground all winter, in a sunny, well pro-tected spot. But this is a risk, even when covered with oak leaves to keep out frost. Plant bulbs three to four inches deep in light, sandy soil with sunny exposure. Water pro-fusely in dry season.

Rock Gardens: Try Leptospermum prostra-tum. For color, variety Heavenly Blue, among Aubrietias, Arabis and Alyssum.

WHAT TO DO IN MAY

PACIFIC CENTRAL

Last month in which lawns can be safely put in before hot summer season. Along the Pacific Coast lawns can be put in during summer if given careful attention.

Plant out tubers of Dahlias. Plant seeds of Asters, Cosmos, and other full blooming flowers. Garden pests are sometimes bad during May and June. Plants should be carefully watched.

Sow seeds of late summer blooming plants. Rooted cuttings of Chrysanthemums, or plants from pots, may be set out in garden. May is California's month of Roses; spray to keep down aphis. For fine bloom, remove the two side buds, leaving center bud.

Annuals to be planted this month: Giant Zinnias in pastel shades, also small pompons. Try some of the California sunshines, as well as the giants. Plant annual Phlox for brilliant border display. Sow broadcast or in rows very thinly. Plant all annuals where they are to bloom. Sow seeds thinly; water regularly during summer; use thin mulch of well screened peat. Get Water Lilies planted early in May.

Thin out annuals planted earlier this year. Plant seeds of Columbines and Primroses for next year. If these fail to germinate there will be time to repeat the sowings later.

Set out Petunias, both the large double ones and small single varieties; put some in your window boxes. Plant Lily-of-the-Valley pips now. Sow Rudbeckia seeds to replace perennials for late bloom. Scatter Shirley Poppy seed and annual Gypsophila in any bare spots. Take up and divide Violets now for bloom next winter.

PACIFIC SOUTHWEST

Chrysanthemums go in this month. The nurseries have the rooted cuttings in pots. As soil should be freshly turned. Should contain much moisture. Plant seeds thinly, not deeply; cover lightly, firm soil, provide moisture constantly during germination.

Spray your Roses for thrips and aphis; keep this fight up regularly every week. Keep planting Gladioli—those you plant now should bloom in late July.

For your summer flowers, plant Zinnias, Asters, Marigolds, Cosmos, Nasturtiums. Good edging plants, if you have a sunny, dry location, are: Verbenas, Lantanas and Petunias.

For shady patios, these evergreen shrubs are good to try: Myrtus communis microphylla, Pittosporum tenuifolium, Pittosporum nigricans, English Laurel, Viburnum sandankwa (suspensum), Rhus ovata. For low growing shrubs: Juniperus conferta, Juniperus sabina tamariscifolia, Hypericum moserianum. Camellias should be in all patios.

For herbaceous material, try: Columbine, Lilies, Daylily, Heliotrope, Azaleas, Cyclamen, Cineraria, Heuchera, Violas, Pansies, Violets, Lobelia, Fuchsia, Agapanthus, and spring bulbous flowers.

These are good for low hedges: Japanese Boxwood, Myrtus communis compacta. Both are good for shade or partial shade.

These annual vines may be planted now, for flowers this summer: Morning Glory, Bugle Vine, Balloon Vine, and the Gourds. Keep watering regularly.

PACIFIC NORTHWEST

Best planting month. At seed sowing time, soil should be freshly turned. Should contain much moisture. Plant seeds thinly, not deeply; cover lightly, firm soil, provide moisture constantly during germination.

Good common annual flowers of dwarf growth to fill in bare spots in your rockery are: Ageratum, Brachycome, Cacalia, Gomphrena, Lobelia, Nemesia, Nemophila, Sweet Alyssum, Virginia Stocks.

For fragrance, try these annuals: Abronia, Angels Trumpet, Candytuft, Evening Scented Stocks, Flowering Tobacco, Mignonette, double Nasturtium, Petunia, Pinks, Sweet Peas, Scabiosa, Sweet Alyssum, Sweet Sultan, Verbena, Stocks.

Other good rock plants which have been found suitable for the Northwest, especially the district between Seattle and Tacoma, are: (For shade) Anthemis styriace (Alpine Daisy), Arenaria balerica, Alpine cyclamen, Oxalis oregana (rose), Linaria arquitriloba (lilac).

Good shrubs for the Puget Sound district are: Snowberry, Rhododendron, Syringa, Spiraea, Honeysuckle, Salal, Oregon Grape, Blue Huckleberry, Red Huckleberry, Wild Currant. Because of the good drainage insured by the sandy soil in this locality, shrubs of all kinds do extremely well with proper fertilizing. The above give many possibilities for low growing shrubs, both for bloom and their foliage. The latter is green all year, excepting the Wild Currant and Red Huckleberry.

WHAT TO DO IN JUNE

PACIFIC CENTRAL

Continue to plant Gladiolus bulbs. Good time to set out Dahlia bulbs. Lawns can still be sown to grass seed in regions tempered by close proximity to Pacific Ocean. Keep up cultivation of soil. Watch plants for plant pests. Seeds of flowers can still be sown in the open, but germination is sometimes uncertain.

Chief work in June is maintenance. Water, cultivate, remove spent flowers. Pinch back Chrysanthemums for bushy growth. Cut back Delphiniums to ground and water them. Divide, replant Bearded Iris. Prune spring flowering deciduous shrubs early this month. Roses may be planted this month from pots.

Trees: Watch for pests. Borers may be at work on your Pines, Cypress, and Thuya.

In limited space it may be necessary to remove bulbs before leaves all wither. Tuberous Begonias may still be planted. Prune Climbing Roses vigorously after blooming, removing old blooms, cutting out weak growth, cutting back canes to within three buds of main stem. Prune Rose bushes in California gardens, removing superfluous growth.

Cultivate soil deeply to conserve moisture during dry season. Keep Roses sprayed or dusted for mildew control.

Give Rhododendrons and Azaleas plenty of water this month. Put mulch of half decayed leaves around roots. Hydrangeas need much water now. Dig in decayed manure around roots. Prune back Mock Orange, Lilacs, Spiraea, Kerria and other spring flowering shrubs. Dig in plant food; keep well watered. Examine for pests; spray.

PACIFIC SOUTHWEST

An important garden activity this month is the planting of seeds and seedlings. Set out Zinnias, Asters and Cosmos, if you sowed them in boxes last month. Keep seedlings moist while planting, to protect from heat. Cover for three days with pots to prevent drying out. Scatter snail poison. Rooted Chrysanthemum plants are on the market, if you did not make cuttings from your old plants. Pinch off tip of new plants — you'll have more flowers this fall. Cut back blooming Dahlias. Watch tubers for insects. Nip out tips of new plants.

For bloom this summer, sow seeds of Nasturtiums (along the coast, not around Riverside, El Centro, etc.). Southern California's variance of climatic conditions greatly affects blooming periods of annuals. Near Los Angeles, Santa Barbara or San Diego you may sow seeds of Zinnias, Asters, Cosmos, Marigold and Portulaca in June. Keep setting out Gladiolus. They come into bloom in 60 to 70 days. Prune deciduous shrubs. Spray Roses. Watch for red spider on Dahlias and Chrysanthemums. Separate and reset Iris now. Apply fertilizers to plants and shrubs growing vigorously. Barnyard manure is good for shrubs, vines, perennial plants; commercial plant food, however, is easier to use and reacts more quickly. Add humus or leaf mold to shady garden where Begonias, Ferns, Fuchsias, etc., are growing. Peat is fine for Camellias, Azaleas. Begin planning your winter garden. Make a list of perennials for your next year's border, and plan to sow seed for them next month.

PACIFIC NORTHWEST

Cultivate much in June. Look out for insect enemies this month. Spray or dust at first sign of trouble.

Watch your Sweet Peas; moisten well. Avoid sprinkling the vines, however; this fosters mildew. If mildew attacks them, dust with flowers of sulphur early in the morning. Keep Sweet Peas from going to seed if you want blooms all summer and fall.

Prune your annuals, especially those of spindling growth. Pinch out center shoots for more compact growth and extra blooms. Snip off all fading flowers in garden to prevent seed production.

In late June, take up Tulip bulbs; store in cool, dry, dark place for summer. Separate bulb clusters according to size.

Cut back your perennial Chrysanthemums, from 1 to 1½ feet from the ground. Fertilize the lawn early this month. Water plentifully right after fertilizing.

June is the month of Roses in the Northwest. Disbud all your Roses. Pick off all lateral buds when still tiny and let strength go into the terminal bud to produce perfect Rose. Protect from intense sunshine and rain; cover choicest blooms for protection. Watch for sucking insects, chewing insects and bacterial diseases. (See Plant Pests.)

Perennials: Plant seed of perennials in Northwest for full grown blooming plants next season. Give young plants plenty of room and make a note to transplant them in fall or late winter to permanent location.

Watering: Start irrigating or sprinkling in earnest now.

WHAT TO DO IN JULY

PACIFIC CENTRAL

This is the month that is "in between" seasons. The garden should be cleaned up, cutting down old flower stalks, removing rubbish. Practice slow irrigation, permitting water to penetrate deep down, rather than too much superficial irrigation on the surface.

Seeds of Salpiglossis, Schizanthus, Snapdragon, Cosmos, Lobelia, Stocks, and others may be sown, if bloom in fall is desired. Give special attention to watering Gladioli and Dahlias; they need much moisture as they come into bloom.

Be careful not to let weeds go to seed; many still ripen if merely cut down. Put on compost heap to rot. Cultivate, dig, and water around shrubs, trees, vines moved this year.

German Iris may still be planted. Sow in flats, etc., seeds of: English Daisy, Canterbury Bells, Cineraria, Delphinium hybrid, Primrose, Pansy (var. hortensia). Seeds which may be sown out are: Candytuft, Pot Marigold, Cornflower, Sweet Sultan, Phlox, Portulaca, African and French Marigolds, Nasturtium, Zinnia.

Mulch soil with peat moss or leaf mold to hold moisture in the ground. Cultivate closely between plants where no mulch is given, for conservation of moisture. When cultivating, work in a little commercial fertilizer once every two months.

For large specimen blooms of Chrysanthemums, remove all side buds and some leaves near terminal to allow strength to go to main terminal bud, called the crown. Stake at this time. Thin out the branches of small-flowered border Chrysanthemums where clumps are too large and not subdivided. Work in good commercial fertilizer between plants now.

PACIFIC SOUTHWEST

Be generous with watering and busy with the cultivator. Keep Dahlias well watered if in sun, and nip off growing tips if you wish many flowers and a bushy plant. For exhibition blooms, keep extra buds picked off, allowing three to a plant. When fertilizing Dahlias, soak ground first, apply fertilizer one foot away from main stalk.

Cut off extra buds of Chrysanthemums for large flower heads. Cut old plants back after July 15th. Keep plants watered; feed judiciously — make a circular trench one foot away from plant after soaking ground; sprinkle half a trowel of commercial fertilizer once in two weeks.

Apply barnyard fertilizer to shrubs this month. Cultivate soil around shrub, make basin; allow water to run in it. Then fill basin with manure. Do not dig in. Phlox needs much moisture; will grow in partial shade. Start perennials and winter blooming annuals now. They will bloom next spring and summer, too, depending on varieties sown. For the coming winter, sow Stocks, Violas, Nemesias, Calendulas, Pansies.

Gladiolus may still be planted. Keep Zinnia blossoms picked, also Asters, Cosmos and many other flowers. Give roots much water if weather is hot. Spray Chrysanthemums and Dahlias for insects. Be sure all plants are staked and tied. Add peat and leaf mold to shady garden, if you have Fuchsias, Begonias, Azaleas, Camellias, Ferns. For a large shady garden, plant deciduous flowering shrubs: Redbud, Flowering Dogwood, Kerria, Mock Orange, Bridal Wreath, Weigela, etc.

PACIFIC NORTHWEST

Plant Viola and Pansy seed this month, for winter and early spring flowers. Plant perennials of all kinds and biennials in July for next season's bloom. Shade ground where you plant seed now to keep surface from drying out and killing young seedlings. A good shade can be made by spreading freshly cut lawn clippings over area where seeds are planted. No soil should be visible. When seeds want to come out, the sun will have dried the clippings so that they can come through easily. Save leaves this fall and you will save money next year on fertilizer requirements.

This is a good time to start the compost bed with plant refuse and lawn clippings, too.

Dig tulips early in July and store in a cool, dry place until October; then replant. Water, fertilize and cut lawn regularly. Soak it good; and when you fertilize, water at once.

Sow annual flower seeds now! Your last chance in Northwestern gardens. Late fall will be colorful if you sow now. Do not delay.

Look over your rock garden. If it is not thriving, how is the soil? Best mixture for rock plants and alpines is one-half peat moss, one-fourth leaf mold and one-fourth garden loam. Never use clay — it packs and bakes; sand washes too easily. Beware of manures and strong fertilizers around tiny plants. Keep soil cool, moist and porous.

Clip back the more rank growing rock plants, such as Helianthemum, Veronicas, etc. Leave a neat mat growth. After clipping, water well and work in a little leaf mold or peat moss around the roots for fast growth.

WHAT TO DO IN AUGUST

PACIFIC CENTRAL

Sow seeds of biennial plants, such as Columbine, Hollyhock, Foxglove, Canterbury Bells, to get bloom next year. Seeds of many perennials may also be sown at this time, to secure good growing plants for possible next year's bloom.

Plant Bearded Iris, Cyclamen, Freesia, Callas. This is your last month for nipping Chrysanthemum shoots. Sow seeds of Snapdragon, Cineraria, Winter - blooming Stocks, Pansies, Violas, Calendula, Virginia Stocks, Lavender Primrose, Cornflower, Mignonette, for late winter blooming.

Cut back Roses moderately.

Some flowering and evergreen shrubs which may be propagated at this time are: Lilacs, Mock Orange, Weigela, Veronicas, Oleander, Snowball, Tamarisk, Deutzia, Forsythia, Cornus, Kerria, Jasminum, Privet, Laurel and Fuchsias.

Certain perennials may be subdivided now and planted in a frame. These are Geum, Alyssum, Aubrietia, Dianthus, Scabiosa, Oriental Poppy, Columbine. Shade for two weeks, and water moderately.

Insert Carnation cuttings in sand. Sow Delphinium seeds. Your Climbing Roses will need tying in and removal of surplus shoots.

Seeds of the following may be sown in August: English Daisy, Delphinium, Forget-Me-Not, Pyrethrum roseum, Statice, Ranunculus (mixed), early-flowering Sweet Peas, and Lobelia. Keep the seed beds and frames shaded and moderately watered.

PACIFIC SOUTHWEST

This is the trying month for southern gardens. Irrigate carefully. For shrubs, make mound of soil around bush, three feet away; flood with slow stream from hose. Next day, cultivate, leaving dirt mulch. Let water run until soil will take no more moisture. Run a furrow between rows of annuals and perennials; let water run down. Soil must become saturated. Always cultivate within a day or two. Mulches of peat, leaf mold, shredded cow manure, bean straw, are all excellent.

Last month to plant winter flowering annuals for flowers in December-January. Plant seed in boxes or flats; transplant to another box when seedlings are two or three inches high. Protect boxes against heat, with covering, until seeds germinate. Sow seeds of such annuals as Stock, Calendula, Pansies, Violas, Sweet Peas, Primulas, Nasturtiums, for abundance of flowers in December-January. Start all sorts of perennials now, for the rockery, garden, potted work, and lathhouse plants.

See that stakes for Dahlias and Chrysanthemums are high enough. Keep bushes well watered, and, for abundance of flowers, nip off growing end of side shoots. Spread some good commercial fertilizer. Water before and after applying. Set Gladiolus corms in partial shade —you should have blooms by latter part of October or early November.

Do not put seedlings out into garden proper this month; transplant to another flat, or pot up from the first flat.

PACIFIC NORTHWEST

Divide large clumps of German Iris. If done now all of them will bloom next year. For color in your Iris beds, or elsewhere, during fall, scatter seeds of Virginia Stocks, Sweet Alyssum, Little Gem, Nemophila, Nemesia. They bloom in six or seven weeks, with good weather.

Snip off blooms of your annual flowers as soon as they are past their prime. Extra blooms will result. Annuals common to the Northwest appreciate a good watering once a week, Sweet Peas especially, if they are to bloom vigorously until late fall.

Plant perennials early this month. New seed matures at this time. Soil is warm, fall rains and natural hardening-off weather benefits them before winter rest, and in spring they emerge properly equipped by nature to bloom in their regular season. Spray, dust and bait the remainder of this year. Clean up waste plant material. Remove annuals that have finished blooming. Cut back perennials. Keep weeds out.

Do not prune Camellias in fall. Shape up, trim back just after flowers are over and before new buds are formed in July and August. Camellias can be grown successfully from Seattle to San Diego. Require even temperature, much water, semi-shade, acid soil.

Are you seeding a new lawn this fall? Sow seed between September 1st and 15th. Work up ground now, fertilize, and keep watered. This germinates native grass and weed seeds, and you can destroy them by cultivation before planting lawn seed.

WHAT TO DO IN SEPTEMBER

PACIFIC CENTRAL

Still time to sow winter blooming Stocks, Snapdragons, Pansies, Violas. Plant Bearded Iris, early Gladiolus, and many others of the bulbous plants, such as Crocus, Cyclamen, Watsonia, Calla, Snowflake, Freesias, all species of Iris, Ixia, Anemone, Calochortus, Ranunculus, Scilla, many of the Lilies, some of the Daffodils and Jonquils.

Seeds of Delphiniums can be sown early this month to obtain strong, vigorous plants for early spring blooming. Seeds of a number of perennials may be sown early in September to get growth during winter for possible bloom the next year. Dig up soil full depth of spade to prepare for winter rains.

Sow grass seed for lawns before end of month if good grass stands are desired before winter sets in. A good month in which to reinvigorate old lawns. Rake vigorously; remove old and dead grass; sow seed; cover with light mulch.

Good perennials for seaside gardens, which may be planted now: Agrostemma, Michaelmas Daisy, Hibiscus, Phlox subulata, Verbena erinoides. For shaded nooks: Japanese Anemones, Columbines, Foxglove, Violet, Campanula, Coral Bell. Hypericum is good for sunny banks, also Transvaal Daisy. Perennials for the rockery: Campanula pusilla, Chrysanthemum maui, double white Shasta Daisy, Gaillardia, Coreopsis, Verbena erinoides. For quick color among the annuals: Calendulas, Shirley Poppy, Pansy, Nigella, Nemophila (Baby Blue-Eyes, a native wild flower of California), Candytuft, Clarkia, Godetia. For bedding: annual Saponaria calabrica.

PACIFIC SOUTHWEST

Beginning of second planting season. Month of preparation for winter and next spring. Plant out material from pots and cans. Give Chrysanthemums much attention from now on — plenty of water; a possible mulch. Pick off extra buds and be sure stakes are tall enough.

Reset Iris Germanica and put in new plants. Set this Iris in full sun. Prick out Calendulas, Snowdrops, Tulips, bulbous Iris, Ixias, Oxalis, Sparaxis, now. Plant in shade or partial shade; cover if planted in sun. Ready to be set in now are: Watsonias, Montbretias, Madonna Lilies, Baby Gladioli, Antholyza.

Be careful of your watering now; allow foliage to dry off before sundown. September's temperature is variable, with high day temperatures, and sometimes drops of 30 degrees at night. Irrigate in the morning.

Keep up the fight against aphis, snails. Give winter blooming shrubs a little fertilizer; keep watered.

Stock or any flowering plant and transplant to another flat or box. If growth is strong, plant in pots. Keep Camellias watered; add peat moss; do not cultivate deeply.

Primroses, Violas, Pansies may be started now to bloom in early spring. Sow in some plants with your bulbs, to bloom when bulbous plants are through. Wait until next month to plant wild flower seeds and most of the annuals for spring color. Sow Nemesia now to bloom in February. Among the perennials, plant Snapdragon now.

Purchase bulbs of Narcissi, Freesias, Ranunculus, Anemones, Grape Hyacinths, Snowflakes, Snowdrops, Tulips, bulbous Iris, Ixias, Oxalis, Sparaxis, now.

PACIFIC NORTHWEST

This month the spring flowering bulbs appear on the market — Hyacinths, Snowdrops, Scillas, Muscari, Crocus, Narcissus, Tulips, etc. Prepare now for planting them.

Lawns: This is your last month for Northwestern lawn making. Lawns seeded after the 20th are seldom satisfactory. Plant lawn seed as early this month as possible.

Pull out annual flowers that are through blooming, to keep from going to seed. Let best plants produce seed, of course. Self-grown annuals will come into bloom earlier than others next season.

Transplant evergreen trees and shrubs now.

Stake and support the tall things in your garden in September to keep them from breaking down in the first storm. Examples: Chrysanthemums, Michaelmas Daisies.

Plant Iris now (Tall Bearded, Japanese and Siberian). Don't plant too deep. Rhizomes on Bearded Iris should lie near surface; only roots are covered.

Divide Peony roots now, or move those wrongly located.

Secure a number of wired wooden plant labels (easy to write on), for labeling Dahlia roots when dug for winter storage later in fall. Use labels for marking Gladiolus bulbs to keep colors and varieties separate. Also for marking trees, shrubs, plants.

Did you make notes last April or May about the placing and color arrangement for your bulbs? Look them up now, and plan for next spring. Inspect bulbs for storage rot or disease signs. If they show any signs "dip" them before fall planting.

WHAT TO DO IN OCTOBER

PACIFIC CENTRAL

Plant bulbs of Daffodils, Narcissi, Tulips, Hyacinths, Lilies, and many of the smaller bulbous plants as early as ready in the market. Should fall season be very warm, it might be well to wait until November before planting out, to prevent too early blooming. Early blooming Gladiolus can still be planted. The large-flowered Gladiolus can also be planted out for early blooming.

Last month in which lawns can be put in with absolute safety.

Seeds of flowers sown during this month must be sown under glass. Seeds of Forget-Me-Nots for late winter blooming can be sown in the open.

For riotous color in a garden corner during the winter months, sow Pansies, Violas, and winter flowering Stocks this month.

Clean up perennial border. Cut back hardy Asters, Phlox, Delphiniums, Hollyhocks. Dig and subdivide larger clumps to fill any existing spaces. Dig in leaves or decayed matter; fertilize border. Weed, cut and water lawn regularly. Seeds of hardy annuals to sow in open ground this month: Eschscholtzias, Lupines, Godetias, Nemophilas, Poppies, Larkspurs, Scarlet Flax, Hollyhocks.

October is one of the best fall months in which to seed your lawn. Do not delay until ground is too cold. Put in cuttings of Geraniums, Penstemons, Lavender. Hoe over beds filled with dormant bulbs.

Watch Chrysanthemums for aphis, mealy bugs, ants. Mulch with tobacco meal.; stake plants well; spray, taking care to avoid damaging blooms.

PACIFIC SOUTHWEST

Repot your house plants now. Pot up Begonia slips which have rooted. Prepare those bulbous plants as you wish to grow in pots. Set bulb with tip at surface. Provide drainage. Set in dark for six weeks or until pot is full of roots. Bring to light gradually. For growing bulbs in water and stones: Narcissi, Soleil d'Or, Chinese Lily, Paper Whites, Grand Monarch.

Reset such perennials as Shasta Daisy, Phlox, Heuchera, Columbine, Geum. Plant more Calendulas and Nasturtiums for January bloom. Sow hardy annuals: Poppies, Larkspurs, Scabiosa, Sweet Alyssum, Godetia, Clarkia, Nemophila, Nemesias.

Lawn can still be renewed. Let water dry off before night. This prevents new grass from rotting. Iris may still be reset and new ones planted.

Generally speaking, October is the month of bulb planting in the Southwest. For fern beds, under trees, in the shady border: Scillas (Blue Bells), Chionodoxas, Snowdrops, Snowflakes, French-Roman Hyacinths. Plant Crocuses in the shade.

Perennial border: Replace old perennials with Calendulas, Stock, Dimorphothecas, Violas, Primroses, Pansies. Plant a few Narcissus bulbs in border. Drop Nasturtium seeds (tall variety) around German Iris. For covering the bulb beds, try annual Phlox, Nemesia, Linaria, Aubrietia, Virginia Stock, Nemophila, Alyssum, Clarkia, Godetia.

Water your Roses, but do not feed too much. Give Azaleas and Camellias peat; keep watered.

PACIFIC NORTHWEST

October is a good month in the Northwest to start early annual flowers from seed. Scatter seeds thinly over well prepared soil. Let rains cover them. Don't expect much growth this fall or winter. These will give you flowers weeks earlier than spring sown seed. Very satisfactory for this fall planting are: Ageratum, Alyssum, Arctotis, Anchusa, Bachelor Button, Cacalia, Calendula, Clarkia, Calliopsis, Chinese Forget-Me-Not, Euphorbia, Evening Scented Stocks, Larkspur, Lupine, Nemophila, Nigella, Pinks, Poppy, Virginia Stocks.

Plant spring flowering bulbs now. Tulips, Daffodils, Narcissus, Crocus, Hyacinths, Scillas, Grape Hyacinths, Dutch Iris, Spanish Iris, Anemone, Chionodoxa, Eranthis, Galanthus, Ranunculus, Fritillaria, Ixia, Ornithogalum, are all to be planted in the fall.

Dig Gladiolus and Dahlia bulbs; dry and store in frost-proof place that is not too warm. Divide and transplant perennials that make early spring growth. October is month's good weather gives you an opportunity to do much garden work for next season. Your work next spring will be lightened.

Lawns: Cut regularly and fertilize. Use complete fertilizer containing good proportion of phosphates and potash.

Pests: Remove matured plants and waste plant material from garden as early as possible. Add to compost pile; turn under. This destroys many garden pests-to-be for next season.

Gather up leaves as they fall, remove to compost heap, mix with a little earth.

WHAT TO DO IN NOVEMBER

PACIFIC CENTRAL

Good month for transplanting trees and shrubs, after abundant rains, and cool weather have set in. Open up ground. Fertilize heavily with barnyard and poultry manures. Put mulch of straw manure, peat, or leaf mold about perennials, annuals for winter blooming, and half hardy shrubs. The mulch keeps the surface soil from freezing.

Clean up garden thoroughly, either burning all trash and using ash for fertilizer, or placing it in compost heap. Compost material should be treated with lime to kill insects and destroy eggs. Prune deciduous trees and shrubs, Roses, if in dormant condition. Prune broad-leaved evergreens by thinning out centers and cutting back tops. Burn prunings.

Rake old lawns vigorously. Lift sod with fork if very compact. Bulbous plants can still be planted out during this month. Spray fruit trees with cleanup spray such as lime-sulphur in late November, if trees are dormant.

Sow the following now in cold-frames: Perpetual Branching and Dwarf Ten Weeks Stocks; Stokesia cyanea; Statice sinuate and caspia; Antirrhinum (Snapdragon) mixed, tall or medium; Scabiosa, Salvia azurea and S. farinacea, Delphinium (hybrid mixed), and D. chinense, Physostegia, Primula, Pentstemon, Foxglove, Sweet William, Godetia, Lupine (in variety), Larkspur (annual), Phlox (annual), Pyrethrum hybrids, Cineraria, Arctotis, Coreopsis, Dianthus.

These may be planted out now: Violets, single and double; Foxglove, Myosotis, Primroses, Wallflower (mixed), Columbine, Agapanthus, Pansies, Violas.

PACIFIC SOUTHWEST

All seedlings in flats should go out into the garden now for winter blooms. The sooner the better—growth is slow in cold weather. Watch for aphis and snails on the tender shoots for your Madonna Lilies, which are probably up now. Gorgeous berried shrubs are being displayed at the nurseries; now is the time to make your selections. Pyracanthas are most popular; then Cotoneasters.

If your Dahlias are through blooming, cut down. Don't disturb labels—you'll want to refer to them next year. Allow tubers to remain in the ground until February.

The planting of all bulbs may be continued this month. Plant as soon as they arrive. Try Jonquils this fall. Gladiolus corms may be planted, but flowers will come no sooner than if you wait until February.

For Christmas Flowers: November is the time to start bulbs growing in water with stones so that you will have flowers next month. Good varieties to use for this are Chinese Lilies, Paper White Narcissus, and Narcissus Soleil d'Or. The base of the bulb should rest on the edge of two or three stones, the stones being used merely as supports. If the bottom surface of the bulb is covered, the roots will not be able to grow. The best appearance is achieved with three bulbs per bowl. Keep in the dark for two weeks until the roots are started. Bring to the light then. The water should not come up any higher than the base of the bulbs—this avoids a rotting off of the upper part. Paper Whites and Chinese Lilies will bloom two weeks earlier than the variety Soleil d'Or.

PACIFIC NORTHWEST

In the latter part of this month, plant Sweet Peas for next season. Plant seeds deeper than for spring planting. In the Puget Sound country you can have Sweet Peas for more than six months each year if you plant in the fall.

Last chance to plant spring flowering bulbs —Tulips, Narcissus, Hyacinths. Early planting gives best results.

Dig your last Gladiolus and Dahlia bulbs before end of the month and put away in a dark, dry, well ventilated place. Spread them out so they won't spoil. Don't put bulbs in your storeroom until they are dry and clean. They keep better that way.

Save little Glad bulblets or cormels by planting in the fall. Plant in rows or broadcast, covering just enough to hide the bulbs.

Fertilize your lawn sometime this month. Use complete commercial fertilizer high in phosphates and potash.

Rock gardens: Plant Aubrietias, Dianthuses and the mossy Saxifrages now.

Set out Pansy plants for winter blooms. Plant Japan Quince, Snowberry, Oregon Grape. Sow seeds of Clarkia, Candytuft, Larkspur, Sweet Alyssum, Chinese Forget-Me-Not, and other hardy annuals, Plant Kolkwitzia amabili, Buddleia alterfolia, Viburnum carlesi.

Plant Oriental Flowering Trees, upright and drooping varieties, such as Pink Flowering Dogwood (Cornus florida rubra). Set out Hawthorns, Washington thorn and double-flowering red and rose types, for berries. Plant dwarf and prostrate evergreens for winter color in the rockery.

WHAT TO DO IN DECEMBER

PACIFIC CENTRAL

Best month in which to set out deciduous trees and shrubs, fruit trees, and roses with naked roots. Spray dormant trees and deciduous ornamentals with Bordeaux mixture for fungous diseases, lime-sulphur oil sprays for scale and sucking insects, or combination of Bordeaux and lead arsenate to catch both fungous pests and leaf eating insects.

Conifers can be transplanted with safety during this month. Also good month in which to set out all kinds of ornamentals. Seeds of Cornflower, Calendula, Lavender Primrose, Pansies, Violas, and other early blooming flowers can be sown under glass during this month. Most of the bulbous plants can be planted at this time, if fall planting has been delayed.

Much should be done this month in cleaning up the garden. Clear away rubbish; cut off dead tops. Place leaves in a pile to decay, later to be dug into soil for humus. Remove rubbish from base of trees and shrubs. Examine Agapanthus, Crinum and Iris for snails and slugs. Do your winter spraying now.

It's pruning time now. This important work should be done without delay. Cut out dead wood; remove weak growth from Roses, flowering shrubs and trees. Cut back Rose bushes to within one to two feet of ground. Cut out dead wood of flowering shrubs. Prune severely evergreen and berried shrubs.

Look over garden, checking on sections not recently fertilized; arrange to do so now. Citrus trees and other fruit trees and ornamentals should have a good commercial fertilizer worked in around roots.

PACIFIC SOUTHWEST

There are still many bulbs on the market which may be planted now: Ranunculus, Anemone, Tulips, Hyacinths, Lilies, Gladiolus corms (don't overlook the primulinus type when making a selection). Gladioli planted this month should bloom in June.

Give your wooden plant labels a coat of white paint. Paint stakes dark green. Plant Sweet Peas, using the early Spencers for Southern California. Take care with watering Sweet Peas; cold water should not rest against tender stems. Make a trench alongside the row and let the water run into it.

For flowers in March you must rely on plants, not seeds. Nurseries can still supply Phlox, Larkspur, Violas, Pansies, Calendulas, Snapdragons, Stock and many perennials. Prune Roses, and purchase new ones. If you have never grown Roses, plan to do so now. Dig up the soil deep down, add screened cow manure (comes in sacks), and a little sand if soil is hard. Wet down good; cultivate. Be ready to plant in late December or January.

Tulips, Narcissi, Daffodils, Gladiolus, Muscari, Crocus, Amaryllis, Freesias, Iris of all kinds, Montbretias, Ixias, Scillas, Watsonias, Tigridia, Ranunculus, Anemones, Brodiaeas, some Lilies, Calochorus and other native bulbous plants may be left in ground for several years, forming daughter bulbs flowering next season. After three years, take up, clean, dry, store away in dry, cool place. Dig up soil, lime it, fertilize later with balanced fertilizer before replanting in fall or early spring.

PACIFIC NORTHWEST

Plan your next year's garden now. Send for the new seed and plant catalogues and select the new things you want to try. Make a diagram or drawing of your garden and mark locations for your plants. Avoid confusion by planning ahead for color schemes, arrangement, etc.

If you are planting evergreens, are you taking care to leave a depression in the soil around them so that water shed by the foliage will run back toward the trunk?

You still have time to plant a few seeds for early bloom next year. Sweet peas may be planted before mid-December, during good weather; also Sweet Alyssum, Clarkia, Marigold, Ageratum, Snapdragon, Cosmos, California Poppy, Arctotis, Blue Lace Flower, Calendula, Godetia, Centaurea cyaneus and imperalis, Candytuft, Calliopsis, Cacalia.

If there is mild weather, mow the lawn. Grass should not get too long during the winter.

Spray fruit trees this month with reliable dormant spray, such as lime and sulphur or oil-base spray. This kills many insects, prevents growth of moss and lichens. Cover entire surface of all branches. Spray again in spring.

Northwest gardens and woods reveal several varieties of ferns, beautiful at this time of year. Press fern leaves for table and gift decorations.

If you have not already done so, mulch your lawn this month with ground peat (horticultural peat moss).

Christmas note: Bulbs make good gifts.

121

BLOOM

Calendar

THE FLOWER CHART which appears on the following pages is designed to give a complete year-round garden calendar for the
Pacific West, indicating what flowers and shrubs may be expected
to bloom each month, when to set out plants to produce flowers at
a stated time, and the months in which certain flowering shrubs exhibit special fruits and berries. Here in the West it is possible to
have something in bloom every month in the year provided the
planting scheme is worked out with that aim in view.

While this calendar is based largely upon garden data of the
San Francisco Bay Region, it applies with few exceptions to the
interior of California, to Southern California, and to all sections of
the state where extremes of temperature are not encountered.
Tropical and subtropical plants and shrubs have not been given.
The chart applies also to the Pacific Northwest, but it is wise to substitute hardy broad-leaved evergreens and deciduous shrubs for the
more tender varieties.

The time for planting bulbs remains about the same everywhere
in the West. The bloom of annuals and perennials can be hastened
in the colder sections by sowing the seeds under glass. The planting
of shrubs and trees in containers can be safely done at any time of
the year provided extremes of temperature, much dryness or excessive wetness are not experienced. Deciduous trees, shrubs and
roses with bare roots can be planted from November to April, depending again upon the season. In case of doubt, always ask your
local nurseryman.

To use this calendar to best advantage it is suggested that the
home gardener obtain a blank notebook and divide it into monthly
divisions. By a study of his garden, together with this calendar of
bloom, he can then make his own *planting* calendar, jotting down
under the correct headings the varieties he needs to plant in order
to round out his garden.

FOR FLOWERS IN JANUARY

NAMES	COLORS	WHEN TO PLANT
ANNUALS		
Lavender or Chinese Primrose (Primula malacoides)	Lavender-mauve	Set plants in October, November. Plant seeds in August.
Cornflowers—Single and Double varieties (Centaurea cyaneus)	Pink, rose, blue	Set plants in September, October. Plant seeds in August.
Royal Sweet Sultan (Centaurea imperialis)	White, rose, purple, lavender	Set plants in September, October. Plant seeds in August.
Cape Marigold—in variety (Calendula officinalis)	Orange, yellow, cream	Set plants in October, November. Plant seeds in August.
Virginia Stocks (Malcomia maritima)	Red, white, crimson, rose, lilac	Sow seeds all year.
Pansies	All colors	Set plants in October. Plant seeds in August and March.
Violas	Blue, white, lilac, apricot, yellow	Set plants in October. Plant seeds in August.
Mignonette Hybrids	Yellow, white, pink	Sow seeds in September, October.
Winter-blooming Stocks—Nice strain *Mathiola*	Lavender, purple, pink, white, red	Set plants in September, October. Plant seeds in August and September.
PERENNIALS		
Violets—in variety	Blue, pink, violet, mauve	Set plants in November.
English Primrose (Primula acaulis)	Pale yellow, blue	Plant clumps September to November.
Cotyledons—in variety (Hen-and-Chickens)	White, yellow, red, purple, orange	Divide roots October, November.
Pink Saxifrage (Saxifraga crassifolia)	Deep pink	Plant clumps October.
Aubrietias—in variety (Purple Cress)	Purple, lilac, rose, lavender	Plant clumps October, November.
Libonia floribunda	Scarlet, yellow	Plant clumps October, November.
Christmas Rose (Helleborus)	White	Divide roots September, October.
Forget-Me-Not (Myosotis)	Blue, pink, indigo	Set plants in October, November.
Mesembryanthemum—in variety	Pink, rose, white, yellow, red	Divide plants October to January, set new plants November, December.
BULBOUS PLANTS		Plant Bulbs
Spring Snowflake (Leucojum vernum)	White	Plant from September to November.
Wild Crocus—Spring-blooming	Yellow, white, lavender	Plant October, November.
Dutch Crocus	Purple, blue, white	Plant October, November.
Paper-white Narcissus		Plant from September to December.
Jonquils	Golden yellow	Plant from September to December.
Winter Aconite (Eranthis hyemalis)		Divide roots October to December.
Narcissus—(Chinese Sacred Lily)		Plant from September to December.
Amaryllis Family (Hippeastrum)	Red, orange	Plant from September to November.
Common Calla (Zantedeschia Aethiopica)	White	Plant from September to December.
Winter-blooming Oxalis	Rose, white	Plant from September to December.
Winter-blooming Iris (Iris stylosa)	Blue	Plant from September to December, and March to April.
Dutch Hyacinth	Many colors	Plant from September to October.
Cyclamen	White, pink, rose, salmon, red	Plant from September to October.
EVERGREEN FLOWERING SHRUBS		Plant Any Time
Silver Wattle* (Acacia decurrens dealbata)	Golden yellow	Blooms January to March.
Bailey Acacia* (Acacia baileyana)	Golden yellow	Blooms December, January.
Australia Beach* (Eucalyptus polyanthemos)	White	Blooms December to May.
Cassia* (Cassia tomentosa)	Golden yellow	Intermittent bloom.
Blue Gum* (Eucalyptus globulus)	Yellowish white	Blooms December to May.
Australian Mock Orange* (Pittosporum undulatum)	White	Blooms December to July.
Flowering Oak* (Chorizema ilicifolia)	Orange-yellow	Blooms December to March.
Pin-cushion Flower* (Hakea laurina)	Crimson	Blooms December to March.
Hakea elliptica*	White	Blooms December to March.

Not recommended for the Northwest.

NAMES	COLORS	WHEN TO PLANT
Orange Cestrum* (Cestrum aurantiacum)	Orange-yellow	Blooms December to February.
Night-blooming Jasmine* (Cestrum nocturnum)	Creamy yellow	Blooms December to April and intermittently.
Aloe*—in variety	Scarlet	Blooms December to March.
Honey Flower* (Melianthus major)	Chocolate-red-brown	Blooms December to February.
Tree Cineraria* (Cineraria maritima)	Yellow	Blooms December to March.
Poinsettia* (Euphorbia pulcherrima)	Vermilion-red	Blooms November to March.
Bauhinia purpurea*	White-red-purple	Blooms December to May.
Buddleia asiatica	Purple-yellow	Blooms December to March.
Daphne (Daphne odora)	White, pink	Blooms December to May.
Bouvardia*	Pink, white, yellow, scarlet in variety	Blooms September to January.
DECIDUOUS FLOWERING SHRUBS		**Plant November to April**
Japanese Magnolia (Magnolia soulangeana)	White, purple	Blooms December to April.
Japanese Quince—in variety (Cydonia japonica)	White, scarlet, pink, rose	Blooms January to April.
Double Pink-flowered Apricot (Prunus mume)		Blooms January, February.
Purple-leaved Plum (Prunus pissardi)	Purple, pink	Blooms January to April.
FLOWERING VINES		**Plant November to April**
Evergreen Trumpet Creeper* (Bignonia venusta)	Orange, crimson	Blooms December to February.
Australian Pea Vine* (Dolichos lignosus)	Magenta	Blooms December to June.
Parrot's Bill (Clianthus puniceus)	Deep red	Blooms December to February.
Copa de Ora*—(Cup of Gold) (Solandra guttata)	Golden yellow	Blooms December to April

FOR FLOWERS IN FEBRUARY

NAMES	COLORS	WHEN TO PLANT
ANNUALS		
Pansies	Many colors	Set plants in October, November. Sow seeds in August and September.
Violas	Blue, white, lilac, apricot, yellow, purple.	Set plants in October, November. Sow seeds in August and September.
Lavender or Chinese Primrose (Primula malacoides)	Lavender-mauve	Set plants in October, November. Sow seeds in August and September.
Winter-blooming Stocks—Nice strain	Lavender, purple, pink, white, red	Set plants in October. Sow seeds in August and September.
Snapdragons	Many colors	Set plants in November, December. Sow seeds in August and September.
PERENNIALS		
Primula polyantha	Red, blue, cream, yellow, orange	Divide clumps from October to December or after blooming.
Primula kewensis	Yellow	Plant clumps in October, November.
Primula acaulis	Pale yellow, blue	Plant clumps from September to November.
Violets	Blue, pink, lilac, mauve	Set plants in December-January or after blooming.
Aubrietia—in variety	Purple, lilac, rose	Plant clumps from October to January.
English Daisy (Bellis perennis)	Rose, pink, white	Plant clumps and new plants from October to January.
Mesembryanthemum—in variety	Pink, rose, white, yellow, red	Divide clumps from October to January.
Myosotis (Forget-Me-Not—in variety)	Blue, pink, indigo	Set plants in October, November.
Zanzibar Balsam	White, red, pink, yellow	Set plants in January.
BULBOUS PLANTS		
Dwarf Iris (Iris pumila)	White, yellow, blue, purple	Plant from August to November.
Squills (Scilla campanulata)	Blue, white, lilac, pink	Plant October, November.
Spring Snowflake (Leucojum vernum)	White	Plant from September to November.

* Not recommended for the Northwest.

NAMES	COLORS	WHEN TO PLANT
Spring-blooming Wild Crocus	Yellow, white, lavender	Plant from October to December.
Dutch Crocus	Purple, blue, white	Plant from October to December.
Dutch Hyacinth	Many colors	Plant in September, October.
Roman Hyacinth	White, pink, blue	Plant in September, October.
Jonquils	Golden yellow	Plant from September to December.
Daffodils—Trumpet varieties	Yellow	Plant from October to December.
Narcissus	White and colored cups	Plant from October to December.
Poeticus and Poetaz varieties		
Narcissus—Leedsii hybrids	Cream-white	Plant from September to December.
Winter Aconite	Blue	Divide roots October to December.
(Eranthis hyemalis)		
Shooting Star	Pink, brown, yellow, rose	Plant in September.
(Dodecatheon)		
Winter-blooming Oxalis	Rose, white	Plant from September to December.
Cyclamen	White, pink, rose, salmon, red	Plant October, November.
Wake-Robin	Violet, white, greenish	Plant September to November.
(Trillium)		
EVERGREEN FLOWERING SHRUBS		**Plant Any Time**
White Ironbark*	Pink	Blooms January to April.
(Eucalyptus leucoxylon)		
Knife-leaved Acacia*	Golden yellow	Blooms January to April.
(Acacia cultriformis)		
Acacia pravissima*	Soft yellow	Blooms January to April.
Sydney Golden Wattle*	Golden yellow	Blooms February, March.
(Acacia longifolia)		
Broad-leaved Wattle*	Yellow	Blooms February, March.
(Acacia pycnantha)		
Kangaroo Thorn*	Clear yellow	Blooms February to April.
Acacia armata)		
Bottle Brush*	Bright red	Blooms January to June.
(Callistemon lanceolatus)		
Buddleia officinalis	Lilac-orange	Blooms February, March.
Flowering Currant	Deep pink	Blooms February to April.
(Ribes sanguineum)		
Bridal Veil Broom*	White	Blooms February to April.
(Genista monosperma)		
French Pussy Willow	Golden yellow—deciduous	Blooms February to April.
(Salix)		

FOR FLOWERS IN MARCH

NAMES	COLORS	WHEN TO PLANT
ANNUALS		
Cornflower	Pink, rose, blue	Set plants in late January.
(Centaurea cyaneus)		Seeds should be sown under glass in December-January.
Cape Marigold	Orange, yellow, cream	Set plants in January, February.
(Calendula officinalis)		Sow seeds under glass in December or January.
Cineraria hybrida	Purple, rose, salmon, white, pink	Plant in October, November.
Star Cineraria	Blue, white, rose	Plant in October, November.
(Cineraria stellata)		
Snapdragon	All colors	Set plants in January.
(Antirrhinum)		Sow seeds in November.
Forget-Me-Not—in variety	Blue, pink, indigo	Set plants in December, January.
(Myosotis)		
Lavender or Chinese Primrose	Lavender-mauve	Set plants in January.
(Primula malacoides)		
Gilias—in variety	Light blue, lilac, yellow	Sow seed in fall or early spring.
Mignonette Hybrids	Yellow, white, pink	Sow seed in January.
Virginia Stocks	Red, white, crimson, rose, lilac	Sow seed in January.
(Malcomia maritima)		
Pansies	Many colors	Set plants in January.
		Sow seeds in December or earlier.
Violas	Blue, white, yellow, lilac, apricot	Set plants in January.
Imperial Stocks—Gillyflowers	Red, pink, yellow, purple	Set plants in January.
Annual Candytuft	White, lilac, rose, purple	Sow seed in fall or early spring.
(Iberis)		
Nasturtium—Vine and Tom Thumb varieties	Many colors	Sow seed in January, February.
PERENNIALS		
Sweet Alyssum	White	Sow seed in January.
Alyssum maritimum)		

* *Not recommended for the Northwest.*

NAMES	COLORS	WHEN TO PLANT
Golden Tuft (Alyssum saxatile)	Golden yellow	Set plants in January, February.
Gypsophila elegans	White	Set plants in January.
Kenilworth Ivy (Linaria cymbalaria)	Lilac-blue	Set plants in January.
Mourning Bride (Scabiosa)	Lavender, blue, rose, pink	Set plants in December-February.
Periwinkle (Vinca minor)	Blue	Divide clumps October to December.
Primula kewensis	Yellow	Set plants in January.
English Primrose (Primula auricula)	Rose, violet	Set plants in January.
Saxifraga—in variety	Many colors	Set plants in September, October.
Wall Cress (Arabis albida)		Divide clumps October-December. Set plants in January.
Aubrietia	Purple, lilac, rose	Set plants in January.
Siberian Wallflower (Cheiranthus allioni)	Bright orange	Set plants in January.

BULBOUS PLANTS

NAMES	COLORS	Plant Bulbs
Iris tingitana	Pale lilac, yellow	Plant in September, October.
Iris oncocyclus and regelia types	Purple, blue, bronze, gray	Plant in October, November.
Moraea Iris	White, yellow, golden yellow	Plant August to November.
Iris—Native species	Yellow, blue, purple, cream	Plant September to November.
Clive Lily (Clivia imantophyllum)	Bright scarlet-yellow	Plant September to November.
Dwarf or Bride Gladiolus	Salmon, red, white, pink	Plant September, October.
Grape Hyacinth (Muscari botryoides)	Purple, blue, white	Plant October to December.
Freesias	Yellow, lavender, pink, white, orange	Plant August, September.
Lily-of-the-Valley (Convallaria majalis)	White	Plant in October.
Cyclamen	White, pink, rose, salmon, red	Set out plants December, January.
Dutch Crocus	Purple, blue, white	Plant October to December.
Spring-blooming Wild Crocus	Yellow, white, lavender	Plant October to December.
Anemone coronaria hybrids	White, pink, rose, deep red, blue, purple	Plant September to November.
Ranunculus—in variety	White, yellow, pink, orange, red	Plant September to November.
Dutch Hyacinths	Many colors	Plant September, October.
Roman Hyacinths	White, pink, blue	Plant September, October.
Babiana	Purple, blue, wine-purple	Plant August, September.
Daffodils—Trumpet varieties	Yellow	Plant October to December.
Narcissus. Poeticus and Poetax varieties.	White and orange-red cups	Plant October to December.
Narcissus. Leedsii and Barri varieties.	Cream-white with colored cups	Plant October to December.
Billbergia	Rose, green	Divide roots October to December.
Winter Aconite (Eranthis hyemalis)		Divide roots October to December.
Lenten Rose (Helleborus orientalis)	White, purple, rose, pink	Plant September to January.
Glory-of-the-Snow (Chionodoxa)	Sky-blue, white	Plant September to December.
Clintonia	Rose-pink, greenish yellow	Plant September to December.
Bleeding Heart (Dicentra spectabilis)	Rose-crimson, white	Plant October, November.
Wake-Robin (Trillium)	White, greenish, violet	Plant in August or September or in February.

EVERGREEN FLOWERING SHRUBS

NAMES	COLORS	Plant Any Time
Blackwood Acacia* (Acacia melanoxylon)	Straw yellow	Blooms March, April.
Ever-blooming Acacia* (Acacia floribunda)	Golden yellow	Blooms February, March and intermittently through the year.
Whorl-leaved Acacia* (Acacia verticillata)	Light yellow	Blooms March, April.
Blue-leaved Wattle* (Acacia cyanophylla)	Golden yellow	Blooms March, April.
Australian Tea Shrub* (Leptospermum laevigatum)	White	Blooms March, April.
White-flowered Bottle-brush* (Melaleuca armillaris)		Blooms March to June.
Red-flowered Bottle-brush* (Callistemon speciosus)		Blooms March to June.
Indian Azalea—in variety (Azalea indica)	Salmon, rose, pink, red	Blooms December to May.
White Heather* (Erica persoluta alba)	Pinkish white	Blooms March, April.
Skimmia japonica	Yellow-white	Blooms March to June.
Aucuba japonica	White	Blooms March to May.

Not recommended for the Northwest.

NAMES	COLORS	WHEN TO PLANT
Carolina Cherry (Prunus caroliniana)	Cream-white	Blooms February to April.
Canary Island Broom (Cytisus canariensis)	Bright yellow	Blooms March to June and intermittently.
DECIDUOUS BLOOMING SHRUBS		**Plant November to April**
Star-flowered Magnolia (Magnolia stellata)	White	Blooms March, April.
Sweet-scented Shrub (Calycanthus floridus)	Reddish brown	Blooms March to May.
Japanese Rose (Kerria japonica)	Yellow	Blooms March to June (practically through year).
Dwarf Flowering Almond (Prunus amygdalus rosea nana)	Pink	Spring blooming.
Double Pink Japanese Plum (Prunus bleiriana)		Spring blooming.
Double Flowering Almond (Prunus triloba)	Pink	Spring blooming.
Flowering Peach—in variety (Prunus persica)	Pink, rose, red, white	Blooms March, April.
Purple-leaved Plum (Prunus pissardi)	Purplish pink flowers	Blooms March to May.
Japanese Flowering Crab (Prunus kaida)	Rose	Blooms March, April.
Golden Bells (Forsythia suspensa)	Golden yellow	Blooms March to May.
FLOWERING VINES		**Plant November to April**
Australian Trumpet Vine* (Bignonia australis)	Creamy white	Blooms March to May.
Yellow Jasmine (Jasminum nudiflorum)	Deep yellow	Blooms February, March.
Daphne mezereum	Lilac-purple	Blooms February to June.

FOR FLOWERS IN APRIL

NAMES	COLORS	WHEN TO PLANT
ANNUALS		
Calliopsis	Yellow, brown, maroon, scarlet	Plant seed under glass in February.
Larkspur (Delphinium ajacis)	Rose, pink, blue	Set plants in March. Sow seeds two months earlier.
Clarkia—in variety	Salmon, rose, pink	Set plants in February, March.
Gilia—in variety	Blue, lilac, yellow	Sow seed in February.
Lobelia—in variety	Light and dark blue, crimson, white	Set plants in March.
Blazing Star (Mentzelia lindleyi)	Golden yellow	Sow seed in October, November.
Nemesia	Many colors	Set plants in February, March.
Pansies	Many colors	Set plants in January, February.
Violas	Blue, white, apricot, yellow, lilac	Set plants in January, February.
Poppies, Shirley Strain (Papaver rhoeas)	Many colors	Sow seed in January, February.
Single Petunia—varieties, Snowball, Rosy Morn.	White, rose-pink	Plant in October, November.
Wild Heliotrope (Phacelia)	Blue, purple, white	Sow seed in October, November or January, February.
Cream Cups (Platystemon californicus)	Cream-white, yellow	Sow seed in October, November or January, February.
Lavender Primrose (Primula malacoides)	Lavender-mauve	Set plants in January, February.
Snapdragons (Antirrhinum)	Many colors	Set plants in February.
Pot Marigold—in variety (Calendula officinalis)	Orange, yellow, cream	Set plants in January, February.
Virginia Stocks (Malcomia maritima)	Red, white, crimson, rose, lilac	Sow seed in January, February.
Zanzibar Balsam	White, red, pink, yellow	Set plants in February, March.
Flowering Flax (Linum grandiflorum)	Red, blue, yellow	Sow seed January to March.
PERENNIALS		
Golden Tuft (Alyssum saxatile)	Golden yellow	Set plants in February.
Coreopsis grandiflora	Golden yellow	Plant clumps October-December. Set young plants in February.

* *Not recommended for the Northwest.*

NAMES	COLORS	WHEN TO PLANT
Poppies—in variety (Eschscholtzia)	Yellow, gold, orange, red	Sow seed in October, November, and January, February.
Creeping Forget-Me-Not (Omphalodes verna)	Blue, white	Set plants in February.
Oriental Poppy—in variety (Papaver orientale)	Orange, red, salmon, pink	Plant clumps August-September. New plants in February, March.
Iceland Poppy (Papaver nudicaule)	Light orange, light yellow, white, orange-scarlet	Plant clumps August-December. New plants in February.
Purple Sage (Salvia leucantha)	White-lavender-purple	Divide roots in February, March.
Mourning Bride—in variety (Scabiosa)	Lavender, blue, rose, pink, red	Set plants in February, March.
Violets	Blue, pink, lilac, mauve	Plant runners January, February.
Pentstemon—in variety (Pentstemon gloxinioides)	Red, pink, white, lavender	Plant clumps in October-January. New plants in February.
Polyantha Primrose (Primula polyantha)	Red, blue, cream, yellow, orange	Set plants in January, February.
Primula auricula	Rose, violet	Set plants in January, February.
Rehmannia angulata	Rosy purple	Plant clumps September-December. New plants in February.
Globe Flower (Trollius)	Yellow	Plant divisions February, March.
Single Daisy (Pyrethrum roseum)	White, red, carmine, pink, rose, lilac, crimson	Plant clumps October-December. New plants February, March.
Siberian Wallflower (Cheiranthus allioni)	Bright orange	Set plants November to February.
Columbine (Aquilegia)	Blue, white, yellow, pink, red	Set plants October to December.
Garden or Clove Pink (Dianthus plumarius)	Pink, rose, white	Plant clumps October-December. New plants January, February.
Maiden Pink (Dianthus deltoides)	Rose, cerise, white	Plant clumps October-December. New plants February, March.
Geum—in variety	Red, golden yellow, orange	Plant clumps October. New plants in January, February.
English Daisy (Bellis perennis)	Rose, white	Plant clumps October-January. New plants January, February.
Cactus—in variety	Rose, crimson, purple, orange, yellow	Plant offsets May-June.
Libonia floribunda	Scarlet-yellow, continuous bloom	Set plants in February.
Mesembryanthemum—in variety	Pink, rose, white, yellow, red	Divide plants October.
Sweet William (Dianthus barbatus)	Pink, rose, maroon, white, scarlet	Plant clumps October-December. New plants January, February.
Carnation (Dianthus caryophyllus)	Red, white, pink, yellow	Plant rooted cuttings January, February.
Leopardbane (Doronicum excelsum)	Bright yellow	Divide clumps September-November. Set new plants March.
Begonia semperflorens—in variety	Red, carmine, rose-red, white	Plant in January, February.
Shasta Daisy—in variety	White	Plant clumps October-January.
Coral Bells (Heuchera sanguinea)	Coral-red, pink	Plant clumps October-December. Set new plants February, March.
Water Lilies (Nymphaea and Lotus)	White, pink, blue, rose, yellow	Plant divisions in February, March.
South African Daisy (Gazania splendens)	White, yellow, orange, scarlet	Plant clumps October-January. Set new plants February.
Blue Bells or Virginia Bells (Mertensia virginica)	Blue	Divide clumps in January, February.
Moss Pink (Phlox subulata)	Lilac, white, pink	Plant clumps October-December. New plants January, February.

BULBOUS PLANTS		Plant Bulbs
Iris—Bearded Iris and German Iris	Many colors	Plant August to March.
Iris oncocyclus and regelia types	Purple, blue, bronze, gray	Plant in October, November.
Dutch Iris	Lavender, yellow, rose, blue, white, orange, cream	Plant July to September.
Iris cristata	Lavender-gold	Plant September to November.
Iris tectorum	Lilac, white	Plant September to November.
Spanish Iris (Iris xiphium)	Bronze, yellow, blue	Plant July to September.
Iris—Native Species	Yellow, blue, purple, cream	Plant January, February.
Tulips—Darwins, Breeders, Cottage	Many colors	Plant October to January.
Anemone coronaria hybrids	White, pink, red, blue, purple	Plant new plants January, February. Bulbs September-November.
Ranunculus—in variety	White, yellow, pink, orange, red	Plant new plants January, February. Bulbs September to November.
Scilla campanulata	Blue, white, lilac, pink	Plant October, November.
Star of Bethlehem (Ornithogalum umbellatum)	White	Plant October, November.
Ornithogalum arabicum	White-black	Plant October, November.
Freesias	Yellow, lavender, pink, white, orange	Plant August, September.
Sparaxis	Scarlet, yellow	Plant September to November.
Babiana	Purple, blue, magenta	Plant September to November.
Tritonia—in variety—Red Freesia	Tan, rose	Plant October, November.
Watsonia—in variety	White, lavender, salmon, pink, coppery red.	Plant July to September.

* Not recommended for the Northwest.

128

NAMES	COLORS	WHEN TO PLANT
Mariposa Lily—in variety (Calochortus)	Creamy white, lilac, yellow	Plant September to November.
Mission Bells (Fritillaria)	Green-brown, purple, orange-scarlet	Plant September to November.
Dog's-Tooth Violet (Erythronium)	White, pink, yellow, cream, rose	Plant September to November.
Brodiaeas—in variety	Crimson, white, blue, yellow, purple	Plant September to November.
Camassia	White, purple, sky-blue	Plant September to November.
Spring Star Flower (Allium)	White, yellow, purple, rose	Plant October, November.
Kaffir Lily (Schizostylis)	Crimson-scarlet	Plant October to December.
Daffodil—Trumpet varieties	Yellow	Plant October to December.
Narcissus—Leedsii and Barri varieties	Cream-white with colored cups	Plant October to December.
Narcissus—Poeticus and Poetaz varieties	White, with orange-red cups	Plant October to December.
African Corn Lily (Ixias)	Blue, white, carmine, red, yellow, orange	Plant September to November.
Lady Tulip (Tulipa clusiana)	White, purple	Plant September, October
Glory-of-the-Snow (Chionodoxa)	White, sky-blue	Plant September to November.
Clive Lily (Clivia imantophyllum)	Bright scarlet-yellow	Plant July to September.
Contonia	Rose-pink, greenish yellow	Plant September to November.
Bleeding Heart (Dicentra spectabilis)	Rose-red, white	Plant October, November.
Winter-blooming Oxalis	Rose, white	Plant October to December.
Lenten Rose (Helleborus orientalis)	White, purple, rose, pink	Plant September to January.
FLOWERING EVERGREEN SHRUBS		**Plant Any Time**
Banana Shrub* (Michelia fuscata)	Brown-purple	Blooms April to June.
Leptospermum scoparium chapmanni*	White, rose, pink	Blooms April, May.
Leptospermum scoparium nicholi*	Carmine	Blooms April, May.
Bottle Brush* (Callistemon rigidus)	Bright red	Blooms April, May.
Pimelia* (Pimelia decussata)	Pink	Blooms April to June.
Japanese Pittosporum* (Pittosporum tobira)	Cream-white	Blooms December to May.
Night-blooming Jasmine* (Cestrum nocturnum)		Blooms January to April and intermittently.
Daphne odora	White, pink	Blooms December to May.
Daphne cneorum—Rose Daphne	Pink	Blooms February to April.
Heather* (Erica persoluta rosea)	Deep pink	Blooms April, May.
Heather* (Erica carnea)	Rose	Blooms March to May.
Osmanthus fragrans*	White	Blooms March to May.
Breath-of-Heaven* (Diosma ericoides)	White	Blooms March to May and intermittently.
Diosma reevesi*	White	Blooms March to June and intermittently.
Texas Umbrella Tree* (Melia azedarach umbraculiformis)		Blooms April, May.
California Lilac (Ceanothus azureus)	Deep blue	Blooms March to June.
California Lilac (Ceanothus spinosus)	Light blue	Blooms March to May.
White California Lilac (Ceanothus verrucosus)		Blooms March to June.
Sand Myrtle* (Leiophyllum buxifolium)	White-pink	Blooms April to June.
Madrone Tree* (Arbutus menziesii)	White	Blooms September to November.
Leucothoe catesbaei	White	Blooms April, May.
Portugal Laurel (Prunus lusitanica)	White	Blooms April to July.
California Cherry (Prunus ilicifolia)	White	Blooms March to May.
Carolina Cherry (Prunus integrifolia)	White	Blooms March to May.
Thunberg's Barberry (Berberis thunbergi)	Pale yellow	Blooms April, May.
Torch Azalea (Azalea kaempferi)	Orange-red	Blooms April, May.
Azalea hexe	Scarlet	Blooms April, May.
Azalea mollis—Flame Azalea in variety	Yellow, orange	Blooms April, May.
Flowering Currant (Ribes ordoratum)	Yellow	Blooms March to May.
Fuchsia-flowered Gooseberry (Ribes speciosum)	Scarlet	Blooms March to June.
Deutzia gracilis	White	Blooms April, May.
Deutzia lemoinei	White	Blooms April, May.

* *Not recommended for the Northwest.*

NAMES	COLORS	WHEN TO PLANT
DECIDUOUS FLOWERING SHRUBS		**Plant November to April**
Pearl Brush (Exochorda grandiflora)	White	Blooms April, May.
Spiraea—Anthony Waterer	Wine-red	Blooms June to October.
Japanese Flowering Cherry (Prunus serrulata)	Pink, white, rose	Blooms April, May.
Prunus cerasus—variety D. H. Veitchii	Cherry	Blooms April, May.
Flowering Crabapple (Pyrus floribunda)	Pale pink, rose	Blooms April, May.
Bechtel's Flowering Crabapple (Pyrus bechteli)	Shell-pink	Blooms April, May.
Sacred Cherry of Japan (Prunus yedoensis)	White-pink	Spring blooming.
Japanese Weeping Cherry (Prunus subhirtella pendula)	Rose-pink	Spring blooming.
Persian Lilac (Syringa persica)	Purple, lilac, rose, blue	Blooms April, May.
Japanese Quince—in variety (Cydonia japonica)	White, scarlet, pink, rose	Blooms January to April.
Red Bud (Cercis canadensis)	Rosy pink	Blooms March to May.
European Red Bud (Cercis siliquastrum)	Purplish rose	Blooms March to May.
Roses	Many colors	Plant dormant plants November to March. Set out potted plants any time.
FLOWERING VINES		**Plant November to April**
Trumpet Vine* (Bignonia violacea)	Lilac	Blooms March to May.
Trumpet Vine* (Bignonia tweediana)	Orange-yellow	Blooms March to May.
Yellow Jasmine (Jasminum primulinum)	Primrose-yellow	Blooms March to May and intermittently
Natal Plum* (Carissa grandiflora)	White	Blooms April, May.
Copa de Ora* (Cup of Gold) (Solandra guttata)	Golden yellow	Blooms March to May.
Akebia quinata*	Purple-brown	Blooms April, May.

FOR FLOWERS IN MAY

NAMES	COLORS	WHEN TO PLANT
ANNUALS		
African Blue Daisy (Arctotis)	Bluish white	Set plants in March.
Chrysanthemum—Annuals in variety	All colors	Sow seed in February.
Clarkia	Salmon, rose, pink	Set plants in March, April.
Nasturtium—Vine and Tom Thumb varieties	All colors	Sow seed in March.
Larkspur (Delphinium ajacis)	Rose, pink, blue	Set plants in March, April.
Farewell-to-Spring (Godetia)	Carmine, crimson, pink	Set plants in March, April.
Baby-Blue-Eyes (Nemophila)	Blue, white	Sow seed from September to February.
Iberis—Annual Candytuft in variety	White, lilac, rose, purple	Sow seed September to November, February to March.
Lobelia—in variety	White, blue, rose, crimson, purple	Plant in March.
Love-in-the-Mist—Variety Miss Jekyll (Nigella)	Blue	Sow seed from September to November, February to April.
Pansies	All colors	Set plants in February, March.
Violas	Blue, white, lilac, yellow, apricot, purple	Set plants in February, March.
Petunias—Large flowered and ruffled varieties	Many colors	Set plants in March, April.
Wild Heliotrope (Phacelia)	Blue, purple, white	Sow seed September to November, February to March.
Phlox drummondii	Many colors	Set plants in March, April.
Painted Glory (Salpiglossis)	Many colors	Set plants in March, April.
Butterfly Plant (Schizanthus)	Many colors	Plant in March, April.
Everlasting Flower (Statice sinuata)	Yellowish white, blue	Set plants in March, April.
Cineraria hybrida	Purple, rose, salmon, white, pink	Set plants in February, March.
Star Cineraria (Cineraria stellata)	Purple, rose, white	Set plants in February, March.

Not recommended for the Northwest.

NAMES	COLORS	WHEN TO PLANT
Snapdragons (Antirrhinum)	Many colors	Set plants in March.
Imperial Stocks—Gillyflowers	Red, pink, yellow, purple, white	Plant in March.
PERENNIALS		
Golden Tuft (Alyssum saxatile)	Golden yellow	Set plants in March, April.
Shasta Daisy	White	Divide clumps from September to January. Set new plants in March.
Baby's Breath ((Gypsophila elegans)	White	Set plants in January, February.
Perennial Candytuft (Iberis sempervirens)	White, lilac, rose	Set plants February, March.
Iberis gibraltarica	Pink-white	Set plants February, March.
Flax (Linum perenne)	Sky-blue	Divide roots in February, March.
Nicotiana affinis and hybrids	White, crimson, rose, purple	Set plants March, April.
Oriental Poppy (Papaver orientale)	Orange, red, salmon, pink	Divide roots August to December. Set plants February, March.
Iceland Poppy (Papaver nudicaule)	light orange, yellow, white, orange-scarlet	Divide clumps August to November. Set new plants February, March.
Violets—in variety	Blue, pink, lilac, mauve	Plant runners January, February.
Periwinkle (Vinca minor)	Blue	Divide clumps October to January.
Yellow Primrose (Primula kewensis)		Divide clumps or new plants January to April.
English Primrose—in variety (Primula acaulis)	Pale yellow, blue and other colors	Divide clumps and new plants January to April.
Single Daisy—in variety (Pyrethrum)	White, red, pink, rose, crimson, lilac	Plant clumps October to December. Set new plants February, March.
Saxifraga—in variety	Many colors	Plant in September to November, or January to March.
Feathered Columbine (Thalictrum aquilegifolium)	Purple white	Plant clumps November to January. Set new plants in March.
Veronica teucrium and other creeping kinds	Blue	Divide clumps October to March. Set new plants in March.
Delphinium hybrida—in many strains	Shades of blue, pink, opal	Plant clumps October to December. Set new plants in March.
Delphinium formosum	Indigo blue, violet	Plant clumps October to December. Set new plants in March.
Verbena	Many colors, pink, red, purple, white	Plant in March.
Siberian Wallflower (Cheiranthus allioni)	Bright orange	Set plants March, April.
Wallflower (Cheiranthus cheiri)	Yellow, brown, russet, purple	Plant clumps October to December. Set new plants March, April.
Columbine—in species and varieties (Aquilegia)	Yellow, blue, white, pink, red, purple	Plant clumps and new plants September to December.
Day Lily—in variety (Hemerocallis)	Orange, yellow, copper	Divide clumps October to January. Set new plants February, March.
Purse Flower (Calceolaria)	Brown, yellow, mahogany	Plant clumps October to December. Set new plants March, April.
Rock Cress (Arabis albida)	White	Divide clumps October to December. Set new plants March, April.
Purple Cress (Aubrieta)	Purple, lilac, rose	Plant February, March.
Cactus—in variety	Rose, crimson, purple, orange, yellow	Division and offsets in April.
Canterbury Bells (Campanula medium)	Purple, rose, pink, white	Clumps and new plants October to December.
Hollyhocks—Single and double varieties	Many colors	Set plants and clumps October to January.
Mesembryanthemum—in variety	Pink, white, rose, yellow, red	Divide plants from October to January. Set new plants February, March.
Catnip (Nepeta mussini)	Lavender-mauve	Plant clumps October to January. Set new plants March to May.
Peony (Paeonia)	Many colors. (Not recommended for Southern California)	Divide clumps October to December.
Garden Pink (Dianthus plumarius)	Pink, rose, white	Plant clumps October to December. Set new plants in February, March.
Sweet William (Dianthus barbatus)	Pink, rose, maroon, scarlet, white	Plant clumps October to December. Set new plants in March.
Carnations—Chabaud's and Marguerite varieties	Pink, rose, white, crimson, red, yellow	Plant in March or October.
Mexican Poppy (Erigeron mucronatus)	Pink-white	Set plants in February, March.
Matalija Poppy (Romneya coulteri)	White with gold centers	Plant clumps October to December. Set new plants in March.
Begonia—Fibrous-rooted varieties	Red, rose, pink, white	Plant rooted cuttings February, March.
Coral Bells (Heuchera sanguinea)	Coral red, pink	Plant clumps October to December. Set new plants February to April.
Forget-Me-Not—in variety (Myosotis)	Blue, pink, indigo	Plant clumps of perennial kinds October to December. Set new plants in February, March.

Not recommended for the Northwest.

NAMES	COLORS	WHEN TO PLANT
Virginia Blue Bells (Mertensia virginica)		Plant clumps October to December. Set new plants in March.
Moss Pink (Phlox subulata)	Lilac, white, pink	Divide clumps October to December. Set new plants February, March.
Sedums—creeping varieties	Yellow, white, pink	Divide clumps October to March.

BULBOUS PLANTS

NAMES	COLORS	WHEN TO PLANT
Iris—Bearded and German Iris	Many colors	Plant June to September.
Spanish Iris (Iris xiphium)	Bronze, yellow, blue	Plant July to September.
English Iris	White, lavender, purple	Plant July to September.
Iris—Spuria hybrids	Yellow, white, purple, blue, lavender	Plant September to January.
Iris ochroleuca	Creamy white	Plant September to January.
Tall Crested Iris (Iris fimbriata)	Lilac-yellow	Plant August to December.
Tulips—Darwins, Breeders, Cottage varieties	Many colors	Plant October to January.
Anemone coronaria—in variety	White, pink, rose, red, blue, purple	Plant bulbs September to November. Set new plants March.
Ranunculus—in variety	White, yellow, pink, orange, red	Plant clumps September to November. Set new plants in March.
Star of Bethlehem (Ornithogalum umbellatum)	White	Plant October, November.
Freesias	Yellow, lavender, pink, white, orange	Plant August, September.
Sparaxis	Scarlet, yellow	Plant September to November.
Babiana	Purple, blue, magneta	Plant September to November.
Watsonia—in variety	White, lavender, salmon, pink, coppery red	Plant July to September.
Mariposa Lily (Calochortus)	Creamy white, lilac, yellow	Plant September to November.
Peruvian Lily (Alstromeria)	Golden yellow, orange-red	Plant September to November.
Lilium umbellatum	Orange-red	Plant October to December.
Lilium hansoni	Bright orange	Plant October to December.
Bleeding Heart (Dicentra spectabilis)	Rose-red, white	Plant February, March.
Oxalis	Rose, white	Plant February, March.
Gladiolus—Large-flowered types	All colors	Plant January-February.

EVERGREEN BLOOMING SHRUBS

NAMES	COLORS	Plant Any Time
Manna Gum* (Eucalyptus viminalis)	White	Blooms May to August.
Small-flowered Bottle Brush (Melaleuca nesophila)	Lavender-rose-pink	Blooms May to September.
Scorpion Senna* (Coronilla emerus)	Yellow-red	Blooms May to July.
Tamarix (Tamarix pentandra)	Pink	Blooms March to June.
Tamarix africana	Delicate pink	Blooms April to June.
Viburnum carlsii	Pink-white	Blooms April to June.
Viburnum odoratissimum	White	Blooms May to June.
Geranium (Pelargonium)	All colors	Blooms April to November.
Fabiana imbricata*	White, intermittent bloom	Blooms May to June.
Veronica hulkeana*	Lavender white	Blooms April to May.
Berberis stenophylla	Golden yellow	Blooms, May, June.
Berberis dulcis	Yellow	Blooms May, June.
Cotoneaster—in different species	White, pinkish white	Blooms May, June and intermittently.
Azalea pontica	Purple-brown	Blooms May, June.
Rhododendron himalayan	White	Blooms April, May.
Rhododendron californicum	Rosy purplish pink	Blooms May, June.
Rhododendron Hybrids	All colors	Bloom May, June.
Pyracantha—Evergreen Hawthorn—in variety	White	Blooms May, June.
Chinese Sacred Bamboo (Nandina domestica)	White	Blooms March to August.
Viburnum rhytidophyllum	Yellowish white	Blooms May, June.
Viburnum tinus lucidum	Pinkish white	Blooms May, June.
Photinia davidsoniae	White	Blooms May, June.
Spanish Bayonet (Yucca filamentosa)	White	Blooms April to June.
Grevillea banksii*	Crimson	Blooms April, May.
Silk Oak Tree* (Grevillea robusta)	Rusty orange	Blooms April, May.
California Tree Lilac (Ceanothus arboreus)	Pale blue	Blooms March to June.
California Lilac (Ceanothus thyrsiflorus)	Lavender-blue	Blooms May to July.
Lilac (Ceanothus cyaneus)	Deep blue	Blooms March to July.
Cape Jasmine* (Gardenia florida)	White	Blooms May to September.

Not recommended for the Northwest.

NAMES	COLORS	WHEN TO PLANT
Mountain Laurel (Kalmia latifolia)	Rose-white	Blooms May, June.
Spanish Broom (Genista hispanica)	Golden yellow	Blooms May to July.
Scotch Broom (Cytisus scoparius)	Bright yellow	Blooms May, June.
Broom (Cytisus racemosus)	Golden yellow	Blooms May, June and intermittently.
Oregon Grape (Mahonia aquifolium)	Golden yellow	Blooms May, June.
California Grape (Mahonia pinnata)	Yellow	Blooms May, June.
Silk Tassel Shrub* (Garrya elliptica)	Greenish white	Blooms April, May.
California Coffee Shrub (Rhamnus californica)		Blooms April, May.
Loquat*	Yellow fruits	Blooms March to May.
Monkey Flower (Mimulus)	Cream, yellow, orange	Blooms May, June.

DECIDUOUS BLOOMING SHRUBS

Plant November to April

NAMES	COLORS	WHEN TO PLANT
Snowball (Viburnum opulus sterile)	White	Blooms May, June.
Wilson's Barberry (Berberis wilsoni)	Golden yellow	Blooms May, June.
Azalea altaclarensis	Bronze-orange	Blooms April, May.
Azalea occidentalis—Western Azalea	White, cream-yellow, rose	Blooms May, June.
Japanese Snowball (Viburnum tomentosum)	White	Blooms May, June.
Spiraea van houtei	White	Blooms May, June.
Bridal Wreath (Spiraea prunifolia)	White	Blooms May, June.
Deutzia scabra	White	Blooms May, June.
Florida Dogwood (Cornus florida)	White-pink	Blooms May, June.
Dogwood (Cornus nuttali)	White	Blooms May, June.
Weigela rosea	Rose-pink	Blooms May, June.
Weigela—variety Eva Rathke		Blooms May, June.
Mock Orange (Philadelphus coronarius)	White	Blooms May, June.
Horse Chestnut (Aesculus hippocastanum)	White-red	Blooms May, June.
Red-flowered Horse Chestnut (Aesculus carnea)	Red-scarlet	Blooms May, June.
Golden Chain (Laburnum vossi)	Golden yellow	Blooms May, June.
Black Locust (Robinia pseudacacia)	White	Blooms May, June.
Tulip Tree (Liriodendron tulipfera)	Green-yellow-orange	Blooms May, June.
English Hawthorn (Crataegus oxycantha)	Scarlet, white, red in variety	Blooms May, June.
Mountain Ash (European) (Sorbus aucuparia)	White-flowered	Blooms May, June.
Roses	Many colors	Plant naked roots November to March. Set potted plants any time.
Tree Peony (Moutan peony)	Rose, red, white	Blooms May, June.

FLOWERING VINES

NAMES	COLORS	WHEN TO PLANT
Potato Vine (Solanum jasminoides)	White, blue	Blooms May to July.
Japanese Wisteria (Wisteria floribunda)	White, purple, lilac	Blooms May, June.
Chinese Wisteria (Wisteria chinensis)	Blue-violet, white	Blooms April, May.
Wisteria multijuga russelliana	Purple, creamy white eye	Blooms April, May.
Trumpet Vine* (Bignonia speciosa)	Yellow, purple	Blooms April to June.
Yellow Jasmine (Jasminum humile)		Blooms April to June.
Tatarian Honeysuckle (Lonicera tatarica)	Pink, crimson, white	Blooms May, June.
Rosenbergia (Cobaea scandens)	Purple-white	Blooms April, May.
Clematis montana	White	Blooms March to June.
Silver Lace Vine (Polygonum auberti)	Rose-white-green	Blooms April to June.

* *Not recommended for the Northwest.*

FOR FLOWERS IN JUNE

NAMES	COLORS	WHEN TO PLANT
ANNUALS		
Virginia Stocks (Malcomia maritima)	Red, white, crimson, rose, lilac	Sow seed in March, April.
Nemesia	Many colors	Set plants in April, May.
Pansies	Many colors	Set plants in March, April.
Violas	Blue, white, lilac, yellow, apricot	Set plants in March, April.
Poppies—Shirley Strain (Papaver rhoeas)	Many colors	Sow seed in March, April.
Mignonette Hybrids	Yellow, white, pink	Sow seed in March, April.
Stocks—Ten Weeks Strain	Red, blue, pink, white, yellow	Set plants in March, April.
Sweet Peas	All colors	Sow seed September to December, February, March.
Swan River Daisy (Brachycome iberidifolia)	Blue, white, rose	Set plants in March, April.
Sweet Sultan (Centaurea imperialis)	White, rose, purple, red	Set plants in March, April.
Calliopsis	Yellow, brown, red, maroon	Set plants in March, April.
Ageratum	Lavender-mauve, blue, white	Set plants in March, April.
Zinnias	Rose, cream, yellow, white, crimson	Set plants in March, April.
French and African Marigolds	Yellow, orange, brown	Set plants in March, April.
Mimulus—Annual varieties	Many bright colors	Sow seed in February, March.
Snapdragon (Antirrhinum)	Many colors	Set plants in April.
Pot Marigold (Calendula officinalis)	Orange, yellow, cream	Set plants in March, April.
Viscaria	Rose, blue, crimson	Set plants in March, April.
Guinea Flower	Golden yellow	Set plants in March, April.
Portulaca	Many colors	Sow seed in February, March.
PERENNIALS		
Gaillardia	Orange, yellow, red	Plant clumps October to December. New plants in March, April.
Astilbe	White, light pink, light purple	Divide clumps September to November.
Coreopsis	Golden yellow	Plant clumps October to December. New plants in March, April.
African Golden Orange Daisy (Dimorphotheca aurantiaca)	Orange-gold	Set plants in March, April.
Kenilworth Ivy—(Continuous bloomer) (Linaria cymbalaria)	Lilac-blue	Divide roots any time.
Perennial Flax (Linum perenne)	Sky-blue, white	Plant clumps March, April.
Cardinal Flower (Lobelia cardinalis)	Cardinal red	Divide roots October to December.
Lupine (Lupinus perennis)	Blue, white—in variety	Sow seed September to November, February to April.
Hound's Tongue (Cynoglossum)	China blue	Plant clumps September to November. New plants March, April.
Oriental Poppy (Papaver orientale)	Orange, red, salmon, pink	Plant clumps in August to December. New plants in February, March.
Iceland Poppy (Papaver nudicaule)	Light orange, light yellow, white, orange-scarlet	Plant clumps August to December. New plants in February, March.
Perennial Phlox (Phlox decussata)	All colors	Divide clumps October to January.
Salvia farinacea	Light blue	Plant clumps October to December. New plants March, April.
Mourning Bride—in variety (Scabiosa)	Lavender, pink, rose, blue, red	Plant in March, April.
Blue Bonnet (Scabiosa caucasica)	Lavender-mauve	Plant clumps September, October. New plants March, April.
Sea Lavender (Statice latifolia)	Mauve	Plant clumps October to December. New plants March, April.
Pentstemon gloxinioides	Pink, crimson, white, purple	Divide clumps October to December. New plants March, April.
False Dragonhead (Physostegia virginiana)	Pink	Plant clumps October to December.
Cone Flower (Rudbeckia)	Yellow, crimson-purple	Plant clumps October to December. New plants March, April.
Dahlias	All colors	Plant tubers in March.
Single Daisy (Pyrethrum roseum)	White, red, pink, rose, lilac, carmine	Plant clumps October to December. New plants March, April.
Purple Mullein (Verbascum phoeniceum)	Purple, rose, pink, lilac, white—in variety	Plant clumps in October to December. New plants March, April.
Thyme—in variety	Rose, purple, red	Plant clumps October to March.
Torch Lily (Tritoma grandiflora)	Orange-red-yellow	Divide clumps October to March.
Speedwell (Veronica spicata)	Blue, pink	Plant clumps October to December. New plants March, April.

* Not recommended for the Northwest.

NAMES	COLORS	WHEN TO PLANT
Delphinium Hybrids—in many strains	Shades of blue, pink, opal	Plant clumps October to December. New plants March, April.
Delphinium belladonna	Sky-blue	Plant clumps October to December. New plants March, April.
Verbena	Many colors, pink, red, purple, white	Plant in April.
Perennial Aster (Aster subcaeruleus)	Lavender-mauve	Plant clumps October to December. New plants March, April.
Columbine (Aquilegia)	Blue, white, yellow, pink, red	Plant October to January.
Acanthus	White, purple	Divide clumps October to March.
Achusa italica	Deep blue-pink	Plant clumps October to December. New plants March, April.
Chamomile (Anthemis)	Yellow-white	Divide clumps October to December. New plants March, April.
Sea Pink (Armeria babarica)	Pink, purple, white	Divide clumps October to January. New plants March, to May.
Canterbury Bells (Campanula medium)	Pink, purple, rose, white	Plant clumps and new plants October to January.
Blue Bells (Campanula muralis)	Deep blue	Plant clumps September to December. New plants February to April.
Harebell (Campanula rotundifolia)	Blue	Divide clumps October to January. New plants February to April.
Hollyhock—Single and Double varieties	Many colors	Divide clumps October to January. New plants February to April.
Lynchnis chalcedonica	Scarlet	Plant clumps October to December. New plants March to May.
Peony (Paeonia)	Many colors (not recommended for parts of California)	Divide clumps October to December.
Valerian	Lilac, rose	Divide clumps October to December.
Shasta Daisy—in variety	White	Divide clumps October to March.
Maiden Pink (Dianthus deltoides)	Rose, cerise, white	Plant in March, April.
Foxglove (Digitalis)	Rose, white, purple	Plant clumps and new plants October to December.
Sweet William (Dianthus barbatus)	Pink, rose, maroon, white, scarlet	Plant in March, April.
Carnation—in variety (Dianthus caryophyllus)	White, pink, red, scarlet	Plant rooted cuttings March to May.
Balloon Flower (Platycodon grandiflorum)	White, blue, lavender	Plant clumps and new plants February to May.
Sea Holly (Eryngium amethystinum)	Steel-blue	Plant clumps October to December. New plants April, May.
Leopard's-Bane (Doronicum excelsum)	Bright yellow	Set plants in March, April.
Matalija Poppy (Romneya coulteri)	White with golden centers	Plant clumps October to December.
Moss Pink (Phlox subulata)	Purplish pink	Plant clumps October to December. New plants March, April.
Begonia semperflorens—Fibrous-rooted begonias.	Red, carmine, rose-red, white	Plant in March, April.
Transvaal Daisy (Gerbera jamesoni)	All colors	Set plants in February to March.
Canary Bird Vine (Tropaeolum peregrinum)	Light yellow	Sow seed March to May.
Lupine (Lupinus polyphyllus)	White, blue, pink	Sow seeds March, April.
True Monkshood (Aconitum napellus)	Bright blue	Plant clumps October to December. New plants March to May.
Gazania—in variety—South African Daisy	White, yellow, orange, scarlet	Plant clumps October to January. New plants April, May.
Evening Primrose (Oenothera)	Yellow	Divide clumps October to December. New plants March, April.
Potentilla—Variety Miss Willmot	Cerise	Plant clumps October to December. New plants March, April.
Rehmannia angulata	Rosy purple	Plant clumps October to December. New plants March, April.
Sedums—Creeping varieties	Yellow, white, pink	Plant clumps and new plants January to April.
Verbena erinoides	Purplish blue	Set plants in March, April.
Convolvulus mauritanicus	Sky-blue	Set plants in March, April.

BULBOUS PLANTS

NAMES	COLORS	WHEN TO PLANT
Iris siberica	Blue, purple, white	Plant August, September, March, April.
Iris laevigata—Japanese Iris	Blue	Plant August to December, March, April.
Iris kaempferi—Japanese Iris	Many colors	Plant August to December, March, April.
Gladiolus	All colors	Plant January.
Anomatheca	Lilac, crimson	Plant October to December.
Watsonia—in variety	White, lavender, salmon, pink, copper red	Plant August to November.
Chilean Lily (Alstromeria chilensis)	Creamy yellow, buff, apricot, pink, red	Plant September to November.
Peruvian Lily (Alstromeria aurantiaca)	Golden yellow, orange-red	Plant September to November.

Not recommended for the Northwest.

NAMES	COLORS	WHEN TO PLANT
African Lily (Agapanthus umbellatus)	Blue	Plant October to April.
Summer Snowflake (Leucojum aestivum)	White-green	Plant September to November. Plant offsets February to April.
Leopard Lily (Lilium pardalinum)	Brilliant orange	Plant September, October.
Lilium umbellatum	Red	Plant October to January.
Lilium humboldtii magnificum		Plant October to December.
Madonna Lily (Lilium candidum)	White	Plant July-August.
Cannas	Many colors	Plant October to April.
Day Lily (Hemerocallis)	Yellow, orange, copper	Plant October to January.
Common Calla	White—intermittent in bloom	Plant October to December.
Oxalis—Summer-blooming	Rose, white	Plant February to April.
Crinums—in variety	White, pink, red	Plant October to December.
Tuberose	White	Plant February to June.
Naegelia	White, scarlet, yellow	Plant October to December.
Chilean Lily (Alstromeria chilensis)	Yellow, red	Plant October to December.
Spider Lily (Hymenocallis)	White	Plant February to April.

FLOWERING EVERGREEN SHRUBS

Plant Any Time

NAMES	COLORS	WHEN TO PLANT
Acacia decurrens mollissima*	Clear yellow	Blooms June, July.
Acacia julibrissin (Albizzia)*	Pink	Blooms June, July.
Australian Flame Tree* (Sterculia diversifolia)	Red	Blooms June, July.
Jacaranda*	Lilac	Blooms June, July.
Silk Oak Tree* (Grevillea robusta)	Golden yellow	Blooms June, July.
Magnolia grandiflora	White	Intermittent bloom throughout the year.
Lyonothamnus aspleniifolius floribundus*	White	Blooms June, July.
Australian Mock Orange* (Pittosporum undulatum)	White	Blooms December to July.
Melaleuca leucadendra*	Creamy white	Blooms June to October.
Melaleuca hypericifolia*		Blooms May to October.
Cestrum elegans*	Red-purple	Continuous bloom.
Lemon Verbena*	Purplish white	Intermittent bloom.
Geranium*—Single	All colors	Blooms continuously.
Oleander* (Nerium oleander)	All colors	Blooms June to September.
Datura cornucopia*	White	Ever-blooming.
Spotted Rock Rose* (Cistus ladaniferus maculatus)	White, scarlet	Blooms all summer.
Rock Rose* (Cistus albidus)	Lilac-rose	Blooms June to September.
White-flowered Rock Rose* (Cistus salviifolius)		Blooms June to September.
Veronica imperialis*	Purple-crimson	Blooms June to September.
Veronica andersoni*	Bluish violet	Blooms June to September.
Veronica elliptica lewisii*	White	Blooms June to September.
Escallonia rosea*	Deep pink	Blooms June to August.
Berberis gracilis	Buff-orange	Blooms June to August.
Berberis verruculosa	Clear yellow	Blooms June to August.
Berberis elegantissima	Clear yellow	Blooms June to August.
Berberis hookeri	Clear yellow	Blooms May, June.
Coronilla glauca*	Yellow	Continuous bloom.
Yellow Heliotrope* (Streptosolen jamesonii)	Orange-yellow	Blooms June to November and intermittent bloom.
Rhododendron Hybrids	Many colors	Blooms May, June.
Rhododendron catawbiense	Lilac-purple	Blooms May, June.
Rhododendron carolinianum	Rosy purple	Blooms May, June.
Erica stricta	Rosy purple	Blooms June to August.
Osmanthus aquifolium*	White	Blooms June, July.
Ceanothus Gloire de Versailles	Blue	Blooms June, July.
Common Myrtle* (Myrtus communis)	White	Blooms June to August.
Myrtus luma*		Blooms June to August and intermittently.
Diosma purpurea*	Light purple	Blooms June to September.
Toyon (Photinia arbutifolia)	White	Blooms June, July.
Pimelea decussata*	Pink	Blooms June to August.
Pernettya mucronata	White	Blooms May, June.
Tree Poppy* (Dendromecon rigida)	Yellow	Blooms June to August.
Andromeda japonica	White	Blooms June to August.

DECIDUOUS BLOOMING SHRUBS

Plant November to April

NAMES	COLORS	WHEN TO PLANT
Fuchsia*—in varieties	Many colors	Blooms May to November.
Smoke Tree (Rhus cotinus)	Purplish mauve	Blooms June, July.

* Not recommended for the Northwest.

NAMES	COLORS	WHEN TO PLANT
Sugar Bush	Light yellow	Blooms June to August.
(Rhus ovata)		
Oleaster	Yellow-white	Blooms June to August.
(Eleagnus angustifolia)		
Spiraea Anthony Waterer	Wine-red	Blooms June to September.
Pomegranate	Orange-red	Blooms June to August.
(Punica granatum)		
Pink-flowered Locust	Bright rose-pink	Blooms May, June.
(Robinia hispida rosea)		
Yellow Wood	White	Blooms May, June.
(Cladrastis tinctoria)		
Roses	All colors	Bloom April to November.
Dogwood	Creamy white	Blooms May, June.
(Cornus capitata)		
Mexican Mock Orange		Blooms May, June.
(Philadelphus mexicana)		
Aesculus splendens	Red-scarlet	Blooms May, June.
FLOWERING VINES		**Plant November to April**
Solanum wendlandii*	Purple blue	Blooms June to August.
Heliotrope*	Lilac, lavender in variety	Blooms June to September and intermittently.
Mandevilla suaveolens*—Chilean Jasmine	White	Blooms June to September.
Jasminum grandiflorum*—Catalonian Jasmine	White	Blooms June to September.
Clematis montana rubens	Pink	Blooms March to June.
Lantana*—in variety	Creamy white, lavender, orange-yellow, pink, yellow.	Blooms June to November.
Bouvardia humboldtii*—in variety	White, pink	Blooms June to December.

FOR FLOWERS IN JULY

NAMES	COLORS	WHEN TO PLANT
ANNUALS		
Zinnias	Yellow, cream, white, crimson, salmon	Set plants in April, May.
Collinsia	Lilac, rose, blue, white	Set plants in April, May.
Cornflower	Pink, rose, blue, white	Set plants in May.
(Centaurea cyaneus)		
Clarkia	Salmon, rose, pink in variety	Set plants in April, May.
Cape Marigold	Orange, yellow, cream	Set plants in April, May.
(Calendula officinalis)		
Larkspur	Rose, pink, blue	Set plants in April, May.
(Delphinium ajacis)		
Diascia barberae	Rose-pink	Set plants in May.
Blue Lace Flower		Set plants in April, May.
(Didiscus caerulea)		
Godetia—Double and Single varieties	Carmine, crimson, pink	Set plants in April, May.
Helianthus—in variety	Yellow	Sow seed March, April.
(Sunflower)		
Lobelia—in variety	White, blue, rose, purple	Set plants in April, May.
Love-in-a-Mist—variety Miss Jekyll	Blue	Sow seed April, May.
(Nigella)		
Pansies	All colors	Set plants in May. Sow seeds two months earlier.
Violas	Blue, white, lilac, yellow, apricot, purple	Set plants in May.
Petunias—Large-flowered and ruffled varieties	Many colors	Set plants in May.
Portulaca	Many colors	Sow seed March to May.
Poor Man's Orchid	Many colors	Set plants in April, May.
(Schizanthus)		
Stocks—Ten Weeks	All colors	Set plants in April, May. Sow seeds two months earlier.
Imperial Stocks—Gillyflowers	Red, pink, purple, yellow, white	Set plants in April, May.
African Blue Daisy	Bluish white	Set plants in April, May.
(Arctotis)		
Snapdragons	All colors	Set plants in May.
(Antirrhinum)		
Balsam	White, red, pink, yellow	Set plants in April, May.
Balloon Vine	White	Sow seed March, April.
Swan River Daisy	Blue	Set plants in April, May.
(Brachycome)		
Browallia elate—Amethyst	Blue	Set plants in April, May.
Nasturtium—Vine and Tom Thumb varieties	All colors	Sow seed in April, May.
Cockscomb	Crimson, yellow, scarlet	Set plants in April, May.
(Celosia)		

Not recommended for the Northwest.

NAMES	COLORS	WHEN TO PLANT
Ornamental Gourds		Sow seeds in April or May for fruits in late summer and fall.
Virginia Stocks (Malcomia maritima)	Red, rose, white, crimson, lilac	Sow seed in April, May.
Everlasting Flower (Rhodanthe)	Pink, white, red	Set plants in April, May.
Guinea Flower	Golden yellow	Set plants in April, May.
Immortelle (Xeranthemum)	Rose, white, purple	Sow seeds March, May.

PERENNIALS

NAMES	COLORS	WHEN TO PLANT
Verbenas	Purple, crimson, white, pink, scarlet	Set plants in April, May.
Poppies—in variety	Yellow, gold, orange, red	Sow seed in March, April.
Mexican Tulip Poppy (Hunnemannia fumariaefolia)	Yellow	Plant clumps October to December. New plants in May, June.
Helenium—in variety	Yellow, orange, red, copper	Plant clumps October to December. New plants in March, April.
Leptosyne douglasi	Yellow	Set plants in May.
Nicotiana affinis—in variety	White, crimson, rose, purple	Set plants in April, May.
Perennial Phlox (Phlox decussata)	All colors	Divide clumps October to January
Coreopsis grandiflora	Golden yellow	Plant clumps October to December. New plants in April, May.
Scarlet Sage (Salvia splendens)		Set plants in April, May.
Salvia pitcheri	Deep blue	Plant clumps October to December. New plants in April, May.
Purple Sage (Salvia leucantha)	White-lavender-purple	Divide roots in April, May.
Blue Bonnet (Scabiosa caucasica)	Lavender-mauve	Plant clumps October to December. New plants April, May.
Pentstemon—Native species	White, yellow, blue, lilac	Set plants in April, May.
Periwinkle (Vinca minor)	Blue	Divide clumps January to March.
Pyrethrum—in many hybrids—Single Daisy	White, red, pink, rose, crimson, lilac	Plant clumps October to December. New plants April, May.
Cotyledons—in variety (Hen-and-Chickens)	White, yellow, red, purple	Set plants in January to May.
Saxifraga—in variety	Many colors	Set plants in October to December, February to May.
Feathered Columbine (Thalictrum aquilegifolium)	Purple-white	Plant clumps November to January. New plants April, May.
Indian Meadow Rue (Thalictrum dipterocarpum)	Lavender-mauve	Plant clumps November to January. New plants March to May.
Yellow Butterfly (Verbascum olympicum)		Plant clumps October to December. New plants February to April.
Herbaceous Veronica (Veronica longifolia)	Lilac	Plant clumps October to January. New plants February to April.
Delphinium hybrida	Shades of blue, opal, pink	Plant clumps October to December. New plants April, May.
Perennial Aster—Michaelmas Daisy	Pink, blue, purple, mauve, lavender	Plant clumps and new plants September to January.
Dahlias	All colors	Plant tubers in April, May.
Siberian Wallflower (Cheiranthus allioni)	Bright orange	Set plants in April, May.
Wallflower (Cheiranthus cheiri)	Yellow, purple, brown, russet, orange	Set plants in April, May.
Geums—in variety	Golden yellow, orange, red, scarlet	Plant clumps October to December. New plants April, May.
Day Lily (Hemerocallis)	Yellow, orange	Plant clumps October to January. New plants March, April.
Purse Flower (Calceolaria)	Brown, yellow, mahogany	Plant clumps October to December. New plants April, May.
Anchusa italica	Deep blue, pink	Plant clumps October to January. New plants April, May.
Rock Cress (Arabis albida)	White	Plant clumps October to December. New plants April, May.
Aubrietia—in variety	Purple, lilac, rose	Divide clumps October to January. New plants April, May.
Beach Bell (Campanula persicifolia)	Blue, lavender, white	Divide clumps October to December. New plants March to May.
Blue Bells (Campanula muralis)	Deep blue	Plant clumps October to December. New plants March to May.
Chimney Bellflower (Campanula pyramidalis)	Blue, white, lavender	Plant clumps October to December.
Carpathian Blue Bell (Campanula carpatica)	Blue, white	Plant clumps October to December. New plants March to May.
Catmint (Nepeta mussini)	Lavender-mauve	Plant clumps October to January. New plants April, May.
Oenothera—in variety	Yellow	Plant clumps October to January. New plants March to May.
Garden Pink (Dianthus plumarius)	Pink, rose, white	Plant clumps October to December. New plants April, May.

* *Not recommended for the Northwest.*

NAMES	COLORS	WHEN TO PLANT
Begonia—Fibrous-rooted	Red, white, rose, pink	Plant rooted cuttings February to May.
Chinese Forget-Me-Not	Brilliant blue	Plant clumps October to December.
(Cynoglossum amabile)		New plants March to May.
Coral Bells	Coral-red, pink	Plant clumps October to December.
(Heuchera sanguinea)		New plants February to May.
Sun Rose	Pink, white, red, rose, yellow	Plant clumps October to January.
(Helianthemum)		New plants March to May.
Perennial Lupine	White, blue, pink	Plant clumps October to December.
(Lupinus polyphyllus)		New plants March to May.
Platycodon grandiflorum	Steel-blue	Plant March, April.
Globe Thistle	White, blue	Divide clumps March, April.
Francoa ramosa	White, bluish pink	Plant clumps October to January.
Impatiens oliveri	Pale lilac	Plant March to May.
Impatiens sultana	Scarlet	Plant March to May.
Sedum spurium	Purplish pink	Plant March to May.
Aconitum	Deep blue	Plant clumps October to December.
		New plants March to May.
Golden Rod	Golden yellow	Plant clumps October to December.
(Solidago canadensis)		
Centaurea montana	Bright blue	Divide clumps October to January.
		Set new plants March to May.
Poker Plant	Orange-yellow	Plant clumps January to May.
(Tritoma grandiflora)		

BULBOUS PLANTS

NAMES	COLORS	WHEN TO PLANT
Japanese Iris	Many colors	Plant August to December, March, April.
(Iris kaempferi)		
Autumn Crocus	Mauve, white	Plant in July to September.
(Colchicum autumnale)		
Tritonia	Rose, tan	Plant October, November.
Gladiolus—Large-flowered and Primilinum.	Many colors	Plant January, February.
Montbretia	Yellow, orange, scarlet, crimson	Plant October to April.
Tuberous Begonias	White, pink, red, yellow, salmon, orange.	Plant March, April.
Lilium washingtonianum	White	Plant October to December.
Gold-banded Lily	White, golden yellow, crimson	Plant October to December.
(Lilium auratum)		
Regal Lily	White, pink, canary-yellow	Plant October to December.
(Lilium regale)		
Peruvian Daffodil	White, yellow	Plant October to December.
(Ismene)		
Golden Calla	Yellow	Plant October to December.
(Zantedeschia elliottiana)		
Cannas	Many colors	Plant October to April.

EVERGREEN FLOWERING SHRUBS

Plant Any Time

NAMES	COLORS	WHEN TO PLANT
Lemon-scented Eucalyptus*	Creamy white	Blooms June, July.
(Eucalyptus citriodora)		
Jewel Flower*	Light red	Blooms June to September and intermittently.
(Grevillea thlemanniana)		
Cassia artemisioides*	Sulphur-yellow	Blooms June to September.
Lagunaria patersoni*	Pale rose	Blooms June to September.
Metrosideros tomentosa	Red	Blooms June to August.
Spanish Broom	Golden yellow	Blooms June to September and intermittently.
(Genista hispanica)		
Viburnum suspensum	White-pink	Blooms June, July.
Chilean Guava*	White	Blooms June to August.
(Myrtus ugni)		
Eugenia apiculata*	White	Blooms June to August and intermittently.
(Myrtus luma)		
Cestrum aurantiacum*	Orange-yellow	Blooms June to August.
Cestrum elegans*	Red-purple	Blooms June to September.
Rock Rose*	Deep pink	Blooms June to August.
(Cistus crispus)		
Yellow-spotted Rock Rose*	White-yellow	Blooms June to August.
(Cistus laurifolius)		
Veronica formosa*	Pale lilac	Blooms July, August.
Veronica traversi*	White	Blooms July, August.
Escallonia rosea	Pink	Blooms July, August.
Escallonia rubra	Red	Blooms June to August and intermittently.
Darwin's Barberry	Golden yellow-orange	Blooms throughout year.
(Berberis darwini)		
Coral Tree*	Crimson	Blooms June to September.
(Erythrina crista-galli)		
Butterfly Bush—Summer Lilac	Lilac	Blooms June to September.
(Buddleia variabilis)		
Cigar Plant*	Bright red	Blooms June to September and intermittently.
(Cuphea ignea)		
Oleander*	All colors	Blooms June to September.
(Nerium oleander)		
Breath-of-Heaven*	White	Almost continuous bloom.
(Diosma ericoides)		

* Not recommended for the Northwest.

NAMES	COLORS	WHEN TO PLANT
Raphiolepis japonica ovata	White	Blooms June to September and intermittently.
Plumbago capensis*	Sky-blue	Blooms June to November.
Polygala dalmaisiana	Rosy magenta	Continuous bloomer.
Anemone Shrub*	White	Blooms June, July.
(Carpenteria californica)		
Hibiscus*	Many colors (grown in shelter)	Blooms June to August.
Hypericum calycinum*	Golden yellow	Blooms July to September.
English Laurel	White	Blooms June to August.
(Prunus laurocerasus)		
Yucca whipplei	White	Blooms June to August.
Jerusalem Cherry*	White	Blooms June to September.
(Solanum pseudocapsicum)		
DECIDUOUS FLOWERING SHRUBS		**Plant November to April**
Roses	All colors	Bloom April to November.
California Privet	White	Blooms April to November.
(Ligustrum ovalifolium)		
Ligustrum lucidum	White	Blooms July, August.
Hydrangea hortensis*	Pink, white, rose in variety	Blooms June to September.
FLOWERING VINES		
Trumpet Vine*	Red-yellow	Blooms June to August.
(Bignonia cherere)		
Trumpet Honeysuckle*	Orange-scarlet	Blooms July to September.
(Tecoma radicans)		
Trumpet Vine*	Rose-pink	Blooms June to September.
(Tecoma mackensii)		
Solanum rantonneti	Violet-blue	Blooms July, August.
Australian Blue Bell Creeper*	Deep blue	Blooms July, August.
(Sollya heterophylla)		
Star Jasmine*	White	Blooms June, July.
(Rhynchospermum jasminoides)		
Common Jasmine	White	Blooms June to September and intermittently.
(Jasminum officinalis)		
Lantana*—in variety	Yellow, orange, lavender, pink	Blooms June to October and intermittently.
Cobaea scandens	Violet-purple	Intermittent bloom.
Bougainvillea spectabilis*	Magenta	Blooms June to January.
Bougainvillea*—variety Crimson Lake		Blooms June to September.
Hall's Honeysuckle	White-yellow	Blooms June to August.
(Lonicera japonica halliana)		
Chinese Honeysuckle	Orange-scarlet	Blooms June to September.
(Lonicera chinensis)		
Clematis jackmani and Hybrids	Purple, blue, lavender, mauve, white, red	Blooms June to August.

FOR FLOWERS IN AUGUST

NAMES	COLORS	WHEN TO PLANT
ANNUALS		
Cosmos	White, pink, crimson	Set plants in April, May.
Calliopsis	Yellow, brown, red, maroon	Set plants in April, May.
Marigolds—French and African varieties	Yellow, brown, orange	Set plants from April to June.
Annual Flax	Red, blue, yellow, white	Set plants from April to June.
(Linum grandiflorum)		
Nemesia	Many colors	Set plants from May to June.
Shirley Poppy Strain	Many colors	Sow seed April to June.
(Papaver rhoeas)		
Mignonette—in variety	Yellow, white, pink	Sow seed May, June.
Salpiglossis	Many colors	Set plants from April to June.
Zinnias	Rose, cream, yellow, white, crimson	Set plants from April to June. Sow seeds two months earlier.
Asters	Many colors	Set plants in April or May.
Mimulus	Many colors	Sow seed April, May.
Sweet Sultan	White, rose, purple, red	Set plants in March, April.
(Centaurea imperialis)		
Snapdragons	Many colors	Set plants in June.
(Antirrhinum)		
Four-o'Clock	Red, white, yellow	Sow seed May, June.
Pot Marigold	Orange, yellow, cream	Set plants in June.
(Calendula officinalis)		
Viscaria	Rose, blue, crimson	Set plants in May, June.
Ageratum—Blue Floss Flower	Lavender-mauve	Set plants in April to June.
PERENNIALS		
Dahlias	All colors	Plant tubers in March, April.
Verbenas	Many colors—pink, red, purple, white	Set plants from April to June.

* Not recommended for the Northwest.

NAMES	COLORS	WHEN TO PLANT
Alyssum saxatile	Golden yellow	Set plants from April to June.
Shasta Daisy	White	Plant clumps March to June.
Coreopsis grandiflora	Golden yellow	Plant new plants April to June.
Perennial Phlox	Many colors	Plant clumps October to January.
(Phlox decussata)		
Cone Flower	Yellow, crimson, purple	Plant clumps October to December. New plants May, June.
(Rudbeckia)		
Cardinal Flower	Cardinal red	Set plants October to January.
(Lobelia cardinalis)		
Salvia patens	Deep blue	Plant clumps August to October. New plants in May.
Salvia sclarea	Whitish blue	Plant from October to December. New plants April, May.
Mourning Bride—in variety	Lavender, pink, rose, blue, red	Set plants April to June.
(Scabiosa)		
California Fuchsia	Vermilion	Set plants April, May.
(Zauschneria californica)		
Pentstemon gloxinioides	Pink, crimson, white, purple	Divide clumps October to December. Set new plants May, June.
Indian Meadow Rue	Lavender-mauve	Plant clumps November to January. New plants April, May.
(Thalictrum dipterocarpum)		
Thyme—in variety	Rose, purple, red	Plant clumps January to April.
Veronica spicata—Speedwell	Blue-pink	Plant clumps October to December. New plants April, May.
Delphinium hybrida—in many strains	Shades of blue, pink, opal	Plant clumps October to December. New plants March to May.
Perennial Aster	Lavender-mauve	Plant clumps October to December. New plants April to June.
(Aster subcaeruleus)		
Perennial Aster—Michaelmas Daisy	Shades of blue and purple, mauve, pink, lavender.	Plant clumps September to January.
Dimorphotheca aurantiaca	White, blue, yellow, orange, salmon in variety.	Plant clumps October to December. New plants March to May.
Carnations	White, pink, red, scarlet	Plant rooted cuttings March to May.
(Dianthus caryophyllus)		
Acanthys	Purplish white	Divide roots October to March.
Boltonia—False Camomile	White, violet, purple	Divide clumps October to January. New plants March to May.
Cactus—in variety	Purple, crimson, orange, yellow, pink	Divisions and offsets in April to July.
Hollyhock—Single and double varieties	Many colors	Divide clumps October to January. Set new plants February to May.
Mesembryanthemum—in variety	Pink, white, rose, yellow, red	Divide plants October to January. Set new plants April to June.
Scarlet Pentstemon		Plant clumps October to December.
(Chelone barbata)		
Valerian	Lilac, rose	Plant clumps October to January.
Foxglove	Rose, white, purple	Plant clumps and new plants October to December.
(Digitalis)		
Sweet William	Pink, rose, maroon, white	Set plants April, May.
(Dianthus barbatus)		
Sea Holly	Steel-blue	Plant clumps October to December. New plants April, May.
(Eryngium amethystinum)		
Leopard's Bane	Bright yellow	Plant clumps October to December. New plants March to May.
(Doronicum excelsum)		
Matalija Poppy	White with golden centers	Plant clumps October to December.
(Romneya coulteri)		
Moss Pink	Purplish pink	Plant clumps October to December. Set new plants March to May.
(Phlox subulata)		
Chrysanthemum—in variety	Many colors	Plant rooted cuttings April, May.
Begonia semperflorens—in variety	Red, carmine, rose-red, white	Plant April to June.
Transvaal Daisy—in variety	Many colors	Set plants February to March.
(Gerbera jamesoni)		
Torenia—in variety	Indigo, yellow, rose, white	Sow seeds February to May.
Cornflower Aster	Blue	Plant clumps October to December. New plants March to May.
(Stokesia)		
South African Daisy—in variety	Orange, yellow, white, scarlet	Plant clumps October to December. New plants May, June.
(Gazania)		
Rehmannia angulata	Rosy purple	Plant clumps October to December. New plants April to June.
Sedum spectabilis	Bright pink	Plant divisions March to May.
Trachelium caeruleum	Pale mauve	Plant new plants March to May.
Convolvulus mauritanicus	Sky-blue	Plant new plants March to May.
Japanese Anemone—in variety	White, pink, red	Plant clumps October to December.
(Anemone japonica)		
Orange Sunflower		Plant clumps October to December. New plants March to May.
(Heliopsis pitcheriana)		
Potentilla nepalensis	Cerise	Plant clumps October to December. New plants April to June.
Gaillardia	Yellow-orange-red	Set plants February to June.
BULBOUS PLANTS		
Montbretia	Yellow, orange, scarlet, crimson	Plant October to January, February to April
Gladiolus—Large-flowered and Primulinum	Many colors	Plant May to June.

* *Not recommended for the Northwest.*

NAMES	COLORS	WHEN TO PLANT
Tuberous Begonias	White, red, yellow, salmon, orange	Plant March, April.
Tiger Lily (Lilium tigrinum)	Reddish orange	Plant October to December.
Showy Lily (Lilium speciosum rubrum)	White, crimson	Plant October to December.
Japanese White Lily (Lilium speciosum album)		Plant October to December.
Lilium henryi	Bright orange-yellow	Plant October to December.
Gold-banded Lily (Lilium auratum)	White, golden yellow, crimson	Plant October to December.
Regal Lily (Lilium regale)	White, pink, canary-yellow	Plant October to December.
Common Calla	White	Plant October to December.
Sternbergia lutea	Bright yellow	Plant November to January.
Tigridia	White, yellow, carmine, salmon	Plant November to April.
Colchium autumnale—in variety	Mauve, white, rose, lilac	Plant July to September.
Amaryllis belladonna	Bright pink	Plant August-September.
Cannas	Many colors	Plant October to April.

EVERGREEN FLOWERING SHRUBS

Plant Any Time

NAMES	COLORS	WHEN TO PLANT
Scarlet-flowered Eucalyptus* (Eucalyptus ficifolia)		Blooms July to September, December to February
Abelia grandiflora	Purplish white	Blooms July to September.
Tamarix hispida	Pink	Blooms August, September.
Myrtus communis*	White	Blooms August, September.
Dwarf Myrtle* (Mytrus communis)	White	Blooms August, September.
Geranium* (Pelargonium)	All colors	Blooms April to September.
Blue-flowered Veronica* (Veronica decussata)	Deep blue	Blooms August, September and intermittently.
Boxwood Veronica* (Veronica buxifolia)	White	Blooms August, September.
Golden Dewdrop Shrub* (Duranta plumieri)	Lilac-yellow	Blooms August to October.
Yellow Heliotrope* (Streptosolen jamesonii)	Orange-yellow	Blooms June to November and intermittently.
Echium fastuosum*	Violet-blue	Blooms June to September.
Crepe Myrtle* (Lagerstromia indica)	Pink, reddish purple	Blooms July, August.
Jewel Flower Shrub* (Grevillea thlemanniana)	Crimson	Almost continuous bloom.
Australian Flame Tree* (Sterculia diversifolia)	Scarlet	Blooms June to August.
Gold Flower* (Hypericum moserianum)	Golden yellow	Blooms July, August.
Hypericum patulum*	Golden yellow (ground cover)	Blooms July to September.
Lion's Tail* (Leonotis leonurus)	Bright orange	Blooms July to October.
Teucrium fruticans*	Blue-white	Blooms June to September and intermittently.
Rosemary* (Rosemarinus officinalis)	Lavender-white	Continuous bloom.
Fremontia* (Fremontia californica and Fremontia mexicana)	Bronze-orange	Blooms June to August.
Cigar Shrub (Cuphea ignea)	Vermilion, ash gray tips	Continuous bloom.
Bouvardia*—in hybrids	Pink, rose, white	Blooms June to January.
Fuchsias*—in variety	Many colors (deciduous)	Blooms June to December.
Roses	All colors (deciduous)	Bloom April to December.

FLOWERING VINES

Plant November to April

NAMES	COLORS	WHEN TO PLANT
Cape Honeysuckle* (Tecoma capensis)	Orange-red-scarlet	Blooms August to November.
Japanese Wistaria (Wisteria floribunda)	White, purple, lilac	Blooms August, September.
Catalonian Jasmine* (Jasminum grandiflorum)	White	Blooms June to September.
Bougainvillea braziliensis*	Pink-purple	Blooms July, August.
Latana*—in variety	Orange, scarlet, yellow, pink, white, lilac, cream.	Blooms June to January.
Kudzu Vine (Pueraria thunbergiana)	Rosy purple	Blooms July to September.
Perennial Pea Vine (Lathyrus latifolius)	Rose	Sow seed April, May.

SPECIAL FRUITS AND BERRIES

Plant November to April

NAMES	COLORS	WHEN TO PLANT
Snowball (Viburnum opulus sterile)	Scarlet	Bears August to October.
Berberis stenophylla	Blue	Bears August, September.

Not recommended for the Northwest.

NAMES	COLORS	WHEN TO PLANT
Cotoneaster adpressa	Red	Bears August to November.
Scarlet Runner Bean	Scarlet beans	
(Phaseolus multiflorus)		
Tatarian Honeysuckle	Red	Bears July, August.
(Lonicera tatarica)		
Yellow-flowered Currant	Black	Bears August, September.
(Ribes odoratum)		
Purple-leaved Plum	Reddish purple	Bears July, August.
(Prunus pissardi)		
European Mountain Ash	Orange-red	Bears July, August.
(Sorbus aucuparia)		
Natal Plum*	Red	Bears August, September.
(Carissa grandiflora)		
Sugar Bush	Dark red	Bears August to October.
(Rhus ovata)		

FOR FLOWERS IN SEPTEMBER

NAMES	COLORS	WHEN TO PLANT
ANNUALS		
Blue Lace Flower		Set plants April to June.
(Didiscus caerulea)		
Larkspur	Rose, pink, blue	Set plants April to June.
(Delphinium ajacis)		
Lobelia—in variety	White, blue, rose, purple	Set plants May to July.
Petunias—Large-flowered and Ruffled	Many colors	Set plants April to June.
varieties.		
Stocks—Ten Weeks	All colors	Set plants April to June.
Imperial Stocks—Gillyflowers	Red, purple, pink, yellow, white	Set plants April to June.
Cosmos	White, pink, crimson	Set plants April to June.
Zinnias	Yellow, cream, white, crimson, salmon	Set plants April to June.
Asters—in variety	White, red, purple, lavender, pink	Set plants April to June.
Snapdragons	All colors	Set plants in July.
(Antirrhinum)		Sow seeds two months earlier.
Everlasting Flower	Yellow, red, white, rose	Set plants April to June.
(Helichrysum)		
PERENNIALS		
Chrysanthemums—in variety	All colors	Plant rooted cuttings April to June.
Dahlias	All colors	Plant tubers April to June.
Poppies—in variety	Yellow, gold, orange, red	Sow seed April to June.
(Eschscholtzia)		
African Golden Orange Daisy	Orange-gold	Set plants in March to May.
(Dimorphotheca aurantiaca)		
Salvia pitcheri	Lavender-blue	Plant clumps October to December.
		New plants April, May.
Nicotiana affinis—in variety	White, crimson, rose, purple	Set plants from April to June.
Perennial Phlox	All colors	Divide clumps October to January.
(Phlox decussata)		
Blue Bonnet	Lavender-mauve	Plant clumps October to December.
(Scabiosa caucasica)		New plants April to June.
Scabiosa columbaria	Pink-blue-lavender	Plant clumps October to December.
		New plants April to June.
False Dragon's Head	Pink	Plant clumps October to December.
(Physostegia virginica)		
Pentstemon—Native species	White, yellow, blue, lilac	Set plants April to June.
Creeping Veronicas	Blue, pinkish blue	Plant clumps October to December.
(Veronica teucrium and species)		New plants April to June.
Plumbago larpentae	Deep blue	Divide clumps October to December.
		New plants April, May.
Delphinium hybrida	Shades of blue, pink, opal	Plant clumps October to December.
		New plants April to June.
Perennial Aster—Michaélmas Daisy	Pink, blue, purple, mauve, lavender	Plant clumps and new plants September to January.
Geums—in variety	Gold, yellow, orange, scarlet, red	Plant clumps October to December.
		New plants April to June.
Day Lily	Yellow, orange	Plant clumps October to January.
(Hemerocallis)		New plants April to June.
Anchusa italica	Deep blue-pink	Plant clumps October to January.
		New plants April to June.
Anthemis	Yellow-white	Divide clumps October to December.
		Set new plants April to June.
Peach Bell	Blue, lavender, white	Divide clumps October to December.
(Campanula persicifolia)		New plants March to June.
Chimney Bellflower	Blue, white, lavender	Plant clumps October to December.
(Campanula pyramidalis)		

* *Not recommended for the Northwest.*

NAMES	COLORS	WHEN TO PLANT
Oenothera—in variety	Yellow	Plant clumps October to January. New plants April to June.
Garden or Clove Pink (Dianthus plumarius)	Pink, rose, white	Plant clumps October to December. New plants April to July.
Carnation (Dianthus caryophylus)	White, pink, red, scarlet	Plant rooted cuttings March to June.
Mexican Daisy (Erigeron mucronatus)	Pink-white	Divide clumps October to December. New plants April to June.
Begonias—Fibrous-rooted varieties	Rose, pink, white, red	Plant rooted cuttings March to May.
Water Lilies (Nymphaea and Lotus)	White, yellow, blue, pink	Divide roots October, November, April, May.
Sun Rose (Helianthemum)	Pink, white, red, rose, yellow	Plant clumps October to January. New plants April to June.
Sidalcea—variety Rosy Gem	Rose	Set plants March to May.
Francoa ramosa	White, bluish pink	Plant clumps October to January.
House Leek (Sempervivum)	Red, yellow, rose	Plant February to June.
Verbena erinoides	Purplish blue	Plant March to May.
Perennial Cornflower (Centaurea montana)	Bright blue	Divide clumps October to January. New plants April to June.
Poker Plant (Tritoma grandiflora)	Orange-yellow	Plant clumps January to May.

BULBOUS PLANTS

NAMES	COLORS	WHEN TO PLANT
Tuberous begonias	White, red, yellow, salmon, orange, pink	Plant March, April.
Gladiolus—Large-flowered and Primulinum.	Many colors	Plant in May.
Christmas Rose (Helleborus)	White-pink	Plant February to April.
Fairy Lily—Wind Flower (Zephyranthes candida)	Yellow, rose, pink	Plant October to December.
Improved Gold-banded Lily (Lilium aurantum platyphyllum)	White-golden yellow-crimson	Plant October to December.
Tuberose	White	Plant February to June.

EVERGREEN FLOWERING SHRUBS

NAMES	COLORS	Plant Any Time
Pittosporum tenuifolium* (nigricans)	Black	Blooms September to November.
Melaleuca nesophila*	Rose-pink	Blooms May to September.
Pink-flowered Heather* (Erica melanthera)	Light pink	Blooms September to January.
Erica melanthera rosea*	Deep pink	Blooms September to January.
Yucca—in variety—Spanish Bayonet	White	Blooms April to June, August and September.
Eugenia hookeriana*	White	Blooms September to December.
Dwarf Myrtle* (Myrtus communis microphylla)	White	Blooms September, October.

DECIDUOUS FLOWERING SHRUBS

NAMES	COLORS	Plant November to April.
Roses	All colors	Blooms April to December.
Hydrangea hortensis*	Pink, white, rose, blue	Blooms June to October.

FLOWERING VINES

NAMES	COLORS	Plant November to April
Chile Jasmine* (Mandevillea suaveolens)	White	Blooms June to September.
Clematis paniculata	White	Blooms June to September.
Tall Morning-Glory (Ipomea purpurea)	Blue, purple, pink	Blooms June to September.
Silver Lace Vine (Polygonum aubertii)	Rose-white-green	Blooms April to June, September, October.

SPECIAL FRUITS AND BERRIES

NAMES	COLORS	Plant November to April
Japanese Snowball (Viburnum tomentosum plicatum)	Red-black	Bears in September, October.
Darwin's Barberry (Berberis darwini)	Deep-blue	Bears in August, September.
Wilson's Barberry (Berberis wilsoni)	Coral-red	Appears with flowers throughout year. Bears from September to November.
Berberis hookerii	Black-purple	Bears in September, October.
Cotoneaster horizontalis	Bright red	Bears from September to December.
Flowering Currant (Ribes sanguineum)	Black-blue	Bears in September, October.
Pernettya mucronata	White, red, lavender	Bears August to October.
Black Locust (Robinia pseudacacia)	Reddish brown pods	Bears August, September.
Carolina Cherry (Prunus caroliniana)	Black	Bears September to November.
Catalina Cherry (Prunus integrifolia)	Purple	Bears September, October.

Not recommended for the Northwest.

NAMES	COLORS	WHEN TO PLANT
English Hawthorn (Crataegus oxycantha)	Scarlet	Bears September, October.
Hawthorn (Crataegus monogyna)	Red	Bears September, October.
Laurel Sumac (Rhus laurifolius)	White	Bears September, October.
Hall's Honeysuckle (Lonicera japonica halliana)	Black	Bears August, September.

FOR FLOWERS IN OCTOBER

NAMES	COLORS	WHEN TO PLANT
ANNUALS		
Annual Phlox (Phlox drummondi)	Many colors	Set plants April to June.
Balsam	White, red, pink, yellow	Set plants April to June.
Nasturtium—Vine and Tom Thumb varieties.	All colors	Sow seed April to June.
Zinnias	Yellow, cream, white, crimson, salmon	Plant seeds April to June.
Cosmos	White, pink, crimson	Plant April to June.
Calliopsis	Yellow, brown, red, maroon	Plant seeds April to June.
Blue Lace Flower (Didiscus caeruleus)		Set plants April to June.
Lobelia	White, blue, rose, purple	Set plants May to July.
Virginia Stocks (Malcomia maritima)	Red, rose, white, crimson, lilac	Sow seed May to July.
Ornamental Gourds		Sow seed April, May.
Papaver rhoeas—Shirley Strain	Many colors	Sow seed April to June.
French and African Marigolds	Yellow, brown, orange	Set plants April to June.
Blue Floss Flower (Ageratum)	Lavender-mauve	Set plants April to June.
Viscaria—in variety	Rose, blue, crimson	Set plants April to June.
Guinea Flower	Golden yellow	Set plants April to July.
PERENNIALS		
Begonia semperflorens	Pink, rose, white, red, carmine	Set plants April to July.
Perennial Phlox (Phlox decussata)	All colors	Divide clumps October to January.
Salvia pitcheri	Lavender-blue	Plant clumps October to December. New plants April to June.
Scarlet Sage (Salvia splendens)		Set plants April to June.
Salvia patens	Deep blue	Divide clumps October to December. Set new plants April to June.
Purse Flower (Calceolaria)	Brown, yellow, mahogany	Divide clumps October to December. Set new plants April to June.
Dahlias	All colors	Plant tubers March to May.
Chrysanthemums	All colors	Plant rooted cuttings April to June.
Orange Sunflower (Heliopsis pitcheriana)	Golden yellow	Plant clumps October to December. New plants April, May.
Wahlenbergia (Platycodon grandiflorum)	Steel-blue	Plant clumps March, April.
Marguerite	Yellow and white varieties	Plant rooted cuttings March to May.
Verbenas	Many colors—pink, red, purple, white	Plant April to June.
Gaillardia	Orange, yellow, red in variety	Plant clumps October to December. Set new plants April to June.
Helenium—in variety	Yellow, orange, red, copper	Plant clumps October to December. Set new plants March to May.
Morning Bride (Scabiosa)	Lavender, blue, rose, pink, red	Set plants in April to June.
Pentstemon gloxinioides	Red, pink, rose, purple	Plant clumps October to January. Set new plants March to May.
Indian Meadow Rue (Thalictrum dipterocarpum)	Lavender-mauve	Plant clumps November to January. New plants March to May.
Delphinium hybrida—in many strains	Shades of blue, pink, opal	Plant clumps October to December. Set new plants March to June.
Delphinium nudicaule (native)	Orange-red	Plant clumps October to December. New plants April, May.
Perennial Aster—Michaelmas Daisy	Shades of blue and purple, mauve, pink, lavender.	Plant clumps and new plants September to January.
Boltonia—False Chamomile	White, violet, purple	Divide clumps October to January. New plants March to May.
Libonia floribunda	Scarlet-yellow	Continuous bloom. Set plants October to December.
Valerian	Lilac, rose	Plant clumps at any time.

Not recommended for the Northwest.

NAMES	COLORS	WHEN TO PLANT
Transvaal Daisy	All colors	Set plants March to May.
(Gerbera jamesoni)		
Impatiens oliveri	Pale lilac	Set plants March to June.
Sedum spectabile	Rosy crimson	Plant divisions March to May.
Japanese Anemone	White, pink, red	Plant clumps October to December.
(Anemone japonica)		
Gazania	Orange, yellow, white, scarlet	Plant clumps October to December. New plants May to July.

BULBOUS PLANTS

NAMES	COLORS	WHEN TO PLANT
Tuberous Begonias	White, red, yellow, salmon, orange	Plant March to May.
Wild Autumn-blooming Crocus	Blue, white, yellow, lilac	Plant October to December.
Kaffir Lily	Crimson scarlet	Plant divisions February to April.
(Schizostylis coccinea)		
Winter-blooming Iris	Blue	Plant September to December.
(Iris stylosa)		
Gladiolus—Large-flowered and Primulinus varieties.	All colors	Plant May, June.
Common Calla	White	Intermittent in bloom. Plant October to December.

EVERGREEN FLOWERING SHRUBS

Plant Any Time

NAMES	COLORS	WHEN TO PLANT
Pittosporum crassifolium	Wine-colored, maroon	Blooms August to October.
Heather-leaved Bottle Brush*	Yellowish white	Blooms September to November .
(Melaleuca ericifolia)		
Darwin's Barberry	Golden yellow	Intermittent bloom.
(Berberis darwini)		
Aralia seiboldi*		Blooms August to October.
Plumbago capensis*	Sky-blue	Blooms June to November.
Strawberry Tree	White	Blooms September to December.
(Arbutus unedo)		
Bouvardia*—in hybrids	Pink, rose, white	Blooms June to January.
Loquat*		Blooms September to November.
(Eriobotrya japonica)		
Japanese Sacred Bamboo		Blooms September to November.
(Nandina domestica)		
Roses	All colors—deciduous	Bloom April to December.
Fuchsia*—in variety	Many colors—deciduous	Blooms May to December.

SPECIAL FRUITS AND BERRIES

Plant November to April

NAMES	COLORS	WHEN TO PLANT
Pomegranate	Red	Bears October to January.
(Punica granatum)		
Viburnum suspensum	Red	Bears September, October.
Berberis gracilis	Blue	Autumn bearing.
Berberis elegantissima	Blue	Autumn bearing.
Catoneaster pannosa	Scarlet	Bears October, November.
Cotoneaster salicifolia	Bright red	Bears October, November.
Cotoneaster microphylla	Bright red	Bears October to February.
Chinese Evergreen Hawthorn	Scarlet	Bears October to January.
(Pyracantha crenulata)		
Firethorn	Bright red	Bears October, November.
(Pyracantha coccinea)		
Winterberry	Bright red	Bears October, November.
(Ilex verticillata)		
Japanese Sacred Bamboo	Scarlet	Bears September to December.
(Nandina domestica)		
Photinia arbutifolia	Bright red	Bears October to January.
Photinia serrulata	Red	Bears October, November.
Oleaster	Coral-red	Bears September, October.
(Eleagnus angustifolia)		
Eleagnus multiflora	Scarlet	Bears September, October.
Florida Dogwood	Scarlet	Bears September, October.
(Cornus florida)		
Cornus nuttali	Orange-red	Bears October, November.
Skimmia japonica	Coral-red to scarlet	Bears September to November.
Oregon Grape	Blue	Bears October, November.
(Mahonia aquifolium)		
Chilean Guava*	Bronze-purple	Bears October, November.
(Myrtus ugni)		
Myrtus luma*	Blackish	Bears October to December.
Australian Blue Bell Creeper	Deep blue	Bears October to November.
(Sollya heterophylla)		
Portugal Laurel	Black	Bears September to November.
(Prunus lusitanica)		
Flowering Crabapple	Red	Bears October to December.
(Pyrus floribunda)		
Japanese Flowering Crab	Red	Bears October, November.
(Pyrus kaida)		

Not recommended for the Northwest.

FOR FLOWERS IN NOVEMBER

NAMES	COLORS	WHEN TO PLANT
ANNUALS		
Cosmos	White, pink, crimson	Plant April to June.
Cape Marigold	Orange, yellow, cream	Plant in June, July.
(Calendula officinalis)		
Mignonette Hybrids	Yellow, white, pink	Sow seed April to July.
Browallia elata	Amethyst-blue	Plant April, May.
Sweet Alyssum—in variety	White, lilac	Sow seed in August.
(Alyssum maritimum)		
PERENNIALS		
Chrysanthemum	All colors	Plant rooted cuttings April to June.
Dahlias	All colors	Plant tubers April to June.
Begonia—Fibrous-rooted varieties	Red, rose, pink, white	Plant rooted cuttings April to June.
Tithonia	Yellow	Plant February to April.
Mexican Tulip Poppy	Yellow	Plant clumps October to December. New plants May, June.
(Hunnemannia fumariaefolia)		
African Golden Orange Daisy	Orange gold	Plant in March to June.
(Dimorphotheca aurantiaca)		
Kenilworth Ivy	Lilac-blue	Divide roots any time.
(Linaria cymbalaria)		
Purple Sage	White-lavender-purple	Divide clumps April to June.
(Salvia leucantha)		
Cotyledons-Hen-and-Chickens in variety	White, yellow, red, purple	Plant January to May.
Chaenostoma hispida—in variety	Red, yellow, white	Plant March to May.
Mesembryanthemum—in variety	Pink, white, yellow, rose, red	Divide clumps October to January. New plants April to June.
Plumbago larpentae	Deep blue	Divide clumps November to January. Set new plants March to June.
Monkshood	Violet-blue	Plant clumps October to December. Set new plants April, May.
(Aconitum wilsonii)		
Impatiens sultani	Scarlet—continuous bloom	Plant March to May.
Verbena erinoides	Purplish blue	Plant March to May.
Marguerites—in variety	Yellow, white	Almost continuous bloom. Plant rooted cuttings March to June.
Nicotiana affinis and hybrids	Rose, white, purple	Plant April to June.
Cornflower Aster	Blue	Plant clumps October to December. Set new plants March to June.
(Stokesia laevis)		
BULBOUS FLOWERS		
Cyclamen—in variety	White, pink, rose, salmon, red	Plant September, October.
Tigridia	White, yellow, red, carmine, orange	Plant February to May.
Tuberous Begonias	White, pink, scarlet, yellow, salmon	Plant March to May.
Helleborus—Christmas Rose	White-pink	Plant February to April.
EVERGREEN FLOWERING SHRUBS		**Plant Any Time**
Flowering Maple	All colors	Almost continuous bloom.
(Abutilon)		
Berberis knightii	Lemon yellow	Blooms November, December.
Camellia japonica	White, rose, pink, red	Blooms October to December.
Erica melanthera rosea*	Deep pink heather	Blooms October to December.
Erica wilmoreana*	Rosy white	Blooms November, December.
Erica blanda*	Rose	Blooms November, December.
Aloe frutescens*	Scarlet	Blooms November to January.
Geranium*	All colors	Blooms April to December.
(Pelargonium)		
Bouvardia*—in variety	Pink, white, rose	Blooms June to January.
DECIDUOUS FLOWERING SHRUBS		**Plant November to April**
Roses	All colors	Bloom April to December.
Fuchsias*	Many colors	Bloom June to December.
Mexican Tree Dahlia	Lavender-rose	Blooms October to November.
(Dahlia imperialis)		
FLOWERING VINES		**Plant November to April**
Bougainvillea lateritia*	Brick-red	Blooms October, November.
Copa de Ora (cup of Gold)	Ochre-yellow	Blooms October to May.
(Solandra guttata)		
Solandra grandiflora*	Yellowish white	Blooms October to January.
Lantana*—in variety	Yellow, orange, lavender, white, pink, cream	Blooms June to November.
Red Passion-vine*	Brilliant scarlet	Blooms June to November.
(Passiflora manicata)		

Not recommended for the Northwest.

NAMES	COLORS	WHEN TO PLANT
SPECIAL FRUITS AND BERRIES		
Berberis dulcis	Black	Bears October, November.
Australian Mock Orange*	Orange	Bears November, December.
(Pittosporum undulatum)		
Pittsporum crassifolium*	Light yellow	Bears November, December.
Mirror Shrub*	Coral-red	Bears October, November.
(Coprosma baueri)		
Smilax	White pink	Bears November, December.
(Asparagus asparagoides)		
Pyracantha angustifolia	Orange-yellow	Bears November to January.
Pyracantha crenulata yunnanensis	Deep red	Bears November to February.
Aralia sieboldi	Purplish black	Bears November, December.
Common Myrtle*	Black	Bears September, November.
(Myrtus communis)		
Symphoricarpos occidentalis	White	Bears October to December.
Indian Currant	Dark red	Bears October to January.
(Symphoricarpos vulgaris)		
Huckleberry	Black	Bears October, November.
(Vaccinium ovatum)		
California Coffee Shrub	Red-black	Bears September to November.
(Rhamnus californica)		
Rock Cotoneaster	Bright red	Bears September to January.
(Cotoneaster horizontalis)		
Cotoneaster franchetti	Salmon-red	Bears October, November.
Photinia davidsoniae	Orange-red	Bears October, November.
East Indian Currant	Black	Bears September to November.
(Raphiolepis indica rosea)		
Cornus capitata	Scarlet	Bears October, November.
California Grape	Blue	Bears October, November.
(Mahonia pinnata)		

FOR FLOWERS IN DECEMBER

NAMES	COLORS	WHEN TO PLANT
ANNUALS		
Double Cornflower	Deep blue	Set plants in October. Sow seed two months earlier.
(Centaurea cyaneus)		
Sweet Sultans	White, rose, purple, lavender	Set plants in September, October.
(Centaurea imperialis)		
Pot Marigold—in variety	Orange, yellow, cream	Set plants in October.
(Calendula officinalis)		
Pansies	All colors	Set plants in September.
Violas	Blue, white, yellow, lilac, apricot	Set plants in September.
Petunia—Rosy Morn, Snowball varieties	Pink, white	Set plants in September.
Mignonette Hybrids	Yellow, white, pink	Sow seed in September, October.
Winter-blooming Stocks—Nice strain	Pink, lavender, purple, white, red	Set plants in September, October.
Primula malacoides	Lavendar-mauve	Set plants in October.
Virginia Stocks	Red, white, crimson, lilac, rose	Sow seed September, October.
(Malcomia maritima)		
Browallia speciosa	Deep blue	Set plants September to November.
PERENNIALS		
Chrysanthemums	All colors	Plant rooted cuttings April to June.
Scarlet Sage		Set plants April to July.
(Salvia splendens)		
Purple Sage	White-lavender-purple	Divide roots April to October.
(Salvia leucantha)		
Pink Saxifrage	Deep pink	Plant clumps September, October.
(Saxifraga crassifolia)		
African Golden Orange Daisy	Orange-gold	Set plants in March to June.
(Dimorphotheca aurantiaca)		
Marguerites—in variety	Yellow, white	Continuous bloomer, plant any time.
Gazania	Orange, yellow, white, scarlet	Plant clumps October to December. Set new plants May to September.
BULBOUS FLOWERS		
Winter-blooming Iris	Blue	Plant clumps August, September, March, April.
(Iris stylosa)		
Kaffir Lily	Crimson scarlet	Plant divisions in February to April.
(Schizostylis coccinea)		
Cyclamen—in variety	White, pink, rose, salmon, red	Plant September, October.
Narcissus	Paper white	Plant September to December.
Amaryllis Family	Red, orange	Plant September to November.
(Hippeastrum)		

* Not recommended for the Northwest.

NAMES	COLORS	WHEN TO PLANT
Common Calla	White	Plant October to December.
Naegelia—almost continuous bloomer	White, scarlet, yellow	Plant in March to May.
Helleborus—Christmas Rose	White, pink	Plant February to April.
Tritonia—Red Freesia	Red, yellow, in variety	Plant September, October.

EVERGREEN FLOWERING SHRUBS

NAMES	COLORS	Plant Any Time
Eucalyptus ficifolia*	Scarlet	Blooms July to September, December to February.
Acacia baileyana*	Golden yellow	Blooms December to January.
Pittosporum tobira*	Creamy white	Blooms December to February.
Mexican Orange (Choisya ternata)	White	Blooms December and February to June
Flowering Oak* (Chorizema ilicifolia)	Orange-yellow	Blooms December to February.
Hakea suaveolens*	White	Blooms December to February .
Geranium*—Single varieties	All colors	Almost continuous bloom.
Cestrum aurantiacum*	Orange-yellow	Blooms December to February, June to August.
Darwin's Barberry (Berberis darwini)	Golden yellow-red	Almost continuous bloom.
Poinsettia* (Euphorbia pulcherrima)	Vermilion red-yellow	Blooms November to March.
Indian Azalea—in variety (Azalea indica)	Salmon, rose, pink, red	Blooms December to May.
Pink Heather* (Erica melanthera)	Light pink	Blooms September to January.
Camellia japonica	Pink, red, white, rose	Blooms October to December.
Chinese Rice Paper Plant* (Aralia papyrifera)	Creamy white	Blooms November to January.
Aloe frutescens*	Scarlet	Blooms November to January.
Camphor Tree* (Camphora officinalis)	Yellow	Blooms December to February.
Bouvardia—in variety	Pink, white, rose	Blooms June to January.
Jewel Flower Shrub* (Grevillea thlemanniana)	Crimson	Almost continuous bloom.
Cigar Shrub (Cuphea ignea)	Vermilion-ash, gray tips	Continuous bloom.
Bougainvillea spectabilis*	Magenta	Blooms June to February.

DECIDUOUS BLOOMING SHRUBS

NAMES	COLORS	Plant November to April
Japanese Magnolia (Magnolia soulangeana)	White, purple	Blooms December to March.
Roses	All colors	Bloom April to December.
Azalea ledifolia alba	White	Blooms December to February.

SPECIAL FRUITS AND BERRIES

NAMES	COLORS	Plant November to April
Pepper Tree* (Schinus mollis)	Coral-red	Bears December to February.
Dwarf Pomegranate (Punica granatum nana)	Red	Bears October to January.
English Privet (Ligustrum vulgare)	Black	Bears December, January.
Berberis knightii	Blue	Bears December, January.
Golden Dewdrop Shrub (Duranta plumieri)		Bears December, January.
Berberis thunbergi	Bright red	Bears August to January.
Chinese Evergreen Hawthorn (Pyracantha crenulata)	Scarlet	Bears October to January.
Red Passion Vine* (Passiflora manicata)	Yellow-green	Bears December to February.
Asparagus sprengeri	Coral-red	Bears December, January.
Asparagus plumosus	Purple, black	Bears December, January.
Smilax (Asparagus asparagoides)	Dark purple	Bears November, December.
English Holly (Ilex aquifolium)		Bears December to February.
Aucuba japonica		Bears November, December.
Toyon (Photinia arbutifolia)	Scarlet	Bears November to January.
Camphor Tree* (Camphora officinalis)	Black	Bears December to February.
Strawberry Tree (Arbutus unedo)	Red	Bears October to December.
Australian Brush Cherry* (Eugenia myrtifolia)	Red	Bears November, December.
Japanese Sacred Bamboo (Nandina domestica)	Scarlet	Bears October to January.
Solanum pseudocapsicum	Red	Bears November to January.
Cotoneaster microphylla	Bright red	Bears October to January.

* *Not recommended for the Northwest.*

DICTIONARY - ENCYCLOPEDIA

A

ABELIA GRANDIFLORA — (ABELIA). Evergreen. 4-6 feet. Sun or partial shade. Symmetrical, bushy shrub with arching branches; dark-green, ruddy-tinged, oval, acuminate (ending in sharp point) leaves; regular, short-tubular, rosy-white flowers in terminal racemes, blooming July-September. *PROPAGATION*—Green wood cuttings in summer; ripened wood cuttings in early fall; seeds sown in spring. *CULTURE*—Impartial in soil requirements, but prefers a rich, light loam. *GROUPINGS*—Common Myrtle and Dwarf Myrtle, Myrtus ugni, Cotoneaster franchetti, Azara microphylla, Melaleuca decussata, Darwins Barberry, Escallonia montevidensis, Veronica traversi. Plant in the foreground of shrub border; as hedge shrubs; as specimens.

ABIES—(FIR). Conifer. 20-50 feet under cultivation. Sun or partial shade. Very symmetrical, pyramidal in growth; needlelike, usually flattened leaves, dark green and shining above, silvery beneath; ovoid or oblong, medium-sized cones. *PROPAGATION*—Seeds sown in spring; grafted on seedlings, using veneer graft. *CULTURE*—Prefers rich, well-drained, moist soil. Used as specimen trees on large lawns; for framing houses; in large groupings.

SPECIES—**A. nordmanniana — Nordmanns Fir.** Makes a large tree with rather flat branches. **A. concolor—White Fir.** Grayish blue-green twisted leaves. **A. picea—Silver Fir.** Long, light green leaves and purple cones. **A. balsamea—Balsam Fir.** Very stiff branches and short, rigid, sharply pointed leaves. **A. grandis—Grand Fir.** Flat, horizontal branches and flattened leaves.

ABUTILON—(FLOWERING MAPLE). Evergreen. 10-12 feet. Sun and partial shade. Vinelike against walls of houses. Vigorous-growing shrub: maplelike, lobed leaves; large bell-shaped flowers several inches long, yellow, pink, red, white, orange, scarlet, frequently veined, prolific in bloom in fall, but almost continuous. *PROPAGATION*—Cuttings of new wood in spring, or of half-ripened wood in fall; seeds sown in March; cut back in fall to induce new growth. *GROUPINGS*—An individualistic type of shrub; should be grouped alone.

ACACIA. Evergreen. Sun or shade. A very variable class of trees and shrubs, usually upright, bushy, more or less symmetrical; leaves very variable, from phyllodia (petioles expanded into blades) to twice-pinnate, feathery leaves, sometimes both kinds of leaves appearing on the same tree; yellow flowers in spikes, clusters, or borne singly. *PROPAGATION*—Seeds sown generally in March, April; heel cuttings from half-ripened side shoots taken usually in June. *CULTURE*—Acacias are hardy, will endure fairly low temperatures; will tolerate a great variety of soils, growing well in adobe and clay. *GROUPINGS*—Being individualistic in character, they are best planted by themselves, taking care to use only such species in combination together that have similar foliage. They may also be grouped with a few other kinds of trees and shrubs having corresponding foliage; shrubs with white or blue flowers harmonize well with the yellow of the Acacia bloom.

SPECIES—**A. armata—Kangaroo Thorn.** 8-10 feet high, but frequently 15-20 feet broad. Very quick-growing, with arching branches; dark green, narrow spiny leaves; solitary, lemon-yellow flowers borne along sides of branches, blooming February-April. Makes fine hedges; grows in sandy soils. Combines with A. verticillata. **A. baileyana—Baileys Acacia.** 12-15 feet. Beautifully shaped tree, with bluish-gray-green, double pinnate leaves; fluffy balls of golden-yellow flowers borne in December-January. Subject to frost injury when young; place burlap sacking around tree for winter protection. One of the best Acacias for the small garden in the rear shrub border; specimen tree on front lawn; street planting. **A. baileyana purpurea.** Has a beautiful purple cast to foliage. **A. cultriformis — Knife-Leaved Acacia.** 15-20 feet. A very graceful tree, with long, pendulous branches covered with grayish green, triangular knife-edged leaves; numerous golden-yellow flowers in a head, blooming February-April. Used both in the shrub border and as a specimen tree. **A. cyanophylla.** Long, beautifully tinted, bluish-green leaves. **A. dealbata—Green Wattle.** Very tall, growing up to 50 feet, with the feathery type of foliage, and deep-yellow flowers in a head, blooming January-February. Should be grown only as specimen tree or in plantations on large estates; makes a fine hedge. **A. dealbata mollissima.** Similar to the above, but blooms in early summer. **A. floribunda—Golden Wattle.** Usually grows 10-12 feet. Round-headed type, with light-green, single-bladed leaves; golden-yellow flowers borne in fluffy heads, blooming most of the year. Used in rear shrub border; specimen tree; hedges. **A. latifolia (longifolia)—Sydney Golden Wattle.** Similar to A. floribunda, but more sprawling in habit, and with broader leaves; short spikes of lemon-yellow flowers, blooming February-March. Much used as a windbreak; hedge shrub. **A. linearis** and **A. neriifolia** are similar to A. floribunda, but have long, very narrow leaves. **A. melanoxylon—Black**

150

wood Acacia. 30-40 feet. Pyramidal and dense, with curved, yellowish-green leaves, and cream-colored flowers blooming in February-March. Endures alkali. Street tree; specimen tree. **A. pravissima.** Similar to A. cultriformis, with smaller leaves. **A. verticillata — Needle Acacia. Whorl-Leaved Acacia.** Rapidly growing Acacia, similar in growth characteristics to A. armata with which it combines. Has arching branches; dark-green, needlelike, sharp-pointed leaves; short spikes of light-yellow flowers blooming in March-April. Tolerant of both heavy and sandy soils. Used in wide shrub borders; as hedge shrub.

ACANTHUS MOLLIS—(ACANTHUS). Perennial. 3-4 feet. Sun and partial shade. Makes a vigorous, heavy growth; large radical, dark-green, cordate (heart-shaped), pinnatifid leaves; densely flowered, erect, pubescent spikes of large, irregular, hooded, purplish-white flowers, blooming in summer. *PROPAGATION*—Seeds sown in spring; division of clumps October-March. *CULTURE*—Grows best in rich, well drained loam. *POSITION*—Used considerably in foundation plantings, especially with white formal residences; occasional plant in the shrub border.

ACER—(MAPLE). Deciduous, usually round headed, some species growing quite high, up to fifty feet, especially in the interior of California. Sun or partial shade. Light or dark-green leaves, lobed and beautifully veined, frequently highly colored in fall; small flowers like silk tassels, blooming in spring; two-winged samara fruit. *PROPAGATION*—Seeds sown soon after maturity; cuttings of hardwood cuttings; layers; grafting or budding of varieties. *CULTURE*—Grows rapidly, being readily adaptable to untoward soil conditions; prefers a somewhat moist, rich light soil. *GROUPINGS*—Specimen tree to frame the house; excellent street trees on wide avenues.

SPECIES — **A. macrophyllum — Large-Leaved Maple.** Large, round-headed, wide-spreading Native Maple. Large, 3-5 lobed, cordate leaves. Adapted for planting in the wild garden. **A. negundo—Box Elder.** Tall growing, with pinnately divided leaves. Grouping tree. **A. palmatum—Japanese Maple.** Among the finest of the Maples; many varieties. Grows up to 20 feet. Leaves palmately lobed, with some species having finely dissected leaves, sometimes highly colored. Used in the shrub border in groupings; artificially dwarfed species suitable for planting near pools and in the naturalistic garden. **A. platanoides—Norway Maple.** Many garden forms. Tall and spreading, suitable as street tree, specimen tree, in groupings. **A. rubrum—Scarlet Maple.** Upright, dense in growth, with leaves turning an intense scarlet in fall; orange-red flowers. **A. saccharinum—White or Silver Maple.** Tall, with wide-spreading, slender branches, and deeply divided leaves, silvery underneath. **A. saccharum—Sugar Maple.** Makes a large tree with leaves turning an intense scarlet and yellow in fall.

ACHILLEA PTARMICA—(THE PEARL). Perennial. 1-2 ft. Sun. Smooth, serrate leaves; medium-sized, pure white, double, daisylike flowers in loose corymbs, blooming throughout summer. *PROPAGATION*—Division of clumps in fall; cuttings; seed

sown in spring. *CULTURE*—Grows in ordinary, well drained soils. Used as a cut flower, and in the regular flower border.

ACONITUM NAPELLUS— (ACONITE)— (MONKSHOOD). Perennial. 3-4 feet. Sun or partial shade. Hardy, erect plant; finely divided leaves; deep-blue, irregular, hooded flowers in racemes, blooming in June-July. *PROPAGATION*—Division of clumps in late fall or early spring; seeds sown in spring, or better sown in late summer and early fall for bloom the next year. *GROUPING*—Used in the hardy border, combining effectively with Rudbeckia, Helianthus, Coreopsis, Calliopsis, Geum, White Phlox, Lilium washingtonianum, Helenium, Yellow Snapdragon, Yellow and Orange Gladiolus.

ADAMS NEEDLE—(YUCCA).

AESCULUS CALIFORNICA— (CALIFORNIA BUCKEYE). Deciduous. 30-40 feet. Large, digitate (fingerlike), smooth leaves; dense panicles, 3-8 inches long, of fragrant, white or pale rose-colored flowers, blooming in May. *PROPAGATION*—Seed sown in fall; layering. *CULTURE*—Does best in loamy, moist soil. Effective in the naturalistic garden.

SPECIES—**Aesculus hippocastanum—Common Horse-Chestnut.** Deciduous. Tall growing, with large, divided leaves; long panicles of very fragrant, snowy-white flowers blooming in May. Used as a shade tree and along wide avenues. **A. carnea—Pink-Flowered Horse-Chestnut.** Tall, compact tree, similar to the Common Horse-Chestnut, but not so bulky, with flowers varying from flesh color to scarlet. *GROUPINGS*—Fine accent tree in the shrub border; very showy for street plantings.

AFRICAN BLUE DAISY — (ARCTOTIS GRANDIS).

AFRICAN ORANGE DAISY—(DIMORPHOTHECA).

AGAPANTHUS UMBELLATUS— (BLUE LILY OF THE NILE) — (AFRICAN LILY). Bulbous plant. 2 feet. Very hardy; long, dark-green, strap-shaped leaves; deep-blue, funnel-shaped flowers in umbels, blooming through the summer into fall. Many varieties in white and different shades of blue. *PROPAGATION* —Principally by division of clumps in fall or early spring. *CULTURE*— Grows best in rich, light garden loam; will grow in heavy soils. *GROUPINGS*—Plant as single specimens, or in combination in the hardy border with Montbretia, Peruvian Daffodil, Yellow Canna, Crinums, Yellow Butterfly, Yellow Day Lily, Mexican Tulip Poppy, Coreopsis, Yellow Geum.

AGATHEA COELESTIS — (BLUE MARGUERITE). Perennial. 1 foot, but spreading. Sun or partial shade. Hardy plant, with gray-green leaves, and small, daisylike, sky-blue flowers blooming almost continuously. *PROPAGATION* — Seed sown from early spring to late fall; cuttings. *CULTURE*—Grows in ordinary garden loam; cut back after first profuse bloom for fresh start. *GROUPINGS*—Useful in the rock garden and in the perennial border. Combines with Dianthus plumarius, Alyssum saxatile, Perennial Candytuft, Calceolaria, Phlox subulata, Sweet William, Gazania, Zinnias, Cape Marigold, Yellow Iris, Yellow Lupine, Siberian Wallflower.

AGAVE AMERICANA—(CENTURY PLANT). Perennial, native to desert regions. Sun or partial shade. Eventually 15-20 feet, but 4-5 feet without flowering stem. Stiff, thorny plant, with the flowering stem greatly elongated; leaves forming a close rosette, very fleshy, grooved, with sharp teeth along margin, lanceolate, 6-8 inches wide, 5-6 feet long; yellowish, funnel-shaped flowers borne in panicles, blooming after 10-15 years' time. *PROPAGATION*—Usually by suckers appearing at base of plant. *CULTURE*—Grows best in sandy loams, moderately rich, with little water. *POSITION*—Several variegated forms with yellow along margins. Suitable for subtropical and desert gardens; occasionally for accent effects on the shrub border; in tubs for patio gardens. The young plant is very attractive, but becomes unsightly after flowering.

AGERATUM HOUSTONIANUM (A. MEXICANUM)—(BLUE FLOSS FLOWER). Annual. 6 inches-2 feet. Sun and partial shade. Forms a bushy growth; heart-shaped, viscid-hairy gray-green leaves; fluffy heads of lavender-mauve, white to deep-blue flowers in dense clusters, blooming from April-November from successive sowings of seed. *PROPAGATION*—Seeds sown in early spring; cuttings of shapely plants in summer. *CULTURE*—Likes a rich, light, well fertilized loam. *GROUPING*—Tall-growing varieties used in flower border as bedding plant; low-growing varieties like Little Dorrit used as border plants. Combines with Columbines, Clove Pinks, Scabiosa coronaria, Pink Sweet William, Delphinium belladonna, Pentstemon, Moss Pink, Blue Lace Flower, French Marigold, Iceland Poppy, Madonna Lily, Salpiglossis.

AKEBIA QUINATA—(AKEBIA). Half evergreen shrubby climber. 6-12 feet. Sun. Twining, with young branches purplish; pinnate leaves; somewhat cup-shaped, medium-sized, fragrant, purplish-brown and rosy-purple flowers, blooming in April-May; long, oblong berries. *PROPAGATION*—Seeds; green wood and hardwood cutting; layering; root division. *CULTURE*—Best in peaty or sandy loam. *GROUPINGS*—Pretty effect used by itself, but can be combined with Jasminum grandiflorum, Streptosolen jamesoni, Yellow Jasmines, Mandevilla suaveolens, Rhynchospermum (Trachelospermum), Tecoma capensis.

ALASKA DAISY — (CHRYSANTHEMUM LEUCANTHEMUM).

ALBIZZIA JULIBRISSIN. Evergreen. 30-40 feet. Sun. Round-headed, quick-growing tree, pinnatifid leaves with numerous leaflets; heads of pink flowers, dense crowded on the upper ends of the branches, blooming in summer. *PROPAGATION* and *CULTURE*—Same as for Acacia. *POSITION*—A very beautiful specimen tree for lawns and for grouping on large plantations.

SPECIES—**Albizzia or Acacia lophanta.** Evergreen. 6-20 feet. Sun and partial shade. Very rapid-growing tree, round headed; bright-green, pinnatifid leaves, divided into numerous leaflets; numerous spikes of straw-yellow flowers, blooming in summer and intermittently throughout year. *PROPAGATION*—Easily by seeds, tending to seed itself and become naturalized in California. *POSITION*—Much used as windbreaks and for making hedges; fine for covering waste places.

ALMOND—(FLOWERING FRUIT TREES).

ALSTROMERIA AURANTIACA—(PERUVIAN LILY). Bulbous plant with tubers. 3-4 feet. Erect, spreading with bright-green, thin, lanceolate leaves; medium-sized, lilylike, orange-yellow, spotted red flowers in terminal clusters, blooming in June. *PROPAGATION*—Easily by seeds self-sown or sown in early fall; division of roots; planting tubers in fall. *CULTURE*—Grows best in rich, sandy soil. *GROUPINGS*—Best effect in the mixed border, combining with Blue Violas, Swan River Daisy, Ageratum, French Marigolds, Gaillardia, Aconitum, Salvia patens, Lupine, Anchusa, Michaelmas Daisy, Veronica spicata, Peach Bell.

SPECIES—**A. chilensis—Chilean Lily.** 2-4 feet. Leaves scattered, obovate or spatulate; large, irregular, rose, red, or white flowers, blooming in June.

ALTHAEA ROSEA—(HOLLYHOCK). Perennial. 6-12 feet. Sun and partial shade. Erect plant, with spirelike, simple, hairy stems; large, rough, rounded-heart-shaped, wavy-angled, or lobed leaves; large, regular, single with flat-petaled corolla, or double flowers in various bright colors, blooming May-September. *PROPAGATION* — Usually by seeds sown in late summer, producing plants to bloom the next season; division of clumps in fall. *CULTURE*—Grows in any soil, enriched with manure. Subject to rust. Quick growth, dusting with sulphur, planting in new ground, picked off infected leaves—are some remedial measures. *POSITION*—The stately Hollyhock is appropriate along walls, lattice fences, boundary lines, in the background of the shrub border, interspersed among shrubs.

ALWOODI PINKS — (DIANTHUS CARYOPHYLLUS).

ALYSSUM SAXATILE—(GOLD TUFT). Perennial. 12 inches. Sun or a little shade. Compact in growth; gray-green, lanceolate leaves; small, regular, golden-yellow flowers in compact clusters, blooming in April-May. *PROPAGATION*—Seeds sown in early fall or early spring; cuttings; division of roots in fall. *CULTURE*—Grows best in rich, well fertilized, light garden loam. *GROUPING*—Border plant; ground cover plant; in the mixed border; combine with Spanish Iris, Scilla, Brodiaeas, Chionodoxa, Violets, Columbine, Arctotis, Phacelia, Gypsophila, Thalictrum aquilegifolium, Veronica teucrium, Campanula carpatica, Forget-me-not.

SPECIES—**A. saxatile citriodora.** Lemon-yellow flowers. **Alyssum maritimum—Sweet Alyssum.** Annual. 6 inches. White flowers blooming continuously. Easily propagated by seeds sown broadcast.

AMARANTHUS—(AMARANTH)—In variety. Annual. 1-2 feet. Sun. Related to the Cockscomb. Grown for the vividly colored foliage and the showy flower clusters. *PROPAGATION*—Seeds sown in spring. *CULTURE*—Does best in moderately rich.

light soil. *POSITION*—Plant in borders in front of shrubbery. Cultivated kinds exhibit brown, red, bronze-green, orange-red, purple-red, purple-green colorations.

AMARYLLIS—(HIPPEASTRUM).

AMARYLLIS BELLADONNA—(BELLADONNA LILY)—(AMARYLLIS). Bulbous plant with deciduous foliage. 1-2 feet. Sun. Long, dark-green, strap-shaped leaves; long, thick flower stalks bearing umbels of large, regular, tubular, very fragrant, deep-pink flowers, blooming in fall. *PROPAGATION*—Easily by the very large bulbs. Cover lightly in fall or spring; seed. *CULTURE*—Good plant for waste places; tolerant of all soils, but prefers a rich, moderately fertilized loam. *POSITION*—Because of strong color does not group easily with other flowers, but effective in front of dark-green shrubs.

AMPELOPSIS PARTHENOCISSUS QUINQUEFOLIA — (VIRGINIA CREEPER) — (WOODBINE). Deciduous vine. 20-30 feet if partially supported. Sun and partial shade. Strong grower, climbing by tendrils; large leaves divided into five leaflets, turning to glowing colors in fall. *PROPAGATION*—Hard and soft wood cuttings in summer or spring; seeds sown in fall; easily by layering. *POSITION* — Useful for covering garages, outhouses, pergolas, brick and cement walls, dry banks, waste places. *CULTURE* — Gross feeders, requiring well fertilized garden loam.

SPECIES—A. P. tricuspidata veitchii—**Boston Ivy—Japanese Ivy.** Deciduous vine, climbing by disk appendages, fastening themselves tightly to walls, etc. Sun and partial shade. Quick-growing, vigorous, with triloded, bright-green leaves, small at first, large with age, turning to brilliant colors in early fall. Same methods of propagation and same positions used as for Virginia Creeper, clinging easily without support to porous substances such as wood, stone, brick, but not easily to glazed surfaces. Subject to mealy bug and mildew (see Plant Diseases). **A. sempervirens (cissus striata)—Evergreen Ampelopsis.** Climbing, evergreen vine. Similar to Virginia Creeper in form of leaf and growth, but much smaller leaf, dark green, not turning color in fall. Grows in full shade. Fine effect against a white wall.

ANCHUSA ITALICA— (DROPMORE VARIETY). Perennial. 4-6 feet. Sun. Strong, robust plant, awkwardly branching; rough, scurfy, large leaves; gentian blue-pink flowers in panicled racemes, blooming June-October. *PROPAGATION*—Division of roots in fall; seeds sown in March produce flowering plants the first season. *CULTURE*—Easy to grow, tolerant of all soils; avoid too much nitrogenous fertilizer. *GROUPINGS*—Plant in the perennial border, combining with Coreopsis, Gaillardia, Doronicum, Tritoma, Rudbeckia, Orange and Yellow Chrysanthemums, Matilija Poppy, Orange Sunflower, Montbretia, Peruvian Lily, Hemerocallis.

ANDROMEDA (PIERIS) JAPONICA—(ANDROMEDA). Evergreen. Small shrub to large tree according to locality, 3-30 feet. Shade loving. Round-symmetrical shrub, with dark-green, smooth, ovate

leaves; clusters of small, white, bell-shaped flowers, blooming April-May. *PROPAGATION*—Cutting of ripened wood in August; layering; seeds sown in spring. *CULTURE* — Grows in acid, moderately moist, well drained, porous soil, adding peat; dislikes heavy clay soil. *GROUPING*—Excellent for the shady border, combining with Skimmia japonica, Kalmia latifolia, Pachysandra terminalis, Azaleas in variety, Rhododendron, Large-leaved Fuchsias.

ANEMONE CORONARIA — (POPPY-FLOWERED ANEMONE). Bulbous plants with tuberous roots. 12 inches. Bright-green, finely dissected leaves; large, poppylike flowers, 1½-1½ inches across, in various shades and mixtures of red, white, and blue; blooming March-June. *PROPAGATION*—Sow seeds in warm fall or early spring. Often treated like annuals. Plant tubers not too deeply, September-November. *CULTURE*—Anemones do not like heavy soils; thrive in rich, light garden loam, kept moist during blooming period. *GROUPING*—Effective in flower beds combined with Ranunculus, or in mixed borders, combining with Primrose polyantha, Nemesia, Scabiosa, Pyrethrum, Perennial Candytuft, Delphinium chinensis.

SPECIES—A. japonica—**Japanese Anemone—Japanese Windflower.** 2-4 feet. Shade and part sun. Erect, long-stemmed, soft, downy plant, spreading by creeping stolons; large, somewhat coarse, lobed, dark-green leaves; loose clusters of regular, flat-petaled flowers, 2-3 inches across, white, red, pink, rose, according to variety, blooming August-November. *PROPAGATION*—Division of roots in fall and early spring. *CULTURE*—Does best in a peaty or sandy loam, adding well rotted horse manure; will tolerate not too heavy clay and adobe soils; acid soil reaction. *GROUPING*—For the shady or semi-shady borders, combining with Thalictrum in variety, Foxglove, Scabiosa in variety, Tuberous and Fibrous-rooted Begonias, Lilium speciosum rubrum, Lilium auratum, Lilium henryii, Ferns, Fuchsias, Potentilla nepalensis, Moss Pink, Peach Bell.

ANEMONE SHRUB—(CARPENTERIA).

ANTHEMIS TINCTORIA—(GOLDEN MARGUERITE). Perennial. 2 feet. Sun. Heavy-scented plant, bushy, with erect, angular stems; finely divided, light-green leaves; golden-yellow, daisylike flowers, blooming from August well into fall. *PROPAGATION*—Seed sown in spring; stem cuttings. *CULTURE* — Grows easily in any kind of soil. *GROUPING*—Used to brighten up flower border.

ANTIRRHINUM—(SNAPDRAGON). Annual, becoming perennial in California. 1-3 feet. Sun and partial shade. Erect, bushy plant, with smooth, clear-green, medium-sized, lanceolate leaves; medium to large-sized, tubular, two-lipped flowers in loose spikes, white, silver pink, through fawn, orange, to scarlet, blooming from early spring to late fall, often during mild winters in California. *PROPAGATION*—Seed sown from January-September for succession of flowers; softwood cuttings of rust-immune and special flowering plants taken in spring. *CULTURE*—Remarkably adaptable to different soils, but prefers rich, light, well fertilized garden loam. Subject to aphis and to rust; the latter disease is sometimes difficult to control, but clean, fresh soil, dusting young plants

with sulphur, irrigation instead of sprinkling, quick growth, are some remedial measures. Cut back good plants for second bloom. *GROUPING*—Fine for the annual and mixed borders. Many distinct strains; varieties with distinct colors only should be used, using colors together that harmonize. Group, according to color of variety, with Scabiosa in variety, Gladiolus, Pentstemon, Larkspur, Delphinium, Columbine, Primula in variety, Nepeta, Coral Bells, Michaelmas Daisy, Perennial Phlox, Clarkia, Chrysanthemum.

APRICOT—(FLOWERING FRUIT TREES).

AQUILEGIA—(COLUMBINE). Perennial, 2-4
feet. Sun or half shade. Erect, branching plant, with long, slender stems; clear-green, finely divided foliage; loose panicles of yellow, blue, pink, red, or white flowers, the petals contracted into spurs, blooming May-June. *PROPAGA-TION*—Seeds, sown preferably in early fall to make blooming plants next year; seeds sown in spring; division of clumps in fall and spring; self-sow readily. *CULTURE*—Tolerate different soils, but prefer a rich, moist, well fertilized, light loam. Attacked by aphis, root rot (see Plant Pests). Favors acid soil reaction. *GROUPINGS*—Splendid for the mixed border. The newer strains have finely formed, large flowers in rich colors, including Blackmore and Langdon, Mrs. Scott Elliott Hybrids, and others. Group with Delphinium, Thalictrum in variety, Spanish Iris, Perennial Candytuft, Scabiosa in variety, Stocks, Snapdragons, Violas, Astilbe, Coral Bells, Gladiolus, Veronica spicata, Bronze and Purple Iris, and with many of the low-creeping rock plants.

SPECIES—**A. caerulea**—Rocky Mountain Columbine, with blue-white flowers; **A. chrysantha**, golden-yellow. **A. skinneri**, brick-red.

ARABIS ALBIDA—(ROCK CRESS). Perennial.
6 inches, but spreading out, forming a matty growth; gray-green, pubescent, lanceolate leaves, forming a sort of rosette; white, fragrant, radishlike flowers, borne in loose racemes, blooming in early spring. *PROPAGATION*—Seeds sown in fall or early spring; cuttings; division in fall. *CULTURE*—Grows well in any soil. *POSITION*—Useful in the rock garden; in the regular flower border; border plant.

ARALIA PAPYRIFERA — (CHINESE RICE PAPER PLANT). Evergreen. 10-20 feet. Sun and
partial shade. Quick-growing, branching, sub-tropical small tree, with stout, downy branches; very large, five-lobed, very tomentose, gray-green leaves. *PROPAGATION*—Cuttings in spring or early fall; seed sown in early spring, also self-sown. *CULTURE*—Prefers rich, heavy soils, and will tolerate clay, adobe. Subject to mealy bug (see Plant Pests). *POSITION*—Valuable tree for planting as single specimens in close proximity to Spanish residences. Combine with Aucubas and Bamboos.

SPECIES — **Aralia sieboldi** — **Hercules Club.** Evergreen. 4-6 feet. Full shade and part sun. Branching shrub, with dark-green, smooth, shining, incised leaves, 6-8 inches long; very large, umbel-shaped, compound inflorescence, bearing small white flowers, blooming in fall; small black fruits—hence the common name. *PROPAGATION*—Cuttings or seed as in A. papyrifera. *CULTURE*—Requires a rich, well-fertilized loam. Several variegated forms with yellow or white margins. Attacked by mealy bug and scale (see Plant Pests). *GROUPING*—Used primarily in shade border, combining with Rhododendrons, Aucuba, Mahonia, Nandina.

ARBOR VITAE—(THUYA).

ARBUTUS MENZIESII—(MADRONE). Native
evergreen. Usually 10-20 feet under cultivation, up to 100 feet in woods. Interesting native tree, with twisted stems and branches, conspicuous by the reddish-brown or mahogany-colored bark, peeling off continually in large, thin plates; large, leathery, smooth, shining, rounded-oval leaves; numerous small, white, bell-shaped flowers in long panicles, blooming in spring; bright, orange-red fruits in fall. *PROPAGATION*—Cuttings in fall; seed sown in early spring. *CULTURE*—Well drained, ordinary soil; sheltered position, not exposed to drying winds; acid soil reaction; attacked by scale and other sucking insects. *POSITION*—The Madrone gives a picturesque effect planted near a Spanish residence; specimen tree on lawns.

ARBUTUS UNEDO—(STRAWBERRY TREE).
Evergreen. 8-15 feet. Sun and partial shade. Hardy, compact, round-headed tree, with medium-sized, thick, leathery, dark-green, oblong-lanceolate, serrate leaves; small, white, bell-shaped flowers in clusters, blooming September-December; pendulous, red, strawberrylike fruits. *PROPAGATION*—Cuttings of half ripened wood in fall; veneer graft; layering; seeds sown in fall or early spring. *CULTURE*—Any good, well drained garden loam; endures sandy, alkali, and stiff soils. *GROUPING*—Specimen tree and for the shrub border, combining with the Toyon, Eugenia hookeriana, Pittosporum crassifolium, California Cherry, Eucalyptus ficifolia, Dogwood, Melaleuca nesophila, Pyracantha angustifolia, Viburnum sandankwa, Viburnum tinus lucidum.

ARCTOTIS GRANDIS — (AFRICAN BLUE DAISY). Hardy annual. 2-3 feet. Sun. Branching
plant, with thick, gray-green, woolly leaves; wide, daisylike, white-lilac-blue narrow-petaled flowers, blooming June-December. *PROPAGATION*—Seed sown from early spring-July. *CULTURE*—Does best in rich, light, well fertilized garden loam. *GROUPINGS*—Important in the mixed border, combining with Snapdragons, Stocks, Larkspur, Godetia, Browallia, Scarlet Sage, Pyrethrum, Centaurea montana, Coral Bells, Autumn Crocus, Tigridia, Peruvian Daffodil.

ARENARIA — (SCOTCH MOSS) — (IRISH MOSS). Perennial. Sun and partial shade. Trailing
plant with long, dark-green filaments, and minute, white, star-shaped flowers. *PROPAGATION*—Seeds, but mostly by division of matted growth; cuttings. *CULTURE*—Preferably a sandy or peaty loam, moderately fertilized; to maintain moss, water continually, keep soil loose, occasionally apply a mulch of one-tenth fertilizer to one-tenths peat. Subject to sow bugs, pill bugs (see Plant Pests). *USES*—Fine for planting between stepping-stones; in rockeries; near pools, on embankments; in courts in place of grass; in dry watercourses.

154

ARMERIA VULGARIS— (SEA PINK) — (THRIFT). Perennial. 8 inches. Bunches of narrow, grasslike leaves coming from the base of the plant; closely contracted heads of small pink, white, or reddish flowers, subtended by bracts, blooming profusely in summer, but quite continuously throughout the year. *PROPAGATION*—Division of stools at any time; seeds. *CULTURE*—Very hardy, enduring a variety of soils, but preferring a rather light, moderately rich loam. *POSITION*—Edging plant along walks; rockeries; ground cover plant.

ARUNDINARIA— (DENDROCALAMUS).

ASH— (FRAXINUS) — (SORBUS).

ASPARAGUS. Perennials, provided with rhizomatous roots, the plants described being vines or trailing in habit. 3-6 or more feet. Leafy, branching plants, the leaves reduced to bracts, with stems called cladodes substituted for them, often thorny. *PROPAGATION*—Seed sown in early spring; division of roots in fall or early spring; cuttings. *CULTURE*—Prefers a light garden loam, enriched with manures. *POSITION*—Used as greens for flowers, so planted under lath or glass; in mild climates planted outdoors under trees in combination with ferns and other shade-loving plants; porch boxes and pots; for use on trellises, as screens, etc.

SPECIES—**A. plumosus—Asparagus Fern.** Existing in many varieties. Tall, woody, climbing vine, flat fronds of very finely divided, bright-green cladodes; small terminal clusters of small white flowers, blooming in summer; purple-black berries in fall. **A. sprengeri.** Cladodes smooth, pointed, linear; pinkish-white, fragrant flowers, blooming in May-June; bright, coral-red fruits, ripening at Christmas time. **A. asparagoides — Smilax.** Tall, slender, smooth climber, very much branched; smooth, shiny, oval, dark-green cladodes; greenish-white flowers; dark-purple berries.

ASTER— (CALLISTEPHUS). Annual. 1-3 feet. Sun, enduring some shade. Erect, bushy plant, with oval, rather large coarsely toothed leaves; terminal heads of characteristic compositæ flowers, 2-4 inches across, white, through pink, rose, lavender, red, to purple, blooming July-October. *PROPAGATION*—Seeds sown in early spring to July. *CULTURE*—Quite impartial as to soil, but very heavy clay or adobe soils should be lightened by addition of straw manure, wood ashes, compost, peat, etc.; fertilize with manures before planting, with commercial fertilizers when coming into bloom. Several serious plant diseases: Aster Yellows caused by leaf hopper, difficult to control, so grub out infected plants; root aphis, controlled by nico-dust; stem rot, induced by too much moisture in soil. Asters are somewhat uncertain plants, but generally do well in an open, sunny position in an ordinary, rich garden loam. *GROUPING*—Make a splendid effect planted close together in separate colors in flower beds and borders; in the mixed border group with Ageratum, Perennial Phlox, Michaelmas Daisy, Sweet William, Cornflower Aster, Gladiolus, Lilium speciosum album, Blue Lace Flower, Salvia azurea, Scabiosa caucasica. **Perennial Aster—Michaelmas Daisy.** Representing many species of hybrid forms. 2-6 feet. Sun and partial shade, although preferring mostly sunny positions. Erect, tending to make large clumps from the creeping stems; oblong-lanceolate, medium green leaves; numerous, daisy-like flowers in dense heads or racemes white, pink, lavender to deep purple, blooming during summer and fall. *PROPAGATION*—Division of clumps in fall or early spring, using young side shoots; seeds, but seedlings tend to vary; cuttings. *CULTURE*—Drought resistant, grows in any soil, but prefers a sandy loam, not too moist, well fertilized with manures in fall. *GROUPING*—Of value in the perennial and mixed borders, combining, according to color, with Columbine, Hemerocallis, Iceland Poppy, Evening Primrose, Pentstemon, Scabiosa in variety, Siberian Wallflower, French and African Marigold, Regale Lily, Madonna Lily, Tuberose, Snapdragons, Primulinum Gladiolus, and many others.

ASTILBE ROSEA— (ASTILBE). Perennial, 1-1½ feet. Half shade. Bushy plants with slender stems; bright-green, compound, ternately (arranged in threes) pinnatifid leaves; rather dense, feathery panicles of small, white, pink, or purplish flowers blooming in June. Two of the best varieties are Peach Blossom, blush-pink, and Queen Alexandra, deeper pink flowers. *PROPAGATION*—Seeds sown in early spring, blooming the second year; division of clumps September-November. *CULTURE*—Requires a rich, moist, garden loam, adding leaf-mold or peat. *GROUPING*—Pretty in the shade border, grouping with Virginia Stocks, Heuchera, Ferns, light-blue Campanulas, Aubrietia, Columbine, light-colored Begonia semperflorens, Summer Snowflake, Hemerocallis, Summer-blooming Oxalis.

ATLANTIC CEDAR — (CEDRUS ATLANTICA).

AUBRIETIA DELTOIDEA — (FALSE WALL CRESS). Perennial. 6 inches, but wide-spreading, forming dense mats. Sun or partial shade. Gray-green, somewhat scurfy, deltoid (delta-shaped) leaves; numerous, small, radishlike, pale lilac, rose, to deep-lilac flowers, blooming January-April. *PROPAGATION*—Seeds sown in early fall to bloom next year; cuttings in early spring; division of clumps in early fall. *CULTURE*—Grows in any soil, but prefers a moderately rich, calcareous (containing lime), gritty soil; subject to pill bugs, sow bugs (see Plant Pests). Cut back each year for new growth. *GROUPINGS*—A very useful plant for the rock garden, between stepping-stones, to cover embankments, for the perennial and mixed borders. Combine with Primula malacoides, Cornflowers, Violets, deep-blue Forget-me-nots, Dutch Crocus, Narcissi, Winter-blooming Oxalis, Polyantha Primrose.

AUCUBA JAPONICA— (AUCUBA). Evergreen. 4-5 feet. Shade loving. Bushy, branching shrub, with dark-green leaves; inconspicuous flowers; bright-scarlet fruits on plants having female flowers. *PROPAGATION*—Readily by half ripened green wood cuttings; taken any time of year; seeds sown after maturity. *CULTURE*—Requires a well drained, moist, acid soil, enriched with manures; subject to mealy bug (see Plant Pests). *GROUPING*—Both specimen and grouping shrub for the shady border; combine with Mahonia, Rhododendrons, Aralia sieboldii, Hydrangea hortensis.

SPECIES — **A. japonica variegata.** Variegated form with yellow-spotted leaves.

155

AUSTRALIAN BEECH — (EUCALYPTUS POLYANTHEMOS).

AUSTRALIAN BLUEBELL CREEPER—(SOLLYA).

AUSTRALIAN BUSH CHERRY—(EUGENIA MYRTIFOLIA).

AUSTRALIAN HOLLY—(COPROSMA).

AUSTRALIAN MOCK ORANGE—(PITTOSPORUM UNDULATUM).

AUSTRALIAN PEA VINE—(DOLICHOS).

AUSTRALIAN TEA SHRUB—(LEPTOSPERMUM LAEVIGATUM).

AUTUMN CROCUS—(COLCHIUM).

AZALEA. Known also as Rhododendron, but differing in character of growth, foliage, inflorescence, colors of flowers. Full shade, half shade, and sun, according to kind. Under cultivation, Azaleas, especially along the Pacific Coast, usually grow from 2-4 feet, with exceptions. Sturdy, beautifully formed, symmetrical shrubs, with medium-sized to large, light or dark-green, often pilose (hairy) leaves, many species having brilliantly colored foliage in the fall; clusters of regular, small to quite large, single or semi-double flowers, with flat, expanded, or frilled petals, delicately or brilliantly colored. *PROPAGATION*—Seeds sown when ripe, but seedlings not coming true; cuttings of half ripened wood in summer; using gentle bottom heat; hybrid varieties by grafting upon hardy stock in spring, autumn, and early winter; occasionally by layering in spring. *CULTURE*—Requires an acid, well drained, moist garden loam, free from lime, adding peat or leaf-mold to maintain acidity; add limited amounts of fertilizer, especially well rotted cow manure; dangerous to use commercial fertilizers like ammonium sulphate except very sparingly and in solution; mulch of pine needles very beneficial; do not cultivate about roots; place most kinds in positions where they receive a little sun during day.

SPECIES—Deciduous Azaleas, having brilliantly colored blossoms, blooming April-May, either smooth or pilose leaves, turning to very brilliant colorations in fall. Some of the best kinds include—**A. mollis—Flame Azalea**, variable, with yellow, orange, and flame-colored flowers; **A. occidentalis—California Azalea**, tall-growing, with creamy-white, fragrant flowers; **A. altaclarensis**, bronze-orange; **A. kaempferi—Torch Azalea**, indeterminate in blooming; **A. japonicum**, with white, bell-shaped flowers in clusters.

Evergreen Azaleas. These are among the finest Azaleas for average California conditions, especially along the Pacific Coast. Rapid growers, usually blooming each year, with smooth, glistening leaves, often turning to vivid colors in fall, 1-3 feet high and wide-spreading in growth.

SPECIES—**A. indica.** Rapid growing, blooming profusely, with glistening leaves, and large, single or semi-double flowers, 2-4 inches across, in bright colors, blooming December-May. Subject a little to leaf spot, controlled by Bordeaux Mixture, or by picking off leaves. **A. ledifolia alba.** Pure white, large, fragrant flowers, blooming early in December.

A. hinodigiri—Japanese Azalea. Small crimson flowers, blooming December-February. **A. kurume.** White and pinkish-white flowers, blooming December-March; **A. hexe**, semi-dwarf; semi-double, scarlet flowers. *GROUPINGS*—Used with excellent effect in rockeries; foundation plantings; shady and semi-shady shrub borders, combining with Bouvardia, Daphne, Andromeda, Mahonia, Chamaecyparis in variety, Cotoneaster horizontalis, Ferns, Fuchsias with similar colors, en masse, using different species together.

AZARA MICROPHYLLA — (AZARA). Evergreen. 6-10 feet. Full shade and sun. Rather flat-sided, loosely spreading shrub; very small, dark-green oval, glistening leaves; minute, greenish-yellow flowers, very spicily fragrant, blooming February-March. *PROPAGATION*—Cuttings of mature wood in fall; seeds sown soon after maturing. *CULTURE* —Require a rich, well fertilized loam, adding peat. *GROUPING*—Used in foundation plantings; against walls; in the shrub border, especially in part shade, combining with Fuchsias, especially F. thymifolia, Pyracantha crenulata, Small-leaved Barberries, Dwarf Myrtle, Myrtus luma, Nandina, Mahonia, Cotoneaster horizontalis.

B

BABIANA. Bulbous plants. 10-12 inches. Narrow, hairy, plaited leaves; racemes lavender to purple, blooming March-June. *PROPAGATION*—Offsets and seed in fall. *CULTURE*—Prefers a rich garden loam; replant every two or three years.

BABYS BREATH—(GYPSOPHILA).

BACHELORS BUTTON—(CENTAUREA CYANEUS).

BAILEYS ACACIA—(ACACIA BAILEYANA).

BALD CYPRESS — (TAXODIUM DISTICHUM).

BALLOON FLOWER — (PLATYCODON GRANDIFLORUM).

BALSAM—(IMPATIENS BALSAMINA).

BALSAM FIR—(ABIES BALSAMEA).

BAMBOO—(DENDROCALAMUS).

BANANA SHRUB—(MICHELIA FUSCATA).

BARBERRY—(BERBERIS).

BEAUTY BUSH—(KOLKWITZIA).

BEEFWOOD TREE—(CASUARINA).

BEGONIA. Evergreen and semi-deciduous perennials. 1-6 feet. Sun and shade loving according to kind. Large order of plants and sub-shrubs, doing especially well outdoors in California. Characterized by stout, green, succulent, often colored stems and branches; roots fibrous or tuberous; leaves variable, medium-sized to large; flowers either axillary or in few-flowered clusters. *PROPAGATION*—Seed, fine as gold dust; germinates readily in spring if sown on the surface of fine, peaty soil medium in seed pans; easily by cuttings in fall and early spring;

tubers, described below. *CULTURE*—In general require a rich, moist, fibrous loam, fertilized with cow manure preferably, or with processed manures.

SPECIES—**Fibrous-Rooted Begonias.** Comprise the tall, large-leaved kinds, and the low-growing, small-flowered kinds. **B. semperflorens,** with many variable varieties. 6-18 inches. Full sun and partial shade. Bushy, round-symmetrical, with small root stock; ovate, medium sized, glistening, bright-green or reddish leaves; abundant white, pink, rose, or red flowers, blooming prolifically in late spring and summer, and quite continuously. The variety Vernon is the most popular variety; used for borders and for colorful bedding purposes. **Large-leaved Varieties**—Growing 4-6 feet. Semi-deciduous. Full or part shade outdoors; shade or sun in the house. Stout stems and large, smooth, often highly colored leaves; large clusters of medium-sized, pendulous, white, pink to deep red flowers, blooming quite continuously; prolific time of bloom being July-late fall. *PROPAGATION*—Seeds same as for above; easily by cuttings of semi-firm wood in spring and fall. *CULTURE*—Very hardy, free from pests, delighting in a sandy or peaty loam, well enriched with cow manure, kept continually moist. *GROUPING*—One of the best plants for the house; does equally well in half shady foundation plantings and in the shady border under trees, combining with Tuberous Begonias, Ferns, Thalictrum, Azaleas, Rhododendrons, Columbines, Aralia Sieboldii, Azara, Cineraria, small-flowered Fuchsias. **House Plants**—**B. socotrana,** variety Gloire de Lorraine with rose-colored flowers. *PROPAGATION*—Bulblike roots potted up in September-October. **Basket Begonias.** These have single or semi-double pendulous flowers in various colors, and are suitable for baskets or in the open ground in partial shade. **Rex Begonia.** Rhizomatous stem. Grown in the half shady border, in the greenhouse, and as potted plants, chiefly for the foliage which is large, hairy, metallic, with a silver sheen. *PROPAGATION*—Shoot cuttings; leaf cuttings, retaining a portion of the leaf stalk with midrib notched, pinning to sand. **Tuberous Begonia.** Bulbous plants with tubers. 10-18 inches. Best in partial shade, but also in sun. Large, smooth, bright-green leaves; flat, single or double, Camellialike flowers in bright colors, frequently measuring 4-6 inches across, blooming in California along the Pacific Coast from July until frosts in November. *PROPAGATION*—Tubers planted usually in March-April, just barely covered with peaty soil; frequently planted in flats containing rich, light soil; when tubers show pink they are cut out and planted in border; seed sown in March will produce small flowering plants the first year; tubers increase in size each year. *CULTURE*—Prefer a rich, light garden loam, fertilized preferably with well rotted cow manure; keep soil continually moist; very hardy, little subject to plant pests, except leaf spot (see Plant Pests). *GROUPINGS*—Very effective in the shrub border in front of dark-green shrubs; for bedding out; as potted plants for sun porch; for the shady border, combining with Ferns, and the same plants mentioned for Large-leaved Fibrous-rooted Begonias.

BELLADONNA LILY—(AMARYLLIS).

BELLFLOWER—(CAMPANULA).

BELLIS PERENNIS — (ENGLISH DAISY). Perennial. 3-6 inches. Shade and part sun. Fleshy root, making large clumps of fleshy, dark-green leaves; large, densely rayed heads of white, rose, pink, or reddish flowers, blooming February-May. *PROPAGATION*—Easily by division in fall or early spring; seeds in early spring, or self-sown. *CULTURE*—Moderately rich garden loam. *GROUPING*—Used principally as border plant; naturalized in wild garden and lawns; flower borders. Combine with Narcissus, Primula malacoides, Lavender Violas, lavender and pink Winter-blooming Stocks, Cinerarias, Heuchera.

BERBERIS—(BARBERRY). Evergreen and deciduous, 18 inches-6 feet, according to kind. Sun and partial shade. Bushy, branching shrubs; frequently with thorny branches or spiny leaves; variable leaves; small, bell-like, yellow flowers in clusters; usually blue or purplish berries. *PROPAGATION*—Seeds sown in fall; Darwins Berberry and others seed themselves readily; green wood cuttings in June; heel cuttings of half firm wood in early fall. *CULTURE*—Tolerate a variety of soil conditions, except heavy clays; prefers a sandy or peaty soil, well enriched with manures; head back after three or four years. *GROUPING*—Splendid subjects for foundation plantings and in the foreground of the shrub border. Combine with Abelia, Ericas in variety (Heathers), Cotoneasters in variety, Dwarf Myrtle, Myrtus ugni, Chamaecyparis in variety, Azaleas in variety, Breath-of-heaven, different species with each other; specimen shrub for lawns; many species used for making hedges about courts, like Darwins Barberry, Thunbergs Barberry.

SPECIES—**B. darwini—Darwins Barberry.** Evergreen. 4-6 feet. Small, spiny, dark-green, shining, hollylike leaves; golden-yellow flowers blooming profusely during July, again in winter, and scattered throughout year; dark-blue berries. **B. gracilis.** Very dwarf. **B. ilicifolium.** Evergreen. Similar to Darwins Barberry. **B. knightii.** Evergreen. Similar to Darwins Barberry, but with larger leaves, and lemon-yellow flowers, blooming in summer and fall. **B. stenophylla.** Evergreen. 5-7 feet. Wide-spreading, with arching, spiny branches; narrow dark-green leaves. **B. thunbergi—Thunbergs Barberry.** 2-5 feet. Branches brown, spreading, spiny; pale-yellow flowers blooming April-May; brilliant red fruits in combination with bright scarlet fall coloration of leaves. Much used for bordering walks and as low hedge. **B. verruculosa.** Evergreen. 4 feet. Bright-green leaves; clear yellow flowers blooming June-August; black fruit. **B. vulgaris—Common Barberry.** Deciduous. 4-8 feet. Upright or arching branches; pendulous, many-flowered racemes of bright-yellow flowers, blooming May-June; scarlet fruits turning purple. **B. wilsoni—Wilsons Barberry.** Semi-deciduous. 18 inches high, but spreading. Very spiny, with small, light-green leaves, and golden-yellow flowers borne in May-June; translucent, coral-red berries in September-November.

BETULA—(BIRCH). Deciduous. 10-60 feet. Symmetrical, erect, rapid-growing trees, some with weeping pendulous forms; bark often covered with a thin, gray or whitish, parchmentlike covering; leaves bright green, sharply serrate, tapering to a point; small flowers in pendulous catkins; small, conelike fruits. *PROPAGATION*—Seeds sown soon after maturity; layering; budding or grafting of varieties on North American species and varieties. *CULTURE*—Grows in all soils, but best in fertile, acid soil; subject to scale followed by smut disease; wash off tree and follow with oil sprays.

SPECIES—**B. alba**—**European Birch.** Tall, slender tree with pendulous branches, much used on lawns and in groupings in shrub borders. **B. alba pendula laciniata**—**Cut-leaf Weeping Birch.** Low-growing, pendulous variety, with light-green, finely dissected leaves. Suitable as specimen on lawns, or near pools. **B. alba atropurpurea**—**Copper-leaf Birch.** Coppery red leaves.

BIGNONIA — **(TRUMPET VINE).** Evergreen. 20-30 feet or more. Sun loving. Strong and rapid growing, climbing by means of tendrils or somewhat by suction; sends out long runners, covered densely with dark-green, smooth, compound leaves; large, tubular or bellshaped, brightly colored flowers. Species described below. *PROPAGATION*—Cuttings of half mature wood in late spring; simple layering; root cuttings in greenhouse. *CULTURE*—Adapted to a variety of soils, but prefers an open, porous, moist loam, well fertilized with manures and commercial fertilizers; should be thinned out occasionally; remove all superfluous branches and weak shoots; keep well watered at all times; subject to mealy bug (see Plant Diseases). *POSITION*—Fine for covering walls of residence, making festoon growths; for covering stone and brick walls and embankments, arches and pergolas.

SPECIES—**B. australis.** Creamy white, blooming March-May. **B cherere.** Orange-scarlet, blooming June-August. **B. speciosa.** Yellow, purple, blooming April-June. **B. tweediana.** Orange-yellow, blooming March-May. **B. venusta.** Orange-crimson, blooming December-February. **B. violacea.** Lilac, blooming March-May.

BIRCH—**(BETULA).**

BIRDS NEST CYPRESS—**(CHAMAECYPARIS NIDIFERA).**

BLACK LOCUST—**(ROBINIA).**

BLACKWOOD ACACIA—**(ACACIA MELANOXYLON).**

BLANKET FLOWER—**(GAILLARDIA).**

BLUE BELLS—**(CAMPANULA MURALIS)**—**(MERTENSIA VIRGINICA).**

BLUE BONNET—**(SCABIOSA CAUCASICA).**

BLUE FLOSS FLOWER—**(AGERATUM).**

BLUE FORGET-ME-NOT — **(CYNOGLOSSUM).**

BLUE GUM—**(EUCALYPTUS GLOBULUS).**

BLUE LILY OF THE NILE — **(AGAPANTHUS).**

BLUE MARGUERITE—**(AGATHAEA).**

BLUE PALM—**(ERYTHEA ARMATA).**

BLUE SCARAB CYPRESS—**(CHAMAECYPARIS LAW. ALUMI).**

BLUE SPIRAEA—**(CARYOPTERIS).**

BORONIA ELATIOR — **(BORONIA).** Evergreen. 4 feet. Sun. Hardy, drought resisting shrub, with pinnate heatherlike leaves; somewhat bellshaped flowers, colored reddish-brown, red, or purple, blooming April-May. *PROPAGATION*—Seeds; cuttings of half ripened wood. *CULTURE*—Ordinary, well drained soil, free from sourness; cut back after flowering. *GROUPINGS* — Plant both in flower and shrub borders, combining with Blue Larkspur, Lobelia, Purple Violas, Veronica decussata, Genistas, Darwin's Barberry.

BOSTON IVY—**(AMPELOPSIS VEITCHII).**

BOTTLE BRUSH — **(CALLISTEMON)** — **(MELALEUCA).**

BOTTLE GOURDS—**(GOURDS).**

BOUGAINVILLEA. Evergreen vine. 10-20 feet or more. Sun or a little shade. Strong growing vines requiring a warm, sheltered situation, free from frosts, doing well outdoors in California along the Pacific Coast; rather large, ovate, glossy, dark-green leaves; clusters of inconspicuous flowers, blooming from June-February according to species. *PROPAGATION*—Cuttings of half ripened or old wood in April-June; cuttings of young shoots placed in sandy soil in bottom heat. *CULTURE*—Quite drought resistant, growing in any soil, but benefited by addition of manures and peat. *POSITION*—Useful for covering porches, arches, pergolas, walls; foundation plantings, used in equable climates for making hedges.

SPECIES—**B. spectabilis.** Large panicles of rose-purple to magenta flowers, blooming June-February; the kind most commonly grown. **B. spec. lateritia.** Brick-red flowers, blooming October-November. **B. brasiliensis.** Pink-purple flowers, blooming July-August. **Variety Crimson Lake.** Rather tender, with rich crimson flowers, blooming June-September.

BOUVARDIA. Small, evergreen, vinelike shrubs treated as perennials. 3-6 feet or more feet high. Sun and partial shade. Semi-hardy, with smooth, ovate-lanceolate, dark-green leaves; terminal corymbs of regular, slightly fragrant tubular flowers, pink, white, rose, blooming September-January. *PROPAGATION*—Cuttings in March; root cuttings in spring. *CULTURE*—Should grow in a warm, sheltered place; requires a rich, moist, well drained, light garden loam; subject to frost injury. *GROUPINGS*—Useful in the flower and shrub borders, combining with Mexican Orange, Pittosporum tobira, Azaleas in harmonizing colors, Magnolia soulangeana, in foreground of Camellia japonica, Coprosma.

BOX ELDER—**(ACER NEGUNDO).**

BOXWOOD—**(BUXUS SEMPERVIRENS).**

BRACHYCOME IBERIDIFOLIA—**(SWAN RIVER DAISY).** Annual. 6-12 inches. Sun and half shade. Leaves small, pinnately divided and forked; small, daisylike flowers, ray petals white to violet-blue, disk florets yellow or dark colored, blooming June-July. *PROPAGATION*—Seed sown in spring. *CULTURE*—Ordinary garden conditions satisfactory. *GROUPINGS*— Plant in annual or mixed borders, combining with Lupine, Yellow Geum, Columbine, Perennial Flax, Alstromeria chilensis, Hemerocallis.

BRAZILIAN MORNING-GLORY — (IPOMOEA SETOSA).

BREATH-OF-HEAVEN—(DIOSMA).

BRIDAL VEIL SHRUB—(GENISTA MONOSPERMA).

BRIDAL WREATH— (SPIRAEA PRUNIFOLIA).

BROOM—(CYTISUS).

BUCKEYE—(AESCULUS).

BUDDLEIA VARIABILIS—(BUTTERFLY BUSH)—(SUMMER LILAC). Evergreen. 10-15 feet. Sun and partial shade. Loose-spreading, rampant grower: long, lanceolate, silver-gray leaves; long, compact spikes of fragrant, lilac-purple flowers, blooming June-September. *PROPAGATION*— Green wood cuttings in spring; hard wood cuttings in fall; seed sown in spring. *CULTURE*—Grows in any soil. *GROUPING*—Combine with Buddleia globosa, Matilija Poppy, Cassia in variety, Yellow Heliotrope.

SPECIES— **B. globosa.** Evergreen. Compact, round-headed shrub; medium-sized, orange-yellow flowers in dense terminal heads, blooming in May. Same groupings as for the Butterfly Bush.

BUSH HONEYSUCKLE — (LONICERA NITIDA).

BUTTERFLY BUSH—(BUDDLEIA).

BUTTERFLY FLOWER— (SCHIZANTHUS).

BUXUS SEMPERVIRENS — (ENGLISH BOXWOOD—BOXWOOD). Round-headed, compact, symmetrical shrub of slow growth, but growing to 25 feet; medium-sized, roundish oval, dark-green, smooth and shining leaves. *PROPAGATION*—Mature wood cuttings in early fall; layering. *CULTURE*—Requires a rich, light, well fertilized, well drained loam. *POSITION*—Very amenable to pruning, thereby creating various forms to be used for formal effects; in tubs and pots; makes a fine hedge; in the shrub border.

SPECIES—**B. japonica.** More spreading in habit; larger, lighter green leaves. **B. semper suffruticosa.** Dwarf form up to 10 inches; smaller, dark-green leaves. Used for making low hedges about formal gardens, from 4-10 inches high.

C

CALADIUM ESCULENTUM—(ELEPHANT'S EAR). Perennial. Tropical plant. 3-5 feet. Sun or partial shade. Stout-growing plant with tuber-like root, with large, flat, light-green, auricular leaves, frequently with red or pink markings. *PROPAGATION*—Division of roots chiefly. *CULTURE*—Re-

quires a rich, moist soil, fertilized with bonemeal and liquid manure. *POSITION*—Used in pots for conservatories. Can be planted in open, especially near pools; specimen plant on lawns; in shrub border, combining with Banana Tree, Rhododendron, Aucuba, Callas, English Laurel; effective in the patio garden. Several varieties with variegated leaves.

CALCEOLARIA. Perennial or small shrub. Evergreen. 1-2 feet. Sun and partial shade. Much branched, with tomentose, rough leaves; purse-shaped, small or medium-sized, brown, yellow, mahogany, often speckled flowers, blooming profusely in late spring and September-November, but quite continuously throughout year. The greenhouse varieties will bloom in winter if seed is sown in fall. *PROPAGATION*—Herbaceous kinds by seed sown from end of March-September; shrubby kinds by cuttings taken from new shoots. *CULTURE*—Do best in a rich, light loam, well enriched with manures; attacked by black-rot fungus, black spots, aphis, mealy bug; remove and burn badly infested plants. *GROUPING*—Used in the foreground of the shrub border; in window boxes; in the mixed border, combining with Peach Bell, Salvia patens, Deep-blue Delphiniums, Lobelia, Purple Violas, Campanula muralis. The herbaceous varieties make good house plants.

CALENDULA OFFICINALIS — (POT MARIGOLD). Annual. 1-2 feet. Sun or partial shade. One of the Compositae group; hardy, stout growing, with entire bright-green, thickish leaves; flower heads with rows of flat ray petals and tubular disk florets, blooming all year, especially valuable in fall and winter, ranging from lemon-yellow, orange, to deep golden-yellow. *PROPAGATION*—Seed sown from early spring to late fall. *CULTURE*—Grows in any soil, but responds to a moderately rich loam. *GROUPINGS*—For bedding out; in front of shrubbery; for the mixed border, combining with Delphinium, Centaurea montana, Shasta Daisy, Salvia Pitcheri, Purple Stocks, Alyssum saxatile, Aconitum, Anchusa. Campanulas in variety.

CALIFORNIA BIG TREE — (SEQUOIA GIGANTEA).

CALIFORNIA CHERRY — (PRUNUS ILICIFOLIA).

CALIFORNIA GRAPE — (MAHONIA PINNATA).

CALIFORNIA HOLLY—(PHOTINIA ARBUTIFOLIA).

CALIFORNIA POPPY—(ESCHSCHOLTZIA).

CALIFORNIA PRIVET—(LIGUSTRUM OVALIFOLIUM).

CALIFORNIA REDWOOD—(SEQUOIA SEMPERVIRENS).

CALIFORNIA WILD LILAC—(CEANOTHUS).

CALLA LILY—(ZANTEDESCHIA).

CALLIOPSIS. Annual. ½-2½ feet. Sun. Much branched plant, with finely divided leaves; numerous daisy like, medium-sized, spotted, maroon, golden-yellow, dark-purple, crimson flowers, blooming April-September. *PROPAGATION*—Seed sown in early spring to summer. *CULTURE*—Grows in any soil, but prefers a rich, light, well fertilized loam. *GROUPING*—Plant in annual and perennial borders, combining with Coreopsis, Deep-blue Delphiniums, Snapdragons with similar colors, Salvia leucantha, Gold Tuft, Alyssum saxatile, Veronica spicata, Siberian Wallflower.

CALLISTEMON — (BOTTLE BRUSH). Evergreen. 6-12 feet. Sun and partial shade. Bushy shrubs, with linear-lanceolate, long, leathery entire leaves; dense, cylindrical spikes of bright-colored flowers, blooming January-June. *PROPAGATION*—Seeds sown in early spring; cuttings of ripened wood. *CULTURE*—Adapted to most kinds of soil, except heavy clay; drought resistant; alkali resistant; does well in sand. *GROUPING*—Hedge shrub and for dry embankment; striking effect in shrub border, combining with Metrosideros, Melaleuca, Aloes, Hakea laurina, Bridal Veil Broom, Leptospermum laevigatum.

SPECIES—**C. lanceolatus (metrosideros floribunda).** Bright-red flowers. **C. speciosus.** Intensely red flowers with golden stamens. **C. rigidus** and the similar **C. linearis.** Very narrow, linear leaves and deep-red flowers. **C. salignus.** Short spikes of yellow or light-pink flowers.

CALLUNA VULGARIS— (ENGLISH HEATHER). Evergreen. 1-2 feet. Sun. Bushy shrub, with small, needlelike leaves; tubular, purplish-red, or white flowers, blooming in August. *PROPAGATION*—Seed sown in spring; green wood cuttings under glass. *CULTURE*—Requires an acid soil, doing best in fairly moist, rich, sandy or peaty garden loams. *GROUPING*—Foreground of shrub border, combining with Ericas (Heathers), Diosma in species, Pernettya, Dwarf Myrtle; fine in rock garden.

CAMELLIA JAPONICA—(CAMELLIA). Evergreen. Usually 10-15 feet, but occasionally much higher. Sun, but best in partial shade. Rather slow-growing, symmetrical, round-headed tree, with medium-sized, dark-green, very shining, ovate-elliptic leaves; rather large, single, double, or semi-double, waxy-petaled flowers, pure white and in shades of pink, rose, red, blooming from November into spring. *PROPAGATION*—Graft varieties on seedling stock; pot layerage; cuttings from matured wood in summer with bottom heat. *CULTURE*—Do best in a moist climate; prefer a rich, light, well drained, moist, acid loam; mulch of well rotted cow manure and an occasional application of commercial fertilizer are both beneficial. *GROUPING* — Lawn specimens; foundation plantings; in the shrub border, combining with Rhododendrons in variety, Japanese Magnolia, English Laurel, Carolina Cherry, Catalina Cherry, Ceratonia siliqua, Raphiolepis, Pittosporum tobira.

CAMPANULA — (BELLFLOWER). Perennials and biennials. Sun and shade for most kinds. A splendid group of plants, used in the flower border, rockeries, and as border plants. Species and varieties vary in height from a few inches to eight feet. Usually forming dense clumps of variable leaves; small to large, bell-shaped, light to deep-blue flow-ers, blooming in spring, summer, or fall according to kind. *PROPAGATION*—Seeds sown in early fall or spring; cuttings of practically all kinds best in early spring; division of clumps in fall and spring. *CULTURE*—Very hardy, subject to few pests, delighting in a moderately rich, moderately moist, well drained, light loam; the rock plants like a gritty soil with some limestone, but are adaptable to ordinary soils. Positions and groupings described under species.

SPECIES—**C. barbata.** Rock plant. 6-9 inches. Medium-sized, nodding blue flowers. **C. carpatica—Carpathian Bluebell.** 10-14 inches. Full shade. Large, white, lavender to deep-blue flowers, blooming in June. **C. garganica—Star-shaped Campanula.** 4 inches, but spreading, forming tufts of crinkled leaves; light-blue, flat-petaled flowers, blooming in May; border plant and in the Rock Garden. **C. isophylla alba.** Trailing species with rather large, pure white flowers, delighting to be near pools; the variety **Mayi** has blue flowers. **C. medium—Canterbury Bells.** Biennial. 3-4 feet. Sun and a little shade. Erect, with branches spread out candelabra-shape; rather coarse leaves; globular, bell-shaped, white, pink, purple, and lavender flowers, blooming May-June. *PROPAGATION*—Seeds sown in July to produce flowering clumps next year. *CULTURE*—Grows in ordinary soils; fertilized with complete fertilizer; attacked by stem rot in soil; also by sow and pill bugs (see Plant Pests); acid soil reaction. *GROUPING*—Background of the mixed border, combining with Scabiosa, Perennial Aster, Veronica longifolia, Lupine, Oenothera, and with other Campanulas. **C. calycanthema** has the cup-and-saucer form, one bell within another. **C. muralis (portenschlagiana)—Blue Bells.** 9 inches, but spreading. Leaves roundish cordate, dark-green; deep-blue, bell-shaped flowers; blooming in May, June, again in early fall. One of the best of the border plants, doing equally well in sun or shade. **C. persicifolia—Peach Bell.** 1-2 feet. Sun and partial shade. Makes a matty growth, with long, dark-green peachlike leaves; erect stems bearing loose racemes of white, blue, lavender, rather large, bell-shaped flowers, blooming May through September. *PROPAGATION*—Seeds sown in July-August, to produce good blooming plants; division of clumps in fall, using new shoots; cuttings in spring. *CULTURE*—Requires a well drained, well fertilized light loam; attacked by sow and pill bugs (see Plant Pests); should be renewed every few years. Used to advantage in the mixed border, combining with Columbines, Sweet William, Delphinium, Catnip, Perennial Flax, Scabiosa in variety, with other species of Campanula. **C. pyramidalis—Chimney Bellflower.** 5-7 feet. Sun and a little shade. Erect plant with large, smooth, dark-green, ovate-lanceolate leaves; long, pyramidal racemes of medium-sized, bell-shaped flowers with expanded petals, white, pale to deep-blue, blooming July-October. *PROPAGATION*—Seed sown July-August; division of clumps, October-December; root cuttings. *CULTURE*—Requires a rich, well drained, light loam. *GROUPING*—Imposing as accent plant or in groupings in the perennial border; against high white walls; combines with other Campanulas, especially Peach Bell and Carpathian Blue Bell, Coreopsis, Thalictrum in variety, Hemerocallis, yellow Geum, yellow and orange Gladiolus, Francoa ramosa, Shasta Daisy. **C. rotun-**

difolia—Harebell—Blue Bells of Scotland. 8-10 inches. Slender, flowering stems, bearing abundant nodding, deep-blue, small, bell-shaped flowers, blooming in June. For the rock garden or flower border; border plant.

CAMPHORA (CINNAMOMUM) OFFICINALIS—(CAMPHOR TREE). Evergreen. 30-40 feet. Sun or part shade. Robust, fast growing, symmetrical, conical in form, with aromatic, ovate-elliptical, ruddy-tinged leaves; small, yellowish-green flowers in panicles, blooming in June. *PROPAGATION*—Seeds sown after maturity; cuttings of half ripened wood. *CULTURE*—Grows in any soil, but requires moisture; very hardy in California; free from pests. *GROUPING*—Used as street trees; specimen trees; groupings on plantations; in large shrub borders, combining with Pittosporums in variety, English Laurel, Carolina Laurel, Mexican Orange, Veronicas, Photinia serrulata, Laurustinus.

CANARY BIRD VINE (TROPAEOLUM).

CANARY ISLAND PALM—(PHOENIX CANARIENSIS).

CANDYTUFT—(IBERIS).

CANNAS. Bulbous plants growing from rootstocks, horizontally spreading. 3-7 feet. Sun. With stout, erect, unbranched stems; long, broad, bright or dark-green, often colored leaves, prominently ribbed and veined; spikes or racemes of very irregular, medium-sized flowers, in strong colors and shades of red, yellow, orange, salmon, pink, blooming June-September. *PROPAGATION*—Division of rootstocks into budded sections, planting from October-April, according to locality; seeds, not too ripe, soaked in water before sowing. *CULTURE*—Rich, moist, warm garden loam, well enriched with manures during growing season, with balanced commercial fertilizers during blooming period. *POSITION*—Excellent for a variety of positions if not overdone; bold groups in front of shrubbery; in the background of the perennial border; for bedding out; patio garden. Appear to best advantage by themselves.

TYPES—Tall, long-jointed, small flowered Cannas; Italian or orchid-flowered, of medium growth, with flowers having soft and flowing, Irislike outlines; Dwarf French or Crozy Cannas, with rather large flowers.

CANTERBURY BELLS—(CAMPANULA MEDIUM).

CANTUA BUXIFOLIA. Evergreen. 4 feet. Sun and partial shade. Much-branched shrub, with dark-green, smooth or downy leaves; clusters of long-tubular, pendulous, crimson-red flowers, blooming in April-May. *PROPAGATION*—Cuttings of half firm wood under glass. *CULTURE*—Requires a rich, moist, well fertilized light loam. *GROUPING*—Specimen shrub; shrub border, grouping with Choisya ternata, Pittosporum tobira, Spiraeas and Deutzias in variety, Leucothoe catesbaei, Fuchsia-flowered Gooseberry, Pearl Bush.

CAPE HONEYSUCKLE—(TECOMA CAPENSIS).

CARDINAL FLOWER — (LOBELIA CARDINALIS).

CARISSA GRANDIFLORA — (NATAL PLUM). Evergreen. 5-6 feet. Sun. Round-headed, spiny shrubs, with smooth, medium-sized, dark-green leaves, large, fragrant, white, salver-shaped flowers, blooming June-July; edible, plum-like, red fruits. *PROPAGATION*—Seeds sown in early fall; cuttings of ripened wood. *CULTURE*—Warm position; impartial as to soils. *GROUPING*—Foundation plantings; specimen shrub; in the shrub border, combining with Hakeas in variety, Coprosma, Euonymus in variety, Streptosolen jamesoni and Heliotrope for contrast.

CARNATION — (DIANTHUS CARYOPHYLLUS).

CAROB TREE—(CERATONIA SILIQUA).

CAROLINA CHERRY—(PRUNUS CAROLINIANA).

CARPATHIAN BLUE BELL—(CAMPANULA CARPATICA).

CARPENTERIA CALIFORNICA — (ANEMONE SHRUB) (native). Evergreen. 6-10 feet. Sun and partial shade. Compact, round-symmetrical shrub, with elliptic-lanceolate, entire, smooth leaves, bright green above, whitish tomentose beneath; medium-sized, pure white, regular, Anemone-like flowers, blooming in June-July. *PROPAGATION*—Seeds sown in spring; green wood cuttings; suckers; *CULTURE*—Requires a light, well drained soil and sheltered situation; subject to scale (see Plant Pests). *GROUPING*—Specimen shrub; for the naturalistic garden; for the shrub border; combining with Escallonia rubra, Veronica in variety, Coronilla glauca, Dendromecon rigidum, Cestrum aurantiacum, Plumbago capensis, Ceanothus in variety, Hypericum calycinum.

CARYOPTERIS MASTACANTHUS — (BLUE SPIRAEA). Deciduous sub-shrub. 2-3 feet. Sun. Woody stems, with coarsely serrate, soft, hairy leaves; small blue, violet, or white, Spiraealike flowers in axillary racemes, blooming in August-November. *PROPAGATION*—Seeds sown in February; soft wood cuttings in spring. *CULTURE*—Likes a rich, well fertilized, light loam. *GROUPING*—Perennial or shrub borders, combining with Spiraeas in variety, Shasta Daisy, Achillea the Pearl, Iceland Poppy, Perennial Aster, Columbine, Deutzia gracilis, Alstromeria, Bronze Iris.

CASSIA TOMENTOSA — (CASSIA). Evergreen. 10-12 feet. Sun loving and partial shade. Round-headed, bushy, fast-growing shrub, with pinnate, grayish-green leaves, tomentose beneath; medium-sized, salver-shaped, golden-yellow flowers in dense clusters, blooming profusely in summer and spasmodically throughout year. *PROPAGATION*—Seeds sown in fall or spring; cuttings of half ripened stems. *CULTURE*—Adapted to a variety of soil conditions; drought resistant. *GROUPING*—Group with Veronicas, Duranta plumieri, Ceanothus in variety, Sollya heterophylla, Solanum *rantonneti Brooms (Genista) Lion's Tail, Spanish Broom, Yellow Heliotrope. **C. artemisioides.** 10-12 feet. Bushy shrub, gray-pubescent all over, with narrow-linear leaflets; sulphur-yellow flowers in axillary racemes. Endures alkali soil, and does well in sandy soil.

CASTOR BEAN—(RICINUS).

CASUARINA EQUISETIFOLIA—(SHE-OAK) —(BEEFWOOD TREE). Evergreen. 20-30 feet. Sun and partial shade. Erect, fast-growing tree, resembling a conifer, gracefully drooping, slender-branched, leafless; long, slender, jointed, pale-green stems; small, brownish-yellow flowers, blooming in September; small, conelike fruits. *PROPAGATION* —Seeds; cuttings of half ripened wood. *CULTURE* —Does well in all kinds of soils, especially in brackish and alkaline soils. *POSITION*—Street tree; specimen tree on lawns; in groupings with conifers; in groupings. *SPECIES*—C. stricta. Similar to the above, but with erect branches and gray-green stems.

CATALINA CHERRY—(PRUNUS INTEGRIFOLIA).

CATALINA IRONWOOD — (LYONOTHAMNUS).

CATALPA BIGNONIOIDES—(CATALPA)— (INDIAN BEAN). Deciduous. 15-20 feet. Sun. Round-headed tree, with crooked branches; very large, cordate-ovate, bright-green, soft, hairy leaves and with golden, purple, silver, or yellow markings; curious, Bignonialike, tubular flowers, white, marked with purple and yellow, in large, showy panicles, blooming in August; large bean pods. *PROPAGATION*—Seed sown in spring; cuttings in spring; root cuttings and layering. *CULTURE*—Catalpas like an open, porous, moderately rich soil. *POSITION*—Striking specimen tree on lawns; street tree; too individualistic to group with other trees.

CATNIP—(NEPETA).

CEANOTHUS — (CALIFORNIA WILD LILAC). Evergreen, a few deciduous. 1-15 feet. Sun. Low, sprawling shrubs, or tall, fast-growing trees, rapid growing, with small to medium-sized, shiny or somewhat tomentose leaves; small, fragrant, lilac-like, blue, white, or purplish flowers in panicles or racemes. *PROPAGATION*—Seeds sown in spring; cuttings of mature wood in fall; soft wood cuttings in early spring from forced plants. *CULTURE*— Will grow under a variety of soil conditions; some species subject to mealy bug (see Plant Pests); use complete fertilizers; the growth of most Ceanothus is so rapid that continual heading back and thinning out are necessary. *GROUPING*—Specimen trees; in the naturalistic garden; foundation plantings; in the background of the shrub border, combining, according to species, with Cestrum aurantiacum, Streptosolen jamesoni, Lantana, Choisya ternata, Cistus in variety, Carpenteria californica, Fremontia mexicana, species of Ceanothus together, Genistas in variety.

SPECIES—C. arboreus—Mountain Lilac. 12-15 feet. Stout, large trunk, with large, roundish leaves; Pale-blue to white flowers, in short panicles, blooming March-June. **C. cyaneus.** 6-8 feet, with small, glistening leaves; deep-blue flowers in terminal panicles, blooming March-July. **C. Glorie de Versailles.** Deciduous hybrid with large, dark-green leaves, very fragrant blue flowers, blooming in spring. **C. thyrsiflorus.** 6 feet, with small, dark-green leaves, and

lavender-blue or whitish-blue flowers, blooming May-July.

CEDRUS—(CEDAR). Conifers. 20-40 feet or more. Erect, symmetrical, with wide-spreading branches; needle-like leaves arranged in bundles; rather small cones. *PROPAGATION*—Seeds sown in spring; varieties by veneer grafting in late summer or fall. *CULTURE*—Prefer well drained, loamy soil, although standing sandy clay soil. *GROUPING* —Specimen trees on lawns; in groupings alone or with other conifers.

SPECIES—C. atlantica—Atlantic Cedar. Pyramidal, with irregular branches; dark-green, short needles, forming dense bundles. **C. atlantica glauca.** Similar to the type, but with glaucous, silvery foliage. **C. deodora—Deodar—Indian Cedar.** Loosely pyramidal, existing in many varieties; characterized by its perfect habit, pendulous branchlets, and fascicles of soft-textured, dark-bluish or bluish-white needles. A fine avenue tree. **C. deodora repandens.** Weeping variety of Deodar. **C. libani—Cedar of Lebanon.** Large, very symmetrical, cone-shaped tree; dark or bright-green, bluish or silvery needles; brown cones. The three types may be combined with species of Abies and Picea (Spruces and Firs), and with species of Chamaecyparis and spreading types of Juniperus in the foreground. The most effective combinations are to use groups of one species of Cedrus, or several species together, in groups of three, five, seven, etc.

CELOSIA CRISTATA—(COCKSCOMB). Annual. 9-18 inches. Sun. Erect plant, with large leaves; curious spikes of crested or plumy, brightly colored fascicles, the effect extending from July until late in fall. Also a dwarf form with large, velvety cockscombs. *PROPAGATION*—Seed sown in early spring. *CULTURE*—Requires a moist, rich soil. *POSITION*—Should be planted by themselves in beds, in flower borders, or in front of shrubs with dark-green foliage.

CENTAUREA CYANEUS — (BACHELORS BUTTON) — (CORNFLOWER). Annual. 2-3 feet. Sun. Branching plant with slender branches; leaves grayish-green with white, woolly hairs; single or double, thistlelike blue, pink, rose, white flowers, blooming July-October. *PROPAGATION*—Easily by seed sown in early spring; seed self-sown. *CULTURE*—Grows in any moderately rich soil. *GROUPING*—Used in both the annual and mixed borders, combining, according to color harmonies, with Coreopsis, Yellow Geum, Dimorphotheca aurantiaca, Snapdragons in variety, Scabiosa in variety, Salvia farinacea, Perennial Aster in variety, Lupines.

SPECIES—C. candidissima and **C. gymnocarpa** —Dusty Millers. Perennial. 2-3 feet. Sun. Erect, branching plant covered with soft, velvety, white hairs. Grown principally for the finely cut, silvery foliage. *PROPAGATION*—Seeds; cuttings. *CULTURE*—Likes a moderately rich garden loam. *POSITION*—Bedding plant and in the flower border. **C. imperialis (moschata)—Sweet Sultan.** Annual. 1½-2 feet. Sun. Erect, branching plant, with bright-green, pinnatifid, dentately lobed leaves; long flower stems surmounted by large cornflowerlike blooms, having the fragrance of musk; red, lavender, purple, white, yellow; blooming June-September. *PROPA-*

GATION—Seeds sown in early spring. *CULTURE* —Grows in ordinary well fertilized garden soil; add lime; very hardy. *GROUPING*—For the annual and mixed borders, combining with Swan River Daisy, Cynoglossum, Perennial Aster, Larkspur, Blue Lace Flower, Gypsophila, Scabiosa in variety, Asters. **C. montana—Mountain Bluet.** 1-2 feet. Sun and partial shade. Perennial. Woolly, branching plant, with long, lance-ovate, dark-green leaves, silvery-white when young; flower heads with purple and deep-blue florets, blooming in summer. *PROPAGATION* —Seed sown in fall and spring; division of clumps October-January; cuttings. *CULTURE*—Grows in any soil, seeding itself. *GROUPING*—Used in the perennial and mixed borders, combining with Calendula, Orange and Buff Snapdragons, Yellow Stocks, Iceland Poppies, Coreopsis, Cotyledons, Francoa ramosa, Golden Calla, Achillea the Pearl.

CENTURY PLANT—(AGAVE).

CEPHALOTAXUS PEDUNCULATA — (JAPANESE YEW). Conifer. 10-15 feet under cultivation. Sun and partial shade. Very symmetrical, cone-shaped tree, with spreading, pendulous branches; shining, dark-green, flattened leaves; drupelike, reddish or greenish-brown fruits. *PROPAGATION*— Seed sown in spring; cuttings in August; veneer grafting in summer. *CULTURE*—Does best in a somewhat moist, but well drained sandy loam. *POSITION*—Planted in tubs; specimen tree for lawns; accent tree in conifer groupings.

CERATONIA SILIQUA — (CAROB TREE) — (ST. JOHN'S BREAD). Evergreen. 20-30 feet. Sun or shade. Gracefully branched, rather open, with shining, oval, medium-sized leaves; inconspicuous red flowers; large, edible bean pods. *PROPAGATION*—Grown from seeds and budded to varieties; cuttings of ripened shoots with bottom heat. *CULTURE*—Drought resistant; adapted to a variety of soils. *GROUPING*—Used in the shrub border, combining with Pittosporum tenuifolium, Japanese Magnolia, Choisya ternata, Aucuba, Escallonia berteriana, Eucalyptus polyanthemos, Euonymus in variety, Mahonia japonica, Prunus integrifolia.

CERCIS SILIQUASTRUM—(JUDAS TREE)— (RED BUD). Deciduous. 15-20 feet. Sun and part shade. Round-headed, much branched tree, with medium-sized, light-green, heart-shaped leaves; small, purplish-rose, pea-shaped flowers in short racemes, blooming March-May; many-seeded bean pods. *PROPAGATION*—Readily by seeds sown in spring; with gentle bottom heat; layering; green wood cuttings from forced plants in early spring. *CULTURE*—Does best in a rich, sandy loam; requires thinning out once a year. *GROUPING*— Specimen tree for lawns; street tree; naturalistic garden; shrub border, combining with Magnolia stellata, Ceratonia siliqua, Pearl Bush, Spiraeas in variety, Deutzia gracilis, Prunus caroliniana, Choisya ternata. **C. canadensis.** Of coarse growth, with rosy-pink flowers; for the wild garden; likes a rich, sandy, moist soil. **C. siliquastrum alba.** White-flowered species.

CESTRUM AURANTIACUM — (ORANGE CESTRUM). Evergreen. 4-6 feet. Sun and a little shade. Bushy shrub, half climbing, with smooth, ovate leaves; panicles of short-tubular, salver-shaped, bright orange-yellow flowers, blooming June-August. *PROPAGATION*—Cuttings of half firm wood in early fall or February-April. *CULTURE*— Requires a rich, well fertilized, well drained, light soil; cut back vigorously after flowering. *GROUPING*— For the shrub border, combining with Iochroma in variety, Choisya ternata, Yellow Heliotrope, Duranta, Genista andreana, Osmanthus fragrans, California Lilac, Buddleia officinalis.

SPECIES—**C. elegans.** Half climbing evergreen. 10-15 feet. Fast growing, in sun or shade; dark-green, ovate-lanceolate, rough, pubescent leaves; long-tubular, crimson flowers, blooming June-September and spasmodically thereafter. *PROPAGATION* and *CULTURE* of this and succeeding species same as for Orange Cestrum. *POSITION*—For the shrub border, but group mostly with dark-green foliage shrubs. **C. fasciculatum.** Like the above, but blooming in spring, more compact, and with nearly globular flowers. **C. nocturnum—Night-blooming Jasmine.** 10-12 feet. Fast growing shrub, with slender, brownish branches; long, elliptical, smooth leaves; small, creamy-yellow, tubular flowers, very fragrant at night, blooming several times a year. Requires frequent severe pruning and thinning out. For the background of the shrub border, combinations the same as for Orange Cestrum.

CHAMAECYPARIS—(RETINOSPORA). Conifer. Varying in size from the dwarf and low growing juvenile Japanese Cypresses to the very tall and broad Lawson Cypress. Either sun or partial shade, but full sun may injure the foliage of some of the Japanese kinds. Vary in shape from the semi-symmetrical, loose-spreading species, as in the Silver Cypress, to the very compact and symmetrical Scarab Cypress. The distinguishing characters include: small, scalelike leaves, frequently turning to bronze, reddish, violet, or steel color in winter; inconspicuous flowers; small, globular cones. *PROPAGATION*—Seeds sown in spring; easily by cuttings from mature wood in fall, early spring, or in early winter with bottom heat; veneer grafting upon seedling stock. *CULTURE*—Most species prefer a moderately moist, rich, well drained, sandy or peaty loam; dead, dried material from inside shrub should be removed; attacked by root borers (see Plant Pests). *POSITION*— Specimen shrubs for lawns and in formal gardens; in foundation plantings and shrub borders, grouping with evergreens, with each other, and with other conifers of similar character. Grouping conifers include species of Juniperus, Thuya, Taxus (Yew), Cedrus. Grouping evergreens include Barberries, Ericas, Diosma, Nandina domestica, Azara, Cotoneaster horizontalis, microphylla, and franchetti, Azaleas in variety, Pernettya, species of Myrtus, Veronica buxifolia and traversi. Dwarf species and varieties are suitable for the rock garden.

SPECIES — **C. Lawsoniana — Lawson Cypress.** Tall growing, up to 60 feet under cultivation; spreading and pendulous branches; flattened, frondlike branchlets; bright-green leaves; **C. law. alumni— Blue Scarab Cypress.** 5-8 feet. Columnar in habit, somewhat flat-sided, with very glaucous, dark-green leaves having a bluish, metallic sheen. Used as accent shrubs, near corners or entrances of residences. **C. law. nidifera—Birds Nest Cypress.** 1-2 feet, but spreading 3-4 feet. Beautiful sprays of shining, bright-green foliage, spreading from the center. There are many other distinct forms. **C. obtusa— Hinoki Cypress.** Beautifully shaped tree, usually 6-8 feet unless dwarfed, with frondlike, flattened, pendulous branchlets, and bright-green, shining leaves. Many varieties, including Aurea, with a golden tinge to foliage; Pygmaea and Nana, dwarf forms, suitable for rockeries; Gracilis, with pendulous branches. **C. pisifera plumosa—Plume Cypress.** 6-8 feet. Of dense, conical habit, with slender branchlets of feathery appearance; bright-green, scalelike leaves. The variety Aurea has a golden tinge. **C. pisifera squarrosa—Silver Cypress.** 6-8 feet. Rather densely branched, with spreading, feathery branches, and linear, silvery leaves. The variety Nana, less than a foot high, is used in the immediate foreground. **C. stewartii.** 6-10 feet. Compact and columnar in habit with bright-green, gold-tinted foliage having a golden tinge. **C. wisseli.** 6-10 feet. Very upright, slender shrub, with frondlike branches, and blue-green leaves. A fine accent shrub and for formal effects. Many other forms, corresponding more or less to those described above.

CHAMAEROPS—(FAN PALMS). 5-10 feet under cultivation. Erect trunk, often fibrous, with the dark-green, glistening, fanlike fronds, with the margins of the petiole spiny; yellow, green, or white flowers borne profusely in spring or summer, followed in warm regions by datelike fruits. *PROPAGATION*—Seeds; suckers from about the base of the trunk. *CULTURE*—Drought resistant, but soil should be irrigated occasionally; adapted to a wide range of soils, but prefers a rich, sandy loam. *POSITION*—Palms in cold countries are restricted to tub specimens, but do exceedingly well along the Pacific Coast and in the interior of California. Excellent for use in patio courts, as specimens on lawns, for grouping in sub-tropical gardens. *SPECIES*—**C. excelsa— Windmill Palm—Fortunes Palm.** Very stout trunk, clothed with old leaf sheaths, the fronds rather far apart. **C. humilis.** Lower growing, with short trunk, the fronds rather close together.

CHEDDAR PINK—(DIANTHUS CAESIUS).

CHEIRANTHUS CHEIRI—(WALLFLOWER). Half shrubby perennial. 2-3 feet. Sun loving, but endures a little shade. Woody plant, with ribbed stem, and dark-green lanceolate leaves; medium-sized, mustardlike flowers in dense clusters, yellow, brown, russet, to mahogany, blooming May-September. *PROPAGATION*—Seeds in early fall and early spring; cuttings of half firm wood in spring. *CULTURE*—Grows in any soil, but prefers a rich, well fertilized, light loam; prune back after flowering. *GROUPING*—Combining in the mixed border with Anchusa, deep-blue Delphinium, Campanula persicifolia and other Campanulas, Violets, Gold Tuft, Veronica spicata, Hemerocallis, Purple Violas.

SPECIES—**C. allioni — Siberian Wallflower.** Perennial. 1 foot. Sun. Bushy plant, with stiff stems; dark-green, lanceolate leaves; terminal racemes of bright-orange flowers, blooming in spring and summer. *PROPAGATION*—Seeds sown in February; division of clumps in fall; cuttings. *CULTURE*—Similar to that of Wallflower. *GROUPING*—For the perennial and mixed borders, combining with deep-blue Delphinium, Lobelia, Salvia

pitcheri, Purple Sage, Orange Day Lily, blue Perennial Asters, Peach Bell, Japanese Iris.

CHILEAN GUAVA—(MYRTUS UGNI).

CHILEAN JASMINE — (MANDEVILLA SUAVEOLENS).

CHIMNEY BELLFLOWER — (CAMPANULA PYRAMIDALIS).

CHINESE FORGET-ME-NOT— (CYNOGLOSSUM AMABILE).

CHINESE RICE PAPER PLANT — (ARALIA PAPYRIFERA).

CHIONODOXA— (GLORY-OF-THE-SNOW). Bulbous plant. 3-6 inches. Sun or partial shade. Narrow, linear leaves; small, blue or white, bell-like flowers in short racemes, blooming in February, March, April. *PROPAGATION*—Seeds, usually self-sown; offsets from bulbs, planted September-December. *CULTURE*—Prefers a rich, light garden loam. *GROUPING*—For the flower border, combining with Scilla, Muscari, Dwarf Iris, Cyclamen, Trillium, Babiana, Primula malacoides, Violets, Violas.

CHOISYA TERNATA—(MEXICAN ORANGE). Evergreen. 4-6 feet. Sun or partial shade. Very compact, round-symmetrical shrub; medium-sized, glossy, tri-parted leaves; terminal clusters of fragrant, white, orangelike flowers, blooming in winter, summer, and intermittently. *PROPAGATION*—Firm wood cuttings taken after blooming period; seed sown in spring. *CULTURE*—Grows in any soil, but does best in rich, light, moderately moist, well fertilized loam. *GROUPING*—Specimen shrub; formal accent shrub; grouping shrub, combining with Veronicas, Raphiolepis, Pittosporum tobira, Cestrum aurantiacum, Escallonia in variety, Ceanothus in variety, Genistas, Sollya heterophylla, Evergreen Viburnums.

CHORIZEMA ILICIFOLIA — (FLOWERING OAK). Evergreen. 2-3 feet, but spreading. Sun and slight shade. Bushy shrub, with drooping, slender branches; small, dark-green, spiny, hollylike leaves; small, pea-shaped, brilliant orange-red flowers, blooming in winter and early spring. *PROPAGATION*—Cuttings of half firm wood in spring; stratified seeds sown in spring. *CULTURE*—Drought resistant; likes a rich, sandy loam. *GROUPING*—Foreground of shrub border, combining with Mahonia aquifolium, Wilsons Barberry, California Cherry, Catalina Cherry, Pyracantha angustifolia, Solanum rantonneti, Bridal Veil Broom, Cuphea ignea.

CHRISTMAS BERRY—(PHOTINIA).

CHRISTMAS FLOWER—(EUPHORBIA).

CHRISTMAS ROSE—(HELLEBORUS).

CHRYSANTHEMUM HORTORUM — (COMMON CHRYSANTHEMUM). Perennial. 3-6 feet. Sun, but will endure a little shade, especially in very warm regions. Erect plants with light to dark-green, often smooth and glistening, thin or thick, medium-sized to large, lobed or cleft leaves; flowers in many colors consisting of series of ray petals, with or without a raised boss in center, blooming from September until cut down by frosts. *PROPAGATION*—Cuttings from tender shoots appearing in March; half firm stem cuttings of special varieties; division of clumps, but not usually satisfactory; by seed for new varieties. Cuttings are inserted in sand in shallow flats, with a layer of several inches of soil in bottom of flat; rooted cuttings in April or May are removed carefully and transferred to thumb pots, the best method, or are transferred to open ground; the plants from thumb pots are later transferred to open ground. If grown as potted plants, they are transferred to 3, 4, 5, or 6 inch pots respectively; soil for pots should be enriched with either manure, preferably rotted cow manure, or with balanced fertilizers. *CULTURE*—Set out new plants each year; soil should be a rich, medium-heavy, garden loam, well fertilized with barnyard or poultry manures in the fall, or before planting; liquid manure applied during the growing season will produce sturdy stems, fine foliage, and well filled out buds; beneficial to apply balanced, commercial fertilizers when plants are coming into bloom; do not use liquid manure after color begins to show in bud. Keep the soil continually moist throughout growing and blooming periods; a mulch of straw manure or of peat about the plants is very beneficial throughout the winter and growing season; add some lime. Set plants about 2-2½ feet apart; stake with redwood or cedar stakes. Pinch back shoots of garden types when 6 inches high and keep pinching back laterals until about the first of August. *DISBUDDING*—Two types of buds: center crown bud and clusters of axillary buds. For the large-flowered varieties either the crown bud, or, more often, a plump axillary bud is retained; for the garden type one or more of the axillary buds are retained. With large-flowered varieties cut out all laterals to form single stem, or leave 2-5 laterals; in disbudding leave a few down the stem in case of accident. Disbudding in the greenhouse or lathhouse is a highly specialized business. Plant should be cut down to ground after blooming period. *PLANT DISEASES*—Chrysanthemums are quite hardy, but are usually subject to a few pests. Insect pests are: aphis, thrips, red spider, tarnished plant bug, midges, caterpillars, leaf-tier. Fungous pests are: damping-off disease of seedlings; mildew (bad in shade); various leaf spots and blights (see Plant Pests). Plants are generally quite healthy with right soil conditions, plenty of moisture, and fertility. *POSITION*—As potted plants they are fine for porch and conservatory decoration. For the garden they are invaluable for the foreground of the shrub border; in special beds and borders by themselves; in the background of the perennial or mixed border for fall color. According to color harmonies, chrysanthemums may be grouped into two general classes: those with pink, white, rose, lavender, etc., colors; those with yellow, brown, bronze, white, reddish, violet-purple, terra cotta, etc., colors. A few combinations with other flowers include Salvia pitcheri, Calceolaria, Salvia patens, Delphinium, Orange Sunflower, Zinnias, Cosmos, Plumbago larpentae, Monkshood, Nicotiana, Cornflower Aster, Kafir Lily. Pick flowers with long stems; last a long time in house if water is renewed each day, and if bottom leaves and sluff is removed.

TYPES—Two general classes of large-flowered Chrysanthemums: reflexed or recurved class in which the petals are curved more or less backward; the incurved class, globular in form, in which the petals incline toward the center. In addition to the incurved type, the Japanese forms include the Japanese Hairy or Ostrich Plume, and spidery, stringy, fluffy, and twisted petal forms. These types are often grown in the greenhouse, under lath, or under cheesecloth frames to preserve purity of color. Types of Garden Chrysanthemums: the Single type resembles a Daisy, is from 2-3 inches across, and consists of several series of ray petals arranged about a central disk. The Pompon type embraces a number of varying forms, all more or less compact, ranging from the tiny, buttonlike Baby Mums to medium-sized varieties with petals fluted, quilled, or flattened. The Japanese Anemone type presents many varieties with flowers either loose or stiff in texture, the outer series of ray petals being long and narrow, with the short tubular in the center grouped closely together upon a raised boss. Flowers intermediate in character between the Pompon and large-flowered varieties are classed as Decoratives.

SPECIES—**C. leucanthemum hybridum—Shasta Daisy.** Perennial. 1-2 feet. Sun and partial shade. Stout, spreading, floriferous plant, with smooth, dark-green, lanceolate leaves; large, daisylike, pure white, golden centered flowers, blooming April-September. *PROPAGATION*—Division of roots October-January; seeds. *CULTURE* — Grows in any moderately rich soil. *GROUPING*—For perennial and mixed borders, combining with a number of flowers. **Alaska.** One of the best; also smaller flowered fringed varieties. **Summer Chrysanthemums.** Annuals. 1-2 feet. Single and double, yellow, white, or golden flowers, blooming all summer. *PROPAGATION* — Seeds sown in spring. *CULTURE* — Grows in any ordinary loam. *GROUPING*—Used in the annual and mixed borders, combining with orange and yellow flowered flowers, or massed alone. **C. pyrethrum aureum—Golden Feather.** 6-8 inches. Annual, with yellowish, divided foliage, turning bright green; small white flowers. Propagation and culture same as for above. Used for carpet bedding, and as edgings.

CIGAR PLANT—(CUPHEA).

CINERARIA. Annual, but semi-perennial in California. 1-2 feet. Shade and semi-sun. Stout-stemmed, bushy plant, with large, roundish, dark-green, velvety leaves; large, regular, Daisylike flowers with wide, flat petals, vividly colored in shades of pink, white, red, orange, purple, salmon, etc., blooming in February, March, and in summer. *PROPAGATION*—Seed sown in August or September to produce early blooms; seed sown in early spring to produce summer blooms, not so fine as the earlier blooms; cuttings; division of plant in fall (in California); tend to seed themselves. *CULTURE*—Favor a rich, light loam, fertilized with cow manure or other well balanced manure; plants tend to bloom a second time; peat and leaf mold beneficial; subject to leaf miner (difficult to control) and to aphis, sow and pill bugs (see Plant Pests). *GROUPING*—Fine for the shady border, planted in masses, or combined with Fuchsias, Columbine,

Foxglove, Polyantha Primrose, Violets, Violas, English Daisy.

SPECIES—**C. stellata—Star Cineraria.** Medium-sized, star-shaped flowers, taller than the above, with a longer blooming season. **Tree Cineraria.** Perennial. 6-8 feet. Stout-growing, round-headed shrub, with very large, yellowish-green, roundish, velvety leaves, and great clusters of small yellow flowers, blooming profusely in spring and summer. Used as specimen shrubs and in the shrub border as an accent shrub.

CINNAMOMUM—(CAMPHORA).

CINQUEFOIL—(POTENTILLA).

CISSUS STRIATA—(AMPELOPSIS SEMPERVIRENS).

CISTUS—(ROCK ROSE). Evergreen. 2-6 feet. Sun. Dense in growth, much branched, with leathery, tomentose, often crinkly leaves; flowers resembling single roses, 2-4 inches across, blooming in summer and early fall. *PROPAGATION*—Seeds sown after maturity; layering; cuttings of medium hard wood in spring or late summer. *CULTURE*—Prefer a light, well drained, moderately fertilized soil containing limestone; attacked by mealy bug (see Plant Pests). *GROUPING*—Used in the shrub border and in rockeries; according to color of flower combines with Echium fastuosum, Sweet Lavender, Lagunaria pattersoni, Leucadendron, Pittosporum crassifolium, Purple Sage, Viburnum rhytidophyllum.

SPECIES—**C. landaniferus maculatus—Spotted Cistus.** Large white, waxy petaled flowers with red spot in center of each flower; does well in sandy soil. **C. laurifolius.** Flowers white with yellow blotch. **C. salvifolius.** Small white flowers. **C. crispus.** Medium sized, deep rose-colored flowers.

CLARKIA PULCHELLA — (CLARKIA). Annual. 12-18 inches. Sun or light shade. Branching, erect plant, with smooth, light-green leaves; terminal racemes of medium-sized, four-clawed, lobe-petaled flowers, colored lilac, rose, white, pink, blooming April-August. *PROPAGATION* — Seeds sown January-April. *CULTURE*—Grows in ordinary light garden loams. *GROUPING*—Plant in the annual or mixed border, combining with Arctotis, Larkspur, Nigella, Pansies, Nicotiana, Nepeta mussini, Dianthus plumarius, Virginia Bells.

SPECIES—**C. elegans.** 2-6 feet. With glaucous, reddish stems; single, but usually double, Carnation-like, orange, salmon, white, creamy-yellow, crimson flowers. Cultural requirements, blooming period, and flower combinations same as for C. pulchella. Several highly developed strains.

CLEMATIS. Deciduous vine. 10-20 feet or more. Sun loving, but enduring slight shade. Small flowered species are the strongest growers. Twining around supports, with opposite, entire, lobed, or pinnately compound leaves; regular, apetalous, medium to large-sized flowers, with colored sepals. *PROPAGATION*—Seeds sown in spring; cuttings of soft wood in summer; layering; grafting of hybrid kinds. *CULTURE*—Requires a rich, well drained, light loam, containing some lime, fertilized with horse or cow manure. *POSITION*—The more vigorous small-flowered kinds useful for covering walls, fences, embankments, trees, residences, arches, pergolas and other garden structures; the large-flowered hybrids are more suitable for training against pillars, trellises, arches, etc.

SPECIES—**C. languinosa.** slender growing, with smooth leaves, woolly beneath; few-flowered clusters of large flowers, 4-6 inches across, blooming June-September. Many varieties, from white, mauve, lilac, blue to violet-blue. Best known varieties: **Jackmani,** with rich purple flowers; **Ramona,** with rich blue flowers; **Henryi,** with creamy white flowers; **C. montana,** a tall grower, with small, white, Anemonelike flowers, blooming March-June, combining with Pink Cherokee Rose and with lilac Japanese Wisteria. The variety **Rubens** has reddish leaves and pink flowers. **C. paniculata—Japanese Sweet Autumn Clematis.** Small white flowers in axillary and terminal racemes, borne in August-September. **C. virginiana—Virgins Bower.** Small white flowers in leafy panicles, blooming in summer.

CLIANTHUS PUNICEUS—(PARROTS BILL). Evergreen. 5-12 feet. Sun and partial shade. Much branched, vinelike shrub. Very smooth, with dark-green, pinnatifid leaves having 16-28 leaflets; short dense racemes of large, crimson, irregular flowers, like a parrot's bill, blooming in winter. *PROPAGATION*—Cuttings of medium-hard wood in spring; seeds. *CULTURE*—Requires a rich, well fertilized loam. *GROUPING*—Used either in the shrub border or for training against supports; combine with Coprosma, Euonymus in variety, Aucuba, Pittosporum undulatum, Portugal Laurel. The variety C. puniceus magnificus has bright scarlet flowers, blooming December-February.

CLOVE PINK — (DIANTHUS CARYOPHYLLUS).

COBAEA (ROSENBERGIA) SCANDENS — (CUP AND SAUCER VINE). Evergreen shrubby climber. 10-20 feet. Sun. Usually treat as annual, climbing by tendrils; rapid growing, with pinnate leaves; solitary, light violet or greenish-purple, bell-shaped flowers, blooming in April-May. *PROPAGATION*—Seeds sown in early spring in moist earth, edge down. *CULTURE*—Should be grown in poor sand. *POSITION*—Good for covering porches, arbors, etc.

COCKSCOMB — (CELOSIA CRISTATA) — (ERYTHRINA).

COCOS PLUMOSA — (COCOS PALM) — (QUEEN PALM). 30-40 feet, 10-12 inches thick. Erect, ringed, spineless trunk, surmounted by a cluster of drooping, pinnatifid fronds, the top having a beautiful umbrella effect. Grown principally in southern California, although doing fairly well as far north as the San Francisco Bay Region area. *PROPAGATION*—Seeds sown in hotbed in spring. *CULTURE*—Requires a well drained, not too moist, light, sandy loam, fed occasionally with manure. *POSITION*—Grown in patio courts; on lawns; in groupings with sub-tropical plants. *SPECIES*—**C. australis.** A little coarser in growth, but better adapted to the San Francisco Bay Region.

COFFEE BERRY—(RHAMNUS).

COLEUS. Annuals or perennials. 1-2 feet. Sun loving. Erect, branching plant, grown chiefly for the leaves which are furrowed serrate, or dentate, colored red, yellow, purple, bright green, frequently blotched or variegated; small blue or lilac flowers in terminal panicles. *PROPAGATION* — Seed in spring; short cuttings from new wood at any time of year. *CULTURE*—Requires a rich, fibrous loam, fertilized with manures; subject to mealy bug (see Plant Pests). *POSITION*—Used in window boxes and as potted plants for sun porches, conservatories, etc. Sometimes planted outdoors in warm, sheltered positions.

COLUMBINE—(AQUILEGIA).

CONE FLOWER—(RUDBECKIA).

CONVOLVULUS TRICOLOR—(COMMON MORNING GLORY). Annual. Trailing or climbing plants. Sun. Robust growing, hairy plant; linear to oblong, smooth or pubescent leaves; large, tubular flowers; azure, blue, varicolored, often striped and spotted, blooming normally in fall, but also in spring and fall if seed is sown in succession. *PROPAGATION*—Seed, which should be scraped before sowing. *CULTURE*—Grows rampantly in any soil; gives best results in moist, rich, rather light soil. *POSITION*—Very useful for covering waste places, outhouses, garages, fences, etc.

SPECIES—**C. mauritanicus.** Perennial. 6 inches, but spreading 3-4 feet. Sun and slight shade. Slender, much branched stems, with round-ovate, light green leaves; small, salver shaped, azure-blue to violet-purple flowers, borne in great profusion, blooming in winter and in other seasons intermittently. *PROPAGATION*—Division of roots in fall, spring; cuttings; seeds. *CULTURE*—Grows in any soil, but prefers a moderately rich, light loam; should not be overfertilized; cut back old growths to induce new shoots. *POSITION*—For the rockery; embankments; in front of the shrub or hardy border.

COPPER-LEAF BIRCH — (BETULA ALBA ATROPURPUREA).

COPROSMA BAUERI — (AUSTRALIAN HOLLY) — (COPROSMA) — (MIRROR SHRUB). Evergreen. 15-20 feet. Sun and partial shade. Fast growing, half climbing shrub, with thick, stout trunk and branches; medium sized, round, smooth, glistening, dark green leaves; inconspicuous flowers; coral-red berries. *PROPAGATION*—Seed sown after maturity; cuttings of ripened wood in spring. *CULTURE*—Grows in any moderately rich, light soil. *GROUPING*—Effective against a white wall, if kept thinned out; as a background for bright hued flowers; in foundation plantings and the shrub border, combining with Pittosporums in variety, Portugal Laurel, Cherry Laurel, Veronicas in variety, California and Catalina Cherry, Viburnum odoratissimum.

SPECIES—**C. baueri variegata.** Gracefully drooping shrub, with leaves broadly blotched creamy yellow. Will grow in any soil, enduring alkali, clay, or adobe. **C. cunninghami.** Erect in growth, with smaller, narrower leaves.

CORAL BELLS—(HEUCHERA).

CORAL GEM—(LOTUS BERTHOLETTI).

CORAL TREE—(ERYTHRINA).

CORCHORUS—(KERRIA).

COREOPSIS GRANDIFLORA—(COREOPSIS). Perennial. 1½-2 feet. Sun. Spreading plant, with long, smooth, dark green, lanceolate leaves; large, daisylike, golden yellow flowers, blooming April-September. *PROPAGATION*—Seeds sown in early spring; division of roots in fall; best to treat plant as annual, setting out in spring. *CULTURE*—Drought resistant; grows in any soil, but best moderately fertilized, light loam; very hardy, but subject to sow bugs (see Plant Pests). *GROUPING*—For the perennial and mixed borders, combining with Blue Cornflowers, blue Salvias in variety, Myosotis in variety, Delphinium, Centaurea montana, Blue Scabiosa, Anchusa italica, Blue Larkspur, Gaillardia.

CORYLINE—(DRACAENA).

CORNFLOWER—(CENTAUREA CYANEUS).

CORNUS—(DOGWOOD). Deciduous. 8-25 feet under cultivation. Sun or shade equally well. Erect, vigorous in growth, with smooth or pubescent, ovate to elliptical leaves; highly colored in fall; terminal cymes of medium to large, showy flowers, blooming in May, June; reddish or scarlet fruits. *PROPAGATION*—Seeds, germinating the second year; mature wood cuttings in fall; nearly ripened wood in summer; varieties grafted in spring or budded in July. *CULTURE*—Will grow under a variety of climatic and soil conditions. *GROUPING*—Effective planted in front of dark green conifers; in the regular shrub border, especially in combination with Spiraeas, Weigelas, Red-flowered Horse-Chestnut, English Hawthorn, Pomegranate, Pink-flowered Locust, Deutzias.

SPECIES—**C. capitata — Large-Flowered Dogwood.** Large, creamy white flowers. **C. florida—Flowering Dogwood.** White or pinkish flowers, 3-4 inches wide. **C. florida rubra—Pink-Flowered Dogwood.** Deeper pink flowers. **C. kousa—Japanese Dogwood.** Large, creamy-white flowers. **C. nuttali—Native Large-Flowered Dogwood.** Tall growing tree, with white and pinkish flowers, 4-6 inches across. **C. mas—Cornelian Cherry.** Small tree, with small yellow flowers in opposite, sessile umbels.

CORONILLA GLAUCA — (CORONET SHRUB). Evergreen. 2-4 feet, but spreading. Sun loving, rangy in shade. Round-headed, much branched shrub, with gray-green, pinnate leaves, small, pea-shaped, golden-yellow, very fragrant flowers, in umbels, blooming continuously. *PROPAGATION*—Cuttings of half ripened wood; seed. *CULTURE*—Grows best in sandy, well fertilized soil. *GROUPING*—Hedge shrub; in the shrub border, combining with Polygala, Solanum rantonneti, Veronicas in variety, Genistas in variety, Duranta plumieri, Ceanothus in variety.

SPECIES—**C. emerus—Scorpion Senna.** 3-5 feet. Dense, symmetrical shrub, with large yellow flowers tipped with red. Blooming May-July.

CORTADERIA ARGENTEA — (PAMPAS GRASS). Perennial. 3-10 feet. Sun. Reedlike, with long, slender, swordlike, light-green spiny leaves; large, dense panicles of silvery white or purplish, fluffy flowers, blooming in fall. *PROPAGATION*—Seeds; division at any time. *CULTURE*—Does best in moderately rich, moist soil; avoid over-stimulation. *POSITION*—Used on lawns; near pools; in Spanish Gardens; for sub-tropical effects.

SPECIES—**C. quila.** Has longer, more flexuous, nodding branches, more graceful, lavender plumes.

COSMOS BIPINNATUS—(COSMOS). Annual. 6-10 feet. Sun and partial shade. Erect, much branched, smooth plant, with finely dissected leaves; medium to large single and double flowers; pink, *PROPAGATION*—Seeds sown in April. *CULTURE*—Grows best in moderately rich, sandy loam. *GROUPING*—Plant between shrubs; in the background of the mixed border, combining with Pentstemon, Shasta Daisy, Lavender, Michaelmas Daisy, rose, white, crimson, blooming August-December. Matilija Poppy, Rehmannia angulata, Regal Lily.

COTONEASTER. Evergreen and deciduous. 1-20 feet, according to species. Sun and slight shade. Quick growing shrubs, with gracefully arching branches; small, oval, smooth or tomentose leaves, turning to brilliant colors in fall; small, regular, white or pinkish-white flowers, solitary or in cymes, blooming in April-July; followed by red, scarlet, or salmon-red berries, according to species, often persistent throughout winter. *PROPAGATION*—Seeds sown in fall, often self-sown; cutting of half ripened wood in August; layering in fall; grafting of special varieties on Quince, Hawthorn, etc. *CULTURE*—Not particular in soil requirements; avoid too moist and very shady situations; apply manures in fall; attacked by aphis, scale, deciduous kinds of blight (see Plant Pests). *POSITION*—As specimen shrubs; those of medium height in foundation plantings; in the immediate foreground, middle ground, or background of shrub border, according to species; many as hedge shrubs. Cotoneasters combine well with small-leaved shrubs, including Berberis in variety, Ericas (Heathers in variety), Diosma, Small-Leaved Veronicas, Abelia, Common Myrtle, Myrtus luma, Pernettya; different species of Cotoneaster with each other. The Dwarf Cotoneasters are frequently used as "fillers"; on embankments; along steps; at intersections of walks; as ground covers; over walls; near pools; rockeries.

SPECIES—**C. acuminata (nepalensis).** Semi-deciduous. 8-10 feet. Deep scarlet berries in September, October. **C. adpressa.** 8-10 inches, but spreading several feet; wavy margined leaves; red berries in August. **C. franchetti.** Evergreen. 4-6 feet. Arching branches; thick, wrinkled leaves; pinkish-white flowers; salmon-red berries in September, October. **C. horizontalis—Rock Cotoneaster.** Semi-deciduous. Very low growing, but widely spreading, with horizontal, flat branches; dark-green, round-oval, glistening leaves, highly colored in fall; pinkish-white flowers; dark-red berries along upper sides of branches, appearing in September, persistent until January. Easily propagated by layering. **C. harroviana.** Evergreen. 10-12 feet. Somewhat similar to **C. pannosa,** but with large, dark-green leaves and large, rose-red berries in September. **C. microphylla.** Low, prostrate, evergreen shrub, 1-2 feet, but spreading out; grows flat against walls; densely branched;

very small, bright-green leaves, densely tomentose beneath; profusely flowering, followed by bright-red fruits in October, persisting until February. **C. pannosa—Silver Cotoneaster.** Evergreen. 8-10 feet. With arching branches; light-green, feltlike leaves; bright-red berries in October. **C. salicifolia—Willow-Leaf Cotoneaster.** Semi-deciduous. 5-7 feet. Bushy shrub, with very long, gracefully arching branches; dark-green, willowlike leaves; bright-red fruits in October, November; attacked by Pear Blight (see Plant Pests). **C. schneideri.** Very similar to **C. franchetti. C. thymifolia.** Similar to **C. microphylla,** but very dwarf.

COTTONWOOD—(POPULUS).

CRABAPPLE—(FLOWERING FRUIT TREES —PYRUS).

CRAPE MYRTLE—(LAGERSTROEMIA).

CRATAEGUS—(HAWTHORN). See also **PYRACANTHA.** Deciduous. 20-40 feet. Sun and slight shade. Rather symmetrical, bushy, often spiny trees; bright-green, smooth, sharply serrate, pinnatifid or lobed leaves, brilliantly colored in fall; small white, red, or rose flowers in corymbs, blooming in spring and early summer; red or scarlet fruits called Haws, persistent into winter. *PROPAGATION*—Stratified seeds in spring; cuttings of hard or soft wood; double varieties grafted in July upon American species. *CULTURE*—Partial to heavy limestone clay, but does well in average, well drained, somewhat moist soils, enriched with manures; pruning back and thinning in fall; subject to scale and smut (see Plant Pests). *POSITION*—Specimen trees for lawns; for large groupings, using different species and varieties together; very effective planted with conifers; as an occasional planting in wide shrub borders, especially in combination with late blooming Flowering Fruit Trees, Spiraeas, Mock Orange, Deutzias, Weigelas, Japanese Quince, Maples (Acer) in variety, Oaks (Quercus) in variety, and other deciduous trees and shrubs; hedges.

SPECIES—**C. oxyacantha—English Hawthorn —Scarlet Hawthorn.** Single and double-flowered forms, with white, red, rose, or scarlet flowers, frequently varying on the same tree. **C. cordata—Washington Thorn.** Slender leaves and shining, bright coral-red flowers; **C. monogyna.** Many varieties, with single and double, pink or deep-red flowers; red or yellow fruits. **C. carrierei.** With reddish flowers and orange or brick-red fruits. Many other species and varieties with weeping or upright forms, variegated foliage, and variously colored flowers.

CREEPING FIG—(FICUS REPENS).

CREEPING JUNIPER — (JUNIPERUS PROCUMBENS).

CROCUS—(DUTCH CROCUS). Bulbous plant. 4-8 inches. Sun and partial shade. Erect plant, with linear, grasslike leaves; funnel-shaped flowers, white, lilac, rose, purple, deep blue, blooming January-April. *PROPAGATION*—Seed in early spring; offsets from corms planted September-December. *CULTURE*—Require a rich, acid, moist, well fertilized, light loam; replant after several years. *GROUPING*—For rockeries; on terraces; as border plants; for naturalizing on lawns; in the flower border, combining with Spring Snowflake, Narcissi, Jonquils, Dutch Hyacinth, Mignonette, Myosotis in variety, Gold Tuft.

SPECIES—**Autumn-Flowering Crocus.** Full sun in sheltered situations. Like Dutch Crocus, but blooming in fall.

CRYPTOMERIA JAPONICA—(JAPANESE CEDAR). Conifer. 20-60 feet under cultivation.
Sun and partial shade. Erect, symmetrical, pyramidal tree, with straight, slender trunk; whorled, spreading branches; spirally arranged, awl-shaped, bluish-green leaves. *PROPAGATION*—Seeds sown in spring; cuttings of growing wood. *CULTURE*—Does best in a rich, moist, loamy soil.

SPECIES—**C. japonica elegans.** 25-30 feet. Sun and partial shade. Rapid-growing, very symmetrical, round-headed tree; horizontal branches with pendulous branchlets; soft, linear, bright-green leaves, turning rapidly to a bronzy red, accentuated when winter approaches. *PROPAGATION*—Seeds; half firm wood in fall and spring. *POSITION*—Both kinds grown as specimen trees on lawns, and as grouping trees on large plantations.

CUP AND SAUCER FLOWER—(CAMPANULA CALYCANTHEMA).

CUP AND SAUCER VINE—(COBAEA SCANDENS).

CUP OF GOLD—(SOLANDRA).

CUPHEA IGNEA—(CIGAR PLANT). Evergreen. 2-3 feet, but spreading. Sun. Very floriferous, dense, branching shrub; dark-green, entire, lanceolate leaves; racemes of irregular, long, tubular, cigar-shaped, bright-red flowers, with dark ring at tip, and white mouth, blooming almost continuously. *PROPAGATION*—Cuttings of half firm wood in fall and spring; seeds. *CULTURE*—Easy to grow in any ordinary, moderately fertilized soil. *POSITION*—For the rock garden; as an occasional plant in both the flower and shrub borders.

CUPRESSUS — (CYPRESS). Conifers. Mostly large and tall growing, graceful in habit, very hardy in California, especially along the Pacific Coast as far north as the San Francisco Bay Region area, and in parts of the interior. Sun and partial shade. Aromatic, scalelike leaves; yellow flowers; medium-sized, many-seeded cones, ripening the second year. *PROPAGATION*—Same as for Chamaecyparis, to which it is closely related. *CULTURE*—Adapted to a variety of soil conditions, but prefers a deep, sandy loam; quite drought resistant; Italian Cypress subject to root borer (see Plant Pests). *POSITION*—Confined usually to large grounds; grouped by themselves or with pines, cedars, and other similar conifers; used as windbreaks and for making high hedges; for naturalistic plantings if headed back and judiciously pruned.

SPECIES—**C. arizonica**—Arizona Cypress. 40-50 feet. Forming a compact, pyramidal head; gray-green, glaucous leaves; grows well in sandy soil. **C. guadalupensis** — Guadalupe Cypress. Wide-spreading, tall tree, with slender, drooping branchlets, and bluish-green leaves. **C. macrocarpa**—Monterey Cypress. 40-60 feet. With erect or horizontally spreading branches, forming a broad, beautifully contoured, spreading head; lustrous, dark-green leaves. **C. sempervirens fastigiata—Italian Cypress.** The true type has erect branches, forming a narrow, columnar head, with dark-green foliage. *PROPAGATION*—Grafting on seedling stock to secure straight, narrow effect. *CULTURE*—Does best in moderately rich, fairly moist, ordinary soils. *POSITION*—Has a variety of uses: as a formal accent shrub; for grouping on lawns, usually in three's; avenue tree; foundation plantings at corners; to create vistas. Low-growing Creeping Junipers at base.

CUT-LEAF WEEPING BIRCH—(BETULA).

CUTTINGS—(See Garden Movies).

CYCLAMEN. Bulbous plant. 8-10 inches. Partial shade best. Forming a rosette of dark-green or variegated, smooth, reinform leaves; irregular, large, orchidlike flowers, spotted, striped, in pure colors and shades of red, white, salmon, pink, rose, blooming December-April. *PROPAGATION*—Seed sown July-January, taking 15 months to bloom; offsets from corms, planted half way in soil, either in small pots or in open ground in sheltered situation, from September-March; potted plants in the house in December may be transferred to the garden. *CULTURE*—Rich, light, acid garden loam, having acid soil reaction, adding peat or leaf mold; fertilize with rotted cow manure. Grown usually in the greenhouse, but can be grown in the shady border. *GROUPING*—Combines effectively with Ferns, Azaleas, Cinerarias, Dutch Crocus, Hyacinths, Lenten Rose, Dicentra.

CYDONIA JAPONICA — (JAPANESE QUINCE). Deciduous. 3-6 feet. Much-branched shrub, with spiny branches, irregular in growth; glistening, smooth, ruddy leaves; large, regular, white, rose to scarlet flowers in clusters, blooming January-April; fragrant, yellowish-green fruits. *PROPAGATION*—Seed, stratify and sow in spring; root cuttings in fall or early spring; hard wood cuttings in fall. *CULTURE*—Grows in any soil, but prefers a rich, light, moist, well fertilized loam; should be thinned out each year. *GROUPING*—Specimen shrubs; for the shrub border, combining with Pomegranate, Magnolia solangeana, Bridal Veil Broom, scarlet and flame-colored Azaleas, Red-Flowered Peach, Pittosporum tobira, Red-Flowered Fuchsias. Choose shrubs with desired color, propagating from these.

CYNOGLOSSUM FURCATUM — (HOUND'S TONGUE)—(BLUE FORGET-ME-NOT). Perennial. 1-3 feet. Bushy plant, with ovate-lanceolate leaves; numerous-flowered racemes of regular, Forget-me-not-like flowers, blooming in summer. *PROPAGATION*—Seeds sown in early spring; division of clumps September-November. *CULTURE*—Hardy, growing in ordinary soils. *GROUPING*—Plant in mixed flower border, grouping with Dimorphotheca aurantiaca, Perennial Flax, Iceland Poppy, Torch Lily, Yellow Columbine, Doronicum excelsum, Lilium pardalinum.

SPECIES—**C. amabile**—Chinese Forget-me-not. Like the above, but with larger, brilliant blue flowers.

CYPRESS—(CUPRESSUS).

CYTISUS (GENISTA)—(BROOM). Evergreen. 4-12 feet. Sun and slight shade. Fast growing, densely branching shrubs; leaves unifoliate or trifoliate, very much reduced in size, bright green; terminal heads and racemes of small to medium-sized, irregular, pea-shaped, fragrant yellow flowers, blooming in early spring and summer, and intermittently throughout the year; fruit a pod. *PROPAGATION*—Seeds sown in May; cuttings of tender shoots under cover. *CULTURE*—Grows in any soil, naturalizing easily; drought resistant; fertilize with manures. *GROUPING*—For the shrub border, the taller sorts like Canary Island Broom and Scotch Broom used in the background, with C. andreanus and C. racemosus in foreground; combine with Veronicas in variety, Acacia in variety, Sollya heterophylla, Salvia leucantha, Solanum wendlandii, Streptosolen, Echium fastuosum, Iochroma; in rockeries; parking strips; dwarf species in window boxes; hedge shrubs.

SPECIES—**C. racemosus—Dwarf Easter Broom.** 3-4 feet. The best species for the average garden, with silver-tipped branches, silky, pubescent leaves, and golden-yellow flowers, blooming quite continuously. **C. canariensis—Canary Island Broom.** Tall growing; many flowered, dense, short racemes of golden-yellow flowers. **C. scoparius—Scotch Broom.** Large shrub with bright yellow flowers in loosely arranged racemes. The variety andreanus has yellow flowers with mahogany-colored wings. **C. albus.** Low-growing form with few leaves and small white flowers.

D

DABOECIA POLIFOLIA (CANTABRICA)— (IRISH BELL HEATHER). Evergreen. 1½-2 feet. Sun. Heatherlike shrub, dense and compact; small, elliptical, shining, dark-green leaves; long, terminal racemes of tubular, purple or white flowers, blooming June-October. *PROPAGATION* — Seeds sown in spring; cuttings of half ripened wood under glass. *CULTURE*—Requires an acid, peaty, sandy, moderately fertilized, garden loam. Several varieties of various colors. *GROUPING*—Adapted for use in rockeries; in the shrub border, combining with species of Erica (Heather), Diosma in variety, small-leaved Barberries, Calluna vulgaris.

DAFFODIL—(NARCISSUS).

DAHLIA. Bulbous plant growing from tubers in clusters. 2-6 feet. Sun loving. Erect, with stout green stems; opposite, large, pinnate, bright green leaves; small to very large flowers, consisting of variously shaped petals in series, surrounding a central yellow disk, blooming from June-November, having a wide range of colors, represented by many different forms described below. *PROPAGATION*—Usually by small tubers together with portion of stem containing one or several eyes; seeds for new varieties, and for Single Dahlias, sowing early in the year; cuttings of medium-soft stems with some varieties. *CULTURE*—Will grow in any soil, except very heavy clay, but prefers a rich, moist, fairly light loam, well enriched with manures before planting tubers; liquid manure in limited quantities during growing period beneficial; add peat, leaf mold, or sharp sand to lighten heavy soils; a little lime is also necessary; as plants come into bloom add small quantities of well balanced, commercial fertilizers; a mulch of

straw material or of peat about plant is good; keep well watered at all times. *PLANTING*—Dahlias do best in a cool, moist climate, indifferently in a hot, dry climate. Dig a basin before planting. In fairly light soil, place tuber almost flat, 4-6 inches below surface; in heavier soils plant shallower; keep soil moist and loose about growing shoot. Tie stem to redwood stake or to stout bamboo. *DISBUDDING* —Pinching back when stem is six inches high will tend to throw out laterals; disbud and remove side laterals for large flowers; remove old blooms, cutting down to low laterals; pick flowers with long stems. Dahlias may be left in the ground over winter, but it is usually best to lift tubers, cleaning them thoroughly, and storing in a cool, dry place. *DISEASES* —Dahlias are usually very hardy, but are attacked by certain pests: aphis, diabrotica sow bugs, mildew (see Plant Pests). Tubers will rot if too much water collects about them. After the blooming season, cut down stalks close to ground, collect and burn all rubbish. *GROUPING*—Dahlias, especially the large-flowered kinds, appear to best advantage when planted in large beds by themselves, or when planted in the foreground of shrub borders. The miniature Pompons, the small-flowered Collarettes, and some of the single-flowered kinds with small flowers may be planted in the flower border, grouping with fall-blooming perennials having harmonious color relations.

TYPES—**Anemone.** A single-type Dahlia with disk tubular flowers. **Cactus.** Rather compact, large flowers, with rolled, pointed petals extending back to the center. **Semi-Cactus** or **Hybrid Cactus.** Looser in form, with very large flowers having flattened, twisted, pointed petals, extending to the center. **Collarette.** With eight petals around the edge, in addition to a collar of small petals opposite each petal. **Decorative.** Including Formal, Informal, and Miniature Decoratives. Flowers are very large, with flat petals extending to the center. **Peony.** With rather large, loose-textured flowers. **Pompon,** including Decorative Pompons and Miniature Cactus—Small flowers, several inches in diameter, rounded and very compact, with quilled petals. **Show** or **Ball.** With rather large, rounded, dense-headed flowers, having quilled petals; Hybrid Show has more flattened petals. **Single.** Varying from small to quite large flowers, with a circular row of large flat petals surrounding a yellow center.

SPECIES—**Dahlia imperialis—Tree Dahlia.** Deciduous. 8-12 feet. Sun and partial shade. Tuberous rooted, tall, erect, with thick, jointed, knotty stems; large, light-green, 2-3 pinnately divided leaves; large, single, nodding, lavender-rose-white flowers, resembling Single Dahlias, blooming in October-November. *PROPAGATION*—Usually by division of stems in fall and early spring; seeds sown in spring. *CULTURE* —Grows in any soil, but prefers a moist, rich loam. *POSITION*—In groupings; as accent plant; in the background of shrub border.

DAPHNE. Deciduous or Evergreen shrubs. 1-5 feet. Sun loving, but endures some shade in very warm regions. Symmetrical, round-headed shrubs, with medium-sized, smooth, glossy leaves; very fragrant, rather small, regular flowers in short clusters, blooming according to species in winter and spring. *PROPAGATION*—Seeds sown after maturity; cuttings of mature wood in fall; soft wood cuttings from forced plants; veneer grafts; layering. *CULTURE*—Does best in a good, light, acid garden loam with acid reaction. Daphne odora blooms best in poor soil, kept slightly moist.

SPECIES—**D. cneorum—Rose Daphne** or **Garland Flower.** Evergreen. Very low, spreading growth, with dark-green leaves, and many-flowered heads of pink flowers, blooming February-April. Suitable for rockeries. **D. mezereum.** Deciduous. 4 feet. Lilac-purple flowers, appearing before the leaves, blooming February-April, followed by scarlet fruits. **D. odora—Daphne.** Flowers in dense, terminal heads, white, pink, to purple, according to variety. Existing in several varieties.

DARWINS BARBERRY — (BERBERIS DARWINI).

DATE PALM—(PHOENIX).

DAY LILY—(HEMEROCALLIS).

DELPHINIUM — (PERENNIAL LARKSPUR).

Perennial. 1-8 feet, according to species and kind. Sun loving, but endures slight shade. Usually erect, but also semi-decumbent kinds, with bright or dark-green, medium-sized to large, frequently cleft or deeply incised leaves; medium to large-sized, somewhat irregular, spurred flowers, white, opalescent, and in shades of blue and pink, also with a characteristic "bee" in center; spikelike inflorescence in various forms; blooming period extends from April until late fall. *PROPAGATION*—Cuttings of medium firm stems of hybrids in spring; division of clumps October-December, and in early spring; seed of hybrids sown in late summer to produce good clumps in fall; seed sown in spring to produce summer-blooming plants. *CULTURE*—Grows in a variety of soils, but prefers rich, well drained, rather light soils, fertilized with manures during growing period, with well balanced commercial fertilizers during blooming period; peat or leaf mold should be added to heavy soils; wood ashes, bone meal, and limestone are also beneficial; avoid overstimulation with manure; keep mulch about plants; stake to stout bamboo or to Redwood stakes; principal troubles are: mildew, blight, root rot, sow and pill bugs, snails and slugs (see Plant Pests); cut down old flower stalks for second bloom. *GROUPING*—The stately Delphinium is one of the finest of all the perennials for the perennial and mixed borders, combining with a number of flowers, including: Columbine, Pentstemon, Salpiglossis, Snapdragons, Stocks, Pyrethrum, Scabiosa in variety, Hemerocallis, Breeder Tulips, Lilies in variety, Gladiolus.

SPECIES—The different strains of Hybrid Delphiniums are legion in number. The English plant breeders have produced many distinct strains running into many varieties. The inflorescence is usually quite compact and of the candelabra form; the Wrexham strain is perhaps the best known. In America the spike is more open with large, multicolored flowers. Delphiniums are apt to run out after several years, so should be renewed; division of clumps is not always satisfactory; plant 1½-2 feet apart.

SPECIES—**D. ajacis—Larkspur.** Annual. 3-4 feet. Sun and light shade. Erect, bushy plant, with light-green, finely dissected leaves; densely flowered racemes or spikes of rose, blue, white, or violet flowers, blooming April-October. *PROPAGATION*—Seed sown successively from January-July. *CULTURE*—Hardy, growing in a variety of soils, but prefers a rich, well fertilized, sandy loam. *GROUPING*—For the annual and mixed borders, combining with Blue Lace Flower, Hybrid Delphiniums, Clarkia, Snapdragons, Pentstemon, Coral Bells, Candytuft, Thalictrum in variety. **D. belladonna.** 2 feet. Perennial. Of medium growth, with light-green, finely divided leaves; large, sky-blue flowers. **D. cardinale.** Native perennial. 2-3 feet. Leaves smooth, deeply cleft, fleshy leaves; many-flowered racemes of bright-red flowers with yellow limbs, blooming May-July. **D. grandiflorum chinense — Butterfly Delphinium.** Low, sprawling form, with deep blue or pale blue in many-flowered racemes, blooming in summer.

DENDROCALAMUS LATIFLORUS—(JAPANESE GIANT BAMBOO).

Bamboo is also known under various generic names as Bambusa, Arundinaria, Phyllostachys. Evergreen or dying down to culm in winter. 2-20 feet, according to kind. Sun and slight shade. Usually large, but some dwarf, with stout, erect, often woody, sheathed canes; usually long and narrow, light-green, dark-green, or variegated leaves, often sharply serrate or pubescent. *PROPAGATION*—Usually by division of clumps before new growth sets in; seldom by seeds. *CULTURE*—Likes a deep, rich, moist loam, fertilized occasionally with manures. *POSITION*—Against walls; in amongst shrubbery; by streams and naturalistic pools; in the Japanese Garden; for use as screens; along boundary lines. Some varieties send out long runners; only those kinds adapted to a particular site should be selected. *OTHER KINDS*—**Arundinaria nitida.** 8-10 feet. Very slender, purple-black stems; short, narrow leaves. **A. japonica.** 10 feet. Rather long and broad leaves, smooth and shining above, white and finely pubescent beneath. **Bambusa vulgaris—Feathery Bamboo.** Tall growing, with rough, long, narrow leaves. The variety **aurea-variegata** has golden-yellow canes. **Phyllostachys aurea—Golden Bamboo.** 10-15 feet. Very erect, with golden-yellow canes. This is one of the best kinds for the average small garden.

DEODAR—(CEDRUS DEODARA).

DEUTZIA. Deciduous. 2-6 feet. Sun or partial shade. Bushy, with roughly pubescent, lanceolate, dark-green leaves; pure white, regular, medium-sized flowers in corymbs or panicles, blooming in May-June. *PROPAGATION*—Seed sown in spring; green wood and hard wood cuttings. *CULTURE*—Impartial in soil requirements. *GROUPING*—Good for spring effects in the shrub border, harmonizing with Snowball, Spiraea in variety, Weigela in variety, Cornus florida, English Hawthorn, Oleaster, Pomegranate.

SPECIES—**D. gracilis.** Slender growing, 2-3 feet, with smooth, bright-green leaves. Does best in partial shade. **D. lemoinei.** Spreading to 3 feet. Like the D. gracilis, but more vigorous. **D. scabra.** 6 feet. Rough, hairy-leaved shrub; dull-green leaves; bluish-white flowers. Many varieties of the above.

DIANTHUS—(PINK). Perennial. 3-12 inches or more, according to kind. Sun loving. The genus Dianthus contains the well-known Pinks, Carnations, and Sweet Williams, and many species of rock plants. In general they are low growing, spreading to form thick mats of tufted, narrow, linear, light to gray-green, glaucous leaves; fragrant flowers range in size from tiny Pinks to large Carnations, colored white and shades of rose, pink, red, blooming from spring into fall. *PROPAGATION*—According to kind may be propagated by seed, sown in fall or spring; division October-December; layering any time; stolens. *CULTURE*—Varied in soil requirements, the Garden Pinks and Carnations requiring a rich, light, fairly moist garden loam, well fertilized with manures; the alpine and rock garden species require a well drained, moderately fertilized, light, gritty soil, containing some limestone; subject to stem rot, induced by too much moisture, sow and pill bugs—otherwise very hardy. *POSITION*—According to kind as border plants, in the mixed border, and in rockeries.

SPECIES—D. barbatus—Sweet William. 10-20 inches. Sun or light shade. Forming a dense mat of light to dark-green, often colored leaves, and dense, round-headed cymes of hairy-petaled, medium-sized flowers, blooming over a long period, ranging in color from white, rose, pink, maroon, to deep scarlet. *GROUPING*—Useful as border plants and in the mixed border, combining according to color with Snapdragons, Delphiniums, Stocks, Arabis albida, Pentstemon, Carnations, Phlox subulata, Perennial Phlox, Petunias, Larkspur. **D. caryophyllus—Carnation—Spice or Clove Pinks.** Listed under such strains as Marguerite, Rivieri, Chabaud. Very fragrant, large flowers, white, pink, scarlet, crimson, yellow, blooming from summer into fall. The well-known Florist's Carnations are best under glass, although doing quite well outdoors in warm, protected situations. These are propagated readily by cuttings during spring or fall. Carnations are best planted by themselves in beds or in flower borders. **Alwoodi Pinks.** Crosses between D. caryophyllus and D. plumarius, combining the qualities of both. **D. chinensis.** Medium-sized, pink and lilac, fragrant flowers with fringed petals. The variety **Heddewigii** has rather large, fringed, single and double flowers in many bright colors, but without fragrance. **D. caesius—Cheddar Pink.** Fragrant, small, rose-pink flowers on short stems, blooming in July; gray-green foliage. A rock garden plant. **D. deltoides—Maiden Pink.** A dainty, low growing plant, with diminutive, white, cerise, or crimson flowers, blooming in spring and early summer. Useful between stepping-stones and as a border plant. Easily propagated by seeds and by cuttings. **D. plumarius—Scotch Pink—Garden Pink—Pheasant's Eye Pink.** Both single and double, very fragrant white, pink, rose, medium-sized flowers, blooming in spring and summer. Easily propagated, very useful as a border plant, for bedding out, or for the mixed border, combining with flowers having soft and pastel shades.

DIERVILLA—(WEIGELA). Deciduous. 6-8 feet. Sun and slight shade. Hardy, fast growing, muchly branched, with large, rough, elliptical-oblong, bright-green leaves; small clusters of medium-sized, regular tubular flowers, white, and shades of pink and red. *PROPAGATION*—Seeds, but do not come true; cuttings of half ripened wood in summer; hard wood in fall; suckers in spring. *CULTURE*—Should be cut back after blooming; impartial in soil requirements. *GROUPING*—Grouping with Spiraeas and

Deutzias in variety, Snowball, Cornus florida and in variety, Mexican Orange, Flowering Cherries. *VARIETIES*—Eva Rathke—Red Weigela; D. rosea—Pink Weigela.

DIGITALIS PURPUREA—(FOXGLOVE). Biennial or perennial. 4-6 feet. Semi-shade, but grows in sun. Erect, rather massive, stately plant, with stout, green stem; medium to very large-sized, downy, rough, oblong-ovate, crowded leaves; long, terminal, one-sided spikes of drooping, rather large, tubular, inflated flowers, the throat hairy and spotted, white, purple, lilac, rose, yellow, blooming June-September. *PROPAGATION* — Seeds, sown preferably in summer for flowers the next year; division of clumps in fall. *CULTURE*—Grows in any soil, but prefers a rich, well fertilized, light garden loam; harbors sow bugs, snails, etc. (see Plant Pests). *GROUPING*—In the perennial border, alone or grouped with Hollyhock, Canterbury Bells, Pentstemon, Shasta Daisy, Matilija Poppy, Begonias in variety, Evening Primrose, Impatiens oliveri.

DIMORPHOTHECA AURANTIACA—(AFRICAN GOLDEN DAISY). Annual. 18 inches. Sun. Bushy plant, with glaucous blue, linear-oblong leaves; large white, salmon, red, yellow, orange, daisylike flowers, blooming July-January. *PROPAGATION*—Seeds sown in April. *CULTURE*—Likes a rich, well fertilized, loamy soil. *GROUPING*—For the mixed border, combining with Iceland Poppy, African Blue Daisy, Blue Salvias, Michaelmas Daisy, Plumbago larpentae.

DIOSMA ERICOIDES— (BREATH-OF-HEAVEN)—(DIOSMA). Evergreen. 4-5 feet. Sun and partial shade. Round-headed, compact shrub, with small, aromatic, dark-green, needlelike leaves; minute, white, star-shaped flowers, borne singly, blooming profusely in summer, but almost continuously. *PROPAGATION*—Seeds; cuttings of short-jointed young shoots in April. *CULTURE*—Grows in most ordinary, moderately fertilized soils. *GROUPING*—Used as formal accent shrubs; in the foreground of the shrub border, groupings with Ericas (Heathers) in variety, Melaleuca ericifolia, and M. armillaris, Berberis Darwini.

SPECIES—D. purpurea. 1-2 feet. Lavender-purple flowers. **D. reevesi** Similar to D. ericoides, but with larger flowers.

DODONAEA VISCOSA. Evergreen. 10-15 feet. Sun. Linear to oblong, resinous leaves; small greenish flowers. Grown mostly in southern California. *PROPAGATION*—Half ripened wood; seeds. *CULTURE*—Grows in ordinary soils. *POSITION*—In the shrub border.

DOGTOOTH VIOLET—(ERYTHRONIUM).

DOGWOOD—(CORNUS).

DOLICHOS LIGNOSUS—(AUSTRALIAN PEA VINE). Perennial. 10-15 feet. Sun. Rapidly growing, shrubby vine, with rough, lanceolate leaves; racemes of white or rosy purple, pea-shaped flowers, blooming in summer, and quite continuously. *PROPAGATION*—Seed, sown in fall or spring; cuttings. *CULTURE*—Grows in any soil, not too rich. *POSITION*—Good for covering embankments; screen plantings; for covering outbuildings, etc.

DORONICUM EXCELSUM — (LEOPARDS BANE). Perennial. 2 feet. Sun loving, and partial shade. Erect plant, with long, lanceolate leaves; slender flower stems, surmounted by large, daisylike flowers, blooming April-July. *PROPAGATION*— Seeds sown in early spring; division of roots in fall. *CULTURE*—Grows best in rich, light, well fertilized loam; hardy, quite immune to pests. *GROUPING*— For the perennial and mixed borders, combining with Calendula, Alyssum saxatile, Scabiosa caucasica, medium blue Delphinium, Calceolaria, Spanish Iris, Lavender Bearded Iris.

DOUBLE PINK-FLOWERED APRICOT— (FLOWERING FRUIT TREES).

DOUBLE PINK JAPANESE PLUM—(FLOWERING FRUIT TREES).

DOUGLAS FIR—(PSEUDOTSUGA).

DOUGLAS SPRUCE—(PSEUDOTSUGA).

DRACAENA (CORDYLINE)—(D. AUSTRALIS)—(DRACENA PALM). 10-20 feet. Sun or partial shade. Palmlike tree, with erect, woody, rather plated or ridged, thick trunk; great bunches of blue-green, strap-shaped leaves, turning brown upon maturity, appearing near top of trunk, but radical in young plants; large clusters of yellowish-white flowers; small blackish berries. *PROPAGATION*—Easily by seeds sown in spring. *CULTURE* —Grows in any soil, but soil should be enriched with manure. *POSITION*—Fine near corners of Spanish residences; in corners of patios; avenue trees.

DURANTA PLUMIERI — (GOLDEN DEWDROP SHRUB). Evergreen. 8-10 feet. Sun loving, and partial shade. Loose growing shrub with drooping branches; medium-sized, smooth, ovate-elliptic, dark-green leaves; small, somewhat irregular, lilac flowers in loose racemes, blooming August-October; brown drupe fruits. *PROPAGATION*—Seeds; cuttings of half firm wood under glass with bottom heat. *GROUPING*—Specimen tree; for the shrub border, grouping with Abelia, Common Myrtle, Hypericum moserianum, Pittosporum tenuifolium, Plumbago capensis, Viburnum lucidum, Acacia floribunda.

DUSTY MILLER — (CENTAUREA CANDIDISSIMA).

DUTCH CROCUS—(CROCUS).

DWARF DATE PALM—(PHOENIX ROEBELENII).

DWARF FLOWERING ALMOND—(FLOWERING FRUIT TREES).

E

ECHIUM FASTUOSUM—(ECHIUM). Evergreen. 6-8 feet. Sun. Round-headed, bushy, compact shrub; large, pale gray-green, soft, pubescent leaves; dense, compact, many-flowered spikes of small, brilliant blue, star-shaped flowers, with exserted stamens, blooming June-September. *PROPAGATION*—Seed sown when mature; cuttings of half firm wood. *CULTURE*—Grow in rather sterile soil for good blooms. *GROUPING*—Used in the shrub border, occasionally as a specimen shrub; group with

Genista, Spanish Broom, Cassia, Cistus salvifolius, Yellow Heliotrope, Hypericum calycinum, Fremontia.

EGYPTIAN LOTUS— (NELUMBIUM).

ELEAGNUS. Deciduous and Evergreen shrubs. 6-15 feet. Sun and slight shade. Bushy, often spiny, spreading shrubs; entire, scurfy leaves, clothed with brown or yellowish scales; fragrant, inconspicuous flowers; bright-colored, edible fruits. *PROPAGATION*—Seeds stratified, germinating the second year; cuttings of both mature and half ripened wood; layering; root cuttings. *CULTURE*—Grows in any good, well drained, moderately fertilized soil; endures alkali and adobe. *POSITION*—Used primarily as contrast shrubs in the shrub border.

SPECIES — **E. angustifolia — Oleaster.** Deciduous. 10-15 feet. Oblong-lanceolate, long, silvery leaves; fragrant yellow flowers blooming in June; coral red-yellow berries. **E. argentea—Silverberry.** Evergreen. Reddish-brown branchlets; leaves silvery on both sides; fragrant yellow flowers; silver-coated berries. **E. multiflora (longipes).** Deciduous. 6 feet. Colored branchlets; hairy, elliptic-ovate, scaly leaves; fragrant, yellowish-white flowers; pendulous, scarlet fruits. **E. pungens.** Evergreen. 6 feet, but spreading 10 feet. Spiny with brown branchlets; oblong-ovate leaves, smooth above, silvery beneath. **E. pungens variegata.** Has yellowish-white margins.

ELEPHANT'S EAR—(CALADIUM).

ELM—(ULMUS).

ENGLISH BOXWOOD—(BUXUS).

ENGLISH DAISY—(BELLIS).

ENGLISH HAWTHORN — (CRATAEGUS OXYACANTHA)

ENGLISH HEATHER—(CALLUNA).

ENGLISH HOLLY—(ILEX).

ENGLISH IVY—(HEDERA).

ENGLISH LAUREL — (PRUNUS LAUROCERASUS).

ENGLISH PRIVET—(LIGUSTRUM).

ERANTHIS HYEMALIS—(WINTER ACONITE). Bulbous plant. 5-8 inches. Half shade. Tuberous root stock, with palmately dissected leaves; small, bright-yellow flowers, blooming January-March. *PROPAGATION*—Division of roots in fall. *CULTURE*—Grows in any good, garden loam. *GROUPING*—For the mixed border, combining with Violets, Spring Snowflake, Aubrietias, Christmas Rose, Violas, Primula malacoides, Mignonette, Myosotis in variety, Dutch Crocus.

ERICA—(HEATHER). Evergreen. 1-10 feet, according to kind. Sun and partial shade. Generally bushy shrubs, with needlelike, light to dark-green leaves; small to medium-sized, short or long tubular and bell-shaped, white, pink, or reddish flowers, blooming in winter, spring, or fall, according to species. *PROPAGATION*—Short cuttings of growing wood, December-April. *CULTURE*—Prefers a light, acid, loamy soil, containing peat or leaf mold; cannot tolerate lime in soil; subject to scale (see Plant Pests); tannic acid or alum in solution will counteract lime; prune back after flowering. *GROUPING*—Specimen shrubs for lawns; foundation plantings; hedges for the shrub border, combining with Diosma, small-leaved Barberries, Cotoneaster franchetti, C. microphylla, and C. horizontalis. Myrtus ugni, Chamaecyparis in variety, different species of Erica with each other.

SPECIES—**E. blanda.** Medium long, tubular, rose-colored flowers, blooming November-December. **E. carnea.** Very dwarf, with bright, rosy-flowered, broadly bell-shaped flowers, blooming March-May. **E. mediterranea—Mediterranean Heather.** 4-6 feet. Globular-shaped, densely branched shrub, with dark-green leaves, and short tubular, purplish-rose flowers, blooming in winter and intermittently. The variety E. med. hybrida grows 1 foot high. The Mediterranean Heather is sometimes used as an accent shrub in formal gardens. **E. melanthera—Pink Heather.** 8-10 feet. Rather symmetrical, with light pink-white, small, bell-shaped flowers, blooming indefinitely in fall and winter, sometimes intermittently. Specimen shrub, for the shrub border, and for making high hedges. **E. melanthera rubra.** Like the type, but with deep pink flowers. **E. persoluta alba.** 2-3 feet. With pretty, round bell-shaped, medium sized white or pink flowers, blooming in early spring. **E. persoluta rosea.** More slender in growth, with deep, pink flowers. **E. wilmoreana.** 3-4 feet. Long, tubular, rosy-white flowers, blooming November-December. **E. regerminans.** 3-4 feet. Deep pink-lavender, bell-shaped flowers, blooming November-December. **E. veitchii.** 4-6 feet. Short, tubular, white flowers with black centers, blooming in winter. Fine for making hedges.

ERIGERON MUCRONATUS. Erroneously called Michaelmas Daisy. Perennial. 6-8 inches, but spreading. Sun or partial shade. Quick growing plant, making a dense mat; lanceolate, bright-green leaves; dense clusters of small, white-purple-rose flowers, blooming profusely in summer, and continuous. *PROPAGATION*—Division of clumps at any time; seeds sown in early spring. *CULTURE*—Grows in any soil. *POSITION*—Rockeries; over walls; to cover embankments.

ERYNGIUM AMETHYSTINUM— (SEA HOLLY). Perennial. 2-3 feet. Sun. Erect, rigid, spiny plant, with steel-blue or purplish stems; stiff, spiny, dark-green, deeply cut leaves; small, bristly, bright steel-blue flowers in crowded heads, blooming June-September. *PROPAGATION*—Seed sown in early spring best method. *CULTURE*—Grows best in moderately rich, sandy loam. *GROUPING*—Used in rockeries; as an occasional plant in the mixed border.

ERYTHEA EDULIS—(GUADALUPE PALM). 10-20 feet under cultivation. Sun or partial shade. Stout stem, with thick, cork bark, fibrous sheaths, and wide fronds or blades, divided into 70-80 lanceolate segments; numerous pale-colored flowers, blooming in spring; black, shining fruits. *PROPAGATION*—Seeds. *CULTURE*—Rich, moist, open soil, fertilized with manure.

SPECIES—**E. armata—Native Blue Palm.** 20-40 feet. Erect, slender palm; very glaucous, bluish leaves; segments 30-40, slightly hairy; petiole deeply grooved; reddish-brown fruits. A fine palm for average California conditions.

ERYTHRINA CRISTA-GALLI — (COMMON CORAL TREE)—(COCKSCOMB). Semi-deciduous. 6-8 feet under cultivation. Sun loving, requiring plenty of heat. Bushy and woody shrub, with a very short trunk, the new branches springing up each year from the root; leaves medium sized, shining, pinnately 3-foliate; terminal racemes of large, pea-shaped, brilliant crimson flowers, having a large keel, blooming June-September. *PROPAGATION*—Cuttings of growing wood; occasionally by seeds. *CULTURE*—Requires rich soil and frequent watering; cut off old flowering stalks. *POSITION*—Specimen shrub; group with foliage shrubs.

ERYTHRONIUM — (DOGTOOTH VIOLET) —(FAWN LILY). Bulbous plant. 4-12 inches. Half shade. Dainty, native plants, with radical, oblong-linear leaves; small, lilylike, light-colored flowers, blooming in early April. *PROPAGATION*—Offsets plant September-November; seeds sown in spring. *CULTURE*—Grows best in a moist, well drained soil, rich in humus and leaf mold; cover surface. *POSITION*—Erythroniums naturalize themselves easily in woodland regions, on grassy slopes, and in the shady flower border.

ESCALLONIA. Evergreen. 10-15 feet. Sun and partial shade. Rapid growing, bushy, loosely branching shrubs; medium-sized, ovate or linear-ovate, dark or bright-green, resinous leaves; short or long, dense terminal racemes of small, regular, short tubular, fragrant flowers, white, pink, or red, blooming prolifically June-August, but also intermittent, with E. montevidensis blooming in winter. *PROPAGATION*—Seeds; easily by cuttings of young shoots in summer; half woody cuttings. *CULTURE*—Grows in any soil, but thrives best in rich, moist, light loam, fertilized with manures; prune back vigorously after flowering. *GROUPING*—E. montevidensis and E. berteriana are used in foundation plantings at corners, the other species being extensively planted in the shrub border, combining with Duranta plumieri, Mexican Orange, Ceratonia siliqua, Eugenia myrtifolia, Myrtle, Pittosporum tobira, Prunus integrifolia.

SPECIES—**E. berteriana.** Very large, dense clusters of white flowers, blooming in summer. **E. langleyensis.** Low and spreading with deep pink flowers. **E. macrantha.** Sometimes called E. rubra, with red or rose-colored flowers. **E. montevidensis.** Large clusters of white flowers, blooming in winter. **E. organensis.** Similar to E. montevidensis, but with delicate pink flowers. **E. rosea.** Trade name for tall growing shrub with pink flowers. **E. rubra.** Dark-red flowers.

ESCHSCHOLTZIA CALIFORNICA — (CALIFORNIA POPPY). Perennial. 12-18 inches. Sun. Semi-erect, with gray-green or blue-green, lacy, finely dissected leaves in tufts; medium to large sized, saucer-shaped, yellow, orange, copper-gold, scarlet, or carmine flowers, blooming in April and during the summer. Several well defined varieties. *PROPAGATION*—Easily by seeds sown in October, November, January, February. *CULTURE*—Grows in any soil, but favors a moderately rich, light loam. *POSITION* —Best to plant in bold masses; in parking strips; in wild garden.

EUCALYPTUS. Evergreen trees of robust growth, up to 100 feet or more under cultivation. Usually rapid in growth, with stout, thick trunk, which is deeply ridged, persistent, or covered with thin bark that peels off periodically; long, simple, entire, beautifully formed, often glaucous leaves, varying in shape from roundish, falcate, to lanceolate; fluffy, pink, white, yellow, or reddish flowers, with calyx and corolla forming a cup, the colored stamens exserted; blooming in summer, winter, or spring, according to species; fruit a fleshy capsule. *PROPAGATION*—Seed sown in flats in May or June, transferring the seedlings to the open field the following spring; cuttings of young, firm side shoots in summer. *CULTURE*—Remarkably adapted to a variety of soils, including stiff clay and adobe, or sandy soils: alkali and drought resistant to a certain degree. Many species will endure freezing temperatures if not too low. They make great demands upon the soil in both moisture and fertility, but their growth can be curbed somewhat by cutting off main lateral roots about eight feet from butts. Many kinds of hardy shrubs like Veronicas, Melaleucas, Leptospermum, Escallonias, etc., can be grown under Eucalypti, provided soil is heavily fertilized. *POSITION*—Some of the less vigorous growing kinds make delightful settings for Spanish and Mediterranean residences. A few species are described below. Excellent street and avenue trees. Used on large plantations they make excellent backgrounds.

SPECIES—E. citriodora—Lemon-Scented Eucalyptus. Usually 20-30 feet, with deciduous, rather white bark; medium-long, linear, grayish-green, fragrant leaves. **E. ficifolia—Scarlet-Flowered Eucalyptus.** 20-30 feet. Persistent, dark-furrowed bark; large, firm and thick, ovate-lanceolate leaves; large clusters of reddish flowers, blooming periodically in summer and fall. The color of flower varies from pink to crimson or scarlet; for distinct colors grafted varieties should be used. **E. globulus—Blue Gum.** The well-known species with flaky bark and long, bluish-green leaves. The variety Compacta is a round-headed tree, not so tall growing, with glaucous leaves. **E. polyanthemos—Australian Beech.** Well branched tree, irregular in growth, with dark-brown or gray persistent bark; roundish and silvery leaves; very profuse bloom. **E. viminalis—Manna Gum.** Very graceful tree, with flaky, white bark, and long, bluish-green leaves. One of the best for planting near residences. Other shrubs doing well under Eucalypti include: Euonymus, Callistemon, California Cherry, Spanish Broom, Laurustinus, Arbutus unedo; among the flowers—Verbenas, Calendula, Petunias, Marguerites, Shasta Daisy.

EUGENIA MYRTIFOLIA — (AUSTRALIAN BRUSH CHERRY). Evergreen. Usually 12-15 feet, but may grow 25-30 feet. Symmetrical, pyramidal tree, with gracefully contoured branches; rather large, oblong-lanceolate, glossy leaves, young leaves ruddy tinged; small clusters of fluffy, creamy-white, fragrant flowers, blooming September-December; edible, red fruits. *PROPAGATION*—Seed, often self-sown, sown after maturity; firm or partially ripened shoots with bottom heat. *CULTURE*—Grows in any soil, but prefers a rich, moist, well drained, well fertilized loam. *GROUPING*—Used at corners and entrances in foundation plantings; as specimens on lawns; as hedge shrub and windbreak; in the shrub border, grouping with Pittosporums, Euonymus, Choisya, Portugal Laurel, Duranta, Veronicas, Azara, Daphne, Hydrangea, Raphiolepis.

SPECIES—E. hookeriana. Similar to the above, but hardier, with larger leaves, more open in growth, the branches forming whorls. Young plants of E. myrtifolia are subject to frost injury; protect the first year during winter with sacking.

EUONYMUS (EVONYMUS) JAPONICUS. Evergreen. Usually 6-10 feet, but may grow to 20 feet. Sun and partial shade. Erect, smooth shrub; shining, obovate to narrow-elliptic leaves. There are many varieties with variegated foliage, showing markings of silver, white, or yellow. *PROPAGATION*—Easily by cuttings of half ripened wood in fall or spring. *CULTURE*—Grows in a variety of soils; fertilize with manures. *POSITION*—Chief value of this shrub lies in its foliage effect; foundation plantings, and in the shrub border where it is grouped with broad-leaved shrubs; also hedge shrub.

EUPHORBIA PULCHERRIMA — (POINSETTIA) — (CHRISTMAS FLOWER). Evergreen. 6-10 feet or higher. Sun. Erect, branched shrub, with green, stout stems; large, entire, lanceolate leaves, the lower leaves a bright green, the upper leaves a flaming red, forming the so-called flower (variations to pink and white); blooming period November-March. *PROPAGATION* — Hard wood cuttings in April; seed sown in May, flowering the first year. (See Bailey's Cyclopedia of Horticulture.) *CULTURE*—Requires a rich, moist, well fertilized, light loam; plant in a warm, sheltered place; cut back old flowering stems. *POSITION*—Excellent in connection with Spanish residence and in patios; does best in southern California, but gives good results farther north if given full protection; striking in foundation plantings, grouped with deep green foliage.

EUROPEAN LARCH—(LARIX).

EUROPEAN MOUNTAIN ASH — (SORBUS AUCUPARIA).

EVENING PRIMROSE—(OENOTHERA).

EVERGREEN AMPELOPSIS—(AMPELOPSIS SEMPERVIRENS).

EVERGREEN GRAPE—(VITIS CAPENSIS).

EVERGREEN HAWTHORN—(PYRACANTHA).

EVERLASTING—(STATICE).

EVERLASTING PEA — (LATHYRUS LATIFOLIUS).

EXOCHORDA GRANDIFLORA (RACEMOSA)—(PEARL BUSH). Deciduous. 8-10 feet. Sun. Slender, spreading shrub, with bright-green, smooth leaves; racemes of large, pure white, regular flowers, blooming in April-May. *PROPAGATION* —Seeds; layering; soft wood cuttings from forced plants. *CULTURE*—Well drained, fertilized, loamy soil. *GROUPINGS*—Used in the shrub border, combining with Spiraea in variety, Japanese Flowering Cherry, Flowering Crabapples, Japanese Quince, Red Bud, Weigela.

F

FALSE ACACIA—(ROBINIA).

FALSE DRAGON'S HEAD — (PHYSOSTEGIA).

FALSE WALL CRESS—(AUBRIETIA).

FAN PALM—(CHAMAEROPS).

FAWN LILY—(ERYTHRONIUM).

FEATHERED COLUMBINE — (THALICTRUM).

FEATHERY BAMBOO — (DENDROCALAMUS).

FERTILIZERS. Plant foods containing chemical elements in certain chemical combinations known as salts. These must be present in the soil in available form to be used by plants. Calcium in the form of slacked lime, limestone, gypsum, egg shells, calcareous rock, etc., acts as a catalytic agent in rendering unavailable salts available by combining with essential plant food elements. Further, the plants cannot make use of these salts unless in solution, in the proper degree of concentration. There are two general classes of fertilizers: organic plant foods, coming chiefly from barnyard manures, poultry manure, guano, compost material, and green manures (legume crops); inorganic plant foods, containing the same elements found in manures, but derived from inorganic sources, and usually present in higher percentages.

The three most essential elements are nitrogen, potassium, phosphorus as phosphoric acid. Nitrogen in the form of a nitrate is found organically in both barnyard and green manures, poultry manure, guano, bone and blood meals; inorganically is found in ammonium nitrate, sulphate of ammonia, and in other combinations. The legumes, like White Clover in lawns, Vetch and Alfalfa, supply an abundance of nitrogen to the soil through the growth of nitrifying bacteria found in nodules on the roots, drawing free nitrogen from the air, thus releasing nitrogen to the soil. Nitrogen enters largely into the formation and growth of leaves and stems.

Phosphorus is found in various manures in small amounts, in wood ash, but is highly concentrated in super-phosphate, ammonium phosphate, raw phosphate rock, bone black, bone meal, fish scrap. It aids in root development, in the production of flowers, and in the formation of seeds. Whereas fertilizers with high content of nitrogen are added to the soil during growth of plants, fertilizers high in both phosphorus and potassium are added after the plant has practically made its vegetative growth. Potassium produces sturdy stems, promotes healthy growth, and also enters into the formation of flowers and fruits. Present in small amounts in animal manures and wood ash, in large amounts in muriate and sulphate of potash, tobacco, stems, kainite, kelp ash (sea weed), nitrate of potash, and carbonate of potash.

The plant also requires many other chemical elements, but usually these are present in the soil in sufficient quantities to satisfy the needs of the plants. However, plants and shrubs are sometimes greatly benefited by the addition of sulphur and of iron to the soil. A complete fertilizer containing high percentages of the three essential elements, and other elements such as magnesium, chlorine, zinc, iodine, etc., in very small quantities, makes the ideal fertilizer. Commercial fertilizers usually consist of high percentages of mineral fertilizers; some brands contain both animal and mineral fertilizers. Analysis of plant food elements, together with their respective availability, will indicate the value of any particular fertilizer. Soils in general are benefited by periodical applications of fertilizers, something in excess of what the plants actually require. Lesser amounts of commercial fertilizers than of manures are applied; with certain plants and shrubs these should be first put into solution. Complete data upon the subject can be obtained from companies dealing in fertilizers, and from your State Agricultural Experiment Station.

In addition to their fertilizer value, animal manures if containing some straw material tend to produce humus (decayed vegetation), lightening heavy soils. Manures also contain nitrifying bacteria, useful in the formation of nitrates, without which plants could not grow. Moderately fresh manures give free ammonia. There are several good bacterial soil cultures on the market, valuable in both decomposing rubbish and in adding nitrates to the soil.

Time and methods of application of fertilizers have an important bearing upon securing the best results from their use. Fresh and half rotted manures containing straw should be spaded in the soil in fall just after first rains. Well rotted manures may be applied during the growing season of shrubs and plants. Commercial fertilizers and concentrated preparations of manures are added as plants come into flower. Do not neglect the matter of fertility in the soil, for the success of the garden is largely dependent upon how shrubs and plants flourish.

FICUS. Tropical, evergreen plants including the Rubber Tree, the Banyan Tree, and the Creeping Figs. **Ficus elastica—India Rubber Tree.** 6 up to 20 feet under favorable conditions. Partial shade best. Erect, with stout, milky green stem; large, smooth and shining, entire, leathery, elliptical leaves, tinged red when unfolding; fruit or flowers do not form outdoors. *PROPAGATION*—Single-eye cuttings January-May; layering and notching, covering with sand. *CULTURE*—Requires a rich, moist, well drained soil, fertilized with manure. *POSITION*—Fine for patios; in foundation plantings at corners. *GROUPING*—With Aucuba, Rhododendron, Banana Tree, Caladium, Mahonia in variety, Aralia sieboldii. **F. repens (pumila)—Creeping Fig.** Sun or partial shade. Of rapid growth, with stout stems, large, ovate, wavy-margined, brightly colored leaves, red, clinging by means of suckerlike appendages to wood, cement, stone, stucco, and brick walls. *PROPAGATION*—Easily by cuttings or by layering. *CULTURE*—Grows in most soils, but prefers a rich, well fertilized, light loam. The variety Minima, growing in full shade, has very small, dark-green leaves, clinging very closely to the wall; grows more slowly than F. repens.

FIG MARIGOLD— (MESEMBRYANTHE-MUM).

FIR—(ABIES).

FIRETHORN—(PYRACANTHA).

FLAGS—(IRIS).

FLAX—(LINUM).

FLOWER BORDERS. The flowering plant should be considered in its entirety—habit and form of plant; form and color of flower; color, size and texture of leaf. These considerations help in putting the plant into its proper place in the flower border. Flowers do not appear to best advantage planted in regular rows. It is the relation of one flower to another that brings out the beauty of each, and that, in certain flower combinations, creates the most beautiful floral effects. However, a narrow flower border planted to one variety is pleasing. Panel beds in Formal Gardens may also be planted to one kind of flower. To bring out the relations existing between different flowering plants, the principal features of foliage, flower, and fruit are given in the Dictionary under each heading.

There are several distinct kinds of borders:

Annual Border. Consists entirely of annuals. As soon as one lot of flowers is through blooming, they should be taken up and be replaced by another lot. By careful planning, flowers may be had in bloom the greater part of the year, every season in California.

Hardy Border—Perennial Border. Consists entirely of perennials and biennials, and possibly the tall growing bulbous plants like the Lilies. The different kinds form small groups, selected and so placed that no space is left void of flowers for any length of time. It is important that flowers in adjacent groups harmonize in both size and texture of leaf and in color of flower. There is no set regularity in the planting, an occasional tall growing plant being placed among the low growing flowers, to introduce pleasing contours.

Mixed Border. Consisting of annuals, perennials, and bulbous plants, is in many respects the best type of border. The border is divided into sections, the perennials and tall growing bulbous plants occupying most of the background, with the low growing annuals, bulbous plants, and border plants occupying the foreground. Such a border with proper planning is assured of continuity of bloom throughout the year. The bulb border is devoted chiefly to bulbous plants, with occasional plantings of low growing flowers in between; the bulbs after flowering are frequently followed by annuals.

Annual borders are interesting when bordering front walks and driveways. Perennial and mixed borders appear to best advantage along straight walks, or as adjuncts to Formal Gardens. A narrow flower border is excellent between the lawn line and shrub border. Borders 1-2 feet wide are used to skirt strips of lawn and walks, and are planted to low growing bulbous and flowering plants. Annual borders may vary from 2-4 feet. The minimum width for the Perennial or Mixed Border is 4 feet, with 15-20 feet the maximum. Plants 6-8 feet high obviously cannot be planted in narrow borders.

Strong primary colors—red, yellow, blue—are seldom used together, although modified colors may harmonize. The complementary or opposite colors in the color wheel—green, violet, orange—or, better still, shades and tints of these colors, contrast favorably with the primary colors—red, yellow, and blue respectively. Following the order of the color wheel, we also find that yellow-orange goes with blue-violet, red-violet with yellow-green, orange-red with blue-green. The neighboring colors of an opposite color also harmonize with its complement: yellow with violet-red and violet-blue; blue with orange-red and orange-yellow. Finally, each color with the two neighboring colors: orange with orange-red and orange-yellow; yellow with orange-yellow and yellow-green; green with yellow-green and blue-green. These are representative rather than all the possible combinations.

Besides these combinations there are many other possible color combinations. A strong color should be combined with a light color. Gray-green foliage, white in a flower, dark-green foliage between conflicting colors, white-flowered plants—are all harmonizing factors, acting as a sort of leavening influence. Blue goes with light pink, gold, salmon, yellow; lilac with deep gold, primrose yellow; lavender with pink, pale blue, and pastel shades; crimson with purple, gold; scarlet with violet, blue, white, black, gold; yellow with brown, russet, and a touch of deep blue; magenta (purplish pink) with gold, and green as a screen. Some shades and tints of the same color do not go together very well, as with blues, pinks, and reds.

The possibilities of color combinations are infinite. The combinations of flowering plants and of shrubs throughout the Dictionary are suggestive. At all times a definite color scheme should be had in mind before starting a flower border. All colors of some flowers like Petunia, Verbena, Nemesia, Phlox drummondi, and others can be used in mixed plantings, but flowers like Sweet William, Snapdragon, Stock, Tulip, Gladiolus, Pentstemon, and many others should be planted in variety.

FLOWERING CURRANT—(RIBES).

FLOWERING DOGWOOD—(CORNUS).

FLOWERING FRUIT TREES. These beautiful spring-blooming trees, some native to North America, but many native to the Orient and to Siberia, are very useful in giving color and character to the shrub border, and for planting as specimen trees on lawns. They are grouped either under Prunus (Stone Fruits) or under Pyrus, but, for the sake of convenience, they have all been grouped under the above term. The different characteristics of representative species and varieties are given under separate headings. The different shapes of trees, from erect and vertical, round-headed and spreading, to weeping kinds, make them stand out above other spring-blooming shrubs; the variable foliage, frequently turning to brilliant colorations in fall, the colored fruits of some species, the clusters of delicately tinted or bright-hued flowers—all are striking characteristics.

The Crabapple and Flowering Peaches should usually be planted in the corners of shrub border; the taller, more erect Flowering Cherries can be planted in the middle of the border. Very pretty effects can be secured by planting spring-blossoming flowers beneath the trees, having harmonizing color relations.

The edible fruit trees under both genera should by no means be discounted in favor of the regular Flowering Fruit Trees, for no tree is more attractive than the apple on the front lawn. In fact, all of the various nuts and fruits are attractive enough either in the shrub border or in the home orchard. *PROPAGATION*—Usually by grafts on seedling stock of native species; by seeds for seedling stock; root grafting; layering. *CULTURE*—Adapted to a variety of soils, but most species prefer a rather moist, well drained, rich loam, fertilized with manures and balanced fertilizers. Most of the species are quite hardy. Some of the more serious pests include: aphis, wooly aphis, codling moth, slugs, leaf-spots, scale, root-borers (see Plant Pests).

SPECIES—Under Prunus are the Flowering Plums, Cherries, Peaches, Almonds, and Apricots. **Prunus amygdalus rosea nana—Dwarf Flowering Almond.** 3-4 feet. Low, spreading bush, with double pink flowers, blooming in March. Combine with Pearl Bush, White Lilacs, Sacred Cherry of Japan. **P. bleireiana — Double Pink Japanese Plum.** 10-15 feet, with purple-tinted leaves, turning to reddish bronze later in season, and medium-sized, semi-double flowers, delicately fragrant, blooming in March. **P. cerasus — Japanese Flowering Cherry.** Usually 10-20 feet. In both single and double forms, with flowers mostly white, light and deep pinks, a few red and rose-red, many having a delicate fragrance. Many named varieties of Japanese Cherry, some of exceeding beauty. **P. cerasifera pissardi—Japanese Redleaf Plum.** 20-30 feet. Round-headed, bushy tree, with large, ovate, purplish leaves; clusters of purplish-pink flowers, blooming January-April; wine-colored plums. The variety **purpurea** has dark-red leaves, variegated with yellow and bright rose; variety **nigra**, with dark-purple leaves; variety **vesuvius**, with large, highly colored, luminous, purple leaves. This species with its varieties is well adapted for street planting, and is also used as an accent tree in shrub border. **P. mume—Double Pink-Flowered Apricot.** 6-10 feet. Finely serrate, broadly ovate leaves; fragrant, light-pink flowers, blooming as early as February in California. **P. persica—Flowering Peach.** 6-15 feet. Growth and habit like the Common Peach; large, single and double, light and deep-red, cerise, maroon flowers, blooming in late March and April. *CULTURE*—Flowering Peaches should be given plenty of room; cutting off branches in flower will not affect the bloom for the next year; prune heavily after flowering; attacked by peach leaf curl, controlled by spraying with lime sulphur or with bordeaux mixture in late Fall and again as leaves begin to appear in spring. *GROUPING*—Blooming so early in the season, Flowering Peaches may safely be planted with harmonizing trees and shrubs blooming later in the year; combines with white-flowered deciduous shrubs. **P. serrulata—variety fugenzo or Veitch's Cherry.** 6-15 feet. Hardy, with arching branches bearing ovate leaves, turning to brilliant fall coloration; large, double, rose-pink flowers in clusters of three, blooming in April. **Pendula—Japanese Weeping Rose-Flowered Cherry.** Usually 4-6 feet, but widely spreading, with oblong-oval, sharply serrate leaves; very floriferous, with pendu-

lous clusters of small rose-pink flowers, blooming in early spring. Effective at ends of vistas; near pools; specimen trees on lawns. Should be supported with frames. **P. triloba—Flowering Almond.** 6-10 feet. Sturdy growing, with soft-hairy, serrate leaves; white and clear pink, single and double flowers, blooming in March or April. **P. yedoensis.** One of the most popular Flowering Cherries in Japan; slightly fragrant, pink to white flowers, blooming in April. Variety **taizanfukun.** Double, light-pink flower. **Pyrus.** This genus, also called **Malus,** for the apple group, includes apples, pears, and crabapples. **P. baccata—Siberian Crab.** Similar to P. pulcherrima. Small, round-headed tree, 10-20 feet, growth hard and wiry, spreading; bright-green, smooth leaves, turning to brilliant coloration in fall; clusters of white flowers, blooming in April; yellow or red, pealike, translucent fruits. **P. ioensis,** variety **bechteli—Bechtels Crab.** 15 feet. Rapid growing, round-headed tree; applelike leaves, turning to bronze tints in fall; large, roselike, deliciously fragrant, apple-blossom-pink flowers in drooping clusters, blooming in April-May. Fine avenue and specimen tree. **P. kaido.** 10-15 feet. Erect tree, not so wide spreading as other crabs; ruddy-tinted leaves; the flower buds resembling cherry blooms, colored a crimson, opening out rose-red, blooming as early as March; the red fruits are carried well into winter. Used widely as street trees and in the shrub border. **P. halliana.** 6-15 feet. With a loose, open crown; long-ovate, glabrous leaves; rose-colored flowers, blooming in May; brownish-red fruits, the size of a pea. The variety **parkmanii** has double flowers. **P. pulcherrima (floribunda).** 8-12 feet. One of the showiest and most popular of the crabapples. Very bushy, with shining, ovate leaves; profuse rose-red flowers, turning white, blooming in April and May. The variety **scheideckeri** is a small tree of pyramidal habit; slightly pubescent, oval leaves; large, semi-double, bright rose-pink flowers, red in the bud, produced abundantly in spring; red fruits. **P. spectabilis—Chinese Flowering Apple.** 15-25 feet. Erect, with vaselike head; oval, smooth leaves; bright-pink flowers, coral-red in the bud, blooming in April-May; reddish-yellow, sour fruits. Much used as specimen trees, street trees, and in shrub groupings. *moruc*

FLOWERING GOOSEBERRY—(RIBES). *mulberry tree moracede*

FLOWERING MAPLE—(ABUTILON).

FLOWERING OAK—(CHORIZEMA).

FLOWERING TOBACCO—(NICOTIANA).

FORGET-ME-NOT—(MYOSOTIS).

FORSYTHIA SUSPENSA — (GOLDEN BELLS). Deciduous. 6-8 feet. Sun. Spreading, semi-climbing, floriferous shrub, with slender, arching branches; long, smooth, broad-ovate leaves; small clusters of golden yellow-orange, medium sized, bell-shaped flowers, blooming March-May. *PROPAGATION*—Seeds; green wood and hard wood cuttings in season; easily by layering. *CULTURE*—Does well in ordinary, rich garden loam. *GROUPING*—Used for spring border effects, grouping with Spiraea in variety, Deutzia in variety, Mock Orange, Pittosporum tobira, Ceanothus in variety, White-Flowered Japanese Cherries, Choisya ternata.

FORTUNES PALM — (CHAMAEROPS EXCELSA).

FOUR-O'CLOCK—(MIRABILIS).

FOXGLOVE—(DIGITALIS).

FRAXINUS—(ASH). Deciduous. 20-50 feet. Sun and partial shade. Many European and Asiatic kinds. Hardy, erect, symmetrical trees; large, odd-pinnate leaves; small greenish or white flowers in panicles, blooming in spring; winged fruits. *PROPAGATION*—Seeds sown in fall, or stratified and sown in early spring; rare varieties budded in late summer, grafted in spring. *CULTURE*—Favors any moderately moist soil. *POSITION*—Specimen tree for lawns; avenue plantings; groupings for large plantations.

FREESIA HYBRIDA. Bulbous plant. 6-8 inches. Sun loving. Growing from corms, forming large clumps; bright-green, grasslike leaves; slender stems bearing numerous, fragrant, tubular or funnel-shaped flowers, white, yellow, lavender, pink, orange, blooming May-June. *PROPAGATION*—Easily by offsets; seeds, blooming after several years. *CULTURE*—Requires a light, rich, well fertilized loam; leave in ground to multiply. *GROUPING*—Edgings of mixed borders; as ground cover; combine according to variety with Dutch Hyacinths, Bride Gladiolus, Aubrietias, Cornflower, Myosotis, Lavender Primrose, Violas, Stocks.

FREMONTIA MEXICANA—(FREMONTIA). Semi-deciduous. 12-15 feet. Sun. Stiff, upright, pubescent tree, the branches and leaves covered with stellate-pubescence; small, palmately lobed, scurfy leaves; large, bronze-orange, cup-shaped, Hibiscus-like flowers, blooming in June. *PROPAGATON*—Seeds; green wood cuttings under glass in summer. *CULTURE*—Prefers a dry hillside with soil not too rich; water sparingly; subject to scale (see Plant Pests). *GROUPING*—Makes a striking effect in the shrub border, either alone, or grouped with Toyon, Rhamnus, Dendromecon rigidum, Manzanita, Ceanothus cyaneus, Garrya elliptica.

FUCHSIA—(JEWEL FLOWER). Deciduous and semi-deciduous shrubs. 6-10 feet, but much higher trained against walls of residences. Shade and partial shade for most kinds; along the Pacific Coast in California may grow in tempered sun, especially the small-flowered varieties. Rapid growing, usually much branched, often with arching branches; beautifully formed and veined, opposite or alternate, pale to deep-green, small to large, ovate to lanceolate, frequently colored leaves; axillary clusters of single or double, highly colored flowers, with tubular corollas, the petals convolute, sepals colored, and long, exserted stamens and pistils; flowers pure white, through shades of pink, rose, and salmon, to deepest purple, claret, and prune; bloom profusely in late spring, again in summer, and through late fall; flowers vary in size from the tiny, single, deep rose flowers of F. thymifolia to the large double varieties. *PROPAGATION*—Easily by cuttings of half ripened wood, preferably in August, but may be rooted in sand all year, except in winter. Fuchsias are easy to hybridize, resulting in many hundreds of new varieties. *CULTURE*—Requires a rich, well drained,

moist, light loam, well fertilized with cow manure, although balanced commercial fertilizers are satisfactory; keep well watered at all times; add soot occasionally; addition of peat or leaf mold is beneficial; prune heavily in late fall, heading back and thinning out; attacked by aphis, mealy bug, white fly, scale, leaf spot, red spider, although generally hardy (see Plant Pests); sprinkling overhead will inhibit red spider. *GROUPING* — Fuchsias, when properly trained to stakes, make good specimen shrubs; also make excellent hedges; used in the naturalistic garden, combining effectively with shade loving plants and shrubs, such as Rhododendrons, Azaleas, Ferns, Fibrous-rooted Begonias, Tuberous Begonias, Aucuba, Impatiens oliveri, Hydrangea hortensis; foundation plantings, either as specimen shrubs, or trained against walls, trellises. Single and double varieties are usually kept separate, taking care to combine colors that harmonize. Used as potted plants for conservatories in cold regions.

SPECIES—Many interesting species, including: **F. procumbens,** trailing, with small, orange-purple flowers; **F. fulgens,** with long, tubular, red flowers; **F. corymbiflora,** with long, tubular, deep-red flowers; **F. magellanica** and hybrids, with small, red or purple-red flowers, including the variety of **gracilis,** with slender-tubed, scarlet flowers. **F. thymifolia.** Very gracefully drooping, tall growing, with very small, shining, bright-green leaves, and tiny, deep rose-colored flowers; suited especially to the naturalistic garden. In addition to these there are the **Baby Fuchsias,** similar in all respects to the large-flowered kinds, but with very small flowers.

G

GAILLARDIA — (BLANKET FLOWER). Annuals and perennials. 1-2 feet and spreading. Sun loving, but endures slight shade. Gray-green, lobed, variable leaves; large, daisylike flowers, bronze, claret, brown, crimson, red; flowers bloom through summer well into fall. *PROPAGATION* — Seed sown in early spring; division of clumps in fall. *CULTURE*—Very hardy, tolerating most soils, avoid fertilizers containing too much nitrogen; attacked by sow bugs (see Plant Pests); drought resistant, growing well on sandy banks. *GROUPING*—Plant in mixed border, combining with Anchusa, deep-blue Delphinium, russet Snapdragons, Peach Bell, Yellow Geum, Salvia patens, Veronica spicata, yellow and bronze Chrysanthemums.

GALANTHUS NIVALIS — (SNOWDROP). Bulbous plant. 6-12 inches. Sun and partial shade. Erect plant, with grasslike leaves; medium-sized, white, pendulous flowers, blooming from November-March, according to species. *PROPAGATION*—Easily by offsets planted from September-November. *CULTURE*—Requires a rich, moist, light loam; tends to naturalize itself. *GROUPING*—Interesting in the mixed border, or in rockeries; combine with Primulas, Violets, Aubrietia, English Daisy, Myosotis, Dwarf Iris, Scilla, Jonquils, Winter Aconite.

GARDEN HELIOTROPE—(VALERIAN).

GARDENIA FLORIDA—(GARDENIA). Evergreen. 3-5 feet. Garden type of the well-known greenhouse Gardenia. Sun loving, but protect from too much sun. Bushy. Loose-spreading shrub, with dark-green, glossy leaves; large, waxy, double, Camellialike, very fragrant, pure white flowers, blooming July-September. Gardenias for the florist trade can be made to bloom in winter, and intermittently throughout the year. *PROPAGATION* — Half ripened wood under glass. *CULTURE*—Does best in rich, light, well fertilized garden loam, adding leaf mold; grow in warm, sheltered place; too much fog will injure buds. *GROUPING* — Combine with Daphne, Skimmia japonica, Andromeda, japonica, Bouvardia, Camellia.

GARDEN PINK — (DIANTHUS PLUMARIUS).

GARLAND FLOWER — (DAPHNE CNEORUM).

GARRYA ELLIPTICA — (TASSEL SHRUB).
Native evergreen. 6-8 feet. Bushy shrub, with medium-sized, gray-green, elliptical, hollylike leaves, densely tomentose beneath; greenish, yellow-white flowers in long, pendulous catkins, blooming November-February. *PROPAGATION*—Seeds; cuttings of half ripened wood under glass; layering. *CULTURE* —Grows well in ordinary, well drained soil; somewhat drought resistant. *GROUPING*—At home in the naturalistic garden, grouping with Eleagnus angustifolia, Eleagnus pungens, Manzanita, Rhamnus, Mahonia pinnata, Lemonade Berry, Rhus ovata, Fremontia, Echium.

GAZANIA — (SOUTH AFRICAN DAISY).
Perennial. 4-6 inches. Sun. Bushy growth, forming stout clumps, with short, stout stems bearing linear, crowded leaves, woolly beneath; numerous, large, daisylike, brilliantly colored, often black-spotted flowers, orange, yellow, scarlet, varicolored, or white, blooming continuously from April-January. *PROPAGATION*—Easily by seed sown in late winter or early spring; cuttings of shoots in spring; division of clumps October-January. *CULTURE*—Grows in any soil, but prefers a rich, light, moderately fertilized soil. *GROUPING*—Used in parkings; over embankments; in the mixed border, combining with Salvia patens, Anchusa, Purple Violas, Purple Sage, herbaceous Veronicas, Indigo, Myosotis, Peruvian Lily.

GENISTA—(CYTISUS).

GENISTA HISPANICA—(SPARTIUM).

GENISTA MONOSPERMA—(BRIDAL VEIL SHRUB).
Evergreen shrub. 4-8 feet. Sun. Drooping, with slender, grayish branches, almost leafless; small, trifoliate, silky leaves; small, fragrant, pea-shaped flowers in short, lateral racemes, blooming February-April. Propagation, culture, and position same as for Cytisus. *GROUPING*—For the shrub border, combining with early, spring-blooming shrubs.

GERANIUM—(PELARGONIUM).

GERBERA JAMESONI—(TRANSVAAL DAISY).
Perennial. 12-18 inches. Sun. Rosette formation of long, lanceolate, gray-green leaves; long, curving flower stems, bearing large, daisylike, narrow petaled flowers, colored salmon, rose, amber, ruby, red, and many intermediate colors, blooming June-November. *PROPAGATION*—Seeds sown in early spring; division of roots in fall. *CULTURE*—Require a well drained, light, moderately fertilized loam; fertilizers should contain more phosphoric acid and potash than nitrogen; do not water too much. *GROUPING*—Best to group Gerberas by themselves in beds or flower borders, but possible to combine with Viscaria, Ageratum, border of Phlox subulata, Blue Lace Flower, certain colors of Snapdragon.

GESNERIA—(NAEGELIA).

GEUM. Perennial. 18 inches. Sun loving, but tolerates some shade. Hardy plants, with rosette formation of large, rough, strawberrylike leaves; long flower stalks, bearing double roselike flowers, in shades of red, yellow, orange, blooming June-October. *PROPAGATION*—Seeds sown in early fall or early spring, producing blooming plants the first year; division of clumps in fall. *CULTURE*—Grows well in most light soils; attacked by sow bugs (see Plant Pests). *GROUPING*—For the mixed border, combining with Peach Bell and other Campanulas, Tritoma, deep blue Michaelmas Daisy, Salvia patens, Lobelia, Aconitum, Cornflowers, Swan River Daisy, Purple Sage. *VARIETIES*—G. **atrosanguineum.** Orange-scarlet. **Lady Bradshaw.** Double scarlet flowers. **G. Lady Stratheden.** Golden-yellow flowers. Many fine alpine species for the rock garden, with colors ranging from orange-yellow to coppery scarlet.

GILLY FLOWER—(MATTHIOLA INCANA).

GINKGO BILOBA—(GINKGO)—(MAIDENHAIR TREE)—(KEW TREE).
Deciduous. Usually 20-30 feet, but may attain 80 feet. Sun and partial shade. Erect, rather slender tree, sparsely branched; clusters of gray-green, thickened, fan or wedge-shaped leaves, notched at apex; a very picturesque tree; flowers as catkins blooming in spring; evil-smelling fruits containing an edible nut. *PROPAGATION*—Seeds, stratified in fall, sown in early spring; varieties by grafting. *POSITION*—Street and avenue tree; specimen tree on lawns; in large groupings; occasional tree in wide shrub border.

SPECIES—G. **variegata.** Variegated leaves. **G. pendula.** Weeping species. **G. laciniata.** Cut-leaved kind.

GLADIOLUS. Bulbous plant, growing from corms. 2-3 feet. Sun loving, but some kinds endure partial shade. Erect plant, with long, sword-shaped, bright-green leaves; medium-sized to large flowers, borne in spikes, the perianth tube funnel-shaped, six-parted, somewhat two-lipped, the segments being unequal, expanded, or hooded, in several strains with edges ruffled or laciniated, with many colors of flowers, blooming April-November. *PROPAGATION*—Easily by corms or cormels appearing about the base of the old corm; the cormels, usually produced in great numbers, can be sown in drills, taking two to three years to produce sizable corms; seed sown in early spring; the corms are planted October-December for spring blooming, from March-September at intervals of several weeks apart for summer and fall blooming, thus giving a long succession of bloom; marble-size corms planted in late fall give sizable stalks and flowers; corms 1-2 inches in size give the longest stalks and largest blooms. *CULTURE*—Will grow in most kinds of well drained soils, but prefer a rich, rather light soil, fertilized with manures in fall or before planting; add a balanced commercial fertilizer just before blooming period; provide a mulch of peat, straw, or manure over surface of soil in winter; leave corms in ground for several years, or remove after withering of leaves, clean thoroughly, storing in a cool, dry place; dip corms in solution of bordeaux to protect against molds; stake to stout bamboo stakes, or tie to lines of string; not subject to serious pests, but attacked by aphis, bulb rot (due to too much moisture or fungous organisms in soil), rust on leaves, snails and slugs (see Plant Pests). *POSITION*—Plant in bold masses in the foreground of shrub borders, in narrow flower borders; in large beds, taking care to group according to correct color relations; in the regular flower border, possible combinations being given under various flower headings. Unsightly old flowers should be removed, the flower stalk being cut off after flowering; the large-flowered Gladioli and Primulinums should be kept separate. *TYPES*—Great progress has been made in recent years in the development of both varieties and strains of Gladiolus, the varieties running up into the hundreds. Much work has been done in crossing species with species, strains with species, and between hybrids, raising the form of the flower to a high degree of perfection, with beautiful gradations of color in the flower itself. Some of the best-known types and species are:

Large-Flowered Type. With straight or slightly ruffled edges. **Ruffled** and **Lacinatus Types,** the latter with slightly divided segments. **G. primulinus.** The hooded type, tall growing, with long flower stalks bearing narrow flowers having a distinct hood over lower segments, with light colors—saffron, yellow, orange, etc. **Early-Flowering Type—G. colvillei.** Very prolific in bloom, with short spikes, the petals open or flaring, white, pink, blush, rose-crimson; the **Bride** and varieties are representative; useful for cutting. Other early blooming kinds include: **G. lemoinei.** Highly colored yellow, red and purplish flowers. **G. triste.** Yellow and terra cotta, blooming in March.

GLEDITSIA TRIACANTHOS — (HONEY or SWEET LOCUST). Deciduous. 60-100 feet or more. Sun and partial shade. Round-headed, spiny trees, forming a loose head, with gracefully spreading branches; of rapid growth; large, light-green, finely pinnate leaves, turning yellow in fall. *PROPAGATION*—Seeds sown in spring, first soaked in hot water; rare kinds grafted in spring. *CULTURE*—Drought resistant, thriving in almost any soil; prune heavily in fall. *POSITION*—Street and avenue tree; specimen tree on large plantations. **Bujotii** variety. Slender, pendulous branches, and narrower leaves.

GLORY-OF-THE-SNOW — (CHIONODOXA).

GLOXINIA. Bulbous plant, growing from tubers. 6-10 inches, but bushy. Sun. Rather crinkly, dark-colored leaves, of a rich, soft, velvety texture; large, tubular or bell-like flowers, in white, red, purple, and intermediate shades, also blotched or spotted, blooming in late summer and early fall. *PROPAGATION*—Seeds sown in a warm temperature in early February; leaf and stem cuttings of choice kinds. (For full details see Bailey's Cyclopedia of Horticulture). *CULTURE*—Require a rich, warm, rather moist,

light soil; old tubers can be used after plants have grown a year. *POSITION*—Potted plants in conservatories and sun porches.

GODETIA — (SATIN FLOWER). Annual. 1-2 feet. Sun and slight shade. Erect, slender branching plant; bright-green, lanceolate leaves; large, expanded, single and double, satiny flowers, white, crimson, pink, mauve, to purple, sometimes variegated, blooming June-October. *PROPAGATION*—Seeds sown in early spring. *CULTURE*—Grows in rather poor, sandy soil. *GROUPING*—Generally look best by themselves in the annual or mixed border, but can be combined with Clarkia, Larkspur, certain colors of Snapdragons and Stocks, Rehmannia angulata, Diascia barberae, Pentstemon.

GOLDEN BAMBOO—(DENDROCALAMUS).

GOLDEN BELLS—(FORSYTHIA).

GOLDEN CHAIN—(LABURNUM).

GOLDEN DEWDROP SHRUB—(DURANTA).

GOLDEN FEATHER—(CHRYSANTHEMUM PYRETHRUM AUREUM).

GOLDEN MARGUERITE—(ANTHEMIS).

GOLDEN WATTLE—(ACACIA FLORIBUNDA).

GOLD TUFT—(ALYSSUM).

GOURDS—(BOTTLE GOURDS)—(LAGENARIA VULGARIS). Annual. Indefinite in growth, doing best in sun. Squashlike vines, with large, tubular, pumpkinlike, yellow flowers, blooming in August; curious large or small fruits resembling dippers, apples, clubs, pitchers, eggs, oranges, pears. *PROPAGATION*—Seed sown in spring. *CULTURE*—Require a rich, light, well fertilized soil. *POSITION*—Used for covering fences, arbors, slopes, walls, unsightly places, over patio walls, the gourds remaining in place on tops of the walls. The gourds may be placed in bowls for patio and house decoration.

GRAFTING AND BUDDING. The objects of grafting or budding ornamental trees, shrubs and plants are: To perpetuate the same kind of variety; to reinvigorate the plant; to produce a more vigorous tree. Budding is the process of inserting a single bud into the growing wood of the plant; grafting is the insertion of a twig bearing several buds. The *CION* (*SCION*) is the portion of one plant inserted into another plant called the *STOCK,* usually rooted. The stock is usually a native species of the same genus. The stock and cion maintain each its own individuality. The bark and wood tissues of the two merely knit together.

A cross-section of a small-sized twig will reveal several layers of tissues—the firm, outer bark and the green, inner bark composed of soft, growing tissue, containing the region of new growth called the cambium layer. With either budding or grafting, the cambium layers of both stock and cion must come into contact. Portions of the bark and wood are retained in budding, the incision being made in such a way that the growing tissues of both stock and bud come directly into contact. To protect the union, grafting wax, raffia, wax thread, and binding cloth are employed. The cions and buds should never be permitted to dry out; keep moist by placing in moist moss or sacking. The budding knife, saw and other grafting tools should be sharp, making clean, quick strokes.

The time to graft is usually in fall before the tree becomes completely dormant, or in the spring when the sap begins to flow. Budding is done when the plant is in an active, growing condition, in spring or in June in warm regions, in summer or early fall in cold regions. In California, roses and other stock are budded about June. Choose strong, vigorous wood of the previous season's growth with plump, matured buds. Never use water sprouts.

Veneer Grafting. Simple in operation and largely used with ornamental stock; consists of cutting out a chip from stock and fitting in a cion of equal size. Stock is headed back when cion is growing nicely. **Side Grafting.** Similar to the veneer cut, but with a diagonal cut. **Cleft Grafting.** Used largely with fruit and nut trees, and with some ornamentals; consists in splitting a fairly large-sized branch or trunk of a tree, cut off square. Two cions, cut wedge-shaped, are inserted at either end, the bark of the stock and cion coinciding. All cut surfaces are thoroughly covered with grafting wax. If both cions grow, the weakest cion is cut out at the end of the first year. **Whip or Tongue Grafting.** Used with small stocks, the stock and cion being of equal size. Both are cut diagonally, employing a long, straight cut. A vertical cut upward is then made in both. The two parts are fitted together and tied with raffia or waxed string. This method is also used in root grafting. **Splice Grafting.** Stock and cion of equal size are cut with a diagonal cut as in whip grafting. The two parts are joined together and tied, or held together by a pin; used with Rhododendrons. **Saddle Graft.** The stock is cut in the form of a wedge. The cion is then split upward and fitted over the wedge. **Side Grafting.** A modification of the veneer graft, in which a diagonal cut is made in the stock and the cion inserted in it. There are other forms of grafting, but these are principally modifications of the above.

Shield Budding. The commonest kind of budding. Cut buds downward from bud stock, with budding knife. Cut off leaves, leaving a portion of the petiole. A "T"-shaped cut is first made in the stock, the cuts being just through the bark, not into wood. Frequently the bud is inverted to shed water. The bud should fit flatly; any bark protruding above the bud should be removed. Buds are usually inserted on the north side of plants. The budded part is covered with raffia, leaving the bud exposed. If the bud is taking, it will appear alive and fresh, if not, it will be dried up and brown; the bud should take in about ten days, then the raffia is cut. If done in fall, should be late in season to prevent killing of bud. In **Patch** or **Flute Budding,** more difficult to do, squares from the cion and stock are fitted together. In **"H"-Budding** an "H" is cut in stock and cion is fitted in.

GRAND FIR—(ABIES GRANDIS).

GRAPE HYACINTH—(MUSCARI).

GRASSES. Both annual and perennial kinds. Low or tall growing. Mostly in sun, but some enduring part shade. Grown mostly for the ornamental leaf blades, growing from stout culms or clumps. The tall growing kinds are effective in the shrub border, while the low growing kinds can be used in the flower border, or near pools. *PROPAGATION*—Usually by division of clumps in fall or spring; seeds sown in spring. *SPECIES*—Many kinds of ornamental grasses. Among the annuals, growing from 18 inches to 3 feet, are:

Jobs Tears—Coix lachryma. Broad, cornlike leaves, and hard, shining, pearly seeds. **Purple Fountain Grass—Pennisetum rueppelianum.** Gracefully drooping, bright-green leaves and long, purplish plumes. **Pennisetum longistylum.** With very graceful, greenish-white plumes. **Cloud Grass—Agrostis nebulosa.** Very graceful plant with mistlike blooms. **Quaking Grass—Briza maxima.** Used for grass bouquets. **Eragrostis elegans.** Feathery panicles. Among the perennial kinds, usually tufted, are: **Crimson Fountain Grass—Pennisetum macrophyllum atrosanguineum.** 4 feet. Gracefully recurved, dark metallic, coppery-bronze leaves, and tawny crimson plumes. **Hardy Fountain Grass—Pennisetum japonicum.** 4 feet. Narrow, bright-green leaves, and cylindrical flower heads, tinged with bronze purple. **Eulalia japonica variegata.** Long, narrow leaves, striped green, white, pink, or yellow. **Zebra Grass—Eulalia japonica zebrina.** Long blades marked with broad yellow bands across the leaf. **Variegated Ribbon Grass—Phalaris arundinacea variegata.** 12-15 inches. Border plant. **Blue Fescue—Festuca glauca.** A dwarf, tufted grass, with blue-green foliage. Pampas Grass, Reeds, and Bamboos are described under separate headings.

GRECIAN BAY LAUREL—(LAURUS).

GREEK JUNIPER — (JUNIPERUS EXCELSA STRICTA).

GREEN WATTLE—(ACACIA DEALBATA).

GREVILLEA. Evergreen. A variable class of shrubs, the different species being described below. Sun and partial shade. *PROPAGATION*—Seeds sown December-March; cuttings of ripened shoots in sand with bottom heat. *CULTURE*—Grows in any soil, but prefers rich, well fertilized, sandy loam.

SPECIES—G. banksii. 4-8 feet. Slender growing tree, with rusty-tomentose branches; pinnatifid, feathery leaves, 4-8 inches long; long, dense, terminal racemes of red flowers, blooming in June. *POSITION*—Distinctly a specimen tree. **G. robusta—Silk Oak.** 20-30 feet. Very loose branching tree, with smooth, glistening, twice or thrice-pinnatifid leaves; racemes of showy, short tubular, orange flowers, blooming in June. Subject to scale and mealy bug (see Plant Pests). *POSITION*—Specimen tree on lawns; street and avenue tree. **G. thelemanniana—Jewel Flower Shrub.** Round-headed shrub, close and dense, with young growths soft-tomentose; soft-textured, pale-green, linear pinnate leaves; terminal clusters of crimson, green-tipped, Honeysucklelike flowers, prolific in bloom in December, almost continuous thereafter. *GROUPING*—Specimen shrub; hedge shrub for courts; for the shrub border, combining with such fine-leaved shrubs as Erica persoluta alba, Diosma, and with some of the Chamaecyparis.

GUADALUPE PALM—(ERYTHEA EDULIS).

GYPSOPHILA PANICULATA. Perennial. 1-3 feet. Much branched plant, with lanceolate-linear leaves, and tiny, prolific white flowers, borne in summer. *PROPAGATION*—Treated as annual with seeds sown in fall or spring. *CULTURE*—Thrives in moist, moderately rich, light soils. *POSITION*—For rockeries; in the flower border, planted freely with other flowers; excellent in bouquets.

SPECIES—**G. grandiflora—Babys Breath.** Annual. Similar to the above, but seed is sown broadcast in early spring; repeat sowings for longer season of bloom.

H

HAKEA. Evergreen. 8-12 feet, under cultivation. Sun. Unusual shrubs, with varied forms and leaves; fluffy flowers, blooming in winter or spring, followed by very hard, persistent capsules. *PROPAGATION*—Very dry year-old seeds, sown in winter or early spring; cuttings taken from ripened shoots. *CULTURE*—Drought resistant; impartial in soil requirement, but does best in light, moderately fertilized, well drained soils; avoid too much moisture. *GROUPINGS*—The several species do not group well together, but they may be grouped with Spanish Broom, Genistas in variety, Lavender, Garrya elliptica, Madrone, Rhamnus, Fremontia, Eleagnus pungens, Chorizema.

SPECIES—**H. laurina—Sea Urchin.** Long, lanceolate leaves; crimson flowers with golden-yellow stamens. **H. elliptica.** Prominent chiefly for the rich bronze color of the young shoots; compact, round headed, with white flowers in globose heads. **H. suaveolens.** Round headed shrub, with long, narrow, rigid leaves, spiny tipped; fragrant, white flowers.

HARDENBERGIA MONOPHYLLA — (HARDENBERGIA). Evergreen. 6-10 feet or more. Sun. Climbers and sub-shrubs, vigorous and floriferous; medium-sized to long, lanceolate, dark-green leaves; small, pea-shaped, purplish flowers in dense racemes. *PROPAGATION*—Seeds sown in spring; green wood cuttings under glass in spring. *CULTURE*—Grows in most soils, but best in open, porous, peaty soil; rather drought resistant. *GROUPING*—Used for trailing over walls and embankments; for training against trellises, pergolas, arches, etc. Combines well with Bignonias in variety, Tecoma capensis, yellow and white Jasmine, Mandevilla suaveolens, Vitis capensis, Streptosolen jamesoni, Cestrum aurantiacum.

HAREBELL — (CAMPANULA ROTUNDIFOLIA).

HAWTHORN—(CRATAEGUS).

HEATHER—(ERICA).

HEDERA HELIX — (ENGLISH IVY). Evergreen, shrubby vine. Climbs to great heights. Will grow in sun, but prefers shade. Strong growing, with stout stems, climbing by aerial rootlets; dark-green, large, 3-5 lobed leaves, pale or yellowish-green beneath; inconspicuous, greenish-yellow flowers; black fruits. *PROPAGATION*—Cuttings of half-ripened wood any time of year. *CULTURE*—Grows in any soil, but prefers a rich, moist, well fertilized, rather light loam. *POSITION*—Used for covering embankments, walls, trunks of trees, walls of houses; in hanging baskets. *SPECIES*—Several species with small leaves, variegated leaves, or with colored foliage.

HELENIUM AUTUMNALE — (SNEEZEWORT). Perennial. 2-5 feet. Sun. Well branched plant, with large, rough, lanceolate leaves; golden-yellow, Sunflowerlike flowers with greenish-yellow disk-florets, blooming July-November. *PROPAGATION*—Division of clumps in fall; seed sown in spring. *CULTURE*—Grows in most ordinary soils; benefited by fertilizer. *GROUPING*—Used in the perennial and mixed borders, combining with Mexican Tulip Poppy, Salvia pitcheri, Veronica longifolia, Carpathian Bluebell, Perennial Aster, Anchusa.

HELIANTHEMUM VULGARE — (SUN ROSE). Evergreen perennial. 3-6 inches, but spreading several feet. Makes a dense, matty growth, with dark-colored, wirelike stems; crowded, small, dark-green, ovate leaves; medium-sized, single, roselike flowers in loose racemes, pink, rose, yellow, white, deep red, blooming June-October. *PROPAGATION*—Division of clumps October-January; seeds sown after maturity; green wood cuttings. *CULTURE*—Grows in any soil, especially in sandy, rocky, or limestone soils; fertilize occasionally; cut back severely once a year. *POSITION*—For planting over walls, in rockeries, on waste lands, embankments, as border plant.

HELIANTHUS—(SUNFLOWER). Annual and perennial. 3-10 feet. Sun. A very variable genus, erect in growth; ovate, rough, hairy, sessile leaves; single or semi-double, red or yellow flowers, blooming from July-fall. *PROPAGATION*—Seeds sown in early spring; division of clumps in fall. *CULTURE*—Grows best in rich, calcareous, light, moist garden loam. *GROUPING*—Plant in the background of the mixed border, combining with Delphinium, Anchusa, Chimney Bellflower, Purple Sage, Goldenrod, Platycodon grandiflorum, Montbretia. Many North American species and hybrids.

HELICHRYSUM BRACTEATUM — (STRAW FLOWER). Annual, 2-3 feet. Stout, branched plant, with oblong-lanceolate, bright-green, stiff leaves; pomponlike, stiff flower head, blooming throughout fall into winter. *PROPAGATION*—Seed sown broadcast in spring. *CULTURE*—Thrives in any kind of soil. *POSITION*—Plant by themselves or with other kinds of Everlastings.

HELIOPSIS PITCHERIANA — (ORANGE SUNFLOWER)—(OX-EYE). Perennial. 3-4 feet. Bushy plant, with coarsely serrate, lance-ovate leaves; large, golden-yellow, Sunflowerlike flowers, 3 inches across, blooming in July-August. *PROPAGATION*—Seed sown in early spring; division of clumps in fall. *CULTURE*—Grows in any soil; fertilize with manure in fall. *GROUPING*—For the perennial border, combining with deep blue Delphinium, Anchusa, blue Lupin, blue Scabiosa, Tritoma, Centaurea montana, Shasta Daisy.

HELIOTROPE—(HELIOTROPIUM). Evergreen or semi-deciduous shrub or vine. 4-20 feet, according to kind. Sun and slight shade. Bushy plant, with oval, soft-pubescent, rather rough-wrinkled, dark-green leaves; dense trusses of small, regular, salver-shaped, very fragrant flowers, white, pale lilac, blue, to deep lilac, blooming profusely in summer, but quite continuous in California. *PROPAGATION*—Cuttings of soft wood from strong shoots from potted plants. *CULTURE*—Prefers a rich, moist, well fertilized, light loam. *GROUPING*—For use in window boxes, pots, and in the shrub border, combining with Streptosolen, Genistas in variety, Orange Cestrum, Choisya, Myrtus in variety, Tritoma, orange and yellow Lantanas.

HELLEBORUS NIGER — (HELLEBORE)— (CHRISTMAS ROSE). Bulbous plant. 1 foot. Sun, but best in partial shade. Erect plant, with large, palmately divided, bright-green leaves; large, white or greenish-white flowers, flushed with purple, resembling single roses, blooming in January-February. *PROPAGATION*—Division of roots in early fall, or February-April. *CULTURE*—Grows best in rich, light soil, fertilized with cow manure. *GROUPING*—For the wild garden or half shady flower border, combining with Azaleas, Narcissi, Jonquils, Crocus, and other early blooming bulbous plants.

HELXINE SOLEIROLII—(HELXINE). Perennial. Shade. Hardy, creeping plant, with delicate green stems; very small, oval, light-green leaves; forms a dense growth. *PROPAGATION*—Mostly by division of clump. *CULTURE*—Will grow in any soil, but best in loose soil; add peat, but no fertilizer. *POSITION* — Useful between stepping-stones in shade; as a ground cover under trees; in shady courts; in rockeries. Cannot stand bright sun.

HEMEROCALLIS— (DAY LILY). Bulbous plant, forming clumps. 18-24 inches. Sun and partial shade. Strong, robust of growth, with a fleshy, fibrous root; long, broad, narrow, light-green leaves; loose corymbs of long, funnel-shaped, Lilylike, yellow and orange flowers, blooming in June and July. *PROPAGATION*—Seed; division of roots in fall or at any time. *CULTURE*—Grows in most soils, but prefers a rich, fertilized, light loam; divide and replant after several years. *GROUPING*—For the perennial and shady borders, combining with African Lily, Lupine, Hounds Tongue, blue Scabiosa, Torch Lily, Veronica spicata, Aconitum, Purple Iris, yellow and orange Gladiolus, Altstromeria.

SPECIES—**H. flavia.** Yellow flowers. **H. fulva.** Orange flowers.

HEMLOCK—(TSUGA).

HERCULES CLUB—(ARALIA).

HETEROMELES—(PHOTINIA).

HEUCHERA SANGUINEA — (CORAL BELLS). Perennial. 12-24 inches. Sun and partial shade. Stout plant; dark-green, cordate, crenate leaves; racemes of small, crimson, bell-shaped flowers, blooming April-late fall. *PROPAGATION*—Division of clumps October-December; seed sown in late winter or early spring. *CULTURE*—Grows in any soil, but prefers a well enriched, light garden loam; subject to mealy bug; dip infested plants in solution of oil emulsion. *GROUPING* — Border plant; in rockeries; in the mixed border, combining with Dianthus in variety, Columbine, rose-pink Sweet William, Virginia Bells, Iris tectorum, Calochortus, Erythronium, Lavender Primrose.

HIBISCUS. Varying from annuals, perennials, to tall shrubby forms, 6-8 feet high. Deciduous and evergreen. Sun and slight shade. Rather symmetrical, with smooth, dentate, dark-green leaves, palmately veined or parted; large, regular, Hollyhocklike or tubular flowers, blooming in summer and early fall. *PROPAGATION*—Herbaceous kinds by seeds and division of clumps; shrubs by cuttings of ripened wood, layering, root cuttings, grafting of special varieties. *CULTURE*—All kinds require a rich, well drained, well fertilized, light loam.

SPECIES—**H. rosa-sinensis.** Grown in protected situations in warm parts of California; can also be grown as potted shrubs, to be placed in greenhouse in winter. Both single and double-flowered varieties, bright red, orange, yellow, amaranth, magenta, and parti-colored. *GROUPING*—Planted in sheltered patio gardens, or in foundation plantings, grouping with Aucuba, Rhododendron, Azaleas, Aralia sieboldii, Escallonia berteriana, Nandina. **Rose Mallows—Marsh Mallows.** Short and tall forms, with flowers coming in a variety of colors. Grown in wide borders.

HIMALAYAN AZALEA — (RHODODENDRON FRAGRANTISSIMUM).

HINOKI CYPRESS — (CHAMAECYPARIS OBTUSA).

HIPPEASTRUM. Known also as **LARGE-FLOWERED AMARYLLIS,** which it resembles. Similar in growth and in methods of propagation to Amaryllis. Flowers are much larger, without fragrance, several to a stalk, usually in shades of red and orange, blooming from December to summer, occasionally through summer. Quite hardy, may be grown in warm, sheltered gardens, but usually grown in pots and used as house plants, or for patio gardens. *CULTURE*—Potting soil should be a rich, fibrous loam, adding rotted cow manure.

HOLLYHOCK—(ALTHAEA).

HONEY LOCUST—(GLEDITSIA).

HONEYSUCKLE—(LONICERA).

HORSE-CHESTNUT—(AESCULUS).

HOUNDS TONGUE—(CYNOGLOSSUM).

HUCKLEBERRY—(VACCINIUM).

HUNNEMANNIA FUMARIAEFOLIA— (MEXICAN TULIP POPPY). Perennial, usually treated as an annual. 2 feet. Sun. Erect, bushy plant, with feathery, grayish-green, glaucous, finely dissected leaves; large, bright-yellow, poppylike flowers, blooming in summer. *PROPAGATION*—Division of clumps October-December; seeds sown in early spring. *CULTURE*—Plant in dry, moderately rich, light garden loam; adapted to sloping ground. *GROUPING*—Plant in large masses, or in the mixed border, combining with blue Cornflower, Centaurea montana, Cynoglossum, Aconitum, Purple Stocks, Platycodon, Peruvian Daffodil.

HYACINTHUS ORIENTALIS — (COMMON HYACINTH). Bulbous plant. 8-18 inches. Sun loving, but tolerates moderate shade. Stout, succulent stem, with long, bright-green, lanceolate, fleshy leaves; dense spikes of rather large, very fragrant, funnel-shaped to campanulate, 6-lobed, regular, single and double flowers, white, cream, red, pink, yellow, blooming in mild, equable climates from January-May. *PROPAGATION*—Usually by offsets secured by scooping out or notching underside of bulb; seeds for new varieties. *CULTURE*—Grows in ordinary light garden soils, enriched with cow manures or commercial fertilizer; use surface mulch of straw, peat, or straw manure; plant from September-November. For indoor culture, plant in pots; cover surface with about 5 inches of sand to produce long stems; subject to aphis, slugs, snails (see Plant Pests). *GROUPING*—Best planted by themselves, or as a border plant, but can be used in the flower border, combining with Pansies and Violas in definite colors, Scilla, Campanula muralis, Dwarf Iris, Narcissi, Freesias, Aubrietia. Also interesting planted in bold masses in front of shrubbery.

SPECIES—**Roman Hyacinths.** 6-8 inches. Slender plants, with narrow, erect leaves; slender scapes bearing loose racemes of slender, tubular, white, blush to light-blue flowers, blooming in February. *POSITION*—Usually massed in wide, shallow pots for indoor culture; may also be planted out.

HYDRANGEA HORTENSIS (OPULOIDES)— (PINK-FLOWERED HYDRANGEA). Deciduous shrub. 5-10 feet. Best in partial or full shade. Round headed, very symmetrical, with stout, brownish branches; large, broad, ovate-elliptic, sharply serrate, beautifully veined leaves, turning to bronze tints in fall; large, round, dense cymes of large, regular, single and semi-double, pink, white, or rose-colored flowers, blooming June-September. *PROPAGATION*—Hard wood cuttings in open in spring; soft wood cuttings under glass in summer. *CULTURE*—Requires a rich, moist, open, porous loam; add peat or leaf mold; prune rangy shrubs to assume round shape; cut off old blooms; iron filings in soil give blue color desired by some. *GROUPING*—Adapted to a variety of uses: in tubs for formal effects; near steps and in foundation plantings; as specimen shrubs on lawns; in the shrub border, combining with Escallonias, English Laurel, Euonymus, Duranta plumieri, Carpenteria, Magnolia in variety, Nandina, Viburnum in variety.

SPECIES—**H. paniculata**—variety **grandiflora.** 10-20 feet. Rather round headed shrub, with elliptic-ovate, serrate, pubescent leaves; very long, conical-shaped panicles of whitish flowers changing to purple, blooming in August-September. This is the kind universally planted in cold climates.

HYMENOCALLIS — (ISMENE) — (SPIDER LILY). Bulbous plant with Daffodil-like bulb. 1-2 feet. Long, sword-shaped leaves; salver-shaped, spiderlike, fragrant white and yellow flowers, blooming in June-July, one species in winter. *PROPAGATION*—Easily by offsets, planted February-April. *CULTURE*—Grows in ordinary, well drained, rich garden loam. *GROUPINGS*—Plant in the mixed border, combining with Chilean Lily, Peruvian Lily, Hemerocallis, Lupine, Ageratum, Nemesia, Viscaria.

SPECIES — **H. calathina — Peruvian Daffodil.**

The cup in flower is corollalike and is green striped.

HYPERICUM—(ST. JOHNSWORT). Perennial plants and evergreen shrubs. 2-6 feet. Sun and partial shade. Hardy, with succulent or woody stems; large, shining, rich green, sometimes ruddy-tinged, oval leaves; large, regular, Anemonelike, golden-yellow flowers with reddish stamens, blooming June-October. *PROPAGATION*—Seed for perennials sown in July or early spring; division of clumps fall and spring; root cuttings and half firm cuttings of shrubs in spring. *CULTURE*—Will grow in any kind of soil, but favors a rich, well drained, moist soil; endures adobe and clay. *GROUPING*—The low growing kinds like H. patulum are used in parkings, waste places, and to cover dry embankments. The shrubby kinds are planted in rockeries, and in the foreground of the shrub border, grouping with Spanish Broom, Chilean Guava, Eugenia apiculata, Cestrum aurantiacum, Veronicas, Butterfly Bush, Plumbago capensis.

SPECIES—**H. calycinum.** 1 foot. Rather woody shrub, with dwarf, spreading stems, large, bright-yellow flowers, 3 inches across, growing well in dry, stony soil. **H. patulum.** 2 feet. Has tough, spreading roots, making large clumps; large, golden-yellow flowers. **H. moserianum.** Slender, wiry, with gracefully arching branches; clusters of rather small, bright-yellow flowers, 3 inches across; does well in dry, stony soil.

I

IBERIS UMBELLATA—(COMMON ANNUAL CANDYTUFT). 12-15 inches. Sun and slight shade. Branching plant, with long, lanceolate leaves; flat-topped clusters of pink, white, rose, purple flowers, blooming prolifically in spring, and during other seasons by successive sowing of seed. *PROPAGATION*—Easily by broadcasting of seed. *CULTURE*—Grows in ordinary soil. *GROUPINGS*—Used in rockeries; as an edging for flower borders; in the mixed border.

SPECIES — **I. gibraltarica.** Perennial. 12-20 inches. Leaves wedge shaped; large clusters of large lilac-white and pink-white flowers blooming in May. *PROPAGATION*—Treated usually as annual, sowing seeds in early spring; division of clumps in fall. *GROUPING*—Used in the rock garden and in the mixed border, with same combinations as for the annual kind. **I. sempervirens.** Perennial. 1 foot. Long racemes of white flowers blooming in May, the plant forming a woody mat.

ICE PLANT—(MESEMBRYANTHEMUM).

ILEX AQUIFOLIUM—(ENGLISH HOLLY). Evergreen. 10-40 feet, according to location. Sun or partial shade. Symmetrical, densely branched, pyramidal tree; very shiny, spiny-margined, oblong-ovate, very dark-green leaves; inconspicuous white flowers in axillary clusters; large, shining, scarlet fruits in December. The flowers are usually dioecious (male and female flowers appearing upon different trees); necessary to have both staminate and pistillate trees to have berries; twigs bearing pistillate flower buds may be grafted upon staminate trees. *PROPAGATION* — Seeds, germinating the second year; dry, clean, and stratify, sowing in fall; layering in spring. *CULTURE*—Does best in a rich, well drained, rather light soil. *POSITION*—Specimen tree for lawns; foundation plantings near corners and entrances; hedge shrub; for formal effects. There are many beautiful varieties, some with variegated foliage. One variety, **Von Tholl**, with dull-green, leathery leaves, spiny only near the upper part, has both kinds of flowers, and always has berries.

IMPATIENS OLIVERI (OVALIFOLIUM). Perennial in California. 4-8 feet. Shade loving, but grows in sun in San Francisco Bay Region. Shrubby, much branched plant, with stout, green stems; long, smooth, oblanceolate leaves in whorls; large, pale lilac flowers, blooming almost continuously. *PROPAGATION*—Seeds, the plant seeding itself; easily by green wood cuttings at any time except winter. *CULTURE*—Prefers a rich, fertilized, light loam; prune in fall. *GROUPING*—Foundation plantings; for the shady border, combining with Ferns, Rhododendron, Pink Azaleas, Columbine, Begonias in variety.

SPECIES—**I. balsamina**—**Balsam**—**Touch-me-not.** Annual. 1½-2¼ feet. Sun. Erect, very much branched plant, with deeply serrate, lanceolate leaves; Camellialike, double and semi-double, white, spotted, yellow to dark-red flowers, blooming July-November. *PROPAGATION*—Seed sown in early spring. *CULTURE*—Prefers a rich, sandy, moist loam, in an open, sunny position; remove first flowers; permit only a few main branches to develop, removing lower leaves. *POSITION*—Balsams look best by themselves, with a background of dark-green foliage shrubs.

INCENSE CEDAR—(LIBOCEDRUS).

INDIAN BEAN—(CATALPA).

INDIAN CEDAR—(CEDRUS DEODARA).

INDIAN HAWTHORN — (RAPHIOLEPIS INDICA).

INDIA RUBBER TREE—(FICUS ELASTICA).

IOCHROMA. Evergreen. 4-8 feet. Sun and partial shade. Erect, branching shrubs, with arching branches; usually tomentose throughout; large, dark-green, entire, broad-ovate to elliptic-lanceolate leaves; pendulous clusters of long, tubular, purple, blue, white, scarlet, or yellow flowers, blooming profusely during summer and early fall, and intermittently in California. *PROPAGATION*—Half firm wood in fall; cuttings of young shoots under glass in summer; seeds. *CULTURE*—Tolerant of most soils, but does best in a rich, well fertilized, medium-light soil. *GROUPING*—Primarily for the shrub border, combining with Cestrum aurantiacum, Streptosolen, Cassia, Spanish Broom, Genista (Cytisus) in variety, Choisya, Pittosporum tobira, Tritoma.

SPECIES—There are several distinct species, of which **I. grandiflora (purpurea)**, with rich purple flowers, is the most popular.

IPOMOEA — (JAPANESE MORNING GLORY) — (MOONFLOWER). Annuals, but mostly perennials in cultivation. 6-18 feet or more. Sun. Climbing vines, with slender, twining or climbing stems; variable, lobed, or parted leaves; long, funnel-shaped flowers, colored various shades and mixtures of red, purple, blue, yellow, white, blooming June-September. *PROPAGATION*—Seed notched to

hasten germination; perennials from cuttings of well ripened wood in early fall; easily by layering; division of root stalk in fall and spring; root grafting. *CULTURE*—Does best in strong, fertilized soil with plenty of water; cut down each fall for new growth. *POSITION*—Suitable for covering garages, outhouses, fences, pergolas, etc.

SPECIES—**I. hederacea**—**Japanese Imperial** and **Emperor Morning Glory.** Perennial. Many varieties, showing scalloped, fringed, ruffled, double flowers, in a wide range of colors. Especially suited for porches, pillars, arbors, etc.; grown by itself, or with white-flowered Clematis and Jasmine. **I. pandurata** —**Perennial Moonflower.** Broad, funnel-shaped, white flowers with dark-purple throat. Useful for covering stumps, fences, waste places. **I. (convolvulus) purpurea** — **Tall Annual Morning Glory.** Many variations in leaf and flower. **I. setosa**—**Brazilian Morning Glory.** Very vigorous, tall growing, branching plant, covered with stiff, purplish hairs; large, cordate, lobed leaves; many-flowered clusters of salverform, rose-purple flowers, blooming August-October. **I. tricolor.** Annual climber. Type is rose colored, often dashed and blotched. The variety **Heavenly Blue** is used for cut flowers.

IRIS — (FLAGS) — (FLEUR-DE-LIS) — (POOR MAN'S ORCHID). Bulbous plant rising from rhizome, bulb, or bulblike root stock. Varies greatly in height, from dwarf forms 6 inches high to tall forms 5 feet high. Sun loving, but some kinds enduring slight or partial shade. Usually stocky plants, with long, sword-shaped, glaucous, dark-green to gray-green leaves. The perianth of the flower in general is regular, dividing into six segments, the three outer segments called the falls, either bearded or beardless according to kind, broad and reflexed; the three inner petaloid segments, known as standards, rise each on a claw, broaden and overarch, and are usually more delicate in coloring, but blending with that of the falls. The range of blooming periods of different species takes up practically the entire year. Propagation and cultural requirement of different kinds are discussed under separate headings. Iris as a class constitutes a very large number of species, strains, and varieties. The more important representatives are given, and these have been grouped into various classes, convenient for purposes of identification.

I. germanica. The type from which the Tall Bearded Iris has been derived. 2-3 feet. Characterized by erect, much branched, stout stalks; large, purple and white flowers. Used considerably in parking areas. **Tall Bearded Iris.** Together with hybrids of various species known as **German Iris.** Represented by hundreds of varieties, in every variety of form and color of flower, frequently exquisitely fragrant. The blooming period extends from March-June, according to locality. *PROPAGATION*—Usually by division of the rhizomatous clump, selecting the smaller, newer rhizomes for planting out; the rhizomes should be planted preferably in August, but can be planted as late as March; seeds, to produce new varieties. *CULTURE*—The requirements for the Bearded Iris and others in the same class are: Will tolerate a variety of soils, including clay, adobe, gravelly, hillside loams; does well in a moderately fertile, well drained, lime-containing soil with no standing moisture; add bone meal, but avoid too much nitrogenous fertilizer; do not oversaturate the soil, especially when grown with other flowers. After about three years the heart of clump should be cut out, replanting several of the small-sized rhizomes; in planting, set rhizomes flat with half of rhizome exposed, one rhizome in place, or three or four set one foot apart if large clump is desired. Iris are quite drought resistant. After blooming, cut tops one-third and remove withered leaves; leaves may be cut off in fall nearly to rhizome for renewal of growth. *POSITION*—Iris should not be planted in straight rows or in large beds. They are splendid in bold groups in front of shrubbery; in isolated clumps in the background of flower borders, harmonizing with flowers in close proximity; occasionally near pools; in association with garden ornaments. A few species falling naturally in the bearded class, and with practically the same methods of propagation and culture are: **I. japonica (fimbriata)—Tall Crested Iris.** 1-1½ feet. grows in shade. Racemes of lilac-yellow flowers with crimped margins and crested segments, blooming in February. **I. neglecta.** 2 feet. Flowers violet-blue, yellowish, white centered. Blooming in May. **I. tectorum—Crested Iris.** Low growing, with white-crested, blue-purple flowers, blooming in April.

Spuria Type. 4-5 feet. Forming vigorously growing, large clumps, erect, with long stems and grasslike leaves; clusters of large, rather stiff flowers, blooming March-June. *PROPAGATION* — Division of clumps in fall. *CULTURE*—Grows in any soil and in any situation, but does best in a moderately moist soil; tends to overrun the garden unless inhibited. Three principal species are: **I. monnieri.** Bright-yellow flowers. **I. aurea.** Deep yellow. **I. orientalis (ochroleuca).** Pale yellow, bordered with white. These Iris may be planted near naturalistic pools, or in bold groups in front of shrubbery.

Japanese Iris—I. kaempferi (laevigata). Forming root stocks. 2-3½ feet. Sun loving, but a little shade during day is beneficial to prevent scorching of blooms. Produces large, stout clumps; long, narrow, grasslike leaves; tall flower stems, bearing clusters of large, flat-topped, expanded, highly colored, exquisitely penciled flowers, with colors ranging from white, through shades of blue, rose, claret, violet, and purple, blooming in June-July. *PROPAGATION*—Division of clumps in fall or early spring. *CULTURE*—Grows in an acid medium, either directly in shallow water in pools, or in saturated soil along stream beds, near rims of pools, in bogs, in moist soil in shrub beds; fertilized with rotted cow or sheep manure. *POSITION*—Interesting in Japanese gardens; near naturalistic and formal pools; in the shrub border.

Siberian Iris—I. siberica. 2-5 feet. Sun and slight shade. Forming large, stout clumps, the habit of growth and culture being much the same as for Japanese Iris. Leaves long, flexible, and narrow; long, slender stems bearing terminal clusters of medium-sized flowers having roundish segments narrowed down to slender claws, white, pale to deep blue **Perrys Blue** is extensively planted.

Regelia and **Onocyclus Types.** 2 feet. Sun. The Regelia Iris are highly colored, strikingly veined flowers, resembling the Bearded Iris, blooming in March-April. The principal Onocyclus Iris is **I. susiana,** the **Mourning Iris.** Single flowered, of interesting texture and somber colors, due to the interlacing of numerous, very thin veins upon a white or straw-colored ground, producing sky-blue, light gray, brown, almost to black. *PROPAGATION*—Division of rhizomes. *CULTURE*—Requires a dry situation; add lime to soil; take up after leaves have died; plant in early fall. **Winter-Blooming Iris—I. stylosa.** 2 feet. Sun and partial shade. Forms stout clump with many long, narrow, bright-green leaves; small, lilac flowers on short stems, blooming in fall and winter. *PROPAGATION*—Division of clumps in fall. *CULTURE*—Grows in any moderately rich, moist soil. **Dwarf Iris—I. pumila.** 6 inches. Short, linear leaves; stems bearing single, small, white, light-purple, yellow to reddish-purple flowers, blooming in February-March. **I. chamaeiris.** 10 inches. Similar to I. pumila in growth, but with bright-yellow flowers. Both kinds suitable for borders.

Bulbous Iris—I. xiphium—Spanish Iris. 1-2½ feet. Growing from small bulbs. Sun and slight shade. Erect, slender growing plant, with long, very narrow, bright-green leaves; rather large, stiff, bronze, yellow, and blue flowers, the inner segments curled or ruffled, blooming in May-June. *PROPAGATION*—Offsets from bulbs, planted in September-October. *CULTURE*—Requires a rich, moderately moist, well drained soil, fertilized with complete fertilizer. *POSITION*—Fine for inserting amongst yellow, blue, and white-colored flowers in the herbaceous border. **I. xiphioides—English Iris.** 1-2 feet. Sun and partial shade. Rather large flowers of loose texture, white, lavender, purple, blooming in May; requires plenty of water and rich soil. **Holland or Dutch Iris.** 2 feet. Sun and partial shade. Form of flower like that of the Spanish Iris, but not so stiff; Orchidlike in texture, delicately fragrant, in soft tones of lavender, yellow, rose, blue, white, orange, cream, blooming in April-June. *PROPAGATION*—Offsets from bulbs, planted September-November. *CULTURE*—Requires a rich, moist, well drained soil. *POSITION*—Less vigorous in growth, but beautiful in the flower and shrub border, or in small groups in close association with some garden ornament like a jar or bird bath. **Native Iris.** 1-1½ feet. Sun and partial shade. Forming stout clumps, with short-stemmed, small flowers, of fine, loose texture, purple, lilac, lavender, buff, blooming in April-May. Suited to the naturalistic garden and near naturistic pools. **I. douglasii** is the type.

IRISH BELL HEATHER—(DABOECIA).

IRISH JUNIPER—(JUNIPERUS COMMUNIS HIBERNICA).

IRISH MOSS—(ARENARIA).

ISLAND IRONWOOD — (LYONOTHAMNUS).

ISMENE—(HYMENOCALLIS).

ITALIAN CYPRESS—(CUPRESSUS SEMPERVIRENS FASTIGIATA).

IXIA—(AFRICAN CORN LILY). 1-2 feet. Sun. Erect plant, with sword-shaped leaves; spikes or racemes of cup-shaped or star-shaped flowers in many brilliant colors, blooming March-June. *PROPAGATION*—Easily by corms planted September-November or in early spring. *CULTURE*—Grows best in well enriched, sandy loam. *GROUPING*— Plant in the bulb or perennial border, combining with Daffodil, Iris, Siberian Wallflower, Scilla, Ornithogalum, Mariposa Lily, deep blue Delphinium, Violets.

J

JACARANDA MIMOSAEFOLIA — (JACARANDA). Evergreen. 20-30 feet. Spreading tree with umbrellalike top and drooping branches; large, twice-pinnate, feathery, fernlike, silky leaves; many flowered, long, loose, pyramidal panicles of large, short-tubular, two-lipped, soft lilac flowers, blooming in early spring. *PROPAGATION*—Cuttings of half ripened wood. *CULTURE*—Does well in rich, light, moderately fertilized loam, but should be protected from frost. *POSITION*—Specimen tree for patios and lawns; street and avenue tree; accent tree in the shrub border.

JAPANESE ANEMONE—(ANEMONE JAPONICA).

JAPANESE CEDAR — (CRYPTOMERIA JAPONICA).

JAPANESE FLOWERING CHERRY—(FLOWERING FRUIT TREES).

JAPANESE CLEMATIS—(CLEMATIS PANICULATA).

JAPANESE GIANT BAMBOO — (DENDROCALAMUS).

JAPANESE HOLLY—(OSMANTHUS AQUIFOLIUM).

JAPANESE IRIS—(IRIS KAEMPFERI).

JAPANESE IVY—(AMPELOPSIS VEITCHII).

JAPANESE LARCH—(LARIX LEPTOLEPIS).

JAPANESE MAGNOLIA — (MAGNOLIA SOULANGEANA).

JAPANESE MAPLE—(ACER PALMATUM).

JAPANESE MORNING GLORY — (IPOMOEA).

JAPANESE PRIVET—(LIGUSTRUM JAPONICUM).

JAPANESE QUINCE—(CYDONIA).

JAPANESE REDLEAF PLUM—(FLOWERING FRUIT TREES).

JAPANESE ROSE—(KERRIA).

JAPANESE UMBRELLA PINE — (SCIADOPITYS).

JAPANESE WEEPING ROSE — FLOWERED CHERRY—(FLOWERING FRUIT TREES).

JAPANESE WINDFLOWER—(ANEMONE JAPONICA).

JAPANESE YEW—(CEPHALOTAXUS).

JAPAN PAGODA TREE—(SOPHORA).

JASMINUM. Hardy deciduous and evergreen climbers and sub-shrubs. 6-20 feet or more. Usually stout, green stems, growing rapidly and vigorously; usually smooth and glistening, pinnate, bright-green leaves; small to medium-sized, regular, tubular, salver-shaped or star-shaped, mostly very fragrant, yellow or white, sometimes reddish flowers, blooming in different species throughout the year. *PROPAGATION*—Cuttings of nearly matured wood in fall or early spring; easily by layering. *CULTURE* —Grows well in ordinary, moderately fertilized, moist soils, except very stiff soil; prune and thin out once a year. *POSITION*—Useful for covering walls, trellises, arbors, pergolas, etc.; the shrubby kinds for the shrub border; the vines, according to species, combine with Hardenbergia, Clematis in variety, Single Climbing Roses in variety, Akebia quinata, Tecoma capensis, Wistaria in variety.

SPECIES—**J. floridum.** Vine or shrub. Large, golden-yellow, fragrant flowers, blooming in July **J. grandiflorum—Catalonian, Royal or Spanish Jasmine.** Like the Jessamine, with large, very fragrant, white flowers, blooming June-September. **J. humile—Italian Jasmine.** Vine or shrub; dark, glossy green, oblong-lanceolate leaves; medium sized, fragrant, bright-yellow flowers in open clusters, blooming April-June. **J. nudiflorum.** Shrubby; semi-deciduous; single, yellow flowers blooming in winter and early spring. **J. officinalis—Jessamine.** Slender but vigorous climber; clusters of small, fragrant flowers, blooming profusely in summer, but quite continuous in bloom. **J. primulinum.** Strong and quick growing shrub or vine; bright-green leaves; solitary, large, semi-double, bright-yellow, non-fragrant flowers, blooming in late winter and early spring. *GROUPING*—For the shrub border; combine with Pittosporum in variety, Orange Cestrum, Spiraeas and other white-flowered spring-blooming shrubs, Prunus caroliniana, Catalina Cherry, Duranta plumieri, blue Veronicas, Iochroma, Solanum rantonneti.

JEWEL FLOWER—(FUCHSIA).

JEWEL FLOWER SHRUB—(GREVILLEA THELEMANNIANA).

JUDAS TREE—(CERCIS).

JUNIPERUS—(JUNIPER). Conifer. Vary in habit from low prostrate to tall, symmetrical, conical or pyramidal forms. Sun and partial shade. Bushy, leafy shrubs; small, needle or scalelike leaves; insignificant flowers; small, usually glaucous, bluish-black cones. *PROPAGATION* — Seeds, germinating the second or third year; easily by cuttings of nearly ripened wood taken in fall; side grafting. *CULTURE*—Junipers have a wide adaptation to all kinds of soils, tolerating rather dry, rocky, or gravelly soils; do best in sandy and loamy, moderately moist soils; fertilize in fall with manures. *POSITION*— Fine in groupings of conifers, using the dwarf forms at the base of taller growing kinds, harmonizing well with species of Chamaecyparis and Cypress, and with erect species of Juniperus; in foundation plantings, the tall species at corners and entrances; the low growing species in rockeries; as specimen and accent shrubs on lawns and in formal gardens.

SPECIES—**J. communis hibernica**—Irish Juniper. Up to 20 feet under cultivation. Tall growing, very erect, compact, columnar in habit. **J. chinensis femina.** Rather similar to the Irish Juniper in form, but with ends of branchlets nodding. **J. chin. procumbens—Creeping Juniper.** Very prostrate variety, sending out long, fingerlike branches, densely covered with sharp, needlelike, silver-green leaves in whorls. One of the hardiest and best of the low growing Junipers; interesting near pools. **J. chin. pfitzeriana—Pfitzers Juniper.** One of the largest of the spreading kinds, forming a broad pyramid with horizontally spreading branches, the long branchlets nodding; 4-5 feet, but spreading 10-12 feet; light, grayish green leaves. Specimen shrub on lawns, and at the base of large conifers. **J. excelsa stricta— (Greek Juniper).** 6-12 feet. Slow growing, very compact, conical in form; glaucous, blue-green foliage. Used both as specimen and as accent shrub. **J. sabina.** Usually 3-5 feet, but spreading, with slender branchlets and dark-green foliage. The variety **tamariscifolia,** usually 1-2 feet, with dark or bright-green foliage, spreads out evenly all around; excellent along steps and with other conifers. **J. virginiana—Red Cedar.** Tall growing, up to 100 feet, with conical head and spreading or upright branches. Many varieties, including the widely planted variety **tripartita,** procumbent type of irregular habit, 2 feet high but spreading 4-6 feet; densely branched; bright-green, glaucous leaves.

K

KAFIR LILY—(SCHIZOSTYLIS).

KALMIA LATIFOLIA — (MOUNTAIN LAUREL). Evergreen. 4-10 feet. Sun, but prefers partial shade. Dense, spreading, round-headed shrub; large, dark-green, glossy, leathery, elliptic-oblong leaves; yellowish-green beneath; regular, saucer-shaped, exquisitely fragrant, delicately lilac-pink-white flowers in compound umbels, blooming in May-June. *PROPAGATION*—Usually by side grafts on seedlings; layers; seed sown in spring. *CULTURE*—Requires an acid medium; prefers a rich, loamy, sandy or peaty soil. *GROUPING*—Specimen shrub; for the shady border, grouping with Andromeda japonica, Skimmia japonica, Rhododendron, Camellia, Daphne, Raphiolepis, Mahonia, several interesting varieties.

KANGAROO THORN—(ACACIA ARMATA).

KENILWORTH IVY—(LINARIA).

KERRIA (CORCHORUS) JAPONICA—(JAPANESE ROSE). Deciduous. As shrub 4-8 feet, but also climbing to 15 feet. Sun and partial shade. Rangy, loose spreading shrub, with ovate-lanceolate, clear-green leaves; single in type, but usually double, roselike, yellow flowers, blooming profusely in summer, and intermittently. *PROPAGATION*—Easily by green wood cuttings; layering; root divisions. *CULTURE*—Grows in any good garden loam, fertilized with manure. *POSITION*—Used extensively for covering garages, fences, arbors.

KEW TREE—(GINKGO).

KNIFE-LEAVED ACACIA—(ACACIA).

KNIPHOFIA—(TRITOMA).

KOCHIA TRICHOPHYLLA (SCOPARIA)— (SUMMER CYPRESS). Annual. 2-3 feet. Sun. Very compact, round-pyramidal, bushy plant; long, linear, bright-green, silky leaves, turning to purple-red in fall. *PROPAGATION*—Easily by seeds sown in flats or in the open in early spring. *POSITION*—Frequently used in hedge formation along walks; occasionally in the shrub border.

KOLKWITZIA AMABILIS — (BEAUTY BUSH). Deciduous. 2-4 feet. Sun. Resembling Abelia somewhat, with slender, hairy branches; medium-sized, oval, dark-green leaves, densely hairy beneath; small, short-tubular, pink-white flowers, blooming in summer. *PROPAGATION* — Usually green wood cutting in late summer; seeds; layers. *CULTURE*—Ordinary, well drained garden soils. *GROUPING*—Plant in shrub border, grouping with Abelia, Myrtus in variety, Cotoneaster in variety, Heathers, Pernettya, Pimelea, Azara, Eugenia myrtifolia, Daboecia polifolia.

L

LABURNUM VULGARE (ANAGYROIDES)— (GOLDEN CHAIN). Deciduous. 10-20 feet. Sun and partial shade. Erect tree with drooping branches; large, dark-green, trifoliate, elliptic-ovate leaves, silky-pubescent when young; long, drooping, soft-pubescent racemes of large, golden-yellow, pea-shaped flowers, blooming in April-May; long seed pods. *PROPAGATION* — Seed sown in spring; layers; varieties grafted. *CULTURE*—Grows well in ordinary, moderately fertilized soils, including limestone and rocky soils. *POSITION*—Fine specimen tree; accent tree in shrub border; in groupings on large plantations; in combination with Maples, Elms, Oaks, etc.; street and avenue tree.

LAGERSTROEMIA INDICA — (CRAPE MYRTLE). Deciduous. 10-30 feet. Sun. Strong growing, rather round-headed tree, with smooth, brown bark; sessile, elliptic-oblong leaves; panicles of soft-fringed, paperlike, bright-pink, bluish, purplish, or white flowers, blooming profusely in summer. *PROPAGATION*—Seeds sown in spring; cuttings of ripe wood. *CULTURE*—No special soil requirements; blooms well only where it is very warm in summer; prune severely in fall. *POSITION*—Too individualistic to group with other trees; specimen tree; street and avenue tree.

LAGUNARIA PATTERSONI. Evergreen. 20-30 feet. Sun. Rather symmetrical tree, with young parts and inflorescence scurfy-pubescent; large oblong leaves; pale rose flowers resembling Hibiscus, blooming profusely in June. *PROPAGATION*—Cuttings of half ripened shoots. *CULTURE*—Impartial in soil requirements. *POSITION*—Specimen tree; street and avenue tree.

LALAND FIRETHORN — (PYRACANTHA LALANDI).

LANTANA CAMARA — (LANTANA). Semi-deciduous. 10 feet or more. Usually rangy shrubs with hairy, prickly branches; thick, leathery, dark-green, rough, ovate leaves, with strong odor; small flowers in dense terminal heads, orange-yellow, deep pink, lemon-yellow, lilac, and intermediate shades, blooming prolifically in summer, again in winter, and intermittently. *PROPAGATION*—Cuttings of side shoots; sometimes by seed. *CULTURE*—Grows in any moderately fertilized soil; should be pruned back heavily in fall; withstands drought. *POSITION*—Usually best by themselves; frequently trained against house walls.

SPECIES—**L. sellowiana — Lavender Lantana.** Trailing, spreading species, with rosy-lilac flowers, blooming most of the year. *POSITION*—Rockeries, over walls, and in foreground of shrub border. Many trailing and semi-shrubby kinds of Lantana.

LARCH—(LARIX).

LARGE-FLOWERED AMARYLLIS — (HIPPE-ASTRUM).

LARGE-FLOWERED DOGWOOD — (COR-NUS).

LARIX—(LARCH)—(TAMARACK). Deciduous conifer. Usually 20-30 feet under cultivation. Sun and partial shade. Erect, symmetrical, loose spreading; whorled branches with pendulous branchlets; light-green, linear leaves in clusters; bright-purple flowers; medium-sized, pendulous, roundish or ovate cones. *PROPAGATION*—Seeds sown in spring; whip, cleft, or veneer graft for varieties. *CULTURE*—Does best in a rich, well drained loam, kept slightly moist; will grow in clay soils; subject to leaf-eating larvae of moths (see Plant Pests).

SPECIES—**L. decidua—European Larch.** Dark, grayish-brown bark; slender, smooth, yellowish branchlets; bright-green leaves. **L. leptolepis—Japanese Larch.** Branchlets yellowish or reddish brown; short and globular spurs; light or bluish-green leaves. *POSITION*—Specimen trees; contrast effects in conifer groupings.

LARKSPUR—(DELPHINIUM).

LATHYRUS ODORATUS — (SWEET PEA). Annual, climbing by means of tendrils. 6-10 feet. Sun and slight shade. Strong growing vine, with rough, hairy, winged stem; leaves equally pinnate; the long flower stems loosely several-flowered; the large, delicately fragrant, papilionaceous flowers of improved hybrids having large, wavy margined, notched, often hooded standard petals, rather fluted wings and prominent keel; the hybrids of today having many colors, frequently with several colors in the same flower, striped or blotched, the garden kinds blooming in summer, or earlier in the greenhouse. *PROPAGATION*—Seeds best sown in October to produce strong, vigorous plants for early blooming; in cold regions, and heavy soils, best to delay sowing until early spring; often grown in pots for winter protection. *CULTURE*—Requires a rich, well drained, rather light loam, kept moist during growing season, well fertilized with manure in the fall before sowing seed; dig a trench 12-16 inches deep, filling in bottom with 4-6 inches of manure; place a layer of soil over this about 6 inches deep; use liquid manure or complete commercial fertilizer during blooming period. Pick off old blossoms; remove and burn vines after blooming. Sweet Peas are ideally suited to Pacific Coast conditions where they are grown in full sun, but away from white walls which scorch the blooms; benefited by some shade during day. Grown on wire and chicken wire frames, on strong cord, over trellises and arbors; on brush supports. Seedlings eaten by birds and rabbits; protect with close-mesh wire screen; sprinkle solution of soil fungicide over surface of soil infected with soil fungi; mosaic disease causing a blackening of the stems is best controlled by pulling out infected vines; also subject to mildew, aphis, red spider, green worm (see Plant Pests). *TYPES*—Several distinct types and strains, running into many varieties. Only seed of distinct varieties should be sown. Sweet peas make a charming picture when used as a screen planting in the background of the flower border, using colors harmonizing with colors of flowers in the foreground. When through blooming, their place may be taken by vines or tall growing annuals blooming in late summer and fall. The prevailing type is the **Spencer or Orchid-Flowering Sweet Pea**, further divided into **Early or Winter Blooming Spencers** and **Summer Blooming Spencers**; the Early Blooming, in the greenhouse, bloom from November until late in spring; in the garden they bloom from spring into summer. The **Grandiflora** type is also grown to some extent. **Cupid Sweet Peas.** 5-6 inches high, early blooming, have the characteristics and colors of the garden kinds.

SPECIES—**L. latifolius—Perennial or Everlasting Pea.** 4-8 feet. Quick growing vine, with leaves and stems like those of the annual Sweet Pea; large, white, rose-purple, or pink, pea-shaped flowers in racemes, blooming in August, but intermittent in bloom. *PROPAGATION*—Seeds; division of roots; cuttings. *CULTURE*—Grows in any soil; drought resistant. *USES*—Ground cover; for covering embankments; screens; covering supports; shrub border.

LAURUS NOBILIS—(SWEET BAY)—(GRECIAN BAY LAUREL). Evergreen. Sun and partial shade. Growing naturally 40-60 feet, but usually pruned into definite shapes. Symmetrical, compact, bushy shrub; dull green, stiff, lance-oblong leaves; yellow flowers, blooming in spring; succulent, purple, cherrylike fruits. *PROPAGATION* — Seeds, sown soon as ripe; cuttings of well ripened wood in fall; root cuttings; layering. *CULTURE*—Likes a rich, moist garden loam, fertilized several times a year with concentrated fertilizers. *POSITION*—Accent shrubs for formal effects, either in tubs or in the open ground; also in tubs about hotels, residences, and large buildings.

LAURUSTINUS—(VIBURNUM TINUS).

LAVANDULA VERA—(LAVENDER). Perennial Evergreen. 3-4 feet. Sun. Round-headed, bushy plant; linearly-lanceolate, gray-green leaves; many long spikes of small, lavender, sweet-scented flowers, blooming prolifically in summer and intermittently. *PROPAGATION*—Cuttings of one season's growth taken with a heel of old wood in late fall or early spring. *CULTURE*—Grows in any soil, but does best in a sandy, somewhat moist, moderately fertilized loam; adapted to dry, calcareous, and stony soils; prune back each fall. *POSITION*—For the flower and shrub borders where it blends in with a variety of shrubs.

LAVENDER COTTON—(SANTOLINA).

LAWNS—In making a new lawn, first study the soil. It is very necessary that the soil be homogeneous in character for the first 3 or 4 inches. In excavating for a residence, remove the top layer of soil, placing it to one side, later replacing it over the surface of the lawn area. Should the sub-soil be a heavy clay or adobe, and there is no appreciable slope, it is a good practice to run lines of tile a foot down, to carry off excess water. Remove stones, concrete blocks, lath, etc.

The matter of proper grading of land is of paramount importance. The natural contours of land are usually interesting without much modification, but garden sites about new homes frequently require re-grading, and a general cleaning up. Formal gardens demand that the ground be brought to grade in one or more planes. They should never be absolutely level, neither should there be undulating contours. Most of our gardens are small in extent, with a narrow frontage, necessitating almost a level plot of lawn, with a slightly convex surface. The ground should always slope away from the house, unless the house is below the street level, in which case tile drains should be placed about the foundations. Where there is an appreciable slope, the ground should be terraced (graded to produce a combination of level area and slope); a retaining wall may be substituted for the slope. Grass on a steep slope is difficult to cut; the slope should not be greater than in the proportion of 1 to 2.

The ordinary lawn grasses are heavy feeders. Good loams in cities and towns are not plentiful. Heavy clay and adobe soils may be modified by the addition of coarse sand, wood ashes, straw manure, coal screenings, etc., and by working the soil several times. Sometimes the most practical way is to bring in good loam for the surface layer. However, even adobe soil may be made to produce a reasonably good lawn if worked up several times, with plenty of peat added; peat, thoroughly incorporated into the soil, improves the physical properties and conserves moisture. The ideal way to make a lawn is to dig up the ground in fall, leaving it in fallow during winter, in spring cutting out weeds and turning it over several times.

Soils are benefited greatly by the addition of concentrated animal or mineral fertilizers, unless they already happen to be naturally rich. The fertilizers should be added in limited amounts and thoroughly worked in to prevent burning of the grass roots. Limestone and fertilizers containing calcareous materials may be added to heavy soils, except for Bent Grass lawns. Animal fertilizers used as a mulch on the surface add fertilizing elements to the soil. A good practice is to make an additional application of concentrated fertilizer six months after the first application. Some good fertilizers include bone and blood meals, sulphate of potash, ammonium sulphate, superphosphate, guano, nitrate of soda, sheep and poultry manures, barnyard manures, and iron, sulphur, or magnesium if deficient in soil.

It is presumed that the soil has been brought to final grade, and that it is ready for sowing to grass seed. The soil particles should be compacted by rolling with water, iron, or cement roller. Never roll very wet soil. Seed should be sown evenly over the surface, using a rotary motion of the forearm; sow seed first along walks and around rim of lawn; select a quiet day if possible for sowing of seed. Rake seed in lightly. Cover with mulch of peat, pulverized or short-straw manure, light shavings, or other light material, taking care not to cover too deeply; peat and manure give a springy feeling to the turf; lawns put in late in the year may not require top mulch. Spring and early fall are generally the two best seasons for putting in new lawns, although in California lawns may be put in late in the year, depending upon weather conditions.

It is essential that both the surface soil and sub-soil be moist when seed is germinating. Very dry soil should be soaked up thoroughly, preparing lawn area for seeding. Very moist soils should not be watered too frequently. The lawn area should be watered at least once a day, preferably in late morning or early afternoon if nights are cool; very warm days may necessitate watering several times a day; when grass is up pretty well, let the soil be a little toward the dry side. Crowding of grass and oversaturation may cause scalding of grass or fungous troubles. Brown spot in grass controlled by use of soil fungicides. A sprinkling system solves many of the vexing problems of maintaining new lawns.

Kentucky Blue Grass gives a rich, dark-green lawn, making a thick, strong turf that can be maintained for years if properly fertilized and cared for; favors a lime-containing soil. Chewings Fescue, rather shallow rooted, makes a lovely, light green turf in sun or partial shade. Some of the Bent Grasses, especially Cocos Bent, Astoria and Seaside Bents, all with creeping root stocks or stolons, are considerably used for making putting greens and for thick set, close-cropped lawns; require an acid-soil medium; Poa trivialis with one of the Bents makes a good, durable lawn. Pacific Rye and other Rye grasses are used in heavy soils, and where little watering is done; these grasses have the habit of bunching up. A mixture containing mostly Pacific Rye and small amounts of Kentucky Blue, Fescue, Red Top, and Clover if desired will give a good-looking lawn, and one which remains green throughout the year; requires lime-containing soil. White Dutch Clover used alone or mixed with other grasses presents a pleasing green, grows rapidly, and also adds fertility to the soil. Clover seed should not be more than seven per cent of any mixture, and should preferably be sown by itself, using sand as a spreader. There are various shade mixtures on the market where shade conditions prevail. Pacific Rye stands some shade. Bermuda Grass, a very wiry grass with creeping stolons, is used in some regions, but tends to encroach upon the garden; turns brown in winter.

Kentucky Blue, Fescue, and similar grasses are sown at the rate of one pound to 150 square feet; Bent Grass and other very fine seeds, one pound to 250 square feet; mixtures of coarse and fine seeds, one pound to about 115 square feet. The grass may receive its first cutting when blades are about two inches high. Set the roller of the lawnmower a little high; sharpen and adjust the blades properly. Cut the lawn at regular intervals; if cut frequently, the cuttings may be left on lawn. The lawn should be rolled again after six months' time. Fertilize several times a year with some concentrated fertilizer, to maintain a good, rich green color.

LAWSON CYPRESS — (CHAMAECYPARIS LAWSONIANA).

LAYERING (See Garden Movie).

LEMON VERBENA — (LIPPIA CITRIODORA).

LEONOTIS LEONURUS—(LIONS TAIL.) 3-6 feet. Perennial. Erect, branching, and shrubby plant, with rigid, woody stems; long, pubescent, oblong leaves; medium-sized, funnel-form, bright red-yellow and orange-red flowers in axillary whorls, blooming quite continuously. *PROPAGATION*—Division of clumps in fall and spring; cuttings of half ripened wood in spring. *CULTURE*—Grows in any soil; drought-resistant. *POSITION*—Excellent in patio gardens; in the shrub border in combination with foliage shrubs and with shrubs having yellow, orange, and deep blue flowers.

LEOPARDS BANE—(DORONICUM).

LEPTOSPERMUM. Evergreen. 4-30 feet. Sun and some shade. Bushy, broad shrubs, with slender, drooping branches, densely clothed with small, usually rigid leaves; numerous, small, regular flowers; small, hard, persistent nutlets. *PROPAGATION*—Seeds sown in spring; usually by cuttings of young wood in May under glass; cuttings of nearly matured wood in fall. *CULTURE*—Adapted to all soils; drought resistant, growing in alkali and sandy soils. *GROUPING*—Fine along driveways; as hedge shrubs; windbreaks; in the background of the shrub border, grouping with Cotoneasters in variety, different species together, Dendromecon rigidum, Fremontia, Rhamnus californica, Spiraeas, Weigela, Tamarisk.

SPECIES—**L. flavescens.** 10 feet. Small, narrow leaves, and white flowers, blooming in April. **L. laevigatum—Australian Tea Shrub.** 10-30 feet. Fast growing, with immense, rough, scaly trunks; variable, glaucous, gray-green leaves; numerous white flowers, blooming in March-April and intermittently. **L. scoparium chapmanni.** 4-6 feet. Gracefully arching shrub; very small, dark-green, ruddy tinted, ovate leaves; white to rose flowers blooming April-May. **L. scoparium nicholi.** 4-6 feet. Small, purplish leaves and carmine flowers, blooming very profusely in late spring and early summer.

LEUCOJUM VERNUM—(SPRING SNOWFLAKE). Bulbous plant. 1 foot. Sun and partial shade. Strap-shaped leaves; nodding, medium-sized, delicately scented, white flowers, blooming January-March. *PROPAGATION*—Easily by offsets planted September-November. *CULTURE*—Prefers rich, light, well fertilized soil. *GROUPING*—Naturalized in the wild garden; for the bulb border, combining with Crocus, Narcissi, Hyacinths, Winter Aconite, Scillas, and other early blooming bulbous plants.

SPECIES—**L. aestivum—Summer Snowflake.** Quite similar to the above, the flowers blooming in April-June. **L. autumnale—Autumn Snowflake.** Less vigorous in growth, with white flowers tinged with red, blooming in early fall.

LIBOCEDRUS DECURRENS — (INCENSE CEDAR). Native evergreen. Usually 20-30 feet under cultivation. Sun and partial shade. Very straight, symmetrical, rather oblong, free; short branches with flattened branchlets; bright, cinnamon-red bark; bright-green, scented, scalelike leaves with yellowish tinge; small, yellowish flowers; small, light reddish-brown cones. *PROPAGATION*—Seeds

sown in spring; cuttings of half firm wood under glass in late summer or fall; grafting on Thuya and Chamaecyparis. *CULTURE*—Grows well in all well drained soils. *POSITION*—Accent type of tree; specimen trees on lawns; foundation plantings at corners about large residences; for hedge effects.

LIGUSTRUM—(PRIVET). Evergreen or semideciduous. 6-12 feet. Hardy. Sun and partial shade. Bushy, fast growing shrubs, much branched of irregular growth; medium-sized to large, variable, smooth and shining leaves; dense, terminal racemes of regular, fragrant, short-tubular, white flowers, blooming in late spring and summer, sometimes intermittent. *PROPAGATION*—Easily from one-year-old wood in fall or early spring; seeds. *CULTURE*—Grows in most soils, but thrives best in rich, moist, rather light loam, fertilizing with manures in fall; prune in fall. *GROUPING*—The well-known California Privet, English Privet, and others are used considerably as hedge shrubs. The Japanese Privet and many others find a place in the background of the shrub border, grouping with Pittosporum in variety, Escallonia in variety, Carolina Cherry, Choisya ternata, Night-blooming Jasmine, Euonymus, Coprosma.

SPECIES—**L. ovalifolium—California Privet.** Leaves rather small, dark-green above, yellowish-green beneath. Several variegated varieties with yellowish margins. **L. vulgare—English Privet—Common or English Privet.** Darker and larger, glistening leaves; immense trusses of very fragrant flowers. **L. japonicum—Japanese Privet.** Large, glistening leaves; immense trusses of very fragrant flowers. **L. ibota, L. lucidum, L. sinense,** and several dwarf varieties are others of much merit.

LILAC—(SYRINGA).

LILIUM—(LILY). Bulbous plant. Vary in height from 2-8 feet. Some species sun loving, others preferring partial shade. Erect plant, usually with light or dark-green, linear-lanceolate leaves; funnel-shaped, regular flowers, borne singly or in clusters, in many colors, varying in size from several inches to 8 inches across, blooming in summer or fall, according to kind. *PROPAGATION*—Offsets from bulbs planted October-December; bulblets and bulbels planted early in fall; seeds sown in spring. *CULTURE*—Bulbs should be set in rich, light soil; planted on a cushion of sand or of peat, 6 inches deep for large bulbs, 2-4 inches deep for small to medium-sized bulbs; keep soil moist, but not too wet; attacked by aphis, worms, and leaf spot (See Plant Diseases); usually best to lift bulbs each year, clean, and store in cool, dry place. *GROUPING*—The sun-loving kinds are planted in the mixed border, or in masses; the shade loving kinds are ideal in the shady border, combining with Columbine, Thalictrum, Astilbe, Fibrous-rooted Begonias, ferns and other foliage plants and shrubs. In the flower border combine, according to color, with Snapdragon, Stocks, Blue Lace Flower, Salvia farinacea, Scabiosa coronaria, Perennial Phlox, Iris kaempferi.

SPECIES—**L. auratum — (Gold-Banded Lily).** Large flowered, ivory white, studded with chocolate-crimson spots, blooming July-September. **L. auratum platyphyllum.** Similar to the preceding, with larger flowers. **L. album—Japanese White Lily.** White with green band. **Bermuda Lily.** The well known greenhouse Easter Lily. **L. hansoni—Golden Turks-Cap Lily.** Bright orange, blooming in June. **L. henryi.** Very tall, delicately scented, with bright-orange flowers in many flowered clusters, blooming in August-September. **L. humboldtii magnificum.** Native lily, growing 10 feet high, with many flowered clusters of large orange-yellow, spotted reddish purple, blooming June-August. **L. pardalinum—Leopard Lily.** Native. Many flowered clusters of bright orange-scarlet, spotted brownish-purple flowers, blooming June-August. **L. regale—Regal Lily.** A fine lily for a sunny position Large, white-pink-canary-yellow flowers in many flowered clusters, blooming in July. **L. speciosum rubrum—Showy Lily.** A very prolific lily, doing best in sandy soil in partial shade. White-red flowers with crimson markings, very fragrant, blooming in late August-September. **L. tigrinum—Tiger Lily.** The well-known, tall growing, scentless lily, producing bulbels in the axils of the leaves. Deep orange flowers, blooming in August-September. **L. umbellatum.** Several varieties in shades of red, orange, yellow, and crimson. **L. washingtonianum.** Native lily, white-flowered, blooming in June-July. Many other species and varieties of distinct merit. A full account is given in Bailey's Cyclopedia of Horticulture.

LINARIA CYMBALARIA — (KENILWORTH IVY). Evergreen trailing vine, 4-6 feet. Sun, but better in partial or even full shade. Quick growing, bushy plant, with small, light-green, smooth, roundish-cordate leaves; numerous, small, irregular, lilac-blue flowers with yellowish throat, blooming prolifically in summer and quite continuously thereafter. *PROPAGATION*—Seeds sown in spring; division of roots any time. *CULTURE*—Very hardy, free from pests, growing in any soil, but preferring a rich, light, moist loam. *POSITION*—Used in hanging baskets; over walls; to climb any support; in shady borders; rockeries; near pools.

LINUM GRANDIFLORUM — (FLOWERING FLAX). Annual. 1-2 feet. Sun and slight shade. Erect, branching freely, with slender branches and flower stems; numerous, alternate, broadly lanceolate to oblong, sessile, smooth and shining leaves; terminal, salver-shaped, red, blue, and yellow, medium-sized flowers, blooming in summer. *PROPAGATION*—Easily by seeds sown in early spring. *CULTURE*—Grows in enriched, ordinary garden loam. *GROUPING*—For the mixed border, combining with Arctotis, Larkspur, Verbena, Heuchera, Nepeta, Nemesia, Ageratum, Lupine.

SPECIES—**Perennial Flax.** 1-2½ feet. Erect and branching; very linear, acute leaves; small, azure-blue and white flowers, blooming prolifically in summer. *PROPAGATION*—Seeds sown in fall or in early spring, blooming first year from seed; divisions of clumps in fall.

LIONS TAIL—(LEONOTIS).

LIPPIA CITRIODORA — (LEMON VERBENA). Evergreen. 6-10 feet or more. Bushy shrub, irregular in growth; long, sweet-scented, dark-green leaves; many flowered spikes bearing minute, white, fragrant flowers, blooming in summer and fall. *PROPAGATION* — Usually by cuttings of new growth in early spring. *CULTURE*—Grows in any

moderately rich soil; head back occasionally. *POSITION*—Occasional plant.

SPECIES—**L. repens.** Commonly called **Lippia,** a creeping species used as a substitute for grass in lawns; also used around stepping-stones, on waste lands, to cover embankments. The well-known plant with gray-green leaves and small heads of rosy purple flowers; roots by sending out runners from the joints. Lippia will grow in any soil, does not require any fertilizer, and is drought resistant. Small clumps of Lippia are inserted in the lawn area; afterwards the soil is rolled; give sufficient water for runners to grow. Water occasionally during dry season; cut with lawn-mower several times during season; looks poorly in winter but quickly revives in spring.

LIQUIDAMBAR STYRACIFLUA — (SWEET GUM). Deciduous. Usually 20-60 feet under cultivation. Sun and partial shade. Very symmetrical, pyramidal tree, with corky branches and deeply furrowed bark; maplelike, glistening, dark-green leaves, turning to deep crimson in fall; inconspicuous flowers; globose, spiny fruits. *PROPAGATION*—Seeds sown when ripe, or stratified and sown in early spring. *CULTURE*—Requires a rich, moist soil; withstands salt air; very hardy and free from pests. *POSITION*—Plant where winters are not too severe; specimen tree; grouping tree, interspersed among conifers; in street plantings.

LOBELIA ERINUS. Annual. 6-12 inches. Sun and light shade. Trailing, or compact, bushy plants; variable, dark-green, bronzed, or light-green leaves; irregular, small, tubular flowers, borne on slender pedicels, varying from light to deep blue, also maroon, rose, crimson, white, blooming April-November, if seeds are planted successively. *PROPAGATION*—Seeds sown from late winter to July; cuttings; seeds itself. *CULTURE*—Prefers a moist, well fertilized, light loam. *GROUPING*—Edging plant; in rockeries; window boxes; in the mixed border, combining with Gold Tuft, Iceland Poppy, Pot Marigold, Coreopsis, Siberian Wallflower, Freesias, Verbascum phoeniceum.

SPECIES—Many varieties, including: **Crystal Palace compacta.** A compact form with deep blue flowers. **Gracilis.** Creeping, with light-green foliage and light-blue flowers. **Speciosa.** Dark-green foliage and dark-blue flowers, trailing in habit. **Lobelia cardinalis—Cardinal Flower.** 2-4 feet. Sun. Perennial in habit; erect, smooth, glistening plant; large, dark-green, lanceolate leaves; racemous spikes of rather large, slender-tubular, intense cardinal flowers, blooming July-September. *PROPAGATION*—Division of clumps in fall; seeds. *CULTURE*—Plant in moist, moderately rich loam. *POSITION*—Accent plant in rockery, near pools, in perennial border.

LOCUST, SWEET—(GLEDITSIA).

LONICERA — (HONEYSUCKLE). Deciduous vines, nearly evergreen in California, and frequently half shrubby. 10-15 feet or more. Sun and partial shade. Quick growing, with old stems woody; opposite, entire, light to dark-green, or colored leaves; medium-sized to large, irregular, long-tubular, delicately or brightly colored, usually fragrant flowers in pairs or whorls, followed by colored fruits. *PROPAGATION*—Seeds sown in fall, or stratified and sown in spring; green wood cuttings under glass in summer; cuttings of ripened wood in fall. *CULTURE*—Grows in most soils, favoring a rich, light loam, fertilized with manures; prune severely and thin out after flowering. *POSITION*—Effective over walls, trellises, arches, pergolas, etc.; makes a heavy screen; ground cover.

SPECIES—**L. japonica halliana.** Vigorous growing; oblong-ovate, bright-green leaves; white flowers changing to yellow, blooming June-August; black fruits. **L. chinensis—Red Honeysuckle Vine.** Very thrifty vine, with reddish stems; purple-red, ovate leaves; very fragrant, orange-red flowers, blooming in summer and quite continuous; black fruits. **L. sempervirens — Trumpet Honeysuckle.** Smooth, glaucous, oval-oblong leaves; large, orange-scarlet flowers, blooming May-September.

LONICERA NITIDA — (BUSH HONEY-SUCKLE). Evergreen. 4-6 feet. Sun and partial shade. Compact, densely branching shrub, with small, dark-green, smooth, ovate leaves; inconspicuous, yellowish flowers, blooming in spring. *PROPAGATION*—Easily by cuttings of young shoots any time of year. *CULTURE*—Grows best in rich, well fertilized, light loam. *POSITION*—Pruned into definite forms, fine for formal effects. Used considerably for making low, formal hedges around courts, formal gardens, driveways, etc.

LOQUAT — (ERIOBOTRYA JAPONICA). Evergreen. 10-20 feet. Sun and some shade. Rather symmetrical, round-headed, compact tree; thick, leathery, glistening, bright-green, almost entire, alternate, very long and broad leaves, rusty-tomentose beneath; white flowers in large, rusty-woolly panicles, blooming during fall; medium-sized, pear-shaped, edible, yellow fruits, ripening in spring. *PROPAGATION*—Grows easily from seed; grafted or budded in October-November. *CULTURE*—Impartial in soil requirements, but prefers rich, moist, moderately fertilized soils; subject to mealy bug and scale (see Plant Pests). *POSITION*—Used as specimen tree on lawns.

LOTUS BERTHOLETII — (CORAL GEM). Evergreen. Growing flat on the ground. Sun and slight shade. Much branched bush, with a silvery sheen; linear, whorled leaves; many flowered loose clusters of medium-sized, irregular, scarlet or crimson flowers, with recurved, hornlike standard, sharp-pointed keel, and spreading wings, blooming in spring and summer. *PROPAGATION*—Division of clumps fall and spring; cuttings of medium-soft wood at any time. *CULTURE*—Requires a rich, well fertilized, light loam; subject to mealy bug (see Plant Pests). *POSITION*—Excellent over walls; ground cover; foreground of shrub border.

LUPINUS—(LUPINE). Herbaceous annuals and perennials, or woody evergreen shrubs. 1-10 feet, according to kind. Sun, or semi-shade for shrubs. Rapid growing, branching, bushy plants and shrubs; raylike, digitate, bright or dark-green, silky, hairy leaves; pea-shaped flowers in a spike inflorescence, in pure tones and combinations of yellow, blue, white, pink, mauve, rose, purple, blooming April-August. *PROPAGATION*—Easily by seeds sown in fall or early spring; division of clumps in fall; half firm cuttings of Tree Lupines. *CULTURE*—Native herbaceous and shrubby kinds grow well on dry hillsides; hybrid forms delight in rich, well fertilized, sandy, moist, well drained soils; will rot in sour, saturated soil. *GROUPING*—The annual and perennial kinds are used in the mixed and perennial borders, combining with each other, and with Alyssum saxatile, Larkspur, Shasta Daisy, Iceland Poppy, Snapdragons, Siberian Wallflower, Spanish Iris, Alstroemeria in variety, Polyantha Primrose, Myosotis in variety.

LYCHNIS CHALCEDONICA — (MALTESE CROSS). Perennial. 2-3 feet. Sun. Erect, usually hairy stem; oblong-cordate, hairy, clasping leaves; regular, long-clawed flowers in variety; brick-red, scarlet, rose, flesh, and white, blooming in June-July. *PROPAGATION*—Division of clumps October-December; seeds sown in early spring. *CULTURE*—Requires a rich, light loam. *GROUPING*—The perennial and mixed borders, combining, according to variety, with Tritoma, Gaillardia, Delphinium, Sweet Sultan, Purple Mullein, scarlet and carmine Perennial Phlox, Shasta Daisy. Many good species. **L. haageana.** Orange-red, scarlet, or crimson flowers in large clusters in summer.

LYONOTHAMNUS ASPLENIFOLIUS FLORIBUNDUS — (CATALINA IRONWOOD). Native evergreen. 25-40 feet. Sun and slight shade. Erect, semi-symmetrical tree, with large, dark-green, fernlike, smooth, pinnate leaves; large clusters of white flowers, blooming in June-July. *PROPAGATION*—Difficult to propagate, whether by seeds or by cuttings, but basal sprouts most certain. *CULTURE*—Subject to mealy bug and to scale (see Plant Pests); does best in somewhat moist, moderately fertilized garden loam; endures clay and adobe. *GROUPING*—Specimen tree for large lawns.

M

MADRONE—(ARBUTUS).

MAGNOLIA. Deciduous and evergreen. 8-40 feet or more. Sun and partial shade. Erect, stout branched; large, entire, leathery, dark or light-green leaves; large, regular, fragrant, terminal and solitary, white, pink, or purple flowers, blooming from February-August, according to kind. *PROPAGATION*—Seeds stratified and sown in spring; layers of last year's growth in spring; half ripened cuttings under glass; budding and grafting of varieties. *CULTURE*—Likes a rich, well drained, well fertilized, light soil. *POSITION*—The Common Magnolia is used as specimen tree on large lawns, as grouping tree on large plantations, and may be trained to lie flat against wall in foundation plantings. The low growing kinds are used either as specimen trees, or as occasional shrubs in the shrub border, combining with large-leaved shrubs.

SPECIES—**M. grandiflora—Common Magnolia.** Evergreen. 20-40 feet. Symmetrical, round-headed or pyramidal tree, with branchlets and buds rusty-pubescent; large, dark-green, glossy, oblong to ovate leaves, sometimes 8 inches across; large, globular, very fragrant, pure white flowers, blooming prolifically May-August, spasmodically during other seasons; does especially well in the San Francisco Bay Region. **M. soulangeana—Japanese Magnolia.** Deciduous. 8-10 feet. Long, bright-green, narrow leaves; large, long, purplish white flowers, long pointed in the bud, blooming as early as December in California, but indefinite in time of blooming. **M. stellata—Star-Shaped Japanese Magnolia.** Deciduous. Like the above, but with small, star-shaped, white flowers, usually blooming a little later than M. soulangeana.

MAHONIA AQUIFOLIUM — (OREGON GRAPE).
Evergreen. 3-6 feet. Best in partial or full shade. Bushy shrub with many stout stems; large, odd-pinnate, prickly, glossy, dark-green leaves with purple tinge, turning to bronze in fall; large fascicles of small, golden-yellow flowers, blooming in May; dark-blue berries. *PROPAGATION*—Principally by suckers; layers; seeds sown after maturity. *CULTURE*—Endures clay and adobe; grows best in a rich, moist, light, moderately fertilized, acid loam. *GROUPINGS*—For the shady border and in foundation plantings, grouping with Berberis in variety, Catalina Cherry, Huckleberry, California Live Oak, Azaleas, Aucuba, Andromeda, Nandina.

SPECIES—**M. pinnata—California Grape.** 2-5 feet. Similar in growth to the above, but with small, dull, gray-green leaves, short, fascicled racemes of yellow flowers, and blue berries. Suitable for rockeries. **M. japonica—Japanese Mahonia.** 8-12 feet. Very stately Mahonia, with large, beautifully colored, compound leaves in whorls; golden-yellow flowers in fascicles, blooming in May; large, bluish black fruits. *CULTURE*—Favors a moist, rich soil with acid reaction in a sheltered situation. *POSITION*—Specimen shrub especially in patio gardens, and in foundation plantings.

MAIDENHAIR TREE—(GINKGO).

MAIDENHAIR VINE—(MUEHLENBECKIA).

MAIDEN PINK—(DIANTHUS DELTOIDES).

MALCOMIA MARITIMA — (VIRGINIA STOCKS).
Annual. 4-6 inches. Sun and slight shade. Thrifty plants, with light-green, elliptic leaves; many small, regular, white, rose, and red-colored flowers, blooming continuously. *PROPAGATION*—Seed, sown successively from early spring until late fall. *CULTURE*—Does best in light, moderately fertilized loam. *POSITION*—Good border plant; foreground of flower border; for planting in open ground; in the rockery.

MALLOW—(ALTHAEA).

MALTESE CROSS—(LYCHNIS).

MANDEVILLA SUAVEOLENS — (CHILEAN JASMINE).
Evergreen vine. 8-15 feet or more. Sun. With cordate, smooth, bright-green leaves; large racemes of large, funnel-form, waxy white, very fragrant flowers, blooming June-September. *PROPAGATION*—Cuttings of small, stiff side shoots taken close to old wood, placed under glass. *CULTURE*—Needs protected position, requires rich, light, well fertilized loam. *GROUPING* — Grown over arbors, porches, pergolas, trellises, etc., alone, or in combination with Clematis jackmanni and other hybrids, Single Climbing Roses, Plumbago capensis, Tecoma capensis, Heliotrope, Streptosolen, Yellow Jasmine.

MANNA GUM — (EUCALYPTUS VIMINALIS).

MAPLE—(ACER).

MARIGOLD—(TAGETES)—(CALENDULA).

MATILIJA POPPY—(ROMNEYA).

MATTHIOLA INCANA — (STOCK) — (GILLYFLOWER).
Annual, more or less perennial in California. 1-2½ feet. Sun and slight shade. Stiff and branching plant; smooth, bright-green, oblong-lanceolate leaves; racemes of fragrant, small, single, or large double, roselike flowers in many colors, blooming for the greater part of the year, according to strain and time of planting. *PROPAGATION*—Seeds sown in early fall for Winter Blooming Stocks; sown in early spring for Summer Stocks; sown from early spring to early fall for successive flowerings. *CULTURE*—Plant in well drained, rich, light loam, fertilized with complete fertilizer; pinch back young plants; plant close together, rogueing out single flowered plants later, if undesired. The weaker seedlings produce a larger percentage of doubles; also some strains with high percentages of doubles. Will stand quite heavy soils if lightened with sand or peat; subject to stem rot (due to standing water), and to aphis (see Plant Pests). *STRAINS*—**Nice, Giant Perfection,** or **Winter Blooming Stock.** With large, delicately scented flowers, blooming normally sometime in winter, but also blooming in summer. **Brompton Strain,** blooming in fall. **Summer or Ten Weeks' Stocks,** blooming in late spring and summer. **Giant Imperial Stock,** 24-30 inches. Best for summer bedding, blooming a long time. **Matthiola bicornis—Evening Scented Stock.** Grown principally for the sweet perfume of the small, single, mauve-colored flowers at twilight. *GROUPING*—Very effective in both the annual and mixed borders, grouped alone, several varieties together, or combined, according to color harmonies, with Cape Marigold, Sweet Sultan, Daffodils and Narcissi, Violas and Pansies, Peach Bell, Bearded and Dutch Iris.

MATTRESS VINE—(MUEHLENBECKIA).

MAYTENUS BOARIA.
Evergreen. 15-25 feet. Sun and partial shade. Rather symmetrical, with loose spreading branches; arching very gracefully; small, ovate-lanceolate leaves. *PROPAGATION*—Easily from seeds sown fall or spring; suckers. *CULTURE*—Adapted to most soils, but prefers a rich, somewhat moist, light loam. *POSITION*—Street and avenue tree; specimen tree; grouping tree.

MEADOW RUE—(THALICTRUM).

MEDITERRANEAN HEATHER—(ERICA).

MELALEUCA — (SMALL-FLOWERED BOTTLE BRUSH).
Evergreen. 4-12 feet or more. Sun and slight shade. Large, bushy, quick growing shrubs; linear to lanceolate, sometimes colored leaves; short spikes like small bottle brushes of white or bright-colored flowers with long exserted stamens, blooming in summer or fall; hard, persistent seed capsules. *PROPAGATION* — Usually by medium-hard shoots in May; occasionally by seeds. *CULTURE*—Adapted to a variety of soils; drought and alkali resistant; grows well in both sandy and stiff

soils, fertilized with manure in fall. *GROUPING*—Specimen shrubs; fine hedge shrubs; good grouping shrubs, combining with Hypericum, Erica in variety and Diosma with M. ericifolia and M. armillaris, Myrtus in variety with M. hypericifolia and M. decussata, Leptospermum laevigatum with M. nesophila, and with species of the closely allied Metrosideros and Callistemon.

SPECIES—**M. armillaris.** Tall, smooth, very graceful shrub, with slender, arching branches; dark-green, narrowly linear leaves; creamy white flowers in cylindrical spikes, blooming June-October. **M. decussata.** Spreading gracefully with arching branches; small, close-set, bright-green leaves; very small spikes of lilac flowers, blooming August-October. **M. ericifolia.** Very gracefully arching, with heather-like, dark-green leaves; spikes of yellowish flowers blooming in September. **M. hypericifolia—Red Bottle Brush.** Broad shrub, with arching branches; lanceolate, bright-green, colored leaves; large spikes of brilliant red flowers, blooming in summer, but also intermittent. **M. nesophila.** Tall growing shrub, with thick, spongy bark; medium-sized, thick, leathery, gray-green leaves; small, lilac-rose flowers, blooming May-September. **M. wilsonii.** Linear leaves and red flowers, blooming in summer.

MELIA AZEDARACH, variety UMBRACULIFORMIS—(TEXAS UMBRELLA TREE). Deciduous. 20-30 feet. Sun. Erect, round-headed, very compact tree; large, compound leaves; graceful racemes of fragrant, blue flowers, blooming in spring; fruit a yellowish drupe. *PROPAGATION*—Readily by seeds; cuttings of ripe shoots under glass with bottom heat. *CULTURE*—Grows in most soils, and at quite low temperatures. *POSITION*—Used as street tree, and as shade tree.

MERTENSIA VIRGINICA — (VIRGINIA BLUE BELLS). Perennial. 1-2 feet. Sun or shade. Very smooth, leafy plant; leaves rounded to oblong; loose panicle of small, slender, trumpet-shaped, bright-blue flowers, blooming in April-May. *PROPAGATION*—Division of clumps in January-February; seeds sown in spring, blooming the second year. *CULTURE*—Requires a rich, moist, light loam. *GROUPING*—Naturalizes easily under woods; used in the mixed flower border, combining with Erythronium, Daffodil and Narcissus, Lenten Rose, Iris cristata, Columbine, Phlox subulata, Iceland Poppy.

MESEMBRYANTHEMUM—(FIG MARIGOLD). Annual and perennial. From a few inches high to several feet. Sun loving, some species in slight shade. Succulent, prostrate or erect herbs, often with thick, woody stems; usually opposite, three-angled, cylindrical or flat, sometimes glandular-dotted leaves; small to large, delicately tinted or brilliantly colored, white and shades of red, rose, yellow, fluffy, terminal flowers, blooming profusely in fall and winter, but almost continuous throughout year in California. *PROPAGATION*—Seeds sown in spring; most kinds easily by cuttings; division. *CULTURE*—Very drought resistant, and adapted to a variety of soils, especially to sandy loams. *POSITION*—Used for covering embankments, along sea shores, parkings, waste places, rockeries; the newer hybrids are frequently used in the flower border and in window boxes.

SPECIES—**M. aurantiacum.** Similar to M. roseum, but flowers having a beautiful combination of rose-gold-orange in flower. Depending upon position, either trailing, or grows into a perfect sphere. **M. crystallinum—Ice Plant.** Procumbent, with rather flat, ovate leaves, covered with glistening dots and elevations; small white to rose flowers. **M. edule.** Stout growing plant with large thick, fleshy leaves, and large yellow or purple flowers, much used for holding sand. **M. roseum.** Making a dense mat of wiry stems and small, cylindrical leaves; very numerous, rose to magenta-colored flowers.

MEXICAN ORANGE—(CHOISYA TERNATA).

MEXICAN SHELL FLOWER—(TIGRIDIA).

MEXICAN TULIP POPPY — (HUNNEMANNIA).

MICHAELMAS DAISY — (PERENNIAL ASTER—See ASTER).

MICHELIA (MAGNOLIA) FUSCATA—(BANANA SHRUB). Evergreen. 10-15 feet. Sun. Related to the Magnolia. Young growths brown-pubescent; leaves elliptic-lanceolate, smooth at maturity; small, brown-yellow flowers edged with carmine, having a bananalike fragrance, blooming April-June. *PROPAGATION*—Seeds; usually by ripened wood cuttings under glass with bottom heat. *CULTURE*—Sheltered position; plant in a rich, moist, garden loam. *GROUPING*—Planted in the shrub border, grouping with Pittosporum tobira, Choisya ternata, Leucothoe catesbaei, Ceratonia, Escallonia in variety, Eugenia myrtifolia, Magnolia soulangeana.

MIGNONETTE—(RESEDA).

MIRABILIS JALAPA — (FOUR-O'CLOCK). Perennial, usually treated as an annual. 2-3 feet. Sun. Erect, bushy plant, with large and fleshy, Dahlialike root; smooth, ovate-lanceolate leaves; tubular, fragrant flowers, red, white, yellow, or variegated, blooming July-August. *PROPAGATION*—Seed sown May-June; division of clumps in fall. *CULTURE*—Grows in ordinary, moderately fertilized soils. *POSITION*—Hedge plant; as filler in flower border.

MIRROR SHRUB—(COPROSMA).

MOCK ORANGE—(PHILADELPHUS CORONARIUS) — (PITTOSPORUM UNDULATUM).

MONKSHOOD—(ACONITUM).

MOONFLOWER—(IPOMOEA).

MONTBRETIA—(TRITOMA).

MORNING GLORY — (IPOMOEA) — (CONVOLVULUS TRICOLOR).

MORUS ALBA—(WHITE MULBERRY). Deciduous. 20-30 feet. Sun. Round-headed tree, with grayish yellow branches; rather small, light-green, variable, smooth leaves; small white flowers blooming in June; small white or violet, sweet fruits. *PROPAGATION*—Seeds; cuttings of any part of tree rooting easily in fall or spring. *CULTURE*—Grows well in any soil. *POSITION*—Street and avenue tree; specimen tree.

SPECIES—**M. alba pendula — Weeping Mulberry.** Lower growing than type; grafted upon type.

MOUNTAIN BLUET—(CENTAUREA MONTANA).

MOUNTAIN LAUREL—(KALMIA).

MUEHLENBECKIA COMPLEXA — (MATTRESS VINE) — (WIRE VINE) — (MAIDENHAIR VINE). Evergreen vine. 15 feet or more. Sun and partial shade. Rapid growing, making a dense growth, with wirelike, black stems; small, dark-green, smooth, oval leaves; inconspicuous flowers. *PROPAGATION*—Cuttings of short side shoots in summer; layering. *CULTURE*—Grows easily in any soil and under any conditions; fertilize with manure. *POSITION*—Used as screen to cover up unsightly places; on embankments; to form hedge effects.

MULBERRY—(MORUS).

MUSCARI BOTRYOIDES—(GRAPE HYACINTH). Bulbous plant. 6-9 inches. Best in sun, but endures slight shade. Forming good-sized clumps, with radical, linear, glaucous leaves; naked scapes bearing very dense racemes of violet blue to pure blue flowers, blooming February-May. *PROPAGATION*—Seeds sown in spring; offsets planted October-December. *CULTURE*—Grows easily in an ordinary, well fertilized garden loam; may be left in ground for some time before lifting and dividing. *GROUPING*—Border plant; in rockeries; in the bulb and mixed borders, combining with Gold Tuft, Polyantha Primrose, Yellow and Orange Freesias, Dutch Hyacinths, Cape Marigold, Yellow Violas, Mignonette.

MYOSOTIS—(FORGET-ME-NOT). Annual and perennial. 6-12 inches. Sun and half shade. Usually low, creeping plants, often forming dense mats; hairy, dark or light green, lanceolate leaves; short racemes of small, salver-shaped, white, purplish, light to dark-blue flowers, blooming in California in January and February, but in other regions in late spring or early summer. *PROPAGATION*—All kinds seed themselves readily, otherwise sow in fall or early spring; divide clumps of perennials in fall and spring. *CULTURE*—Adapted to all ordinary soils, but favor rich, moist, light, moderately fertilized soils. *GROUPING* — Naturalize readily; group in the flower border with Spring Snowflake, Crocus, Jonquils, Narcissi, Winter Blooming Oxalis, White Dutch Hyacinth.

MYRTUS—(MYRTLE). Evergreen. 2-12 feet, according to kind. Sun and moderate shade. Bushy, symmetrical shrubs, with smooth, glossy, dark-green, ovate to lanceolate leaves; axillary and terminal, very fragrant, white or cream-colored flowers, blooming June-August, but intermittent with some species. *PROPAGATION* — Usually by partially ripened cuttings; ripened cutting in fall; varieties of Myrtle either by cuttings or grafted. *CULTURE*—Favors a rich, light, well drained loam, fertilized with manure; give plenty of water during dry summers; subject to scale (see Plant Pests). *GROUPING*—Accent shrub in formal plantings, especially the dwarf species; foundation plantings; informal shrub border; low hedges for courts. Group different species with each other, and with Small-leaved Veronicas, Diosma, Gardenia, Huckleberry, Bush Honeysuckle, Eugenia myrtifolia, Melaleuca decussata, Pimelea, Ceanothus cyaneus.

SPECIES — **M. communis — Common Myrtle.**

8-10 feet. Loose growing, with scented leaves; very fragrant, cream-white flowers, blooming in summer and intermittently; blue-black berries. **M. communis microphylla — Dwarf Myrtle.** 3-3½ feet. Compact, round-headed shrub; small, dark-green leaves; waxy white flowers, red in bud. The variety **compacta** of the latter is 2 feet high. **M. luma (Eugenia apiculata).** 4-6 feet. Erect, very floriferous shrub, loosely branching; very dark-green, almost blackish, round leaves; very fragrant cream-white flowers, blooming June-August and intermittently; purplish black fruits; **M. ugni—Chilean Guava.** 4-5 feet. Round-headed, compact shrub; small, roundish, very dark-green leaves, bronzy-tinted; cream-white flowers; edible, bronze-purple fruits.

N

NAEGELIA GESNERIA — (NAEGELIA). Bulbous plant. 1-2 feet. Sun and slight shade. Rhizomatous roots; soft-textured, cordate leaves; long, swollen-tubular, red, yellow, white flowers, blooming prolifically in winter, but also almost continuously. *PROPAGATION*—Easily by division of rhizomes planted October-December. *CULTURE*—Ordinary, rich, well drained garden loam. *GROUPING*—For the flower border, combining with the Kafir Lily, Narcissus, Helleborus, Tritonia, Purple Stocks, African Golden Orange Daisy.

NANDINA DOMESTICA — (SACRED BAMBOO OF JAPAN). Evergreen. 5-8 feet or more. Partial or complete shade; not too strong sun. Erect, much branched shrub; the compound leaves arranged in whorls, spreading horizontally, ruddy tinged, the young growth in spring a brilliant red; large trusses of white flowers, blooming in fall; scarlet berries where warm enough. *PROPAGATION*—Usually by seeds; cuttings; rooted stems. *CULTURE*—Requires a rich, light, porous soil. *GROUPING*—Foundation plantings; specimen shrub; in the Japanese and naturalistic gardens. Group with ferns, Azaleas, Japanese conifers, and with the general run of shade shrubs and plants.

NARCISSUS — (DAFFODIL). Bulbous plant. 12-16 inches. Usually sun, but some kinds, especially the Narcissi, will bloom in moderate shade. Leaves strap-shaped, linear; one to several flowers, borne on a scape rising from bulb, the perianth consisting of six equal segments, ascending, spreading, or reflexed, the throat bearing a corona or crown which is long and tubular, or short and cup-shaped. Flowers white, various shades of yellow, orange or red in the ring type of Narcissus, blooming December-April, according to kind. *PROPAGATION*—Natural division; plant bulbs September-December; seeds for new varieties. *CULTURE*—Ideal conditions are: well drained soil, preferably on a slope; a medium heavy loam with surface mulch of manure in fall; leave bulbs in ground for three to four years to multiply; then take up, divide, prepare soil for replanting; fertilize with bone meal just before blooming; do not remove leaves before withered; subject to bulb rot (due to standing water) and to aphis (see Plant Pests). *GROUPING*—Naturalize some species of Narcissus and Jonquils in the wild garden; plant in bold clumps, in front of shrubbery, or combine in the mixed border with Primula malacoides, Violas, Cornflowers, purple and lavender Stocks, Forget-me-not, Winter Aconite, Winter Blooming Iris.

TYPES—**Trumpet Daffodil.** The trumpet or crown is as long or longer than the perianth segments, with the perianth sometimes varying in color from the trumpet, in white and yellow tones. Example: Emperor. **Incomparabilis.** Short, cuplike yellow coronas. Cup or crown less than or nearly equal to length of perianth segments. Example: Sir Watkin.

Small yellow or white corona; white or yellow perianth. Cup or crown less than one-third length of perianth segments. Example: Barii conspicuus. **Leedsii.** Perianth white; short cup or crown, white, cream, or pale citron; fragrant. Example: Mrs. Langtry. **Jonquil.** Reedlike foliage, with scapes 2-4 flowered; rich golden-yellow, very fragrant flowers. Example: Campernelle. **Poeticus—Poets Narcissus.** Pure white perianth and small flat, yellow corona edged with scarlet; very fragrant. Example: Poeticus recurvus—Pheasants Eye. **Tazetta.** Polyantha type. 4-8 flowers on a stem. Example: Paper White Narcissus. **Poetaz.** 4-6 flowers to stem. Like the Poeticus, but with white or creamy yellow perianth and yellow or orange corona; very fragrant. **Double.** Yellow flowers. Example: Von Sion. **N. bulbocodium—Hoop-Petticoat Daffodil.** Slender plant with long, solitary, funnel-shaped, bright-yellow flowers with thin corona.

NASTURTIUM—(TROPAEOLUM).

NATAL PLUM—(CARISSA).

NATIVE BLUE PALM—(ERYTHEA).

NEEDLE ACACIA — (ACACIA VERTICILLATA).

NEEDLE-LEAF HAKEA—(HAKEA SUAVEOLENS).

NELUMBIUM (SPECIOSUM). Commonly called, but erroneously, **Egyptian Lotus.** Large, bulky, aquatic plant, growing from thick rhizomes; large, thick, dark-green, peltate, twisted leaves, rising above the water; large, rather globular, fragrant, pink, white, or reddish flowers, rising well above the water, blooming in summer. *PROPAGATION*—Division of rhizome just after growth has started; seeds. *CULTURE*—Requires rich, well fertilized soil, growing well in mud. *POSITION*—Suited best to growing in large pools.

NEMESIA STRUMOSA — (NEMESIA). Annual. 8-12 inches. Bushy, floriferous plant; smooth, dark-green, linear-lanceolate leaves; terminal racemes of medium-sized, purselike flowers, in rich colors, blooming April-September. *PROPAGATION* —Seed sown January-July for succession of flowers. *CULTURE*—Grows best in rich, well fertilized, light garden loam. *GROUPING*—Plant in annual and mixed borders, combining with Arctotis, Clarkia, Phacelia, Salpiglossis, Snapdragons, Arabis, Anemone, Ranunculus.

NEPETA MUSSINI — (CATNIP). Perennial. 8-12 inches. Sun and slight shade. Spreading, leafy plant; small, heart-shaped, gray-green leaves; dense racemes of small, two-lipped, lavender-blue flowers, blooming May-August. *PROPAGATION*—Division of clumps October-January; cuttings of half firm wood; seeds sown January-May. *CULTURE*—Grows in any soil, but prefers a moderately rich, light loam; cats eat the leaves; cut back in fall. *GROUPING*—Very useful as border plant or in the flower border, combining with French Marigold, Guinea Flower, Gaillardia, Dimorphotheca, Iceland Poppy, Calliopsis, Peruvian Lily, Hemerocallis.

NERIUM—(OLEANDER). Evergreen. 6-20 feet. Sun loving, requiring heat to flower well. Much branched, gracefully arching shrub; thick, dark-green, smooth, shining, long and tapering leaves; in whorls; great clusters of large, regular, salver-shaped, crinkly, single and double flowers in white and rich colors, blooming June-September. *PROPAGATION*—Easily by ripened wood of shoots after blooming period. *CULTURE* — Requires a rich, well drained, light loam, fertilized with manure; do not over-water; prune carefully to prevent breaking; prune heavily and top after third year; subject to mealy bug and scale. *POSITION*—Best effect by themselves, or with large-leaved foliage shrubs; parkings; hedge shrub. Does best in interior valley.

SPECIES—**N. odorum — Sweet-Scented Oleander.** Similar to above but not so robust in growth. **New Zealand Flax—(Phormium).**

NICOTIANA AFFINIS — (FLOWERING TOBACCO). Perennial. 2-5 feet. Sun and partial shade. Erect, pubescent, sparsely branching; large, lance-elliptic, sessile, light-green leaves; long, wandlike stems bearing racemes of very fragrant, long-tubular, star-shaped, white, pink, rose, purple flowers, opening late afternoon, blooming from May well into fall. *PROPAGATION*—Seeds sown March-June; seeds itself. *CULTURE*—Grows best in rich, moist, light loam. *GROUPING*—Plant in mixed and perennial borders, combining with Shasta Daisy, Clarkia, Godetia, Petunias, light blue Delphinium, Columbine, Coral Bells.

SPECIES—**N. alata.** Pure white, night-scented flowers. **Sanderae Hybrids.** Day blooming, in a variety of colors. **N. tabacum—Tobacco.** Annual. 6-8 feet. Very large leaves and white flowers; specimen plant and background of perennial border.

NIEREMBERGIA—(CUP-FLOWER). Perennial, shrubby plant. 6 inches-3 feet, according to species. Sun and moderate shade. Much branched plant, with creeping or semi-erect, slender stems; scattered, linear leaves; tubular, white, tinted lilac or blue flowers, with corolla rotate, blooming prolifically in summer, but quite continuous. *PROPAGATION*—Seeds and cuttings of half firm wood in spring and fall; division of creeping stems. *CULTURE*—Does best in light, moist, moderately fertilized loam. *GROUPING*—For the rockery and the mixed border, combining with Scabiosa caucasica, Pentstemon, Coreopsis, Salvia pitcheri, Aubrietia, Coral Bells, Perennial Lupine. The dwarf species are planted in rockeries and in hanging baskets.

NIGHTBLOOMING CEREUS — (CEREUS GRANDIFLORUS). (See Cactus and Movie.)

NIGHTBLOOMING JASMINE — (CESTRUM NOCTURNUM).

NIGHTSHADE—(SOLANUM).

NORDMANNS FIR—(ABIES NORDMANNIANA).

NORWAY MAPLE—(ACER PLATANOIDES).

NYMPHAEA ODORATA — (WATER LILY). Perennial aquatic. Leaves and flowers floating, spreading 2-5 feet or more. Sun loving, but endures slight shade. Growing from a stout root stock or tuber; long stems bearing at the tips large, flat, roundish or heart-shaped, cleft, bright-green leaves, often reddish beneath; medium to large-sized, fragrant flowers, pure white, and shades of cream, pink, yellow, blue, red, blooming as early as April in California, continuing until late in fall. *PROPAGATION*—Division of clumps preferably February-May according to region; seeds. *CULTURE*—Well adapted for planting in large or small pools and ponds. Small sections of the root stock are planted either in pots or in large redwood boxes; there should be at least a foot of water over the top of the container; planted in soil well enriched with rotted cow manure and a little bone meal; cut off old leaves and flowers; after three or four years' time take up and divide. In most parts of California it is unnecessary to remove plants during winter; in very cold regions the plants are moved to tanks or tubs under glass, or to a separate covered pool. Subject to aphis, leaf minor, leaf spot (see Plant Pests). North America contains many interesting species, and there are many hybrids, varying in their degree of adaptability to different regions.

O

OAK—(QUERCUS).

OENOTHERA BIENNIS GRANDIFLORA (LAMARCKIANA) — (EVENING PRIMROSE). Biennial. 2-6 feet. Sun and partial shade. Erect, stout, branching plant; long, smooth, bright-green, lanceolate-oblong, sessile leaves; large, fragrant, narrow-tubular, bright-yellow flowers; opens at twilight, blooming June-October. *PROPAGATION*—Seeds sown best in early fall, also in early spring; seeds self-sown; cuttings. *CULTURE*—Grows in any moderately rich garden soil. *GROUPINGS*—Splendid in the background of the perennial border, combining with Canterbury Bells, Chimney Bellflower, Anchusa, Lupine, Hemerocallis, Calla Lilies, Statice latifolia.

OLEA AQUIFOLIUM — (OSMANTHUS AQUIFOLIUM).

OLEA EUROPAEA COMMUNIS — (OLIVE). Evergreen. 10-20 feet or more. Sun, and in partial shade for ornament. Bushy, round-headed tree, gray-green throughout; small, lanceolate, willowlike leaves; inconspicuous flowers; ovoid black drupe. *PROPAGATION*—Seeds; grafting of desired variety upon seedlings; usually by cuttings taken from tree in dormant state in January or February. *CULTURE*—Thrives in any kind of well drained, rich soil, fertilized with manure. *POSITION*—Fine specimen tree for patio gardens; lawn plantings; in large shrub borders; as avenue and street tree, the gnarled and twisted trunk and branches of an old tree being very picturesque.

OLEANDER—(NERIUM).

OLEASTER — (ELAEAGNUS ANGUSTIFOLIA).

OLIVE—(OLEA EUROPAEA).

ORANGE, LEMON and other **CITRUS FRUITS.** Evergreen. 6-15 feet. Sun and slight shade. Compact, usually round headed shrubs, with glossy, large, smooth, light to deep green, elliptical or oval leaves; clusters of medium-sized, regular, very fragrant white flowers, often pink or red-tinted in bud, blooming indeterminately according to kind; small to large, orange, yellow and red, round, flat and oblong fruits. *PROPAGATION*—Easily by cuttings of young shoots or of half ripened wood; seeds; grafting. *CULTURE*—Requires a rich, light, well drained loam, fertilized with manure; subject to mealy bug; scale, aphis; black fungus (see Plant Pests). *POSITION*—Valuable in patio and Spanish gardens, and in some kinds of foundation plantings. Grown in tubs or planted out where warm enough. Excellent as avenue and street trees. Group only with shrubs having broad leaves.

ORANGE CESTRUM—(CESTRUM AURANTIACUM).

ORANGE SUNFLOWER—(HELIOPSIS).

OREGON GRAPE—(MAHONIA).

ORIENTAL PLANE TREE — (PLANTANUS ORIENTALIS).

ORNITHOGALUM ARABICUM—(STAR OF BETHLEHEM). Bulbous plant. 1-2 feet. Sun. Erect, with very narrow, glaucous green leaves; regular, somewhat urn-shaped flower with black base, blooming April-May. *PROPAGATION*—Offsets from bulbs, planted October-November; seeds. *CULTURE*—Requires rich, light, well fertilized loam. *GROUPING*—Interesting in the mixed border, combining with Iris in variety, Tulips, Mariposa Lily, Brodiæas, Mission Bells.

SPECIES—**O. umbellatum.** 6-12 inches. Short racemes, many flowered, of small white flowers; used largely in naturalizing.

OSMANTHUS AQUIFOLIUM (OLEA AQUIFOLIUM)--(JAPANESE HOLLY). Evergreen. 10-20 feet. Grows in sun, but best in partial shade. Erect, very compact shrub; large, dark-green, shining, oblong-elliptic, Hollylike leaves, spiny at upper margin; axillary clusters of small, white, regular, very fragrant flowers, blooming in June-July, and quite continuous; bluish drupe fruits. *PROPAGATION*—Cuttings of half-ripened wood in late summer under glass. *CULTURE*—Grows in sheltered position in ordinary garden soil. *GROUPING*—Foundation plantings and in shrub border, grouping with Cestrum aurantiacum, Catalina Cherry, Hypericum, Mahonia, Daphne, Spiraeas, Escallonias, Pittosporum tobira.

OXALIS. Some annuals, but usually with bulbous, tuberous, or perennial root stock. 4-6 inches. Partial shade. Rapidly spreading plant, with reddish stems; cloverlike, digitately compound, bright-green leaves; medium-sized, rose, pink, white flowers, blooming in January-March. *PROPAGATION*—Usually by division in September-December; seeds in fall and spring. *CULTURE*—Grows in moderately rich, light, moist soil. *POSITION*—Used as ground cover.

SPECIES—**Summer Blooming Oxalis.** Rose and white flowers blooming in summer, but spasmodically in other seasons.

OX-EYE—(HELIOPSIS).

P

PACHYSANDRA TERMINALIS. Evergreen, 6-12 inches. Full or partial shade. Spreading, forming a dense mat; thick, glossy, bright-green, wedge-shaped leaves; terminal spikes of small white flowers blooming in May. *PROPAGATION*—Easily by division. *CULTURE*—Grows well in most fairly light soils. *POSITION*—Fine ground cover plant; in rockeries.

PAEONIA — (PEONY). Herbaceous perennial, growing from a fleshy root stock. 2-3 feet. Sun and slight shade. Stout stem, with long, light to dark-green, pinnately compound or dissected leaves; large, terminal, double and semi-double flowers, in many colors and many varieties, blooming in May-June. *PROPAGATION* — Root cuttings; stem cuttings; seeds, sown in September. *CULTURE*—Requires rich garden loam, well fertilized with manures, with an abundant supply of water; liquid manure is good. Subject to stem-rot; burn infected plants. *POSITION*—Best planted by themselves, in the foreground of the shrub border, in large flower borders.

SPECIES—**P. moutan—Tree Peony—Chinese Peony.** 3-3½ feet. Sun. Bushy plants, with dark-green, lanceolate-ovate leaves; large single, or double flowers in many colors, sometimes measuring 12 inches across, blooming in May. *PROPAGATION*—Varieties usually grafted upon P. moutan, or upon P. officinalis; cuttings taken with heel in summer; layering; root grafts in early fall. *CULTURE*—Requires a rich, moist, well drained soil, adding well rotted cow manure or liquid manure. *POSITION*—Plant in beds by themselves, in front of background of dark-green shrubs.

PAINTED DAISY—(PYRETHRUM).

PALM — (CHAMAEROPS) — (ERYTHEA)—(PHOENIX).

PAMPAS GRASS—(CORTADERIA).

PANSY—(VIOLA TRICOLOR).

PAPAVER—(POPPY). Annual and perennial. 6 inches-4 feet, according to kind. Erect plants, with usually hispid, coarsely toothed, pinnatifid leaves; small to large globular, brightly colored flowers, blooming in spring and summer. *PROPAGATION*—Seeds sown in fall or early spring, blooming the same year; division of roots with perennials August-December. *CULTURE*—All kinds require a well drained, moderately rich, light loam, not too moist.

SPECIES—**P. orientale—Oriental Poppy.** Perennial. 3-4 feet. Stout, leafy stem, rough, hairy, large leaves; very large, terminal flowers, the type scarlet with a black eye and purple stamens, also salmon, red, orange, pale pink, blooming April-July. *GROUPING*—For the perennial border, grouping, according to color harmonies, with Pot Marigolds, Purple Sage, Rehmannia, purple and bronze Iris, red and orange Tulips, Star of Bethlehem, Spanish Iris,

Ixias. **P. nudicaule—Iceland Poppy.** Perennial. 1-1½ feet. Usually treated as annual. Slender stemmed, with a tuft of deeply pinnatifid, bright-green leaves; leafless stems bearing single, medium large, delicately fragrant flowers, white, and in light yellow and orange, orange-scarlet, rose-pink, blooming April-July. *CULTURE*—Requires an open, sunny situation in open, porous soil. *GROUPING*—Effective by themselves, or grouped in the mixed border with Myosotis, Cornflower, yellow and orange Snapdragon, Violas, Gold Tuft, Aubrietia, Scilla, Narcissi, Lobelia. **P. rhoeas—Shirley Poppy.** Annual. 1-2 feet. Branching plant, with gray-green, finely divided leaves; more or less fringed flowers, white, through shades of pink to deep scarlet, blooming April-September. *PROPAGATION*—Seed sown in succession January-July. *CULTURE*—Thrive best in a sandy, moderately fertile loam. *GROUPING*—Very showy in large masses by themselves.

PAPYRUS ANTIQUORUM — (PAPYRUS PLANT). Perennial with woody rhizome. 10-15 feet. Sun and moderate shade. Erect, smooth, green, slender stems, long and sedgelike, and linear-lanceolate leaves, forming an umbrellalike top. *PROPAGATION*—Seed; division in fall and spring. *CULTURE*—Requires a rich, well fertilized, moist soil. *POSITION*—Grown near edges of pools, or partly submerged in water; in patio courts; at entrances of residences.

PARROTS BILL—(CLIANTHUS).

PASSIFLORA—(PASSION VINE). Evergreen vine. 10-20 feet or more. Sun and partial shade. Rampant in growth, climbing by tendrils; entire or digitately lobed or parted, glistening, light or dark-green leaves; usually large, axillary, tubular flowers, with flat, expanded corolla; colored yellow, pink, blue, green, or red, blooming through the fall, sometimes intermittently; colored, usually edible fruit. *PROPAGATION*—Easily by cuttings of young wood in summer. Seeds. *CULTURE*—Grows in any soil. *POSITION*—Good for covering screens; waste land; the Red Passion Vine for covering trellises, arbors, garages, etc.

SPECIES—**P. caerulea.** Greenish, white-blue-purple flowers. **P. jamesoni.** Bright-rose or coral-red flowers. **P. (tacsonia) manicata—Red Passion Vine.** Small, leathery, dark-green leaves; medium-sized, brilliant scarlet flowers. Many other interesting species, most of which grow well in California.

PEACH BELL—(CAMPANULA).

PEARL BUSH—(EXOCHORDA).

PELARGONIUM—(GERANIUM). Perennial of various habits of growth, variable in leaf and flower, being vinelike, spreading, or somewhat shrubby. 2-6 feet or more. Sun and partial shade, according to kind. The different types are described below. *PROPAGATION*—Usually by cuttings of half firm stem growth in spring, summer, or fall; division of roots with Pelargoniums; seeds of Common Geraniums, tending to seed themselves; buds inserted in sand. *CULTURE*—Grows in most ordinary, moderately fertilized soils; very hardy, but somewhat subject to frost injury. Pelargonium, especially, are susceptible to excessive heat or cold and to freezing temperatures; subject to aphis, stem rot (too much water), and to leaf spot, otherwise free from pests (see Plant Pests). *POSITION*—Pelargoniums and Geraniums in general are grown in pots, and, when weather is suitable, are inserted in soil, or are placed in porches, patios, courts, etc.; removed and given shelter during cold weather. The Single Geraniums in California are frequently planted in the open, growing well against walls, fences, and in protected shrub borders. Pelargoniums in the open should always have a sunny, protected situation. To insure success with potted plants, first put rooted cuttings into thumb pots, gradually transferring to 3, 4, 5, 6-inch pots respectively (see Garden Movie).

TYPES — **Hortorum Class — Common Bedding Geranium.** 1-4 feet, some climbing. Bushy, round-headed plants; medium to large-sized, thick, leathery, or velvety, roundish to peltate, sometimes particolored leaves; cymelike clusters of close-set, regular, showy, medium to large sized flowers, with rounded or obovate petals, white and vivid shades of pink, rose, crimson, to scarlet, and intermediate shades, blooming prolifically in summer and sporadically during other seasons. *POSITION*—Much used for bedding out, occasionally in the flower border, or in parkings. Rapid growing and hardy. **Single Geranium.** Shrubby or vinelike. Rapid growers, with stout green stems; large peltate, velvety, bright-green, crinkly margined leaves, sometimes variegated; large clusters of rather large flowers in shades of pink, salmon, red, scarlet, blooming prolifically in summer, but almost continuous in California. *POSITION*—Used in almost any position. **P. peltatum—Ivy-Leaved Geranium.** Making a quick, thickset, spreading, almost shrubby growth; medium-sized, shiny, dark-green, peltate leaves; many clusters of irregular, single and double, brilliant pink and red flowers, blooming continuously in California. Should be headed back occasionally. *POSITION*—Planted over walls, embankments, in window boxes, hanging baskets, against trellises, etc. **Pelargonium or Domestic Type.** 2-4 feet. Straggly, upright in growth, with stiff, woody stems; medium large, somewhat folded up, dark-green, triangular, incised, crinkly leaves; large, brilliantly colored or soft-tinted, irregular, finely textured, velvety flowers, varicolored, striped, and blotched, in white, and shades of pink, salmon, red, scarlet, crimson, blooming prolifically from late spring until late in fall. *CULTURE*—Must be pruned very carefully and given support. *POSITION*—Effective in the shrub border or planted in masses in the flower border; as potted plants for the patio garden, courts, etc. **Rose Geranium.** 3-5 feet. Bushy, shrublike plant, with very much incised, crinkly, sweet-scented, roundish leaves; small purplish flowers blooming continuously. According to scent of leaves, known as lemon, nutmeg, apple, etc. An old favorite of the garden. There are many other species and hybrid forms. An extended account of Geraniums and Pelargoniums is given in Bailey's Cyclopedia of Horticulture, and in Robert Sweet's work on "Geraniaceae" in five volumes, 1820-1830, containing over 500 colored plates of species and hybrids then in vogue.

PENTSTEMON GLOXINIOIDES — (PENTSTEMON). Perennial. 2-4 feet. Sun and partial shade. Fast growing, bushy plant, branching from the base; medium-sized, bright-green, shiny, ovate-lanceolate leaves; rather large, long-tubular flowers, red, pink, coral, lavender, and intermediate shades, blooming April-September. *PROPAGATION*—Seeds sown in early spring; division of clumps in spring and fall; cuttings of half hardy wood in spring, summer, and fall. *CULTURE*—Tolerant of most soils, including clay and adobe, but favors a well drained, rich, well fertilized soil; prune back in fall; subject to aphis, stem rot (see Plant Pests). *GROUPING*—Fine for the perennial and mixed borders, combining, according to color of variety, with Clarkia, Gilia, Nemesia, Delphinium, Rehmannia, Pyrethrum, Shasta Daisy, Verbena.

NATIVE SPECIES—Perennial. 6-12 inches. Sunny, dry situations. Many interesting kinds, suitable for rockeries and for the flower border, with narrow, dark-green leaves, and clusters of small, tubular flowers, brilliant violet-blue, pink, blue, purple, violet, blooming usually in summer and early fall. **P. barbatus torreyi.** 4 feet. Tufts of low growing foliage, and brilliant scarlet flowers, blooming in July.

PEONY—(PAEONIA).

PEPPER TREE—(SCHINUS).

PERENNIAL ASTER—(ASTER).

PERENNIAL FLAX—(LINUM PERENNE).

PERENNIAL LARKSPUR—(DELPHINIUM).

PERENNIAL PHLOX—(PHLOX DECUSSATA).

PERENNIAL SWEET PEA—(LATHYRUS LATIFOLIUS).

PERIWINKLE—(VINCA).

PERNETTYA MUCRONATA — (PERNETTYA). Evergreen. 1½-2 feet. Sun. Dense, much branched shrub; small, dark-green, smooth, shining, ovate leaves; very small, pink-white, globose-ovoid flowers, blooming in May-June; large, flat-topped berries, white, red, to purplish black. *PROPAGATION*—Seeds; cuttings of half ripened wood in summer under glass; layers and suckers. *CULTURE*—Does best in a light, acid peaty soil, kept moderately moist. *GROUPING*—Potted plants; in the rock garden; foundation plantings; in the shrub border, grouping with Dwarf Cotoneasters, Pimelea, low growing Barberries, Heathers (Erica), small-leaved Veronicas, Azara, Lonicera nitida, Dwarf Myrtle, and other species of Myrtus.

PERUVIAN DAFFODIL—(HYMENOCALLIS).

PERUVIAN LILY—(ALSTROMERIA).

PETUNIA HYBRID. Annual, but more or less perennial in California. 1-2½ feet. Sun and slight shade. Semi-erect or trailing plants, with stout, viscid-pubescent stem; rather thick, light to dark-green, oblong-oval leaves; small, medium-sized to large, salver-formed, fragrant flowers, variously colored, striped, or blotched, blooming from May until cut down by frost. *PROPAGATION*—Seeds sown in early spring; cuttings of hybrids. *CULTURE*—Requires rich, light, well fertilized soils to produce large flowers, but will tolerate relatively poor soils; prefers sunny situations; cut back old flowering branches; subject to aphis (see Plant Pests). *GROUPING*—Fine in mass plantings on embankments, but also used in flower border, combining with Larkspur, Verbena, Snapdragons, Scabiosa in variety, Anemone coronaria, Gladiolus, Delphinium, Cineraria.

TYPES—**Giant Ruffled** and **Fringed Petunias.** Large flowers, gorgeously colored, frequently delicately veined, with some of the weaker seedlings coming double. Suitable for pot culture as well as for the flower border. **P. nana erecta.** Represented by Rosy Morn, Heavenly Blue, etc., with rather small blooms, blooming prolifically for most of the year; used for edgings; in the foreground of the shrub border; in parkings; along driveways. **Balcony** or **Trailing Petunias.** Less bushy than the other Petunias, with small, gay-colored, white, blue, and pink flowers.

PFITZERS JUNIPER — (JUNIPERUS PFITZERIANA).

PHEASANT'S EYE—(DIANTHUS PLUMARIUS)—(NARCISSUS POETICUS).

PHILADELPHUS CORONARIUS—(MOCK ORANGE)—(SYRINGA). Deciduous. 8-10 feet. Sun loving, enduring moderate shade. Gracefully drooping shrub, with rather stout branches; large, variable, thickish, dark-green, ovate-lanceolate leaves; dense racemes of regular, very fragrant, creamy white, single and semi-double flowers, blooming in May-June. *PROPAGATION*—Seeds sown in spring; often self-sown; hard wood cuttings in fall; suckers and green wood cuttings of some varieties; easily by layering. *CULTURE*—Grows in a variety of soils, but prefers a rich, light loam; prune after flowering. *POSITION*—Inserted occasionally in the shrub border, it presents a most delightful spring effect, and fills the garden with a delicious fragrance. Many interesting species and varieties.

PHLOX. Annual and perennial. 6 inches to 4 feet, according to kind. Creeping and erect forms, smooth or pubescent; leaves variable; salver-shaped flowers in bright colors, blooming in spring, summer, or early fall, according to kind. Representative species are described in detail below.

SPECIES—**P. decussata (paniculata) — Perennial Phlox.** 2-4 feet. Stout stems bearing long, dark-green, smooth, oblong-lanceolate leaves; great trusses of soft to brilliantly colored flowers, white, pink, salmon, scarlet, and intermediate colors, blooming June-November. *PROPAGATION*—Root stocks divided in September-October; take divisions from outside of clump; seed. *CULTURE*—The secret of success in growing Perennial Phlox is to keep the soil moist during the dry season, to provide a mulch of straw manure, peat, or of leaf mold during winter and summer, and to supply manures in fall and well balanced fertilizers in spring; cut down after flowering; divide clumps every two or three years. *GROUPING*—One of the best perennials for the perennial and mixed borders, combining according to color, with Scabiosa in variety, Salvia pitcheri, Pentstemon, Pyrethrum, Michaelmas Daisy, Sweet Wil-

liam, Delphinium, Peach Bell, Petunias in variety. **P. amoena** and **P. subulata—Moss Pinks.** Rock plants forming low matty growths, with mosslike foliage and lavender-pink flowers, blooming in May-June. *PROPAGATION*—Seed sown in spring or by stem cuttings. *CULTURE*—Prefers a somewhat dry, light, porous soil, containing gritty material. Suitable also for the flower border as border plants. **P. divaricata laphami.** With lavender flowers, delighting in moist, shady locations. **Phlox drummondi—Annual Phlox.** 8-10 inches. Sun. Bushy, branching plant, with linear-lanceolate, bright-green leaves; many flowered clusters of bright-hued flowers in many colors, blooming July-October. *PROPAGATION*—Seed sown in March. *CULTURE*—Requires a rich, moist, well fertilized, light loam for best blooms. *GROUPING*—Used as a cover plant in rose beds; in the foreground of the shrub border; in large mass plantings in the flower border, or combined with Viscaria, Verbenas, Petunias, Gypsophila, Snapdragons, Nemesia, Pentstemon.

PHOENIX DACTYLIFERA—(DATE PALM). 20-30 feet under cultivation. Rapid growing, erect, with thick, hairy trunk; long, drooping fronds; thorny leaf stalks; small, yellow flowers; great clusters of small, brown, datelike fruits. *PROPAGATION*—Seeds sown in fall or spring. *CULTURE*—Grows in any soil, favoring sandy soil, fertilizing with manure; withstands slight freezing temperatures; cut off old fronds. *POSITION*—A very regal palm, suited where sub-tropical effects are desired on large estates, but not on small lawns; fine avenue and street tree; for grouping in extensive palm gardens.

SPECIES—**P. canariensis—Canary Island Palm.** Widely grown. Not quite so robust in growth, with slender, gracefully drooping fronds. **P. roebelenii—Dwarf Date Palm.** About 2 feet, with leaves a foot long; linear, soft, dark-green, shining, curved leaflets. Usually in pots in conservatories, hotel lobbies. *CULTURE*—Requires a moist, rich loam, and a sheltered, shaded situation. **P. reclinata.** 25 feet or more. Long, bright-green, rigid leaflets.

PHORMIUM TENAX — (NEW ZEALAND FLAX). Sub-tropical, perennial, shrubby plant. 10-15 feet. Sun and moderate shade. Stout, rigid, with very long, strap-shaped, radical, fibrous leaves, with margin and keel bright red or brownish; long, crooked, reddish purple flower stalk, bearing numerous reddish brown or yellow flowers in fall. *PROPAGATION*—Easily from division of clumps in fall or spring; seeds. *CULTURE*—Grows in any moderately rich, well drained loam; somewhat drought resistant. *POSITION*—Specimen plant; foundation plantings about Spanish residences; in patio gardens; in tubs.

SPECIES—Variety **atropurpureum.** Reddish purple foliage. Variety **veitchianum.** Broad, creamy white striped on a light-green background; variety **atropurpureum nanum.** Dwarf variety.

PHOTINIA (HETEROMELES) ARBUTIFOLIA — (TOYON) — (CALIFORNIA HOLLY)—(CHRISTMAS BERRY). 15-20 feet. Sun and partial shade. Rather symmetrical, bushy, round-headed shrub; large, dark-green, glossy under cultivation, sharply serrate, oblong-lanceolate leaves; large, broad trusses of small, regular, white flowers, blooming in June-July; large scarlet berries persistent through winter. *PROPAGATION*—Seeds sown in fall or spring; seeds self-sown; cuttings of half ripened wood under glass, producing the best plants. *CULTURE*—Grows in any well drained, rather light soil, fertilized with manure; subject to scale, red spider, caterpillars (see Plant Pests); better under cultivation than in native state. *GROUPING*—Foundation plantings; hedges; specimen tree on lawns; in the shrub border, grouping with Arbutus unedo, evergreen species of Prunus, Escallonias, Pittosporums, Catalina and California Cherries, Pyracanthas, Eugenia myrtifolia, Rhododendron californica, Oregon Grape, California Live Oak, Huckleberry.

SPECIES—**P. serrulata.** 10-20 feet. Erect, symmetrical shrub; large, oblong, shining, dark green but ruddy-tinted leaves, yellowish green beneath; large panicles of white flowers, blooming May-July; red berries. Placement, propagation, and soil requirements the same as for Toyon.

PHYLLOSTACHYS—(DENDROCALAMUS).

PHYSOSTEGIA VIRGINIANA — (FALSE DRAGON'S HEAD). Perennial. 1-4 feet. Sun, but best in slight shade. Erect, leafy plant; smooth, medium-sized, oblong, serrate leaves; funnel-shaped, gaping, rosy-pink, lilac, or white flowers, blooming June-October. *PROPAGATION*—Seeds sown in early spring, blooming the same year; division of clumps October-December and in spring; cuttings. *CULTURE*—Requires a rich, light, moist, well-fertilized loam. *GROUPINGS*—Plant in perennial border, combining with Nicotiana, Scabiosa caucasica, lilac and rose Pentstemon, Pyrethrum, Dianthus plumarius, Francosa ramosa, Foxglove, Lupine.

PICEA—(SPRUCE). Conifer. 10-30 feet or more under cultivation. Sun and partial shade. Similar to the Firs, with which they are frequently confused. Erect, symmetrical, pyramidal in growth; whorled, spreading branches; spirally arranged, small, dark-green, sometimes glaucous, flattened leaves; catkinlike, colored flowers; medium-sized, pendent, green or purplish cones. *PROPAGATION*—Seeds sown in spring; by grafting upon seedlings in spring or August. *CULTURE*—Adapted to a variety of soils, but best in a moderately moist, sandy, well fertilized loam; horizontally spreading roots. *POSITION*—Splendid specimen and grouping trees, with same uses as for Abies (which see).

SPECIES—**P. engelmannii—Engelmann Spruce.** Slender, spreading branches; slender, straight leaves. **P. excelsa—Norway Spruce.** Fast growing, with spreading branches and pendulous branchlets; short, dark-green, shining leaves. Many varieties, from very dwarf to tall growing forms. One of the best and hardiest conifers for the average garden. **P. pungens—Colorado Blue Spruce.** Existing in many forms, with bright yellowish-brown branches; rigid, incurved, bluish-green to silvery-white leaves. Should be grown in sheltered situation. **P. orientalis—Oriental Spruce.** Very compact, round headed tree, attaining 10-12 feet under cultivation; small, dark-green leaves.

PIMELEA DECUSSATA (FERRUGINEA) — (PIMELEA)—(RICE FLOWER). 3-4 feet. Sun and slight shade. Symmetrical, very floriferous, round headed, compact, much branched shrub; woody stems, with small, shining, bright-green, ovate-oblong leaves; small, pink flowers, crowded in terminal heads, blooming June-August. *PROPAGATION*—Cuttings of half ripened shoots with bottom heat in March. *CULTURE*—Requires a rich, light, well fertilized loam; stem is weak, tending to break off in heavy wind. *GROUPING*—Foundation plantings; low hedges for courts; specimen shrub in formal garden; for the shrub border, grouping with small-leaved Veronicas, Melaleuca decussata, Azara, small-leaved Barberries, Ericas (Heathers), Myrtus in variety, Pernettya.

PINCUSHION FLOWER—(SCABIOSA).

PINE—(PINUS).

PINK HEATHER—(ERICA).

PINK SAXIFRAGE—(SAXIFRAGA).

PINKS—(DIANTHUS).

PINUS—(PINE). Conifer. Dwarf to tall growing species. Sun and partial shade. Usually symmetrical and pyramidal when young, irregular and often picturesque when old; usually thick, rather rough bark, furrowed or in plates; whorled branches covered with needlelike leaves, arranged in clusters of 2-5, according to species; catkinlike, yellow, orange, or scarlet flowers; brownish, oblong, small to very long cones. *PROPAGATION*—Seeds sown in spring; veneer grafting for rare varieties. *CULTURE*—Usually very hardy, enduring extremes of temperature and a variety of soil conditions. *POSITION*—Specimen tree for lawns; grouping trees on large plantations, with themselves, with other conifers, and with deciduous trees.

SPECIES—**P. canariensis—Canary Island Pine.** A fine ornamental tree. 15-20 feet or more, forming a broad, round-headed top, the whorls of yellowish branches being at some distance apart; long, slender, flexible, light-green leaves in threes, 9-12 inches long; light-brown and glossy cones, 4-8 inches long. **P. coulteri.** Native. 15-20 feet under cultivation. Grayish bark and stout branches, forming a pyramidal head; stout, dark bluish-green leaves; pendent, yellowish-brown cones, 9-14 inches long. **P. densiflora—Japanese Red Pine.** Usually 12-15 feet under cultivation. Rather pyramidal, compact in growth, with orange-yellow branchlets; acute, slender, bright bluish green leaves in twos, 2½-5 inches long; grayish brown cones. **P. jeffreyi—Jeffreys Pine.** Native. 15-20 feet. Short, spreading, ascending, or pendulous branchlets, forming an open pyramidal or spire-like head; acute, pale green leaves, 5-8 inches long; light brown cones, 6-12 inches long. **P. montana—Swiss Mountain Pine.** Very variable in habit, from prostrate form to tall pyramidal tree; dark-brown branchlets; leaves in twos, acute, stout and crowded, dark-green, ¾-2 inches long. The variety **mughus** has twisted branches. Especially suitable for the rock garden, near a cataract, and in the Japanese garden. **P. pinea—Italian Stone Pine.** 12-15 feet under cultivation. Forms a broad, round-topped head, with long, horizontally spreading branches; pale brown branchlets; rigid, bright-green leaves in twos, 5-8 inches long; broadly ovate cones, 4-5½ inches long. **P. radiata—Monterey Pine.** Native. Fast growing up to 50-60 feet. Stout, spreading branches forming an irregular, round-topped head; with brown colored branchlets; thick, furrowed bark; acute, bright-green leaves in threes, 4-6 inches long; small ovate, brownish cones. Endures clay and adobe. **P. sylvestris—Scotch Pine.** Usually 20-30 feet. Pyramidal when young; spreading, frequently pendulous branches, with grayish-yellow branchlets; rigid, twisted, bluish-green leaves in twos, 1½-3 inches long; grayish or reddish cones, 1½-2½ inches long. **P. torreyana—Soledad Pine.** Native. 15-20 feet. Spreading and sometimes ascending branches, with glaucous, smooth, greenish or purplish branchlets; rigid, dark-green leaves in fives, 8-13 inches long; chocolate brown, broadly ovate cones, 4-6 inches long. *SHRUBS* and *CREEPING PLANTS* under Pines: Abelia, Nandina, English Ivy, some of the Pittosporums, Mahonias, English Laurel, Periwinkle, Rhamnus, Evergreen Dogwood, Pachysandra terminalis, Escallonia rubra.

PITTOSPORUM. Evergreen. 10-30 feet or more. Sun and partial shade. Symmetrical, compact, usually round-headed or pyramidal shrubs; smooth, glossy, entire leaves; regular, fragrant flowers, blooming, according to kind, throughout the year. *PROPAGATION* — Seeds sown in early spring; easily by cuttings of half ripened wood in spring. *CULTURE*—Grows well in most soils, but partial to rich, light, well fertilized loam; some species subject to mealy bug (see Plant Pests); thin out occasionally. *GROUPING*—Excellent as specimen trees for lawns; foundation plantings at corners and entrances; hedge shrubs. The Pittosporums in general have wonderful grouping qualities, combining with English Laurel, Portugal Laurel, Carolina Cherry, Choisya ternata, Veronicas, Myrtus communis, Coprosma, Euonymus, Pyracantha crenulata, Daphne, Rhododendron, Toyon, Raphiolepis, Escallonias, Evergreen Viburnums, and different species with each other.

SPECIES—**P. crassifolium—Karo Tree.** Erect, with young parts densely clothed with white or buff downy pubescence; obovate leaves, dark green above, gray beneath; wine or maroon-colored, fragrant flowers, blooming August-October; yellowish, globular fruits with red seeds. **P. eugenioides—Tarata Tree.** Very erect, pyramidal tree, slender branched; shining, yellowish green, elliptic oblong, undulate leaves; inconspicuous greenish-yellow flowers; yellow fruits. Remarkably hardy, making a tall hedge; grows in limestone shale. **P. phillyraeoides—Narrow-Leaved Pittosporum.** 10-20 feet. Slender, open tree, with drooping branches; long, light-green, linear leaves with undulate margins; yellow flowers blooming June-September. **P. rhombifolium—Queensland Pittosporum.** Pyramidal tree, with long, rhomboid, coarsely toothed leaves; white flowers, blooming June-September; bright orange-yellow fruits. **P. tenuifolium (nigricans)—Tawhihi Tree.** 20-40 feet. Dense, pyramidal tree; small, oblong, dark-green, shining, undulate-margined leaves; solitary, blackish flowers, blooming September-November. Susceptible to mealy bug. **P. tobira—Japanese Pittosporum.** 6-10 feet. Rather symmetrical, bushy shrub; thick, leathery, dark-green, shining leaves, pale green beneath; very fragrant white or yellowish flowers, in terminal umbels, blooming December-February; yellowish fruit. **P. undulatum — Victorian Box — Australian Mock Orange.** 20-40 feet. Symmetrical, dense, broad, round-headed tree; long, oval-oblong, dark-green, shining, wavy-margined leaves; very fragrant, orangelike, white flowers in clusters, blooming in winter, early spring, and summer; large, globose, light-orange fruits with reddish seeds. **P. viridiflorum—Cape Pittosporum.** 10-25 feet. Similar to the Japanese Pittosporum, but with greenish and yellowish flowers in dense, compound clusters, blooming December-February.

PLANE TREE—(PLATANUS).

PLANTING — TRANSPLANTING—(See Garden Movies).

PLANT PESTS. Here are a few practical suggestions on how to control the more serious pests that infect ornamental shrubs and plants. Fortunately, the majority of ornamentals are quite immune from pests, at least from serious pests, and, if soil conditions are right, and the plant is healthy, little difficulty is experienced in keeping down pests. However, this does not obviate the careful watching of plants and shrubs for any indications of diseases. Immediate control measures taken will prevent many serious troubles. College and State Experiment Stations will send various pamphlets upon measures of plant disease control upon application. Reliable companies handling fungicides and insecticides can supply pamphlets. It is usually inadvisable to prepare home-made remedies, as proprietary remedies are cheap and more reliable.

Every disease has a specific remedy, although certain preparations on the market are effective against several kinds of troubles. Insects are divided into several classes, according to method of attack: those with sucking mouth parts, causing girdling of plants, yellowing of leaves due to reduction of chlorophyll, resulting in the gradual death of plant; those with biting mouth parts, causing perforations in leaves, destruction of vegetative parts, frequently resulting in death of plant. A few ornamentals, notably Pyracantha angustifolia and several of the Cotoneasters, are attacked by bacterial organisms; the only practicable method of control is removal of infected parts, or complete eradication. Gummosis of Flowering Cherries is controlled by gouging out infected parts, treating with disinfectant, and painting over wound.

Sucking insects are controlled by the use of miscible oils, nicotine preparations, soaps, sulphur, pyrethrum, oily or resinous emulsions, and combinations of these substances. Nicotine preparations are effective against aphis (plant lice); frequently used in combination with volatile oils. Miscible oils and oil emulsions are effective against mealy bug, scale, red spider, mites, white fly, leaf hopper, thrips. Pyrethrum controls aphis, thrips, leaf hoppers. Whale oil soap is used as a spreader with Black Leaf 40 and pyrethrum. Sulphur in the form of lime sulphur controls scale on fruit trees. These preparations are termed contact insecticides.

Biting insects are controlled by poisoning insecticides, such as basic barium fluosilicate, lead arsenate, paris green, hellebore (powder). Effective against caterpillars and larvae of various insects, diabrotica (green ladybug), black slugs on Flowering Fruit Trees, codling moth, beetles, fruit flies, and other similar insects. Hellebore is effective against rose slug. Arsenicals are mixed with bran and some sweetened material in the control of sow and pill bugs, snails, cutworms, grasshoppers, army worms, earwigs, slugs, attacking herbaceous plants. Wire screens, slag, coarse, gritty materials, etc., are other means of protection against snails and slugs. Para-di-chloro-benzene is used to kill insects in soil and tree borers.

Fungicides are used in the control of parasitic fungous organisms, lower forms of plant life, indicating their presence by the white mycelium as in mildew, reproducing by spores (seedlike bodies). Fungi cause: wilting and drying up of vegetative parts; perforations in foliage; blighting and destruction of all parts of plant. Bordeaux mixture (lime and copper sulphate) is the standard remedy for mildew, peach leaf curl, scab, rust, leaf spot, blight, etc. Agricultural sulphur is used for mildew on roses and for red spider. Lime sulphur is used as a clean-up spray in winter for destroying both insect and fungous pests on ornamental and fruit trees. Copper carbonate and preparations of sulphur are also used. It has been discovered that some of the miscible oils are effective against some kinds of mildew.

It is a good practice to have enough of these remedies on hand to meet any emergency. Shrubs and trees subject to plant pests should be sprayed periodically, in fall, spring, and whenever necessary. Some insects, such as aphis, caterpillars and moths, appear during definite seasons; atmospheric conditions exert an influence; condition of plant determines resistance. Cover all parts of shrub or plant; prevent the occurrence of a pest rather than to try and effect a cure after plant becomes badly diseased. Washing off or syringing a shrub or vine will frequently eradicate a pest, especially aphis and mealy bug. Control of ants will also control mealy bug. Many troubles can be overcome by correcting improper soil conditions. Spray materials are applied either in the form of spray or as dust. Full directions are given on packages as to strengths to use; usually one teaspoon to a quart of water is sufficient. Large portable tank sprayers should be used for large gardens and for trees. A bellows duster is good for dusting with sulphur or with pyrethrum. Clean out spray tank with hot water after using. A good time to spray or dust herbaceous plants is early in the morning when dew is on the foliage; volatile oils are only effective on sunshiny days. Roses should be sprayed or dusted every two weeks during spring and summer, where mildew is prevalent.

PLATANUS ORIENTALIS — (ORIENTAL PLANE) — (SYCAMORE PLANE). Deciduous. May grow to 80 feet in height, but usually kept under 20 feet under cultivation. Sun and partial shade. Hardy, round-headed tree with short trunk; dull grayish or greenish white, thin bark, overlaid with darker blotches which peel off in large, thin plates; large, palmately lobed, bright-green leaves, hairy when young; small, greenish flowers in drooping heads, blooming in spring; one-seeded nutlets. *PROPAGATION*—Seeds; cuttings of ripened wood; green wood cuttings under glass; layering. *CULTURE*—Grows in either heavy or light soils, but best in rich, deep, moist loam. *POSITION*—Street tree; specimen tree; for the shrub border, grouping with deciduous trees. Very amenable to pruning.

SPECIES—**P. acerifolia.** Quite similar and is of garden origin.

PLATYCODON (WAHLENBERGIA) GRANDIFLORUM — (BALLOON FLOWER). Perennial. 1-3 feet. Sun and partial shade. Bushy plant; smooth, light-green, lanceolate leaves; large, open bell-like, violet-blue flowers, blooming in June-July, sometimes until September. *PROPAGATION*—Division of clumps February-May; seeds sown in early spring bloom the first year. *CULTURE*—Thrives in poor, dry soil; does well in well drained, moderately rich, sandy loam. *GROUPING*—For the perennial border, combining with Gladiolus primulinus, Peruvian Lily, Hemerocallis, Tritoma grandiflora, Evening Primrose, Coreopsis, Gaillardia. *SPECIES*—**P. japonicum.** Semi-double flowers.

PLEROMA— (TIBOUCHINA).

PLUM—(See Flowering Fruit Trees).

PLUMBAGO CAPENSIS — (PLUMBAGO). Evergreen shrubby vine. Sun and moderate shade. As a shrub spreads out 10 feet; as vine climbs 20 feet. Bushy, floriferous, slender-stemmed shrub; light-green, oblong-ovate leaves; short clusters of medium-sized, sky-blue, Phloxlike flowers, blooming June-November. *PROPAGATION*—Readily from cuttings of half firm wood in fall or spring. *CULTURE*—Grows on dry banks, but best in moist, well fertilized, light loam. *POSITION* — Used in the shrub border; against buildings or walls; on trellises, arbors; combine with Streptosolen; Genistas, Coronilla glauca, California and Catalina Cherries, Coprosma, orange-yellow Lantana, Ceratonia siliqua, Carpenteria.

SPECIES—**P. larpentae.** Perennial. 6 inches, but spreading; dark-green, lanceolate leaves; many indigo-blue flowers, blooming in September. *GROUPING*—For the perennial border, combining with Calendula, Geums, Coreopsis, French Marigold, Hemerocallis, Gold Tuft, Yellow Viola.

PLUME CYPRESS—(CHAMAECYPARIS PISIFERA PLUMOSA).

POINSETTIA—(EUPHORBIA).

POLIANTHES TUBEROSA — (TUBEROSE). Bulbous plant. 2-3½ feet. Sun. Stout growing plant; long, narrow, bright-green, basal leaves; spikes of pure wavy white, very fragrant, narrowly funnel-shaped flowers, blooming during the summer, and intermittently. *PROPAGATION*—Usually by offsets, planting from February-June. *CULTURE*—Grows in ordinary, enriched garden loam. Requires plenty of heat and moisture. *POSITION*—For the flower border, combining with a large number of bulbous and flowering plants.

POLYGALA DALMAISIANA — (POLYGALA). Evergreen. 4-6 feet. Best in partial shade. Bushy, round-headed shrub; glistening, medium-sized, oval leaves; short racemes of pea-shaped, purplish, rosy-lilac flowers, blooming profusely in summer, but almost continuous. *PROPAGATION*—Best by layering; cuttings. *CULTURE*—Grows best in rich, moist, light loam, fertilized with manure. *GROUPING*—Specimen shrub; shrub border, grouping with Genistas, Hypericum, Spanish Broom, Coprosma, Euonymus, English Laurel, Carolina Cherry.

POLYGONUM AUBERTII — (SILVER LACE VINE). Evergreen. 25 feet. Rapid growing vine, bushy; variable, reddish-brown or pale green leaves; small, white, rose or green flowers in long, slender, axillary panicles. *PROPAGATION*—Easily by seeds; division. *CULTURE*—Grows in any soil, but best in rich, light loam. *POSITION*—Useful for quick, abundant growth as screens, for covering porches, outhouses, arbors, etc.

POMEGRANATE—(PUNICA).

POOR MAN'S ORCHID—(SCHIZANTHUS) —(IRIS).

POPPY—(PAPAVER).

POPPY-FLOWERED ANEMONE — (ANEMONE CORONARIA).

POPULUS—(POPLAR)—(COTTONWOOD). Deciduous. 30-40 feet. Sun and partial shade. Soft-wooded, much branched trees; variable, round to oval, entire or lobed, usually smooth, glistening, bright-green, tremulous, serrate leaves; flowers in catkins, blooming in spring. *PROPAGATION*—Easily by hard wood cuttings in spring and fall; weeping variety grafted upon erect kind. *CULTURE*—Grows in any soil, but best in moist, rich lowlands; cut off lateral roots if near drains.

SPECIES—**P. deltoides—Carolina Poplar.** 30-40 feet. Rather broad, branches wide spreading; deeply furrowed or ridged, dark-colored bark. *POSITION*—Specimen and grouping tree; street tree. **P. nigra italica—Lombardy or Italian Poplar.** Straight, narrow, spirelike, used in landscape work for skylines and as accent tree. **P. alba bolleana—Bolles Poplar.** Like Lombardy Poplar, but with deeply lobed, dark-green leaves, snowy white beneath. **P. tremula pendula—European Weeping Aspen.** Slender tree, with drooping, fountainlike sprays; leaves small, thin, round-oval, reddish purple when young. Specimen tree.

PORTUGAL LAUREL—(PRUNUS LUSITANICA).

PORTULACA GRANDIFLORA. Annual. 6-10 inches. Sun. Prostrate or semi-ascending; fleshy, ruddy-colored stems, hairy at joints; short, fleshy, linear-lanceolate leaves; large, regular, brightly colored, bowl-shaped flowers, in many colors, blooming June-August. *PROPAGATION*—Seed sown February-March. *CULTURE*—Requires a fairly rich, sandy loam and the hottest position to give the best results. *POSITION*—For narrow borders, or on dry embankments. Plant alone.

POTATO VINE — (SOLANUM JASMINOIDES).

POTENTILLA—(CINQUEFOIL). Perennial. 1-2 feet. Sun and moderate shade. Semi-procumbent plants, with dark-green, hairy, compound, strawberrylike leaves; regular, medium sized, buttercuplike single and double, maroon, orange, scarlet flowers, blooming June-September. *PROPAGATION*—Hybrid forms only by division of clumps in fall or early

spring; species both by division, and by seeds sown in early spring. *CULTURE*—Favors rather heavy soils, not too moist. *GROUPING*—Excellent for rockeries; embankments; in the hardy border, combining with Gaillardia, Lobelia, Salvia leucantha, Periwinkle, Helianthemum, Platycodon, Globe Thistle.

SPECIES—Variety **Miss Willmott.** With purple, twisting stems, interesting foliage, and cerise-rose flowers.

POT MARIGOLD—(CALENDULA).

POTTING—(See Garden Movies).

PRIMULA—(PRIMROSE). Annual and perennial. 8-18 inches. Best usually in moderate shade. Forming rosettes of leaves; clusters of regular flowers. *PROPAGATION*—Seeds sown in early fall usually, or in early spring; division of clumps with perennials in fall. *CULTURE*—Requires a rich, light, moist, acid, moderately fertilized loam.

SPECIES—**P. malacoides—Lavender Primrose.** 8 inches. Soft, light-green leaves; slender scapes bearing lavender-mauve flowers, blooming December-May; seeds itself readily. *GROUPING*—For the mixed border, combining with Daffodil, Viola, Pansy, Mignonette, Virginia Stocks, Violet, Forget-me-not. **P. polyantha.** 8-10 inches. Rosettes of dark-green, rough leaves; clusters of deep-toned flowers, red, cream, yellow, white, blue, blooming February-May. Fertilize with manure or complete fertilizer. *GROUPING*—Border plant, or for the mixed border, combining with Viola, Daffodil, Narcissus, Cineraria, Freesia, Columbine. Other Primulas—**P. acaulis (vulgaris)—English Primrose.** Blue, yellow. **P. kewensis.** Tall growing, with large clusters of pale yellow flowers. **P. auricula.** Rose, violet flowers.

PRIVET—(LIGUSTRUM).

PRUNING—Ornamental trees and shrubs are pruned: to reinvigorate the shrub and produce new growth; to reduce the amount of woody growth; to induce the formation of fruiting wood; to remove abnormal, diseased, and injured growths; to make them take some desired shape. The tools required are: a strong pair of hand shears, pruning saw, pole shears to reach high limbs, pair of two-foot shears. Tools should be sharp and be properly adjusted. Thinning out the center of a bush permits good circulation of light and air, and reduces the number of branches; heading back tends to produce new stem growth. The usual practice with woody plants is to prune to a lateral or bud, leaving no stubs; with shrubs having succulent growth, this practice is not so essential. Paint over large exposed wounds; small cuts generally heal of themselves.

Time for pruning depends largely upon when the tree or shrub blooms. Spring blooming deciduous and some of the evergreen shrubs are pruned after the blooming period, to induce the formation of flower buds for the next season. Summer and fall blooming shrubs are usually pruned in late fall and winter; the growth in spring produces the new flowers. Many evergreen shrubs which are indeterminate in their blooming periods can be pruned or thinned out at almost any time of year. Directions for pruning are given with many of the trees and shrubs in the Dictionary.

All broken roots and branches of shrubs received from the nursery should be removed. Careful pruning at the start will determine to a great degree the future shape of the shrub. Hedges and trimmed formal shrubs should be pruned several times a year. It is a good practice to go over all trees and shrubs once a year, removing superfluous branches, thinning out, forcing new growth, removing diseased tissue, shaping the shrub.

PRUNUS. Under this heading are included the evergreen species. The deciduous species are listed under Flowering Fruit Trees. 12-25 feet or more. Sun and partial shade. Usually symmetrical trees, with smooth and shining, variable leaves; racemes of fragrant, white, plumlike, regular flowers, blooming in spring; plumlike fruits. *PROPAGATION*—Some species propagate by seeds, stratified, and sown in early spring; ripened wood cuttings of all kinds in fall and spring; layering. *CULTURE*—Most species grow in any soil, but prefer rich, well drained, rather moist soils, fertilized with manures. *GROUPING*—Fine specimen trees for lawns and clipped for formal gardens; tall hedges; for the shrub border, the different species grouping with each other, with Pittosporums, Hakea elliptica, Evergreen Viburnums, Veronicas, Choisya, Cestrum aurantiacum, Duranta plumieri.

SPECIES — **P. caroliniana** — **Carolina Cherry.** Round-headed tree, with large, oblong-lanceolate, deep green leaves, ruddy-tinged; cream-white flowers, blooming February-April; black, shining fruits. **P. ilicifolia—California Cherry.** Rather symmetrical, forming a dense crown; medium-sized, glossy, spiny, Hollylike leaves; cream-white flowers blooming in April; small, purple, cherrylike fruits. **P. integrifolia—Catalina Cherry.** Similar to the California Cherry in growth, but with large, smoother, entire leaves. **P. laurocerasus—English Laurel.** Very compact, symmetrical, cone-shaped tree; large, oval, rather leathery, shining leaves; long racemes of very fragrant flowers, blooming in April-May. *POSITION*—Accent shrub in formal gardens; in foundation plantings at corners and entrances. **P. lusitanica—Portugal Laurel.** Very compact, cone-shaped tree, with very dark-green, shining leaves; long racemes of very fragrant white flowers, blooming in April. Same positions as for English Laurel.

PSEUDOTSUGA TAXIFOLIA — (DOUGLAS SPRUCE)—(DOUGLAS FIR). Conifer. 50-60 feet under cultivation. Sun and partial shade. Symmetrical, pyramidal tree, rapid growing, with ridged, dark red-brown bark, and whorled branches; branchlets pendulous, covered with linear, flexible, dark or bluish-green leaves; orange and red flowers; pendulous cones, 2-4½ inches long. Many varieties. *PROPAGATION*—Seeds sown in spring; grafting of varieties; inarching. *CULTURE*—Grows in many soils, but favors a porous, sandy loam. *POSITION*—Specimen tree; used in groupings with spruces and firs.

PUNICA GRANATUM— (POMEGRANATE). Deciduous. 6-8 feet. Sun loving and moderate shade. Spiny and much branched shrub; smooth, entire, shining, oblong, ruddy-tinged leaves; large, single and semi-double, showy, orange-red flowers, blooming June-August; pomelike, reddish fruits. *PROP-*

AGATION—Usually by hard wood cuttings in fall; layering. *CULTURE*—Prefers a rich, well fertilized loam. *GROUPING*—For the shrub border, grouping with Eugenia myrtifolia, Myrtus luma, Viburnum suspensum, Cornus capitata, Escallonia berteriana, Pittosporums.

SPECIES—**P. granatum nana.** 1 foot. Dwarf, like the type, for the rock garden, in patio gardens, and in the shrub border.

PYRACANTHA — (CRATAEGUS) — (EVERGREEN HAWTHORN). Evergreen. 6-12 feet. Sun and partial shade. Strong, sturdy, bushy shrubs, erect or spreading, with woody, thorny branches, usually long, dark-green, narrow-linear leaves; clusters of small white, fragrant flowers, blooming in spring; brilliantly colored, orange, red or yellowish berries. *PROPAGATION*—Seeds; cuttings of ripened wood in fall; layering; grafting. *CULTURE*—Grows in most soils, preferring a rich, somewhat moist, well fertilized loam. Subject to scale (see Plant Pests). *POSITION*—Specimen tree; foundation plantings; hedge shrubs; grouping shrubs, especially with each other and with a few shrubs such as Chorizema, Mahonia.

SPECIES—**P. angustifolia.** 6 feet, but spreading 10 feet. Very bushy, with grayish green leaves; large, flat, orange-yellow, red berries. Subject to pear blight; propagate from plant immune to disease. **P. coccinea—Firethorn.** 8-10 feet. Bright-red berries. **P. coccinea lalandi.** More robust than the type, with orange-red berries; grows in clay or adobe soils. **P. crenulata—Chinese Evergreen Hawthorn.** Very erect and tall growing, with dark-green, narrow leaves; vivid scarlet, persistent berries. Grows in both sun and shade. **P. gibbsi yunnanensis.** 4-6 feet, but spreading 12 feet. Very hardy, with dark-green foliage and deep red berries; grows in sandy soil. Excellent for covering embankments and for the wide shrub border.

PYRETHRUM ROSEUM — (PAINTED or SINGLE DAISY). Perennial. 1-3 feet. Long, slender flower stems; clear green, finely dissected, fernlike leaves; single and double, daisylike flowers, several inches across, white, and shades of pink, carmine, rose, lilac, salmon, to crimson, blooming April-August. *PROPAGATION* — Seeds sown in early spring; division of roots in fall. *CULTURE*—Like a cool root run, in well drained, rich, loamy soil, well fertilized with manures and balanced fertilizers during growing season; subject to rotting of stems in very moist soil. *GROUPING*—Of great value in the perennial border, combining with pink and rose Sweet William, Iceland Poppy, Pink Pentstemon, Sweet Scabious, Nicotiana, Coral Bells, Dianthus plumarius.

PYRUS—(FLOWERING FRUIT TREES).

Q

QUEEN PALM—(COCOS PLUMOSA).

QUERCUS—(OAK). Deciduous and evergreen. Sun and partial shade. Usually tall growing trees, with massive trunks, and stout, spreading branches; dentate or serrate, usually lobed leaves, sometimes beautifully colored in fall; inconspicuous flowers in catkins; acorn fruits. *PROPAGATION* — Acorns planted soon after maturing; cuttings of half ripened wood; layering; grafting of rare varieties. *CULTURE*—Endures clay or adobe; does best in fairly moist, moderately rich loam; acid soil.

SPECIES—**Q. agrifolia**—**California Live Oak.** 20-30 feet. Round-headed, picturesque tree of dense growth with crooked branches; medium-sized, dark-green, spiny leaves. **Q. chrysolepis**—**Golden-Cup Oak.** With spreading head; leaves bluish or yellowish green above, glaucous and tomentose beneath. **Q. kelloggii**—**California Black Oak.** 100 feet. Open, round-headed tree, with deeply lobed, spiny-toothed, dark-green leaves. **Q. coccinea**—**Scarlet Oak.** 80 feet. Round-topped, open head, with deeply divided leaves, turning scarlet in fall. **Q. rubra.** 80-100 feet. Leaves turn red in fall.

R

RANUNCULUS ASIATICUS — (RANUNCULUS). Bulbous plant. 8-12 inches. Sun loving, but half shade in very warm situations. Erect plant; finely dissected foliage; very double, globular flowers, like enlarged Daisies, in all colors except blue, sometimes variegated, blooming March-June. *PROPAGATION*—Offsets from tubers, planted September-November; plant 2 inches deep in sandy surface soil; seeds sown in early spring. *CULTURE*—Requires a light, well drained loam, fertilized with manure. *POSITION*—Plant in flower borders and beds; usually grouped with Anemone coronaria.

RAPHIOLEPIS OVATA (JAPONICA). Evergreen. 5-10 feet. Sun and partial shade. Very symmetrical, round-headed shrub, with stout, upright branches; smooth, thick, shining, elliptic-oval, dark-green leaves; dense, tomentose racemes of regular, fragrant, white flowers, blooming in June-September and intermittently; persistent, blue-black fruits. *PROPAGATION*—Seeds; usually by cuttings of ripened wood in late summer under glass; layering. *CULTURE*—Grows in any soil, but does best in rich, well drained, light, well fertilized loam. *GROUPING*—Specimen shrub; for formal effects; foundation plantings; foreground of shrub border, grouping with Pittosporum tobira, Evergreen Viburnums, Mexican Orange, Mahonia, Daphne, Rhododendron, Veronica in variety, Azalea in variety.

SPECIES—**R. indica rosea**—**Indian Hawthorn.** Similar to above, but more spreading; pinkish white flowers.

RED BUD—(CERCIS).

RED FREESIA—(TRITONIA).

RED-HOT-POKER PLANT—(TRITOMA).

REDWOOD—(SEQUOIA).

REHMANNIA ANGULATA. Perennial. 1-3 feet. Sun and partial shade. Glandular, soft-hairy plant; pinnately lobed, dentate, dark-green leaves; large, tubular, pilose, rosy purplish brown flowers, blooming in spring and summer. *PROPAGATION*—Division of clumps September-December; seeds sown in early spring. *CULTURE*—Requires a rich, moist, light loam. *GROUPING*—Fine for the perennial border, combining with Nemesia, Purple Sage, Scabiosa, Pyrethrum, maroon and scarlet Sweet William, Shasta Daisy, Snapdragons.

RESEDA ODORATA—(MIGNONETTE). Annual. 6-10 inches. Branching plant, with dark-green, spatulate leaves; close-set, spikelike racemes of very fragrant, yellowish white, green, yellow or reddish flowers, blooming normally in August, but also in other seasons. *PROPAGATION*—Easily by seeds. *CULTURE*—Does best in rich, light loam. *POSITION*—For the annual and perennial borders, combining freely with most flowers.

RETINOSPORA—(CHAMAECYPARIS).

RHAMNUS CALIFORNICA—(CALIFORNIA COFFEE BERRY). Evergreen. 6-8 feet. Sun and partial shade. Round-headed, compact shrubs; large, smooth, thick, oblong-lanceolate, dark-green leaves; greenish, inconspicuous flowers in umbels, small red berries, turning to purplish black. *PROPAGATION*—Seeds stratified, sown in fall; layers; cuttings of ripened wood under glass. *CULTURE*—Drought resistant; grows in any soil. *GROUPING*—Satisfactory for the naturalistic garden, grouping with California Live Oak, Garrya elliptica, Manzanita, Fremontia, Dendromecon, Toyon, Rhus ovata.

RHODODENDRON. Evergreen. Hybrids 5-6 feet; species up to 20 feet. Sun, but best in partial shade. Bushy, round-headed shrubs or small trees; large, smooth, entire, ovate to lanceolate leaves; inflorescence in clusters of regular, white, pink, rose, purple, salmon, to deep red flowers, 2-4 inches across, blooming in May-June. Varieties and species run into the hundreds. Propagation, culture, and position same as for Azalea, which see.

SPECIES — **R. fragrantissimum** — **(Himalayan Azalea).** 10-12 feet. Large, very fragrant, white flowers. Hardy and grows rapidly. **R. catawbiense.** Lilac-purple flowers. **R. californicum.** 15-20 feet. Erect shrub, with dark-green, smooth leaves, and many flowered clusters of rosy purple or pink flowers. Ideal for naturalistic garden. Rhododendrons in general are fine for foundation plantings; in large groupings under open trees, with themselves, or in combination with Aucuba, Hydrangea hortensis, Aralia sieboldii, Kalmia, Andromeda, Skimmia, Camellia.

RHYNCHOSPERMUM JASMINOIDES—(TRACHELOSPERMUM) — (STAR JASMINE). Evergreen vine. 10-15 feet. Sun, but best in half shade. Half shrubby, with dark-green, ovate-lanceolate, smooth leaves; very fragrant, medium-sized, pure white, Jasminelike flowers, blooming May-August. *PROPAGATION*—Cuttings of half ripened wood under glass. *CULTURE*—Does best in rich, light, well fertilized loam. *GROUPING*—Over arches, pergolas, etc.; foundation plantings; combine with Yellow Jasmines, Solanum rantonneti, Clematis in variety, Climbing Roses, Wisteria, Hardenbergia, Tecoma capensis, Plumbago capensis.

RIBES — (FLOWERING CURRANTS)—(GOOSEBERRIES). Deciduous, occasionally evergreen. 4-10 feet. Sun and moderate shade. Bushy, prickly shrubs; small to medium-sized, dark-green, shining, palmately lobed leaves; racemes of highly colored, regular flowers, blooming in spring; colored fruits. *PROPAGATION*—Easily by seeds; Hard wood cuttings in fall; green wood cuttings in summer; mound layering in summer. *CULTURE*—Grow in ordinary, well drained soils; Gooseberries prefer a sunny, dry situation, while the Currants do best in rather moist, half shady situations. *GROUPING*—For the naturalistic garden or the shrub border, grouping with Flowering Oak, Mahonia, Huckleberry, Rhus in variety, Matilija Poppy, Toyon.

SPECIES—**R. aureum.** Yellow-flowered Currant. Fragrant yellow flowers; red or black fruits. **R. sanguineum—Red-Flowered Currant.** Cordate, silky, hairy leaves, red flowers; blue-black berries. **R. speciosum — Fuchsia-Flowered Gooseberry.** Stout, bristly, gracefully arching branches; small glistening leaves; numerous bright-red flowers; red fruits.

RICE FLOWER—(PIMELEA).

RICINUS—(CASTOR BEAN).
Perennial. Sun and partial shade. 10-12 feet. Erect, branching shrub, with large, highly colored, divided leaves, used for its decorative effect. *PROPAGATION*—Easily by seeds. *CULTURE*—Grows in any soil. *POSITION*—For the shrub border and in patio gardens.

ROBINIA PSEUDACACIA — (FALSE ACACIA)—(BLACK LOCUST).
Deciduous. 50-80 feet. Sun and moderate shade. Round-headed tree, with deeply furrowed, deep brown bark and prickly branches; large, odd-pinnate leaves; long racemes of very fragrant, white, pea-shaped flowers, blooming in May-June; long, reddish brown pods. Existing in many varieties. *PROPAGATION*—Seed sown in spring; suckers; cuttings of mature wood; grafting of varieties. *CULTURE*—Grows in any soil; very drought and heat resistant; good for sandy soil. *POSITION*—Specimen tree for large plantations; street tree, but short-lived.

SPECIES—**R. hispida rosea—Rose Acacia.** 1-3 feet. Branchlets and leaf stalks hispid; rose-colored or purple flowers in short racemes, blooming in July. *POSITION*—Specimen tree and in shrub border.

ROCK COTONEASTER — (COTONEASTER HORIZONTALIS).

ROCK CRESS—(ARABIS).

ROCK ROSE—(CISTUS).

ROMNEYA COULTERI — (MATILIJA POPPY).
Semi-deciduous. 3-5 feet. Sun. Much branched, bushy shrub, with gray-green, large, papery, ternately divided leaves; very large, Poppy-like, white flowers with golden-yellow stamens, blooming in May-August. *PROPAGATION*—Root cuttings; seeds, difficult to germinate. *CULTURE*—Does best in well drained, light, moderately fertilized loam. *POSITION*—Used in wide perennial borders; occasionally in shrub border.

ROSA—(ROSE).
Deciduous. Sun loving, but tolerating moderate shade. Varying from low bush forms to climbing roses many feet high. Usually erect and stout growing with prickly stems; odd-pinnate, ovate to ovate-lanceolate leaves; regular, single flowers in species, double and single in hybrids, blooming in spring, summer, or fall, according to kind; colored fruit called a hip or thorn apple. *PROPAGATION*—Seeds, slow to germinate; cut-

tings from firm wood in fall, placed in the open ground; budding of hybrid varieties in July or August on such stock as Manneti, Ragged Robin, Rosa multiflora, etc. Own root stock, however, is usually just as satisfactory as budded stock, but most nursery materials are budded. *CULTURE*—Soil for roses should be a rich, well drained, somewhat heavy loam. Tea roses prefer lighter soils; add straw manure, peat, coal screenings, sand to very heavy soils; add straw manures to soil in fall or early spring; add well balanced commercial fertilizers as roses come into flower; add a small amount of limestone or of wood ashes. Bone meal is beneficial. Roses from the nursery should be pruned back to 6-12 inches from ground; cut off broken branches and roots; leave two to three good canes; cover point of union with about an inch of soil.

Roses should be planted in sunny situations, free from draughts. The life of the rose depends materially upon methods of pruning. Roses should be picked with long stems, cutting with sharp shears down to bud or bud ring. Bushes are normally pruned in late fall or in winter when dormant, but in California the writer has always pruned his roses rather heavily in summer after the first prolific bloom. The farther back bushes are pruned, the stronger the new growths; all weak and superfluous growths should be cut out, retaining several of the most vigorous canes. Climbing roses should be pruned to within three or four buds of the main stem, immediately after flowering and again in late fall. *ROSE DISEASES*—Principal insect pests: aphis, diabrotica, rose beetle, scale, rose slug. Principal fungous diseases: rust, mildew, leaf spot (see Plant Pests). Roses grown in a dry, hot climate are comparatively free from pests; those grown where Coast conditions prevail are more subject to disease, and should be carefully watched and treated periodically.

Rose beds should be regularly watered during the dry season. All prunings and diseased dead leaves should be removed and burned; cut off projecting stubs to prevent die-back of stem. Disbud for large flowers. Remove all sucker growth from the base of stock. Open up ground in spring; keep in constant state of cultivation. A mulch of straw, straw manure, or of peat is beneficial.

Roses are placed in various positions, according to requirements and garden effects desired. The bush type is best in regular beds and in formal plots, part of a geometric design; occasionally they are planted directly in the flower border, and in narrow borders in front of shrubbery. The standard type—roses kept to a long, straight stem, budded at top to the desired variety, and forming a round, bushy head—are placed at pivotal points in the formal rose garden, along either side of a walk, as specimens; some varieties, notably the Isobel rose, may be pruned urn shaped. Climbing roses are trained against house walls and cement, brick, or rock walls, over trellises, arches, pergolas, fences, and into trees. Many climbing roses have been derived from bush types. The more vigorous types of both climbing and bush roses are formed into hedges, the native California Rose, the Prairie Rose, and other species into thickets in the wild garden. The Chinese Rosa hugonis and others are employed as shrubs in the shrub border.

There are several well defined classes of roses which are in extensive use in the gardens of today.

It is inexpedient to give names of varieties within the limits of this book, but reference may be made to articles appearing in SUNSET Magazine and elsewhere, to catalogues specializing in roses, and to Rose books.

Hybrid Perpetual Class. Very vigorous and hardy, erect, tall growing, tolerating heavy soils, cold resistant; dull green, rough, wrinkled foliage. Example: Ulrich Brunner. **Tea Rose Class.** Less vigorous, slender in growth, more spreading; glossy, light-green leaves with tea fragrance. Example: Lady Hillingdon. **Hybrid Teas.** Representing most of the newer hybrids of today, combining the fine qualities of the Tea Rose with the sturdy habit and hardiness of the Hybrid Perpetual. Example: Mme. Caroline Testout. **Pernetiana Class.** For the most part very sturdy growers, prolific and continuous bloomers, with exquisite shades of bronze, yellow, copper, orange. Fine for the Pacific Coast. Example: Daily Mail.

CLIMBING TYPES—**Polyantha** or **Multiflora Class.** Stout, vigorous climbers, with abundant foliage, and clusters of small flowers, blooming a long time. Examples: Cecile Brunner, Rambler Roses.

STRAIGHT CLIMBERS—Vigorous stems, medium to large-sized buds. **Cherokee.** Very vigorous, free blooming roses, pink, white, and red. **Wichuraiana.** Many varieties, trailing or climbing, with single red, pink, rose blooms.

Other classes of importance include the hardy, free flowering and fragrant **Damask** and **French Roses**; **Moss Rose**, with rough-wrinkled foliage, part of the flower covered with mosslike glands; **Austrian** or **Yellow Briars**, almost shrublike, with single, copper and yellow flowers; **Sweet Briars**, with fragrant leaves and light-colored flowers.

ROSE ACACIA—(ROBINIA HISPIDA).

ROSE MOSS—(PORTULACA).

ROSE-OF-HEAVEN—(VISCARIA).

ROSMARINUS OFFICINALIS—(ROSEMARY).
Evergreen. 2-4 feet. Sun. Aromatic, bushy shrub, with narrow, entire leaves; light-blue, irregular, two-lipped flowers, blooming in early spring. *PROPAGATION*—Easily by cuttings of half firm wood at any time; seeds sown in March. *CULTURE*—Likes a well drained, moderately fertilized, light soil, doing well in dry and rocky places. *POSITION*—In either the flower or shrub border; hedge shrub.

ROWAN TREE—(SORBUS).

RUDBECKIA LACINIATA — (CONE FLOWER).
Perennial. 2-7 feet. Sun. Erect plant, with large, cleft leaves; large, sunflowerlike, golden yellow-brown flowers, blooming in August. *PROPAGATION*—Seed sown in spring; division of roots in fall. *CULTURE*—Grows in any moderately fertilized loam. *GROUPING*—For the perennial border, combining with Shasta Daisy, French Marigold, Nepeta, deep blue Perennial Aster, Boltonia, yellow and bronze Chrysanthemums.

S

SACRED BAMBOO OF JAPAN — (NANDINA).

SAGE—(SALVIA).

SALIX BABYLONICA—(WEEPING WILLOW).
Deciduous. 30-40 feet. Sun and partial shade. Long, slender, drooping, olive-green or purplish branches; long, narrow, bright-green leaves; greenish catkins, blooming in spring. *PROPAGATION*—Easily by cuttings; seed sown at maturity. *CULTURE*—Grows in any soil, but favors a light, moist loam. **French Pussy Willow.** 10-15 feet. Long, wide, golden-yellow catkins. *POSITION*—Specimen tree, especially near large pools.

SALPIGLOSSIS.
Annual, almost perennial in California. 1-2½ feet. Sun. Erect, sticky pubescent plant; elliptic-oblong, wavy-toothed or pinnatifid, dark-green leaves; large, tubular, velvety textured, lilylike flowers in bright and gaudy colors, blooming from May into fall. *PROPAGATION*—Seed sown in early spring. *CULTURE*—Requires a rich, light, well fertilized, well drained loam. *GROUPING* — Impressive in front of dark-green shrubbery, and in the mixed border, combining with Salvia patens, deep blue Viola, Lobelia, Veronica spicata, Anchusa, Siberian Wallflower, Common Wallflower, deep blue Delphinium.

SALVIA.
Perennial. 1-3 feet. Sun. Erect, branching plants, with variable leaves and irregular, tubular flowers, blooming in summer or fall. *PROPAGATION*—Seed; division of clumps. *CULTURE*—Will grow in ordinary soils, fertilized with manures.

SPECIES—**S. splendens—Scarlet Sage.** Many varieties. With square stems, smooth, dark-green, oval leaves; terminal, spirelike racemes of intensely scarlet flowers, blooming in California in December, elsewhere July until frost. *PROPAGATION*—Seeds sown in early fall or early spring; cuttings of half ripened wood. *POSITION*—Best with background of shrubs having dark-green, glossy leaves. **S. farinacea.** 2-3 feet. Tomentose plant, with gray-green, lanceolate leaves, and violet-white, purple flowers, blooming in June-July. *GROUPING* — For the mixed border, combining with Yellow Lupine, Yellow Snapdragons, Pot Marigold, deep blue Delphinium, Sea Holly. **S. pitcheri** and **S. azurea**, with deep blue and azure-blue flowers respectively. **S. patens.** 1-2½ feet. Grows from a thick, tuberlike root. Clear green leaves; long flower spikes bearing large, deep blue flowers blooming June-September. *GROUPING*—Border plant and in the perennial border, combining with Coreopsis, Helenium, Heliopsis, yellow Pot Marigolds. **S. leucantha—Purple Sage.** 2½ feet. Shrubby perennial; long, linear-lanceolate, gray-green, pubescent leaves; woolly stems; long spikes of violet-white flowers, blooming in spring, summer, and intermittently. *PROPAGATION*—Division of roots at any time. *GROUPING*—Used to cover embankments and for the perennial border, combining with Coreopsis, yellow and brown Chrysanthemums, Gaillardia, yellow Columbine, Tritoma.

SANTOLINA CHAMAECYPARISSUS—(LAVENDER COTTON).
Perennial. 1½-2 feet. Sun and partial shade. Half shrubby, much branched plant, with aromatic, small, silvery gray leaves; small globular heads of yellow flowers, blooming in summer. *PROPAGATION*—Easily by cuttings taken at any time. *CULTURE*—Does best in rich, light,

well fertilized loam. *POSITION*—Used as edging material; occasionally in flower border.

SATIN FLOWER—(GODETIA).

SAXIFRAGA CRASSIFOLIA — (PINK SAXIFRAGE). Perennial. 8-12 inches. Sun and shade. Stout plant, with very large, broadly ovate, dark-green leaves; racemes of regular, deep pink flowers blooming in winter or early spring. *PROPAGATION*—Usually by division or offsets in fall; subject to mealy bug (see Plant Pests). Many species, mostly rock and alpine plants, many of them forming rather dense mats of mosslike foliage; flowers star-shaped, pink, white, yellow, blooming in winter, spring, and summer.

SCABIOSA. Biennial and perennial. 1½-3 feet high. Sun and moderate shade. Bushy plants with divided foliage and dense heads of irregular flowers, blooming in spring, summer, and fall, according to kind. *PROPAGATION*—Seed sown in early spring, blooming the first year; division of clumps in fall. *CULTURE*—Grows well in ordinary soils, but favors well fertilized, somewhat sandy loam. *GROUPING* —For the perennial and mixed borders, combining with Ageratum, Gladiolus, Madonna Lily, Snapdragon, Perennial Phlox, Sweet William, Stocks, Columbine, using such colors as harmonize.

SPECIES—**S. atropurpurea—Sweet Scabious—Pincushion Flower—Mourning Bride.** Flowers in many colors, blooming from March until late fall. *PROPAGATION*—Sow seed December-June for succession of bloom. Plant separate varieties. **S. caucasica — Blue Bonnet.** 18 inches. Spreading plant, with whitish, linear-lanceolate, cut leaves; large lavender-mauve flowers, blooming June-October. Subject to stem rot in too wet soil. **S. columbaria.** 2 feet. Finely cut, gray-green foliage; lavender-mauve flowers in small globular heads.

SCHINUS MOLLE—(CALIFORNIA PEPPER TREE). 20-50 feet. Evergreen. Sun and partial shade. Round-headed, picturesque tree, with gracefully drooping branchlets; long, smooth, shining, dark-green, pinnatifid leaves; many flowered panicles of small, yellowish white flowers, blooming in early fall; coral-rose berries. *PROPAGATION*—Easily by seed sown in early spring. *CULTURE*—Grows in any rather moist, well drained soil. *POSITION*—Specimen tree; shade and avenue tree

SCHIZANTHUS — (BUTTERFLY FLOWER) —(POOR MAN'S ORCHID). 1-1½ feet. Sun. Erect, slender-branched; bright-green, finely divided leaves; butterflylike flowers; varicolored, blotched flowers in many colors, blooming May-August. *PROPAGATION*—Seeds sown in early spring. *CULTURE*—Grows best in rich, sandy, well fertilized sandy loam. *GROUPING*—Excellent in masses; for the mixed border, combining with Gypsophila, Coral Bells, Virginia Blue Bells, Mariposa Lily, Viscaria, Gerbera.

SCHIZOSTYLIS — (KAFIR LILY). Bulbous plant. 1-2 feet. Sun. Growing from rhizome; linear, sword shaped leaves; large, slender-tubed, Lilylike flowers, crimson-scarlet, blooming October-late December. *PROPAGATION*—Division of rhizomes in fall or spring. *CULTURE*—Grows in rich, light soil,

in sunny, sheltered places. Used as potted plants for the conservatory.

SCIADOPITYS VERTICILLATA—(JAPANESE UMBRELLA PINE). Conifer. Usually 6-15 feet under cultivation. Sun and partial shade. Very symmetrical, narrow, compact, pyramidal-shaped tree; large, linear, dark-green, furrowed leaves; inconspicuous flowers; long, oval cones. *PROPAGATION*—Layering; seeds; cuttings of half ripened wood in summer. *POSITION*—Specimen tree for lawns and in tubs as accent tree. *CULTURE*—Prefers a moist, loamy soil, but will grow in medium clay soil.

SCILLA— (SQUILL) — (WILD HYACINTH). Bulbous plant. 4-8 inches. Sun and partial shade. Slender, graceful plant, with grasslike leaves; nodding, bell-shaped, blue, white, lilac flowers, blooming February-May. *PROPAGATION*—Easily by offsets, planting October-November. *CULTURE*—Plant in light, moderately fertilized loam. *GROUPING*—For the rockery and wild garden; border plant; mixed border, combining with Spring Snowflake, Dutch Crocus, Lavender Primrose, Narcissi, Mignonette, Virginia Stocks.

SPECIES — **S. autumnalis — Autumn Squill—Starry Hyacinth.** Rose-colored flowers before the leaves, blooming July-September.

SCORPION SENNA—(CORONILLA).

SCOTCH BROOM—(CYTISUS SCOPARIUS).

SCOTCH MOSS—(ARENARIA).

SCOTCH PINK—(DIANTHUS PLUMARIUS).

SEA HOLLY—(ERYNGIUM).

SEA LAVENDER—(STATICE).

SEA PINK—(ARMERIA).

SEA URCHIN—(HAKEA LAURINA).

SEQUOIA—(BIG TREES OF CALIFORNIA). Conifer. 50-60 feet under cultivation. Sun and moderate shade. Erect, symmetrical tree, with thick, red, fibrous, deeply grooved bark; variable leaves; yellow-brown flowers; medium-sized cones. *PROPAGATION*—Seeds sown in spring or fall; by stump sprouts with Redwood; varieties by grafting. *CULTURE*—The Sequoias like a rich, open, porous, somewhat moist, well drained, acid soil, but they are adapted to a variety of soils. The Redwood does best in regions where the climate is marked by fogs and cool summer winds. The Big Tree can stand a drier atmosphere and greater extremes of temperature. *POSITION*—Specimen trees for lawn and for framing residences; avenue and street trees; grouping trees, with each other, and with other conifers.

SPECIES—**S. sempervirens — California Redwood.** Conical in shape, open in growth, with branches spreading out horizontally; flattened sprays of light to dark-green leaves. **S. gigantea—California Big Tree.** Young trees pyramidal, very compact; scalelike, gray-green leaves. Variety **pendula—Weeping Big Tree.** Branches strongly recurved, closely covering the stem, producing a narrow, cylindrical effect. Variety **glauca** of both species with bluish green foliage.

SHASTA DAISY — (CHRYSANTHEMUM LEUCANTHEMUM).

SHE OAK—(CASUARINA).

SHRUB GROUPINGS. Like the flower, the shrub should be considered in its entirety in groupings in the shrub border. The various features considered are: leaf characters; form of shrub; color of flower. Leaf characters vary according to smoothness or hairiness; shininess or dullness; large, small, medium-sized; entire or divided. Some trees and shrubs are symmetrical, formal in character, appropriate as accent and pivotal specimens in formal gardens, near corners and entrances of residences, as specimens on lawns, and in special positions in the shrub border. Many shrubs, because of their loose form, are essentially grouping shrubs, and cannot be used as specimens. On the other hand, there are many that can be placed in either class. Shrubs in close proximity in the shrub border should have approximately the same leaf texture, and be near the same size; occasionally a tree or shrub, different in appearance and in character of foliage, is inserted in the shrub border for purposes of contrast or for accent. Shrubs blooming at the same time should have colors of flowers that harmonize.

All shrubs in foundation plantings should have fine texture of foliage and distinctive shapes; low growing shrubs placed at the base of shrubs at corners and entrances make splendid groupings. Shrub borders are also used as a fringe about both the front and rear lawns. Sprawling and low growing shrubs are placed in the immediate foreground, gradating from these to the very tall shrubs in the rear; avoid too great a regularity in the planting, inserting a few shrubs taller than the rest in the foreground; plant in groups of 3, 5, 7, etc., rather than too many individual specimens. Shrubs used in connection with very formal residences may occasionally be clipped; it is much better, usually, to select a specimen tree which already has the desired shape. Grouping shrubs may frequently be pruned to lie flat against a wall. Trees and shrubs with large, broad, smooth leaves should be planted in connection with Spanish and Mediterranean residences and large buildings. Shrubs with finely textured, small leaves can be used about the average residence. Color in foliage is desirable in the shrub border; there should be abundance of bloom in the shrub border about the lawn, to correspond to the floral effects of the flower border, or else shrubs with dark-green foliage can act as a background for the flowers in front. Bearing these points in mind, directions are given in the Dictionary for the proper placement and grouping of trees and shrubs.

SIBERIAN CRAB — (FLOWERING FRUIT TREES).

SIBERIAN WALLFLOWER — (CHEIRANTHUS ALLIONI).

SILK OAK—(GREVILLEA ROBUSTA).

SILVERBERRY—(ELEAGNUS ARGENTEA).

SILVER CYPRESS — (CHAMAECYPARIS PISIFERA SQUARROSA).

SILVER LACE VINE—(POLYGONUM AUBERTII).

SINGLE DAISY—(PYRETHRUM ROSEUM).

SKIMMIA JAPONICA. Evergreen. 4-5 feet. Half shade. Bushy shrub, with yellowish green, smooth, laurel-like leaves; clusters of small white flowers, blooming in April-May; bright coral-red fruits. PROPAGATION—Seeds sown in fall; cuttings of half ripened wood under glass. CULTURE —Prefers a sandy loam, or can grow in peaty loam. GROUPING—For the half shade border, grouping with Andromeda, Aucuba, Azara, Azaleas and Rhododendrons, Raphiolepis, Pachysandra, Kalmia.

SMILAX—(ASPARAGUS).

SNAPDRAGON—(ANTIRRHINUM).

SNEEZEWORT—(HELENIUM).

SNOWBALL — (VIBURNUM OPULUS STERILE).

SNOWDROP—(GALANTHUS).

SNOWFLAKE—(LEUCOJUM).

SOLANDRA GUTTATA—(COPA DE ORO)— (CUP OF GOLD). Evergreen. 15-20 feet. Sun. Large, elliptic-oblong dark-green, smooth leaves, very pubescent beneath; large, long-tubular, fragrant, solitary, ocher-yellow flowers, blooming October-May. PROPAGATION—Cuttings of firm young shoots taken with heel and given bottom heat. CULTURE—Requires a moderately rich, sandy loam, in sheltered situation. POSITION—Beautiful effect against the residence.

SOLANUM — (NIGHTSHADE). Evergreen vines and shrubs. Low growing up to 50 feet. Sun. PROPAGATION—Those described easily by cuttings of half firm wood; seeds. CULTURE—All grow well in ordinary, moderately fertilized loams. POSITION—For covering walls, pergolas, trellises, etc.; rockeries; for the shrub border, grouping with Cestrum aurantiacum, Spanish Broom, Ceratonia, Yellow Jasmines, Cytisus, Berberis.

SPECIES — S. rantonneti. Shrubby vine. 3-6 feet. Erect, bushy, with gray-green, ovate-lanceolate leaves; small clusters of potatolike, violet-yellow flowers, blooming in July-August; large red fruits. S. wendlandii. May reach 50 feet. Leaves somewhat prickly, lobed or trifoliate; large cymes of pale, lilac-blue flowers, blooming June-August. S. jasminoides—Potato Vine. 8-10 feet. Bright-green leaves, and clusters of large white-blue flowers, with long period of bloom.

SOLLYA HETEROPHYLLA—(AUSTRALIAN BLUEBELL CREEPER). Evergreen shrubby vine. 10-15 feet. Round-headed, dense as shrub; slender branched as vine; medium-sized, dark-green, smooth, glossy, variable leaves; terminal cymes of deep blue, small, bell-shaped flowers, blooming July-August. PROPAGATION — Easily by seeds; cuttings of young shoots under glass. Prefers a rich, well fertilized, light loam. GROUPING—As shrub for formal effects; as vine against the house, over pergolas, arbors, etc.; in the shrub border, grouping with Streptosolen, Genistas, Cassia, Spanish Broom, Escallonia montevidensis, Dwarf Myrtle, Lantana.

SOPHORA JAPONICA — (JAPAN PAGODA TREE). Deciduous. 40-60 feet. Sun. Symmetrical, round-headed, spreading tree; odd-pinnate, dark-green, glossy leaves; yellowish white, small flowers in long racemes, blooming July-September; variety **pendula** with slender pendulous branches. *PROPAGATION*—Seeds; root cuttings; layering; grafting. *CULTURE*—Does best in well drained, dry, rather poor soil. *POSITION*—Specimen tree; street tree.

SORBUS AUCUPARIA — (EUROPEAN MOUNTAIN ASH)—(ROWAN TREE). Deciduous. 20-40 feet. Erect tree with drooping branches; pinnate, dull-green leaves, turning orange-red in the fall; flat, broad corymbs of white flowers, blooming in May-June; bright-red fruits. *CULTURE*—Grows in any soil, especially on rocky sites. *PROPAGATION*—Seeds stratified, sown in fall or spring; layering. *POSITION* — Street tree; lawn tree; accent tree in shrub border.

SOUTH AFRICAN DAISY—(GAZANIA).

SPANISH BAYONET—(YUCCA).

SPANISH BROOM—(SPARTIUM).

SPARAXIS—(WAND FLOWER). Bulbous plant with corms. 6-12 inches. Sun. Swordlike leaves; regular, short, funnel-shaped flowers like Ixias, in bright colors, blooming in April-May. *PROPAGATION*—Offsets in fall; seeds in spring. *CULTURE*—Grows in any moderately fertile soil. *GROUPING*—Border plant; mixed border, combining with Delphinium, purple Iris, Peach Bell, Coreopsis, purple Violas, Purple Sage, Larkspur.

SPARTIUM JUNCEUM — (GENISTA HISPANICA) — (SPANISH BROOM). Evergreen. 6-10 feet. Sun and partial shade. Erect, much branched shrub, with almost leafless, rushlike branches; very small, bluish green, trifoliate leaves; large, very fragrant, golden-yellow, pea-shaped flowers, blooming profusely June-September and almost continuously. *PROPAGATION* — Seeds; green wood cuttings. *CULTURE*—Grows well in any soil; alkali resistant; subject to aphis and scale (see Plant Pests); head back severely each fall. *GROUPING*—Specimen on lawns; in the shrub border as contrast shrub, grouping with English Laurel, Aucuba, Arbutus unedo, Ceratonia siliqua, Mexican Orange, blue-flowered Veronicas, Solanum Wendlandii.

SPIDER LILY—(HYMENOCALLIS).

SPIRAEA. Deciduous. 2-6 feet. Sun and moderate shade. Erect shrub, with gracefully arching branches; incised, light to dark-green leaves, frequently turning to bright colors in fall; umbels and racemes of fragrant, white, pink, or red flowers, blooming in spring. *PROPAGATION*—Seed; division of roots; layering; hard wood and soft wood cuttings. *CULTURE*—Adapted to ordinary, well drained, light, moderately fertilized soils; prune after flowering. *SPECIES*—S. billardii. Spikes of bright pink flowers. **S. bumalda,** variety **Anthony Waterer.** Round-headed bush with wine-colored flowers. **S. prunifolia—Bridal Wreath.** White flowers borne along the arching branches. Variety **flora plena.** Double white flowers. **S. van houttei.** The most popular species, with abundant, pure white blooms. Group with Japanese Quince, Tamarisk, Flowering Crabapple, Japanese Cherry and other Flowering Fruit Trees. **S. thunbergii.** A very graceful shrub, with feathery dark-green leaves.

SPRUCE—(PICEA).

SQUILL—(SCILLA).

STAR JASMINE—(RHYNCHOSPERMUM).

STAR OF BETHLEHEM — (ORNITHOGALUM).

STATICE SINUATA—(EVERLASTING). Perennial, treated as annual. 1-2 feet. Sun. Erect, branching, with thick, dark-green, divided leaves; angular stalks bearing dense panicles of papery, blue-yellow-white flowers, blooming in July-August. *PROPAGATION*—Seeds sown in early spring. *CULTURE*—Grows in any soil, requiring little water. *POSITION*—By themselves and for cutting.

SPECIES — S. latifolia — Sea Lavender. 1-1½ feet. Stout growing, with large, broad, dark-green, radical leaves; slender branched panicles of small, filmy, pale violet flowers, blooming in June. *POSITION*—Rock garden; occasional plant in flower border.

ST. JOHNS BREAD—(CERATONIA).

ST. JOHNSWORT—(HYPERICUM).

STOCKS—(MATTHIOLA).

STOKESIA CYANEA — (STOKES ASTER). Perennial. 1-2 feet. Sun. Much branched plant, with purplish, hairy branches; clasping, lanceolate leaves; large, blue flower heads, blooming in August. *PROPAGATION*—Seeds; division in spring. *CULTURE* — Same requirements as for Centaurea. *GROUPING*—For the mixed border, combining with yellow Geum, Coreopsis, Tiger Lily, Tigridia, Doronicum, Gaillardia, Rudbeckia, Calendula.

STRAW FLOWER—(HELICHRYSUM).

STREPTOSOLEN JAMESONII — (YELLOW HELIOTROPE). Evergreen shrubby vine. 6-20 feet or more. Sun and moderate shade. With dark-green, medium-sized, rough-wrinkled, pubescent leaves; medium-sized, tubular, regular, orange-red flowers in corymbose panicles, blooming in summer, winter, and continuously. *PROPAGATION*—Cuttings of half firm wood; seeds in spring. *CULTURE*—Requires rich, well drained, light loam; subject to frost injury. *GROUPING*—Used as vine or shrub, combining with Heliotrope, Iochroma, Solanum rantonneti, lilac-purple Wisteria, Clematis jackmani, Plumbago in variety, Veronica decussata.

SUMMER CYPRESS—(KOCHIA).

SUMMER LILAC—(BUDDLEIA).

SUNFLOWER—(HELIANTHUS).

SUN ROSE—(HELIANTHEMUM).

SWAN RIVER DAISY—(BRACHYCOME).

SWEET BAY—(LAURUS).

SWEET GUM—(LIQUIDAMBAR).

SWEET PEA—(LATHYRUS).

SWEET SULTAN — (CENTAUREA IMPERIALIS).

SWEET WILLIAM—(DIANTHUS).

SYCAMORE—(PLATANUS).

SYDNEY GOLDEN WATTLE — (ACACIA LATIFOLIA).

SYRINGA—(LILAC). Deciduous. 6-20 feet. Sun. Bushy, round-headed shrubs; large, bright-green, opposite, entire leaves; regular, single and double, white, pink, blue, purple, lilac flowers in close-set panicles, blooming in April-May. *PROPAGATION* —Usually grafted or budded stock; green wood and hard wood cuttings; suckers; division. *CULTURE* —Does best in rich, light, moist, well fertilized soil; prune back and thin out after flowering; subject to frost injury; attacked by mildew, borers, leaf spot (see Plant Diseases). *POSITION*—Best grouped by themselves; specimen shrubs for lawns; in the shrub border, harmonizing in respect to foliage and color of flower with spring blooming deciduous shrubs and broad-leaved evergreens.

T

TACSONIA—(PASSIFLORA).

TAGETES PATULA—(FRENCH MARIGOLD). Annual. 6-10 inches. Sun. Bushy, branching plants; dark-green, pinnately cut, pungent foliage; compact heads of tubular, strongly scented flowers, brilliantly colored brown, yellow, orange, gold, blooming from June-late fall. *PROPAGATION*— Seed sown January-May for succession of bloom; seeds itself. *CULTURE*—Grows in ordinary, rich, moist, light, well fertilized loam. *GROUPING*— Used as bedding plant and for the mixed border, combining with Ageratum, Violas, purple Stocks, Pot Marigold, Blue Perennial Aster, Anchusa, Sea Holly, Aconitum.

SPECIES—**T. erecta—African Sun Marigold.** Annual. 1-2 feet. Similar to French Marigold, but with larger leaves, and large, double, sulphur yellow to deep orange, balled flowers, blooming through summer and fall. **Guinea Flower — Carnation Flower.** A new production, with sweet-scented, large flowers. Requirements same as for above.

TAMARACK—(LARIX).

TAMARIX — (TAMARISK). Deciduous. 6-15 feet. Sun and moderate shade. Woody shrubs with slender, arching branches; minute, scalelike leaves; loose, large panicles or lateral racemes of small, light or medium-pink flowers, blooming, according to species, from spring through fall. *PROPAGATION*— Seeds; cuttings of ripened wood in open ground. *CULTURE*—Adapted to many soils; dry land; seaside conditions; salt and alkali soils; sandy soils. *GROUPING*—Windbreaks; hedges; some kinds as specimen shrubs; for the shrub border, combining with Spiraea, Mock Orange, Pearl Bush, Deutzias in variety.

SPECIES—**T. plumosa.** Pinkish flowers, blooming in spring. **T. hispida.** Bluish green, finely pubescent leaves; pink flowers in dense racemes, blooming in summer. **T. pentandra.** Purple branches, pale green foliage, and pink flowers.

TASSEL SHRUB—(GARRYA).

TAXODIUM DISTICHUM—(BALD CYPRESS). Deciduous conifer. 20-40 feet. Sun and partial shade. Tall, pyramidal, rather broad tree, with buttressed trunk, light cinnamon-brown, flaky bark, erect or spreading branches; small, light-green, linear leaves; small, purplish, catkinlike flowers; small, globose cones. Many varieties. *PROPAGATION*—Seeds sown in spring; cuttings under water; grafting of varieties. *CULTURE*—Best in sandy, moist, acid soil. *POSITION*—Specimen tree.

SPECIES—**T. mucronatum—Montezuma Cypress.** Evergreen conifer. Quite similar to the Bald Cypress.

TAXUS—(YEW). Conifer. 10-25 feet. Sun and partial shade. Symmetrical, slow growing trees, with small, dark-green, linear leaves; insignificant white flowers; red berries. *PROPAGATION*—Seeds, germinating the second year; layering; cuttings, but not always satisfactory; best by grafting upon seedlings. *CULTURE*—Does best in a moderately moist, sandy, well fertilized loam. *POSITION*—Specimen shrubs on lawns; accent shrubs for the formal garden; foundation plantings; grouping shrubs, using spreading and erect species together.

SPECIES—**T. baccata—English Yew.** 10-12 feet. With spreading branches, forming a low, broad head; branchlets pendulous. Variety **repandens.** Low growing form, with long, wide-spreading branches, and dull, bluish-green leaves. **T. baccata fastigiata —Irish Yew.** 20-25 feet. Erect, very compact, cylindrical in form; somber, very dark-green, glossy leaves in clusters. **T. baccata aurea—Golden English Yew.** Leaves tinged a golden yellow. **T. baccata fastigiata aurea.** Like Irish Yew, but with yellow-tipped leaves. **T. baccata erecta.** Similar to Irish Yew, but faster growing and with smaller leaves.

TECOMA CAPENSIS— (CAPE HONEYSUCKLE). Evergreen vine. 10-20 feet. Sun and partial shade. Light-green, odd-pinnate leaves; tubular, orange-scarlet flowers in terminal racemes, blooming August-November. *PROPAGATION* — Soft and hard wood cuttings; root cuttings; grafting. *CULTURE*—Prefers a light, moderately fertilized loam. *POSITION* — Over lattice work, pergolas, walls, etc.; combine with white-flowered Jasmines, Clematis jackmani.

SPECIES — **T. mackenii.** Divided leaflets and trumpet-shaped pink flowers striped red. **T. radicans—Evergreen Trumpet Honeysuckle.** Orange-scarlet flowers.

TEUCRIUM FRUTICANS. Evergreen. 5-8 feet. Sun. Much branched, round-headed shrub, with grayish, tomentose, medium-sized, ovate leaves; terminal clusters of Honeysucklelike, light blue-white flowers, blooming profusely in summer and early fall. *PROPAGATION* — Cuttings of half ripened wood in spring. *CULTURE*—Grows in any moderately fertilized soil. *GROUPING*—For the shrub border, grouping with Lavender, Melaleuca ericifolia and M. decussata, Leptospermum chapmanni, Rosemary, Cotoneasters.

THALICTRUM DIPTEROCARPUM—(INDIAN MEADOW RUE). Perennial. 4-8 feet.

SUNSET'S COMPLETE GARDEN BOOK

Sun, but best in partial shade. Erect, with slender stems; large, pale green, compound, Columbinelike leaves; small, lavender-mauve, nodding flowers, blooming July-September. *PROPAGATION*—Division of clumps November-January; seeds sown at maturity and in spring; seeds self-sown. *CULTURE* —Requires a rich, light loam. *GROUPING* — In shady border combine with Begonias, Columbine, Heuchera, Ferns, Campanulas, Impatiens oliveri, Lilies, Japanese Anemone. **T. aquilegifolium — Feathered Columbine — Meadow Rue.** Perennial. 1-3 feet. Feathery, corymbose heads of white-purple flowers, blooming May-August. *POSITION*—Suitable for rockery and for the shady border.

THRIFT—(ARMERIA).

THUYA—(ARBOR VITAE). Hardy conifers. 6-20 feet. Sun and shade. Symmetrical trees of narrow, pyramidal habit, or low and bushy; numerous, flattened, frondlike branchlets; small, scalelike leaves; small, yellowish flowers; small, roundish cones. *PROPAGATION*—Seeds sown in spring; cuttings of shoots in summer; grafting. *CULTURE*— Will grow in poor soils fertilized with manure; better foliage in somewhat moist, loamy soil. *POSITION*—Accent shrubs for formal effects; conifer groupings; foundation plantings; hedge shrubs.

SPECIES—**T. orientalis—Chinese Arbor Vitae.** 4-6 feet. Erect, flat-sided shrub, with bright-green leaves. **T. orientalis berckmanni—Berckmanns Arbor Vitae.** 1-2 feet. Dark-green foliage, tipped with golden yellow. **T. occidentalis — Common Arbor Vitae.** Numerous varieties. Usually 10-25 feet. Either pyramidal or round-headed, with ovate leaves, bright-green above, yellowish-green beneath. The variety **pyramidalis** is frequently used in place of the Italian Cypress. **T. orientalis beverleyensis—Pyramidal Golden Cedar.** 15-20 feet. Tall, pyramidal in shape, with golden tinge to foliage. **Thuyopsis dolobrata.** 8-10 feet. Similar to Thuya, but with broader, much flattened branchlets, and glossy green leaves.

TIBOUCHINA SPLENDENS — (PLEROMA ELEGANS). Evergreen. 8-10 feet. Sun and moderate shade. Erect, bushy shrub, with stiff, brownish stems, large, ovate-oblong, velvety, bright-green and colored leaves; medium-sized, regular, royal purple flowers in clusters, blooming November-January in the open in California, in early summer if used for pot culture. *PROPAGATION*—Side shoots of rather firm wood taken between April and August; subject to frost injury. *CULTURE* — Requires a moderately fertilized, light soil with acid reaction. *POSITION*—Specimen shrub; foundation plantings; occasional shrub in shrub border; patio garden.

TIGRIDIA — (MEXICAN SHELL FLOWER). Bulbous plant. 1-2½ feet. Sun. Narrow, grasslike leaves; irregular, cup-shaped, brilliantly colored, yellow, orange, purple and spotted clustered flowers, lasting but a day, blooming in July-August. *PROPAGATION*—Easily by offsets planted in fall or early spring; seeds. *CULTURE*—Grows in light, rich, well fertilized loam. *GROUPING*—For the mixed border, grouping with Montbretia, Peruvian Daffodil, Platycodon, Aconitum, Peach Bell, Veronica longifolia, Aubrietia, Salvia patens.

TOBACCO PLANT—(NICOTIANA).

TORCH LILY—(TRITOMA).

TOUCH-ME-NOT—(IMPATIENS).

TOYON—(PHOTINIA).

TRACHELOSPERMUM — (RHYNCHOSPERMUM).

TRAILING MYRTLE—(VINCA).

TRANSPLANTING—(See Garden Movies).

TRANSVAAL DAISY—(GERBERA).

TREE ANEMONE—(CARPENTERIA).

TREE DAHLIA—(DAHLIA IMPERIALIS).

TREE PEONY—(PAEONIA).

TRITOMA (KNIPHOFIA) UVARIA — (TORCH - LILY)—(RED - HOT - POKER PLANT). Perennial. 4-6 feet. Sun and slight shade. Makes a vigorous growth from stout culms; long, narrow, flexible, bright-green leaves; dense terminal spikes of irregular, long-tubular, brilliant yellow-orange-red flowers, blooming profusely in summer and fall, more sparsely in winter and spring. *PROPAGATION* — Seeds; easily by division fall and spring. *GROUPING*—Spanish Garden; in the shrub border, grouping with Cestrum aurantiacum, Lavender Lantana, Sea Holly, Iochroma, Purple Sage, Sollya heterophylla, Solanum rantonneti.

TRITONIA—(MONTBRETIA)—(RED FREESIA) and other species. Bulbous plants. 12-18 inches. Sun and slight shade. Erect plant, with sword-shaped leaves; racemes of slender, tubular, yellow, orange, red, scarlet flowers, blooming April-September. *PROPAGATION*—Offsets from corms planted in fall; seed. *CULTURE*—Grows in ordinary, light, well fertilized loam. *GROUPING*—Plant in bold masses in front of shrubbery, or in the mixed border, combining with Blue Iris, Anchusa italica, Blue Lupine, Periwinkle, Helenium, Salvia pitcheri.

TROPAEOLUM MAJUS — (NASTURTIUM). Annual. 6-8 feet. Sun and partial shade. Trailing herbs, vines, or bedding plants, with bright-green, roundish leaves; irregular, spurred, brightly colored flowers, blooming from spring into fall. *PROPAGATION*—Seeds when nearly ripe. *CULTURE*— Grows in any moderately rich, moist loam. *POSITION*—Embankments, over fences, trellises, etc. The dwarf, bushy Tom Thumb varieties are used for bedding out.

SPECIES—**T. peregrinum—Canary Bird Vine.** Annual vine, with irregular, canary-yellow flowers.

TRUMPET VINE — (BIGNONIA) and (TECOMA).

TSUGA CANADENSIS—(HEMLOCK). Conifer. 15-20 feet. Symmetrical, pyramidal tree, with irregularly whorled branches; yellowish-brown, drooping branchlets; dark-green, linear, white-lined leaves; small ovoid cones. *PROPAGATION*—Seeds sown in spring; cuttings of partially ripened wood; grafting of varieties. *CULTURE*—Grows in ordinary, moist, moderately fertilized loam. *POSITION*

215

—Conifer groupings; windbreaks; hedges as backgrounds for garden ornaments, sculpture, etc.

TUBEROSE—(POLIANTHES).

TUBEROUS BEGONIA—(BEGONIA).

TULIPA—(TULIP). Bulbous plant. 2-30 inches according to kind and species. Sun and moderate shade. Erect plant, with showy, glaucous, long, broad, dark or gray-green, gray-blue leaves; flowers usually solitary on long flower stalk from bulb, the perianth campanulate or slightly funnel-shaped, in many colors, often spotted or blotched at base, blooming in spring. *PROPAGATION*—Natural division, either leaving bulbs in soil, or taking them up and planting again October-January; seeds. *CULTURE*—Require a rich, well drained, moderately moist, well fertilized, light loam; attacked by mold in soil, controlled by dipping the bulbs in solution of bordeaux mixture before planting; add manure in fall and commercial fertilizer just before blooming; subject to aphis and attacks by rodents (see Plant Pests).

TYPES—**Early Flowering.** Used for bedding out, with short stems, and small, globe or egg-shaped flowers, soft-colored, some sweet-scented. **Darwin Tulips.** Long, stiff, and sturdy stems; beautiful, chalice-shaped blooms of heavy texture, in many light and deep-toned colors. **Breeder Tulips.** Similar to the Darwin Tulips, with large, cup-shaped blooms, usually gold, bronze, buff, and derivatives. **Cottage or May Flowering Tulips.** Long flower stalks bearing fragrant, long, vaselike or egg-shaped flowers with reflexed edges, in a wide range of colors. **Bizarre,** including the Parrot, Rembrandt, and Bybloemen Tulips, all showing flecking, penciling, or stripes of different colors. **Large-Flowered Double Tulips,** running the entire gamut of colors.

U

ULMUS—(ELM). Deciduous. Mostly tall growing up to 100 feet. Sun and partial shade. Rather symmetrical, much branched trees, assuming various shapes; bright to dark-green, oval, pointed, serrate leaves; inconspicuous greenish-brown flowers in spring; fruit a winged, dry nutlet. *PROPAGATION*—Seeds sown immediately after ripening; layering in fall; suckers; grafting of varieties. *CULTURE*—Grows in ordinary, rather moist soil. *POSITION*—Street trees, specimen tree.

SPECIES—**U. americana—American Elm.** Tall, wide-spreading tree, with light-gray trunk, pendulous branches, assuming many shapes, such as plume form, willowy, feathery, oak tree form. **U. racemosa—Cork Elm.** Round-topped head, with branchlets corky winged. **U. glabra camperdownii—Camperdown Elm.** Dark-green, very large leaves; branches and branchlets pendulous. Interesting as specimen tree, especially near pools.

UMBRELLA TREE—(MELIA).

V

VACCINIUM OVATUM—(HUCKLEBERRY). Evergreen. Native. 5-8 feet. Sun and partial shade. Bushy shrub, with slender, arching branches, dark-green, red-tinged, shining ovate leaves; clusters of small, bell-shaped, rose-red-white flowers, blooming in May; black berries. *PROPAGATION*—Seed sown in fall; layering; suckers. *CULTURE*—Requires an acid, light soil. *GROUPING*—For the naturalistic garden and shrub border, grouping with Barberries, Mahonia, Toyon, Pernettya, Fuchsia-flowered Gooseberry, Flowering Currant, Cotoneaster horizontalis.

VALERIANA CENTRANTHUS—(VALERIAN)—(GARDEN HELIOTROPE). Perennial. 2-4 feet. Sun and partial shade. Erect, branching plant, with smooth, compound leaves; dense clusters of small, fragrant white or pinkish lavender flowers, blooming profusely in summer and intermittently. *PROPAGATION*—Seeds; division in fall. *CULTURE*—Grows in any soil. *POSITION*—Useful for filling in between shrubs, for covering embankments.

SPECIES—Variety **ruber.** A good variety with gray-green foliage and crimson flowers.

VERBENA HYBRIDA— (VERBENA). Perennial. 6-8 inches, but spreading. Sun. Densely branching, with dark-green, wrinkled, dissected leaves; dense, corymbose clusters of medium-sized, salver-shaped, white, pink, red, blue, purple flowers, blooming from May often into winter. *PROPAGATION*—Grows in any soil, but best in rich, light, moderately fertilized loam. *GROUPING*—Border plant; in parkings; foreground of shrub border; in the mixed border, combining with Petunias, Shirley Poppies, rose and red Snapdragons and Stocks, Perennial Aster, Gypsophila.

VERONICA. Evergreen. A great tribe of plants varying from creeping rock plants, herbaceous perennials, to large shrubby forms. Sun and partial shade. The shrubs are bushy, usually round-headed, very compact, with smooth, glossy, entire leaves; many spikes or racemes of irregular, short-tubular, fragrant, blue, white, rose, red flowers, blooming profusely in late spring and summer, intermittently during other seasons. *PROPAGATION* — Easily by seeds, some species self-sown; easily by cuttings of half firm wood in spring or summer. *CULTURE*—Hardy shrubs, but most species favor a well fertilized, light, rather moist loam; prune back after flowering. *GROUPING*—Accent shrubs in the formal garden; foundation plantings; hedge shrubs; low growing species in rockeries; in the shrub border, grouping with Mexican Orange, Raphiolepis, Pittosporum in variety, Evergreen Viburnums, Coprosma, Polygala, Myrtus in variety, Escallonias, Genistas.

SPECIES—**V. buxifolia—Boxwood Veronica.** 2-3 feet. Round and compact, with dark-green, Boxwoodlike leaves; short spikes of small, white flowers, blooming in fall. **V. chathamica.** Trailing, 6 inches high, but 3 feet broad, with flexible, woody branches; pale green, elliptical leaves; dense racemes of lilac-white flowers, blooming July-August. **V. cupressoides—Cypress Veronica.** 4-6 feet. Globose shrub, resembling a small Cypress tree. **V. decussata (elliptica) — Blue-Flowered Veronica.** 5-8 feet. Large thick leaves, and purplish blue flowers in dense, short spikes. The variety *lewisii* has long racemes of large, white-blue flowers. **V. hulkeana.** 2-3 feet. Loose growing shrub, with coarsely serrate, ovate leaves; long panicles of soft lilac-white flowers, blooming in April-May. **V. speciosa imperialis.** 5-6 feet. Stout shrub with large, dark-green leaves; long spikes of large purplish-crimson flowers, blooming June-September. The variety **andersoni variegata** has leaves variegated white, and long spikes of lavender-white flowers. **V. carnea.** Rose-carmine flowers. **V. traversi.** 2-4 feet. Similar to the Boxwood Veronica, but with larger, gray-green foliage. **Herbaceous Veronica: V. spicata—Speedwell.** 2-4 feet. Erect, slender stemmed, with light-green, lanceolate, downy leaves; long, upright racemes of clear blue or pale pink flowers, blooming June-August. **V. longifolia.** Long spikes of intensely blue flowers. For the flower border, combining with yellow and orange-colored flowers. **V. teucrium, prostrata, rupestris,** and many others are rock plants with pale to deep blue flowers.

VIBURNUM. Deciduous and evergreen. 6-12 feet. Sun and moderate shade. Hardy, erect, usually bushy and somewhat round-headed shrubs; rather large, shining, oval to lanceolate leaves; terminal panicles or cymes of regular, fragrant, white or pinkish-white flowers, blooming in spring and summer, some species intermittently; red or black fruits. *PROPAGATION*—Seeds, usually stratified, sown in fall or spring; hard wood cuttings in fall; green wood cuttings in summer; easily by layering; grafting. *CULTURE*—Most Viburnums grow in ordinary soils, but make a better appearance in sandy, well fertilized loam; prune in fall. *GROUPING*—Specimens; foundation plantings; hedges; parkings; shrub border, grouping with Carolina Cherry, different species together, Pittosporums, Cistus, Eleagnus in variety, Escallonias, Toyon, Veronicas, Duranta plumieri, Catalina Cherry.

SPECIES—**V. carlsii.** Half deciduous. 3-4 feet. Much branched, spreading, pubescent shrub; dull green, broadly ovate leaves; very fragrant, salver-shaped, pinkish-white flowers, blooming in spring; **V. tinus—Laurustinus.** Evergreen. Tall with dark-green leaves and densely flowered clusters of pinkish-white flowers, blooming May-August. The variety **lucidum** has larger, finer leaves and larger flowers. **V. odoratissimum.** Evergreen. Tall, with stout, warty branches; large, Laurel-like, bright-green leaves; pure white, fragrant flowers. **V. opulus sterile—Common Snowball.** Deciduous. 10-12 feet. Much branched shrub, with broadly ovate, coarsely dentate-serrate leaves; globose balls of white flowers; scarlet fruits. Grown principally for fruits and fall coloration. **V. rhytidophyllum.** Evergreen. Tall, with stout, upright branches; thick, leathery, dark-green, wrinkled leaves, yellowish tomentose beneath; cymes of yellowish-white flowers. **V. suspensum (sandankwa).** Evergreen. 6-8 feet. Large, shining, very dark-green leaves; rose-pink flowers with spicelike fragrance. **V. tomentosum,** variety **plenum—Japanese Snowball.** Deciduous. Fast growing, tall shrub, with spreading, pubescent branches; broadly ovate leaves; globose balls of white flowers; red, ovoid fruits turning to bluish black.

VICTORIAN BOX—(PITTOSPORUM).

VINCA MINOR — (PERIWINKLE) — (TRAILING MYRTLE). Evergreen. 1 foot. Partial or full shade. Hardy, trailing plant; dark-green, glistening, elliptic-lanceolate leaves; large, solitary, lilac-blue, tubular, salver-shaped flowers, blooming in spring and summer. Many varieties with white, purple,

rose, single or double flowers, or variegated foliage. *PROPAGATION*—Easily by cuttings or division. *CULTURE*—Grows in any kind of moist soil. *POSITION*—Used for ground covers under trees; window boxes, covering banks.

SPECIES—**V. major.** Larger leaves, and larger, blue flowers.

VIOLA TRICOLOR—(PANSY). Annual. Low growing border and bedding plant. Sun and moderate shade. Bushy plant, with oval or heart-shaped leaves; irregular, fragrant, spurred, flat-petaled flowers in many colors, blooming from March into fall. *PROPAGATION*—Seeds sown in August for early blooming, in spring for late spring and summer blooming. *CULTURE*—Pansies should grow in light, sandy or peaty, well fertilized, moist soil; provide mulch for winter protection; attacked by pill and sow bugs, wire worms, snails (see Plant Pests). *POSITION*—The Pansy, existing in many strains and varieties, has been developed to a high degree of perfection in both form and color of flower. Mixed or separate colors may be used in border plantings.

SPECIES—**V. cornuta—Viola.** Annual, but almost a perennial in California. Habit and culture like that of Pansy, but with longer-petaled, narrower flowers, that remain almost pure in color for the variety, in blue-white, light lilac, purple, yellow, apricot, etc., blooming continuously from March to late fall, and during mild winters. *GROUPING*—Same positions as for Pansy, but also in mass plantings in the flower border in combination with Alyssum saxatile, Columbine, Yellow Snapdragons and Stocks, Pot Marigolds, Coreopsis, Iceland Poppy, French Marigold. **V. odorata—Violet.** 4-8 inches. Perennial. Sun and slight shade. Tufted plants with creeping runners; bright to dark-green, cordate-ovate leaves; medium-sized, single or double flowers, in variety white, yellow, lilac, blue, mauve, etc., blooming in April-May, sometimes earlier. *PROPAGATION*—Seeds, usually by cuttings, using short-jointed runners taken in February; division in fall or early April; select good, disease resistant, and prolific plants to propagate from. *CULTURE*—Best in rich, moist, light, well fertilized loam; trim back leaf growth if heavy. *POSITION*—Border plant, or for bedding out in naturalistic garden; combinations much the same as for Viola.

VIOLET—(VIOLA ODORATA).

VIRGINIA BELLS—(MERTENSIA).

VIRGINIA CREEPER—(AMPELOPSIS).

VIRGINIA STOCK—(MALCOMIA).

VIRGINS BOWER—(CLEMATIS).

VISCARIA — (ROSE-OF-HEAVEN). Annual. 12-18 inches. Sun and moderate shade. Much branched plant, with light-green, linear leaves; slender stems bearing medium-sized, salver-shaped flowers, in shades of white, red, rose, blue, blooming June-November. *PROPAGATION*—Seeds sown for succession of bloom from March-July. *CULTURE*—Prefers a rich, moist, well fertilized, light loam. *GROUPING* — For the mixed border, combining with Snapdragon, Virginia Stocks, Madonna Lily, Rosy Morn and Balcony Petunias, Pyrethrum, Coral Bells, Mignonette.

VITIS CAPENSIS — (EVERGREEN GRAPE). 8-15 feet. Sun and partial shade. Strong growing, with large, thick, leathery, roundish, dark-green leaves, colored in fall; small, woolly flowers; globular, glossy, red-black fruits. *PROPAGATION*— Hard wood cuttings; layering. *CULTURE*—Best in light, rich, well fertilized loam. *POSITION*—Used extensively alone or in combination with other climbers in window boxes, over trellises, pergolas, arches.

W

WAHLENBERGIA—(PLATYCODON).

WALLFLOWER—(CHEIRANTHUS CHEIRI).

WAND FLOWER—(SPARAXIS).

WASHINGTON THORN—(CRATAEGUS CORDATA).

WATER LILY—(NYMPHAEA).

WATSONIA. Bulbous plant, growing from corms, somewhat similar to Gladiolus. 3-5 feet. Sun. Erect plant, with long, sword-shaped leaves; large spikes of long-tubular flowers in many colors, blooming from April-September, according to locality. *PROPAGATION* and *CULTURE*—Same as for Gladiolus. *POSITION*—For the mixed border, using correct color harmonies, and combining with same flowers as for Gladiolus.

WEEPING BIG TREE—(SEQUOIA).

WEEPING EUROPEAN ASH — (FRAXINUS PENDULA).

WEEPING MULBERRY—(MORUS).

WEEPING WILLOW—(SALIX).

WEIGELA—(DIERVILLA).

WILD HYACINTH—(SCILLA).

WILLOW—(SALIX).

WINDFLOWER— (ANEMONE JAPONICA).

WINDMILL PALM—(CHAMAEROPS EXCELSA).

WINTER ACONITE—(ERANTHIS).

WIRE VINE—(MUEHLENBECKIA).

WISTERIA. Deciduous vine. 20-30 feet. Sun. Climbing by means of tendrils, with thick woody stems; light-green, odd-pinnate, large leaves; medium to large, pea-shaped, blue, lilac, pinkish or purplish flowers in long, drooping racemes, blooming in April-May, and spasmodically in early fall. *PROPAGATION*—Grafting for varieties; layering in summer; seeds; small root cuttings; cuttings of ripened wood under glass. The spring bloom is borne on short spurs, the fall crop on terminal shoots of the season *CULTURE*—Requires a rich, well drained, rather light, moist garden loam, fertilized with manures in fall, commercial fertilizers in spring; prune

back in fall to short lateral spurs containing 2-3 eyes. Secure scions for grafting from flowering wood.

SPECIES — **W. chinensis** — **Chinese Wisteria.** Rather open racemes, 6-12 inches long, with large, showy, blue-violet corollas. Variety **alba** has white flowers. **W. multijuga**—**Japanese Wisteria.** Long, dense racemes of fragrant, violet or violet-blue flowers. In variety the flowers are single or double, and vary in color from white, rose, to violet.

WOODBINE—(AMPELOPSIS).

Y

YELLOW HELIOTROPE — (STREPTOSOLEN).

YEW—(TAXUS).

YUCCA — (SPANISH BAYONET). Evergreen sub-tropical and desert plants. Sun. Stout, rigid plants, dwarf, or rising to 20 feet, attaining much branched, treelike forms; fibrous, sword-shaped, often leathery leaves; long, erect, thick flower stems, bearing compound panicles of very fragrant, white, cream, or violet-shaded, cup and saucer-shaped flowers, blooming in summer to late fall. *PROPAGATION*—Seeds; offsets; stem or rhizome cuttings. *CULTURE*—Drought resistant; best in sandy loam, but will grow in any well drained, light, moderately fertilized soil. *POSITION*—Used in sub-tropical and desert gardens, with Spanish residences, and in the flower or shrub border as an accent plant. Several interesting native species: **Y. filamentosa—Adams Needle.** Very narrow leaves; creamy white flowers on long stalks; **Y. whipplei.** Clumps of narrow, blue-green leaves; tall flower stems bearing hundreds of pendulous, waxy white flowers.

Z

ZANTEDESCHIA (RICHARDIA) — (CALLA LILY). Bulbous plant with fleshy, spreading root; long and broad, fleshy, dark-green leaves; large, white or yellow, irregular flowers, consisting of spadix with enfolding spathe, surrounding a central spoke of yellow stamens, blooming quite continuously. Varieties with variegated leaves. *PROPAGATION*—Chiefly by division of roots. *CULTURE* —Easy to grow, but requires a moist acid soil; occasional application of manure. *GROUPING*—For hedges, and combined with Caladium, Aralia sieboldii, Aucuba, English Laurel, Carolina Cherry.

ZINNIA ELEGANS. Annual. 2-3 feet. Sun. Stems erect and hairy, with elliptical, rough, clasping leaves; large, double and single, Marigoldlike flowers in well pronounced colors, blooming June-November. *PROPAGATION*—Seed sown in March-April. *CULTURE*—Likes a rich, light, well fertilized, moderately moist loam. *GROUPING*—Makes a fine effect in mass plantings, grouping together varieties that harmonize in color; in the mixed border combine with Anchusa, deep blue Delphinium, blue Cornflower, Salvia patens, Salpiglossis, African Marigold, Pot Marigold, Hemerocallis, Aconitum. **Dwarf Zinnias.** With flowers several inches across, suitable for planting in the foreground of the mixed border.

GLOSSARY

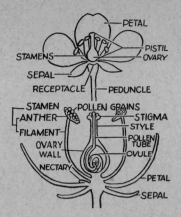

ACUMINATE—long pointed, tapering.

ADPRESSED—closely and flatly pressed against; appressed.

AXILLARY—borne at junction of petiole and stem.

BILABIATE—two lipped.

CALYX—outer circle of floral leaves.

CAMPANULATE—bell shaped.

CILIATE—margin of leaf fringed with hairs.

COMPOUND—leaf with two or more separate leaflets.

CONIFER—tree bearing cones, usually evergreen.

CONVOLUTE—floral envelopes rolled up in the bud.

CORDATE—heart shaped.

CORM—a solid bulblike part.

COROLLA—inner circle of floral envelopes, either separate as petals or united.

CORYMB—a short and broad, rather flat-topped flower cluster, growing on from the apex of the stem.

CRENATE—the leaf margin shallowly round toothed.

CYME—a broad, rather flat-topped flower cluster, with cessation of growth at the apex of stem.

DECIDUOUS—refers to trees and shrubs that lose their leaves in late fall or winter.

DENTATE—with sharp, spreading teeth.

DIGITATE — compound leaf, with the members spread out in a handlike manner.

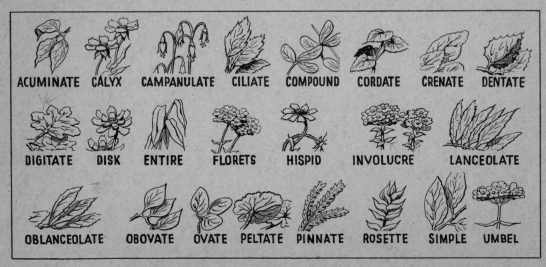

ACUMINATE CALYX CAMPANULATE CILIATE COMPOUND CORDATE CRENATE DENTATE

DIGITATE DISK ENTIRE FLORETS HISPID INVOLUCRE LANCEOLATE

OBLANCEOLATE OBOVATE OVATE PELTATE PINNATE ROSETTE SIMPLE UMBEL

DISK—the central development of floral parts, as in the Daisy.

DRUPE—a fleshy, one-seeded fruit, as in the stone fruits.

ENTIRE—margin of leaf that is not indented.

EVERGREEN—refers to trees and shrubs, excepting conifers, that remain green throughout the year.

FALCATE—sickle shaped.

FASCICLE—clustered, brought together.

FLORETS—individual, usually small, tubular flowers that make up the central disks of daisylike flowers.

GENUS—the first scientific name of a plant, as Phlox in Phlox drummondi; further divided into one or more species.

GLAUCOUS—covered with a bloom or whitish substance that rubs off.

HISPID—leaf or stem covered with stiff or bristly hairs.

INFLORESCENCE—the manner in which flowers are borne.

INVOLUCRE—whorl of small leaves or bracts beneath a flower or flower cluster.

LACINIATE—cut into narrow, pointed lobes.

LANCEOLATE—much longer than broad, widening above the base and tapering to the apex.

LOBED—a portion of a leaf, sepal, or petal, representing a division to about the middle.

OBLANCEOLATE—inversely lanceolate, the broadest part toward the apex of leaf.

OBOVATE—inversely ovate, with the broadest part upward.

OVATE—outline of leaf somewhat oval, with broader end downward.

PANICLE—a branching raceme, the flowers being pedicellate.

PEA SHAPED—the flower shaped like that of Sweet Pea, consisting of a keel, wings and standard; corolla papilionaceous or butterflylike.

PEDICEL—stem of a flower in a cluster.

PELTATE—shield shaped, with leaf attached to its stalk inside the margin.

PERIANTH — the floral envelope considered together, in which there is usually no clear distinction between calyx and corolla.

PETIOLE—leaf stalk.

PETAL—separate leaf of a corolla.

PILOSE—shaggy, with soft hairs.

PINNATE—compound leaf, with leaflets on the sides of a main axis; feather-form.

PISTIL—seed-bearing floral organ.

PUBESCENT—downy covering of hairs.

RACEME—a simple elongated cluster of stalked flowers.

RADICAL—pertaining to leaves springing from base of stem near root.

ROOT STALK — underground, usually thickened stem.

RHIZOME—synonym for root stalk.

ROSETTE—pertaining to a close arrangement of leaves about a shortened stem.

SALVER SHAPED—with a slender tube, abruptly expanded at top; dish shaped.

SCABROUS—rough or gritty to the touch.

SCANDENT—climbing.

SCAPE — one to many flowered, leafless flower stalk, rising from ground.

SCURVY—very rough-hairy.

SEPAL—leaf of calyx.

SERRATE—saw-edge-leaved.

SESSILE—leaf not stalked; sitting.

SIMPLE—opposite to compound; unbranched.

SPATULATE—spoon shaped; broad at top, narrow at base.

SPECIES—the second scientific name of a plant, as drummondi in Phlox drummondi.

STAMEN—the pollen bearing or male floral organ.

STOLON—horizontal stem taking root at the tip.

STRATIFY—to bury hard-shelled seeds in moist soil, or subject them to frost action, to enable them to germinate more readily.

TOMENTOSE—densely woolly.

TRIFOLIATE—of three leaves.

TUBER—a thickened underground part, with buds usually near the top.

UMBEL—cluster of flowers with branches rising from a common point; umbrellalike.

VARIETY—further division of a species into one or more individuals that show certain variations from type; the third scientific name of a plant.

INDEX

Empress of Russia Dahlia — maroon with
orchid edge.